X1C

MW00651873

Turbo Basic™

Owner's Handbook

BORLAND INTERNATIONAL, INC.
4585 SCOTTS VALLEY DRIVE
SCOTTS VALLEY, CALIFORNIA 95066

Table of Contents

Introduction

Turbo Basic is a self-contained programming environment for IBM® personal computers and true compatibles. Following in the footsteps of its famous sibling, Turbo Pascal®, Turbo Basic is a combination editor, fast memory-to-memory compiler, run-time library, and internal linker. Its modern user interface uses windows and pull-down menus. And for maximum speed and memory efficiency, Turbo Basic is written entirely in assembly language.

Some other distinguishing characteristics include the following:

- Floating-point support (full 8087 integration and full software emulation)
- Professional development environment
- New block-structured programming statements
- Full EGA support

A language for both the beginner and the experienced programmer, Turbo Basic's integrated design permits quick program turnaround without sacrificing the powerful features professional programmers demand. It is compatible with IBM's Advanced BASIC (commonly referred to as BASICA) interpreter version 3.00 and Microsoft's GW BASIC™ (with minor exceptions because these are interpreters), and contains many extensions. (In general, from now on we'll refer to Advanced BASIC and GW BASIC collectively as "Interpretive BASIC.")

Programs created with Turbo Basic have access to all the memory available in the target machine—64K for scalars, 64K for strings, available memory for arrays, and more than 64K for programs. The compiler generates true .EXE files that operate 4 to 100 times faster than their interpretive counterparts. And the incorporation of the 8087 support puts the whip to numeric-intensive applications. Turbo Basic also supports all graphics capabilites and extensions of the Enhanced Graphics Adapter (EGA).

Thanks to its advanced flow-control constructs (IF/THEN/ELSEIF/ELSE/ ENDIF blocks, DO/LOOP, CASE/SELECT, CALL/SUB), Turbo Basic programs are easier to write, debug, and maintain than Interpretive BASIC programs. Line numbers are optional; alphanumeric labels can serve as the target of GOTO and GOSUB statements. User-defined functions and procedures allow the declaration of local, static, and shared variables, and permit recursion.

Turbo Basic supports a greatly expanded string range (up to 32,767 characters per string), and does away with long delays of periodic string space "housecleaning." There's a BINARY file mode for low-level file processing and a long integer numeric type for fast, flexible numeric processing. The CALL and REG statements offer a straightforward linkage to assembly language, and there are numerous compiler directives for conditional compilation, error trapping, buffer control, and more.

Turbo Basic is a powerful, Interpretive BASIC-compatible language that produces fast programs quickly.

About this Manual

First, what this manual is not. It isn't a comprehensive introduction to BASIC programming. At last count there were over 15,000 books in print on this subject, and more than 1,000 were about Interpretive BASIC (which has virtually the same syntax as Turbo Basic) in particular. This manual is also not a replacement for information resources such as the DOS and technical manuals for your machine.

Instead, what this manual is is a reference to the program development system known as Turbo Basic. We begin with a brief tutorial about installing the system onto a working floppy or a hard disk, and then discuss how to use Turbo Basic to edit and compile a simple program. Following the tutorial is background material, split broadly between Chapter 3, "Turbo Basic: The Program," and Chapter 4, "Turbo Basic: The Language." Chapter 5, "Turbo Basic Reference Directory," is an alphabetically arranged look-up section of Turbo Basic commands, system variables, functions, statements, and metastatements.

The appendices provide an ASCII chart and keyboard scan codes, and supplemental information about numeric considerations, event trapping, interfacing to assembly language subroutines, compile-time and run-time errors, and the differences between Turbo Basic and Interpretive BASIC.

Typography

The body of this manual is printed in a normal typeface; other typefaces have special meaning.

`Alternate` type is used for example programs and screen output; for example:

```
Dir mask:
```

Italic type emphasizes an important concept or word. In particular, italics are used in syntax descriptions to indicate areas within commands to be filled in with application-specific information; for example:

REG *register, value*

UPPERCASE text denotes part of a BASIC command that must be supplied verbatim; for example:

```
RESUME NEXT
```

Certain characters have special meaning when they appear in syntax descriptions.

Brackets ([ ]) mean that the enclosed information is optional. For example:

OPEN *filespec* AS [#] *filenum*

means that you can include a number sign (#) before the file number or leave it out, at your option. Therefore, both of the following are legal:

```
OPEN "cust.dta" AS 1
OPEN "cust.dta" AS #1
```

Braces ({ }) indicate a choice of two or more options, one of which must be used. The options are separated by vertical bars (|). For example:

```
KEY {ON|OFF}
```

means that both KEY ON and KEY OFF are valid statements, and that KEY by itself is not.

Ellipses (. . .) indicate that part of a command can be repeated as many times as necessary. For example:

READ *variable* [,*variable*]...

means that multiple variables, separated by commas, can be processed by a single READ statement:

```
READ a$
READ a$, b$, a, b, c
```

Three vertically spaced periods indicate the omission of one or more lines of program text; for example:

```
FOR n = 1 TO 10
   .
   .
   .
NEXT n
```

System Requirements

Turbo Basic itself requires MS-DOS or PC-DOS 2.0 or above. In addition, any program you create will require DOS 2.0 or above to execute.

Turbo Basic and the programs you create with it are designed to work on the IBM PC, XT®, or AT® models, or a fully compatible machine. Graphics features of the language are not available without appropriate graphics hardware, such as the Color/Graphics Adapter, the Enhanced Graphics Adapter, or equivalents, and a suitable display.

Acknowledgements

We refer to several different products in this manual; the following lists each one and its respective company:

- Turbo Pascal and SideKick are registered trademarks and Turbo Basic is a trademark of Borland International, Inc.
- GW BASIC and MS-DOS are registered trademarks of Microsoft Corp.
- WordStar is a registered trademark of MicroPro International, Inc.
- IBM, XT, and AT are registered trademarks of International Business Machines Corp.
- MultiMate is a trademark of MultiMate International Corp.
- dBASE is a registered trademark of Ashton-Tate.
- Lotus 1-2-3 is a registered trademark of Lotus Development Corp.

C H A P T E R **1**

About BASIC

Like Maine lobster, maple syrup, and basketball, BASIC is a product of New England. Created in 1964 at Dartmouth College in Hanover, New Hampshire, as a language for teaching programming, BASIC is commonly identified as an acronym for "Beginner's All-purpose Symbolic Instruction Code." (However, cynics think inventors John Kemeny and Thomas Kurtz first came up with a catchy name for their new, easy-to-use language and then worked backward to concoct something it could stand for.)

Students and programmers alike soon found that BASIC could do practically anything that stuffy, awkward FORTRAN could do. And since BASIC was so easy to learn and to work, its programs usually ended up taking less time to write than its FORTRAN equivalents. BASIC was also available on most personal computers, usually in ROM. So BASIC caught on in a big way.

Remarkably, of the dozens of general-purpose programming languages available to programming aficionados, BASIC is still the easiest to learn more than 20 years after its introduction. And better yet, BASIC gets the job done. C and Pascal snobs notwithstanding, BASIC is a no-nonsense language gifted with powerful tools for tackling the specific things that people do most with small computers, namely, working with files and putting text and graphics on a display.

Although their language has its detractors, no one can deny that Kemeny and Kurtz achieved their "BASIC" goal: to make programming more accessible to more people. This leads us to Turbo Basic.

Turbo Basic

Turbo Basic is a compiled BASIC. You may be familiar with IBM's Advanced BASIC (called GW BASIC™ on many compatibles, but which we're now referring to as "Interpretive BASIC"), a popular *interpreted* version from Microsoft. Interpreting and compiling are two basic methods of implementing high-level languages. To understand the important differences between these two approaches, and consequently between Turbo Basic and Interpretive BASIC, requires that we descend briefly to the ground floor of programming.

Back to Basics—Machine Language

Surprisingly, a given computer is only able to execute programs written in its native *machine language.* There are almost as many different machine languages as there are computers, but all are variations on a similar theme—simple operations performed lightning-quick on binary numbers. IBM personal computers use 8086-family machine language because their hardware design is based on that particular microprocessor family.

It is possible, although difficult, to write programs directly in machine language. In the early days of computers (through the early 1950s), machine language was all that there was, so people made do. To save programmers from the rigors of machine language programming, high-level (that is, non-machine) languages were created as a bridge between human beings and the machine language world of the computer.

High-level languages work via translation programs that input "source code" (a machine-readable hybrid of English and mathematical expressions), and ultimately cause the computer to execute appropriate machine language instructions to get the job done. The two basic types of translators are interpreters, which scan and execute source code in a single step, and compilers, which scan source code to produce machine language that is then executed separately.

Interpreters

Historically, BASIC has usually been implemented as an interpreter (a familiar example being Interpretive BASIC itself). One oft-cited benefit of an interpretive implementation is that it permits a "direct mode." A direct mode lets you give a computer a problem like PRINT 3.14159 * 3^2.1, and returns an answer to you as soon as you press the *Enter* key (this allows a $3,000 computer to be used like a $10 calculator).

Additionally, interpreters have certain attributes that simplify debugging. For one thing, it's possible to interrupt an interpreter's processing of a program, display the contents of certain variables, browse through the source program, and then continue execution.

What programmers like most about interpreters is the instant response. There's no compiling necessary; the interpreter is always ready to take a shot at your program. Enter RUN and the effect of your most recent change is on the screen.

Interpreted languages are not without drawbacks, however. For one thing, it's necessary to have a copy of the interpreter in memory at all times—and many of the interpreter's features (and therefore much of its size) may not be necessary to execute a given program.

A subtle disadvantage of interpreters is that they tend to discourage good programming style. Since comments and other formatting niceties take up valuable program memory space, people tend not to use them. Hell hath no fury like an Interpretive BASIC programmer trying to get 120K of program into 60K of memory.

Worst of all, *interpreters are slow.* They spend too much time figuring out what to do, instead of actually doing it.

In executing a program's statements, an interpreter must first scan each statement for content (*What's this human asking me to do here?*), and then perform the requested operation. Statements within loops are scanned redundantly.

Consider this three-line program:

```
10 FOR n = 1 TO 1000
20   PRINT n, SQR(n)
30 NEXT n
```

The first time through this program, a BASIC interpreter would figure out that line 20 means:

1. Convert numeric variable *n* to a string.
2. Send the string to the screen.
3. Move the cursor to the next print zone.
4. Calculate the square root of *n*.
5. Convert the result to a string.
6. Send the string to the screen.

The second time through the loop it will figure it all out again, having totally forgotten what it learned about this line a millisecond ago. Ditto the next 998 passes.

Clearly, if you could somehow separate the scanning/understanding phase from the execution phase, you'd have a faster program. That's what compilers are all about.

Compilers

A compiler is a text-to-machine-language translator that reads source text, evaluates it according to the syntactic design of the language, and produces machine language. The machine language output (called object code) is then run as an independent step. In other words, a compiler doesn't execute programs, it builds them. Interpreters can't be separated from the programs they run; compilers do their job and then get out of the picture.

In working with a compiled language such as Turbo Basic, you'll come to think about your programs in terms of the two major phases in their lives: compile time and runtime. With an interpreter, there's only runtime.

The speed improvement you'll see with Turbo Basic depends on the program. Most programs will run four to ten times faster than the interpretive equivalent. If you work at it, you may achieve a 100-fold speed improvement. On the other side of the coin, programs that spend most of their time shuffling disk files or waiting for input won't show a dramatic speed increase.

Line Numbers and Turbo Basic

Interpretive BASIC needs line numbers so that it can find its way when GOTOs and GOSUBs send execution to a statement that isn't next in sequence. In addition, line numbers are at the core of its editing process.

Although tolerant of them, Turbo Basic has no need for line numbers. Instead of GOTO 5000, in Turbo Basic you'll say something like GOTO *ErrorExit*, where *ErrorExit* is a "label" at the start of the *ErrorExit* routine.

There are compilers and there are compilers. Turbo Basic was designed from the start to be fast. This goal was achieved with an integrated design that keeps the compiler, editor, and program in memory at the same time, eliminating the endless disk drive excursions that cause conventional compilers to make the text-to-test transition 10 or 20 times more slowly.

Turbo Basic's enormous compilation speed (thousands of lines per minute) is such that it retains Interpretive BASIC's interactiveness. Simply press ***R*** and a Turbo Basic program runs.

Note: If you're new to BASIC, continue reading and/or exploring this manual. However, for those seasoned BASIC programmers who are thinking of converting Interpretive BASIC code to Turbo Basic, take a look at Appendix D, "Comparing Turbo Basic and Interpretive BASIC."

C H A P T E R **2**

Touring Turbo Basic

This chapter will get you started using Turbo Basic. We'll begin with some basic operations in Turbo Basic, including installing Turbo Basic, using the menu system, and creating, running, and editing a program. However, before you get started, you should complete and mail in the license agreement at the front of this manual. This agreement allows you to make as many copies of the program disk as you need for your personal use and backup purposes only.

Backing Up Your Disks

For your own protection, make a backup copy of the distribution disk with your file-copy or disk-copy program before you start using Turbo Basic. Make certain all files have transferred successfully, then store the original disk in a safe place.

Files on the Distribution Disk

The files you have just copied from your distribution disk are described here.

TB.EXE The all-in-one development environment/editor/compiler/run-time library. When you type TB and press *Enter*, Turbo Basic is up and running.

***.BAS** Sample Turbo Basic programs.

TBHELP.TBH Contains help screens for using Turbo Basic.

README.COM Use this program to read the README file.

README This text file may or may not be present. If it is, it contains information more current than that contained in this manual. Use README.COM to type this or copy it to a printer.

Installation

For floppy-based systems, copy TB.EXE to a boot disk along with as many DOS utility programs (for example, CHKDSK, FORMAT) as will fit. Use drive *B* to store the source and executable programs you'll be creating.

For hard disk systems, create a new directory off the root called "TB," or something equally appropriate. Copy all the files on the distribution disk into \TB. If you're tight on disk space, copy only TB.EXE. Log into this directory and you're ready to go. A standard configuration with the hard disk addressed as drive *C* and the first floppy as drive *A* requires the commands

```
C>MD \TB
C>COPY A:*.* \TB
C>CD \TB
C\TB>
```

To use Turbo Basic from other places on your hard disk, set up a path statement or copy the file TB.EXE to the directory where you keep system programs such as CHKDSK, FORMAT, and Advanced BASIC (this directory is often called \BIN). (See Appendix I, "Customizing Turbo Basic," for more about setting up paths.) For detailed information about creating and managing subdirectories, consult your DOS manual.

Setting Up an Operating Environment

If you have some special hardware needs or if you're a developer in need of a dynamic environment, being able to set *environment variables* will afford you some choices. Environment variables actually override compiler and/or program options, and are determined by using the SET command in DOS.

Environment variables have an effect on the entire environment in which a program is executed. Thus after setting a variable, it's in effect until you reset it to another value or turn off your machine. If you find yourself setting these values consistently one way, you may want to enter the SET command into a batch file or your AUTOEXEC.BAT file (see Appendix G, "A DOS Primer," for more information).

Turbo Basic's environment variables allow you to override compiler and run-time options for 8087 support and Color/Graphics Adapter (CGA) "snow" checking. For example, in the following example you're setting up your environment for 8087 use by typing at the DOS prompt

```
SET 87=yes
```

where *yes* means you have an 8087; *no* means even if you have an 8087 don't use it. The default setting is *yes*.

In the case of CGA snow-checking, you could type

```
SET CGASNOWCHK=no
```

where *no* doesn't do snow-checking and *yes* does snow-checking. The default setting is *yes*.

When your compiler begins executing or when a generated .EXE file starts executing, it will actually search the *environment variable space* for these variables.

Though it's not necessary to set these variables, they're available when you need them. If you choose not to set them, the current directory searches for files and creates temporary ones to store the default variables.

Starting Up Turbo Basic

When you have a copy of the system on your working disk and you are in the appropriate directory (or disk, if you have a floppy-based system), enter TB at the DOS prompt and press *Enter*:

```
C>TB
```

and Turbo Basic's first screen appears:

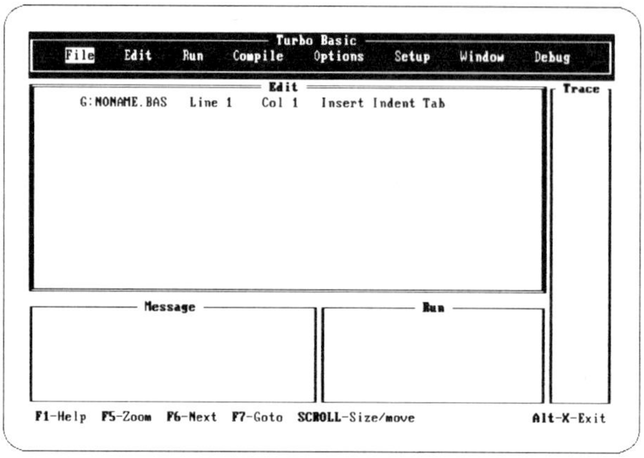

***Figure 2-1** Turbo Basic's Main Screen*

The main menu bar at the top of the screen displays your command options and the four windows, Edit, Message, Trace, and Run. You can choose an item from the menu by pressing the associated highlighted capital letter (for example, *E* for **E**dit) or by moving the highlighted bar with the left and right arrow keys to the desired option and pressing *Enter*. (Note that the highlighted letters of each option on the screen are expressed as boldface in the text.)

Experiment for a minute. Choose the **F**ile command. A series of options related to files "pulls down." To choose one of these options, again, press the first letter of the option or use the up and down arrows to set the highlighted bar and press *Enter*. To return to the options available from the main menu, press *Esc*, which takes you back to the main menu. No matter where you are in Turbo Basic, pressing *Esc* a few times will get you back to the main menu. (For more information, see the section in Chapter 3 entitled "The Main Menu.")

Note that the help line at the bottom of the screen changes according to where you are in the menu system; look here first if you get stuck—it may be all the help you need. If you need additional help, press *F1*.

Some of the items on the main menu have no other options than the one displayed. For example, **C**ompile simply compiles your loaded file; it has neither a pull-down menu nor a pop-up menu. On the other hand, **F**ile has a pull-down menu with several options.

In practice, most of the time you'll be making the same three menu selections over and over:

- **E**dit to create and alter source programs
- **C**ompile to compile source programs into executable form

- Run to execute programs or compile programs if they need it

For a more extensive explanation of the menu system and its pull-down menus, refer to the section in Chapter 3, "The Main Menu."

Editor Survival Kit

Before we get you into writing programs, we'd like you to know something about the editor you'll be using. You need only read this section if you are unfamiliar with either the Turbo Pascal editor, WordStar®, or Multimate™. If you are already familiar with this type of editor, go ahead to the section entitled, "A First Program." (If you want more explanation, refer to the section, "The Turbo Editor," in Chapter 3.)

For those of you who need to learn the editor, take your time and practice a few of the basic features. (Table 2-1 on page 18 summarizes the basic commands.) Then later on you'll be able to concentrate on writing Turbo Basic programs rather than spending your time learning the editor. Keep in mind that help is only a keystroke away—pressing *F1* will bring you context-sensitive help for wherever you happen to be.

Basic Operations

Select **Edit** from the main menu by pressing **E** from anyplace on the main menu bar or press *Enter* when positioned at the **Edit** command.

First take a look at the status line to determine whether you're in *Insert* mode or *Overwrite* mode. Insert mode means all characters entered on the keyboard are inserted at the cursor position; existing text moves to the right of the cursor as you type. When using Overwrite mode, every character typed replaces what is currently under the cursor. You can toggle these modes on and off with the *Ins* key or *Ctrl-V* keys. Select whichever one you find most comfortable to use.

Now type in your name and address as you would on an envelope; for example:

```
Sam Spade
1264 Clinton St.
New York, NY 12345
```

and press *Esc* to finish editing. Then save the contents of the work file by selecting **File** (press *F* when positioned anywhere on the main menu or press *Enter* when positioned at **File**) and then **Save**. Since you didn't name the file previously, the default file name NONAME.BAS was assigned. You can rename the file now by saving what's in the editor under the file name ADDRESS. (If you don't specify an extension, Turbo Basic will give your file a .BAS extension name.)

Now use the **New** option to delete what you have typed into the editor. First press *F* for **File** and *N* for **New**. Now press *E* and type in a list of your five favorite foods, each on a separate line.

```
chicken curry
sushi
blackened fish
chimichangas
lumpia
```

Now end the editing session again (press *Esc*) and select **File** from the main menu, then **Load**. When asked for a file name, type ADDRESS followed by *Enter*. The system asks if you want to save the text in the current work file. You do not, so press *N* (for No) and notice what has happened in the editor window—your favorite foods have been replaced by the ADDRESS file.

Block Operations

While in the Edit window, you can also mark a block of text to be deleted, moved, or copied. Once marked, you can copy the block to another place in the text, delete it from its current spot, or move it to another place in the text.

Marking a block is easy. To try it, first re-select the **Edit** command. With your name and address still in the Edit window, use the arrow keys to position the cursor at the top left corner. Mark the start of the block by pressing *Ctrl-KB*. Now move the cursor to the last character in the last line of your address and mark the end of the block by pressing *Ctrl-KK*.

Now make several copies of this block so that you've got more text to play with. To do this, move the cursor to the end of your address and copy the block by pressing *Ctrl-KC*. Move the cursor to the end of the newly created text and make another copy of the block. Repeat the process until you have a total of ten copies of your address in the Edit window. Use the arrow keys and *PgUp* and *PgDn* to move around the text inside the Edit window.

Now let's mark a new block. Using the status line at the top of the Edit window to determine what line number you're on, insert a new line 4 into the file consisting of 20 letter *X*'s. Now make line 11 a new line of 20 letter *Y*'s.

Your new block will be lines 5 to 10. Mark it with *Ctrl-KB* and *Ctrl-KK* as before. To delete the block, press *Ctrl-KY* and you should now have a line of *X*'s followed by a line of *Y*'s.

Next, mark a new block that consists of these two rows of *X*'s and *Y*'s. Move the cursor to the end of the text, then move the new block here by pressing *Ctrl-KV* (check that it has been moved and not copied by using *PgUp* and *PgDn*).

Block operations can be performed with fewer key presses by using the function keys. The keys and their uses are displayed at the bottom of the screen. Note that the *F7* and *F8* keys mark the beginning and end of a block, respectively. To mark a block, move the cursor to the beginning of a block and press *F7*. Then move the cursor to the end of the block, and press *F8* to mark the end of the block.

Search and Replace

The search-and-replace command comes in handy if you decide to change the name of something in your program after you've written it. For example, to show you how to use this command, let's delete everything currently in the editor (using *Del*, the New option, or by marking a block) and type in this well-known phrase

```
To be or not to be
That is the question
```

Now replace every occurrence of *To be* with *TB*. First press *Ctrl-QA* and then type *To be* when you are prompted for a search string. Press *Enter* and then when prompted for the replacement string, type *TB*. Next, you can choose certain options to be performed during your search. Select option *G* for a global search, select *N* so that the string is replaced everywhere without asking you for confirmation at each occurrence, and select *U* so that it ignores uppercase/lowercase. Press *Enter* after you have selected all your options. The search and replace is carried out and the text transformed to

```
TB or not TB
That is the question
```

If you simply want to find a string in the text, you can use the search command (as opposed to search *and* replace). Press *Ctrl-QF* and you are prompted for a search string. Use the search function to find the first occurrence of *TB* in the preceding text. Then use *Ctrl-L* to find subsequent occurrences.

Table 2-1 Summary of Editor Keystrokes

Keys	Function
Esc	Exits the editor
Arrow keys, *PgUp*, *PgDn*, *Home*, *End*	Moves the cursor
Del	Deletes the character at the cursor position
Ins/Ctrl-V	Toggles Insert/Overwrite mode on and off
Ctrl-KB	Marks the beginning of a block
Ctrl-KK	Marks the end of a block
Ctrl-KH	Unmarks a block
Ctrl-KC	Copies a marked block to the position indicated by the cursor
Ctrl-KY	Deletes a marked block
Ctrl-KV	Moves a marked block to the position indicated by the current cursor position
F1	Help information
F2	Saves file
F3	New file
F5	Zoom
F6	Switches windows
F7	Begin block
F8	End Block

A First Program

Now let's create a short program with the editor. Go to the main menu and select **File**, then **Load**. At the file name prompt, enter MYFIRST and press *Enter*. Now press E to enter the editor. You'll know the Edit window has become active because its window has a double border.

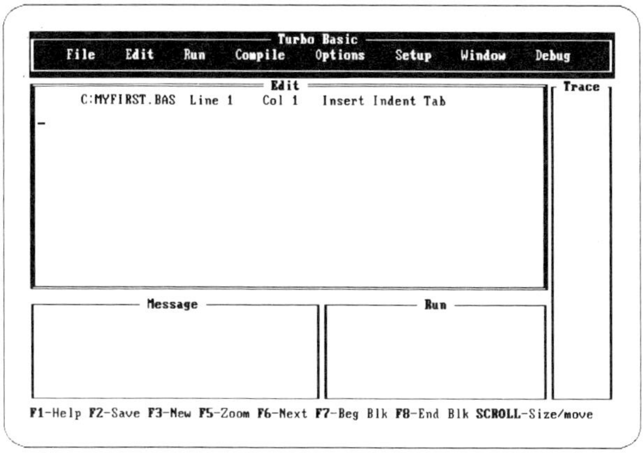

Figure 2-2 *Blank Editor Screen*

Those of you experienced with WordStar or some other program that uses its control sequences, such as the SideKick® Notepad, will find Turbo Basic editing a breeze. Those of you not familiar with this editor should refer to the quick review section earlier in this chapter, "Editor Survival Kit." (If you find you still need more information, refer to the section in Chapter 3 entitled "The Turbo Editor.")

Now type in the program MYFIRST that follows this paragraph. Type as precisely as possible, because Turbo Basic can't do anything other than what you tell it. Some of you may notice a flaw in this program—leave it in; we'll explain why later.

```
WHILE -1
  FOR n = 1 TO 8
    READ a$
    PRINT a$ " ";
  NEXT n
  PRINT
  RESTORE
WEND
DATA Presenting, Turbo Basic --, The, Fastest, BASIC, on, Earth
```

What makes this program look different from BASIC programs you've seen in the past is its lack of line numbers.

Line numbers are an integral part of both the editing and execution of Interpretive BASIC programs. However, since Turbo Basic has a built-in screen editor, and since it's a compiler, line numbers are so much excess baggage. Yet, Turbo Basic is open-minded on the subject. If you like, you can number every line. Or every third line. In order or backward. Or you may choose to number only those lines that are the target of a GOTO or GOSUB. Better yet, you can use named labels.

Doing without line numbers may seem odd at first, but after a few days you'll wonder how you were able to put up with them for so long.

When you've got MYFIRST entered, sit back and admire it for a minute.

You have just created a Turbo Basic source program. Inside the memory of your computer at this moment are the hundred-odd ASCII codes that make up MYFIRST.BAS. So far, only the editor has worked with this text.

This source program, however, is only a means to an end. Before your system's 8086-family microprocessor chip can execute MYFIRST, the source text must be translated, or compiled, into a form that it can understand; namely, 8086 machine language.

The editor's part of the job is now finished, so press **Esc** to leave the editor and return to the main menu. The selection bar becomes visible at the main menu, indicating that you can now select another option.

While the editor is temporarily de-selected, you can't work with it; however, the text of your program is still in memory, ready to be added to or changed at a moment's notice. (A quick press of **E** demonstrates this; pressing **Esc** returns you to the main menu.)

Options

You're about to take the second big step in the program creation process: compiling your source code into executable form. But before you do, you must set a compiler option. Press **O** to choose the **Options** menu (see Figure 2-3).

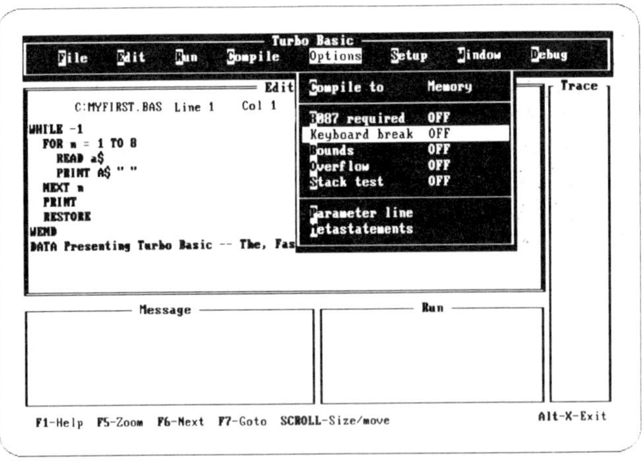

Figure 2-3 Options Menu

As its name implies, the selections in the **Options** menu provide control over certain aspects of the upcoming compilation. At this point, especially if Turbo Basic is your first encounter with a compiled language, some of these selections may seem somewhat mysterious. (The compiler options are discussed in detail in Chapter 3 under the section entitled "The Options Command.")

Right now the only one you're interested in is **Keyboard** break, which is currently turned off. With this option on, however, you can interrupt most programs (stop I/O) generated by the compiler. With this option off, you'll be unable to interrupt (via *Ctrl-Break*) any program generated by the compiler. So to prevent MYFIRST from running forever, press *K* (a toggle switch) to turn on the **Keyboard** break option, and then press *Esc* to return to the main menu.

Compiling

Press *C* to compile MYFIRST (like the editor, the compiler processes the current work file). Quickly and quietly the compiler examines the characters of your program and builds the machine language equivalent. This phase, for even a simple program like MYFIRST, can take some BASIC compilers the better part of a minute.

If the compiler finds something in your source program that isn't acceptable Turbo Basic grammar, it will be noted on the editor status line and you'll be dropped automatically into the editor at the point of the error. If this happens to you, press *Esc* and edit your program. Then exit the editor and recompile: press *Esc*, then *C*.

After the Compile

After a successful compilation, there are two versions of MYFIRST in memory: (1) the source program you've created with the editor, and (2) the resulting executable program 8086 machine language created by the compiler.

In the Message window, Turbo Basic brags about how fast it is and gives some statistics on the compilation (see Figure 2-4).

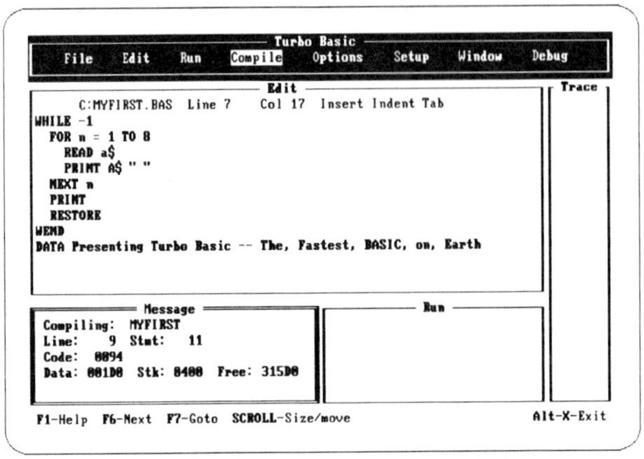

Figure 2-4 Statistics of Compilation

The statistics indicate in Hex bytes the compiled program's code segment size, stack size, and data area size. Also noted are the number of statements and lines compiled, plus the amount of free space left in memory for compilation. (Be assured that you don't need to know anything about hex or stacks or buffers to write Turbo Basic programs, any more than you need to know these things to work with Interpretive BASIC. The information is here if you need it; usually you won't.)

Running the Program

Now that you've translated your source program into machine language, you can run it by pressing *R*. Check out your program output in the Run window (see Figure 2-5).

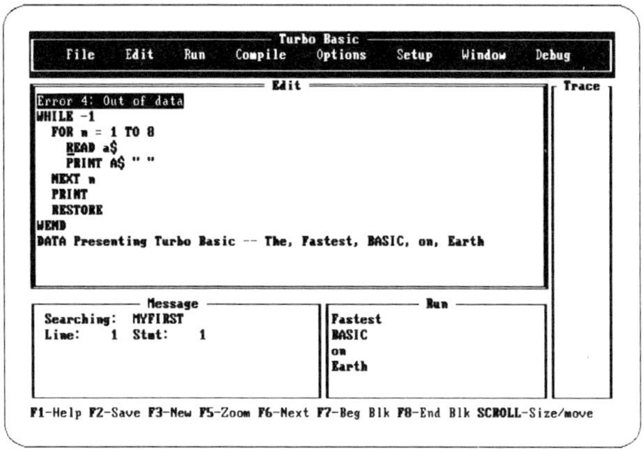

Figure 2-5 Running MYFIRST

Hmmm. MYFIRST ran for a split second and then blew up.

That's because we deliberately included an error in MYFIRST to make a point: The analysis performed by the compiler doesn't figure out everything that might go wrong when the program runs. The compiler mainly checks errors of syntax, such as misspelled commands, superfluous or missing commas, and unmatched parentheses. There's a whole class of bad things that can happen at runtime, from disk failures to attempts to compute mathematical impossibilities such as the square root of a negative number.

Keep in mind that some of your mistakes will be caught at compile time; others won't surface until runtime.

About the Error

In addition to telling you that an Out of Data error occurred, Turbo Basic also shows you *where* it occurred by placing you at the point of error in the editor (see Figure 2-5). Since MYFIRST.BAS is still in memory, this happens quickly.

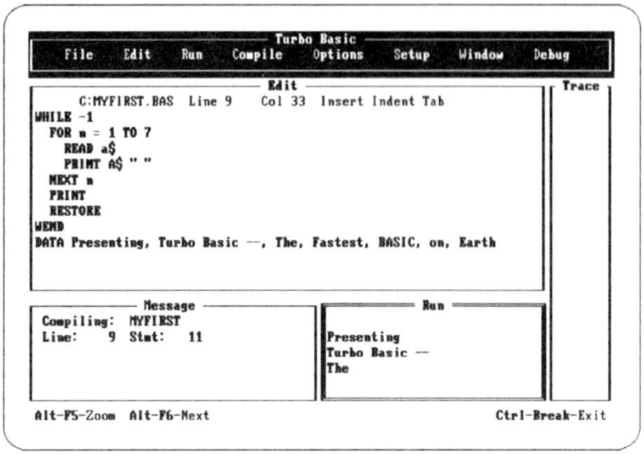

Figure 2-6 Running MYFIRST Successfully

The compiler automatically translates where the error occurred into the corresponding spot in the source file.

What's wrong with this line, of course, is that it should only read seven constants, not eight. Change the FOR/NEXT loop to stop at 7, and you should have a working program.

Press *Esc* and then *R* to first compile and then run the corrected version. Turbo Basic will recognize that you've changed the source program since the last compilation and automatically recompiles MYFIRST before running it. When you get comfortable with the keystrokes involved, you'll find that it takes only seconds to go from editing to executing and vice versa.

Now MYFIRST runs in all its glory. Again, check your output in the Run window and press *Alt-F5* to zoom the window in and out (see Figure 2-6).

When you're comfortable with this program, interrupt it by pressing *Ctrl-Break* and then press *Esc* to return to the main menu.

Saving to Disk

So far everything you've done has been in memory only. If there were a power failure at this instant or your program hung, both the source and executable forms of MYFIRST would be lost. Prudent programmers, therefore, periodically save their source programs to disk with the **F**ile menu's **S**ave command. Do so now. You may notice a burst of activity on the default drive as MYFIRST.BAS is written out. (You can also use the **A**uto save edit option under **M**iscellaneous in the **S**etup menu to automatically save your current file before running a program.)

Use the **Directory** option in the **File** menu to verify that a file named MYFIRST.BAS now exits in the quasi-permanent world of your file system. Pressing *D* causes the quick response:

```
Enter mask
```

Turbo Basic is requesting the sort of file descriptor you might include with DOS's DIR command; for example, *.BAS, or MYFIRST.BAS. Just pressing *Enter* causes every file to appear, as though you had typed *.*.

Saving the Executable Program

Saving the executable (machine language) form of MYFIRST to disk is a different matter altogether. In fact, if you look, you won't see anything on any of the menus for saving an executable program. If you're creating a program for your own use, you may never need to save it. Since it can be created fresh each time by compiling, why bother? However, there will come a time when you'll want a permanent form of a compiled program.

Turbo Basic allows you to generate a stand-alone program (a file with the .EXE extension) that can be executed directly at the DOS prompt. You can do this with MYFIRST by setting the **Compile** to switch in the **Options** menu, as shown in Figure 2-7.

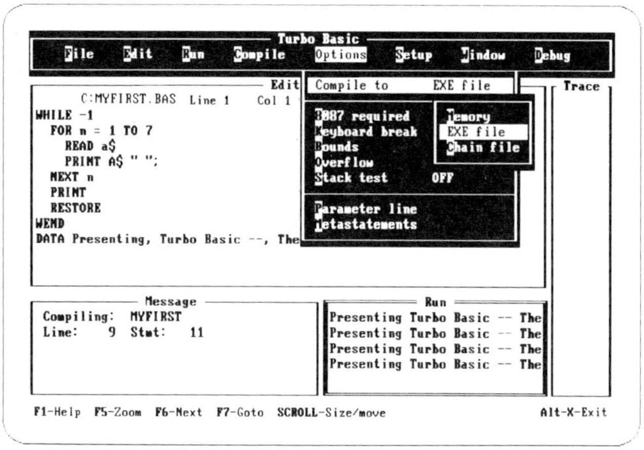

Figure 2-7 Options Menu

First press *O* to get to the **Options** menu, then press *C* for **Compile to**. Select the **Executable** file setting by pressing *E*. This doesn't change anything on disk yet—you've only changed what the compiler will do the next time it is invoked. The default, which is what we've used so far, is to compile to memory.

Press *Esc* to exit the **O**ptions menu, then *C* to recompile MYFIRST. This time it compiles more slowly, because Turbo Basic has to physically write to the disk drive.

To see the resulting file, exit Turbo Basic altogether by first going to the **F**iles menu and then pressing *Q* (for **Q**uit). Once back at DOS level, enter

```
C>DIR MYFIRST
```

You should see both the source and executable forms of your program, MYFIRST.BAS and MYFIRST.EXE, respectively.

Executing MYFIRST from DOS

You probably already know that files with the .EXE extension are directly executable by the operating system. If you enter the file name at the DOS prompt

```
C>myfirst
```

it causes MYFIRST to run, producing the same program you saw before. This time when you interrupt the program with *Ctrl-Break*, you'll be returned to DOS.

Tracing Your Program

Now go back to the Turbo Basic environment and your MYFIRST file by typing TB MYFIRST at the DOS prompt. To give you a taste of everything on the main menu, let's try *tracing* the MYFIRST program.

The Trace window will list any line numbers, labels, or procedure or function names in your program, so add line numbers to MYFIRST so you can trace it.

In order to trace, or step through, your program as it runs, press *D* to go to the **D**ebug menu. Use the arrow keys or press *T* to get to the **T**race option and then toggle it on by pressing *Enter*. Press *Esc* to exit from the **D**ebug menu and then press *R* for **R**un. (Since you've modified your program, it will be automatically recompiled before it is run.) Look at the Trace window to check out your program's tracing.

Note that you can also trace your program by placing the *trace* compiler directive in your program when you write it.

The System Windows

Turbo Basic provides four windows to the programming environment:

- The Edit window lets you create/edit any of your programs.
- The Trace window (when toggled on) lists each program line number, label, and procedure and function name as your program runs it.
- The Message window displays compilation statistics and other messages.
- The Run window displays your program output.

These windows can be used in any configuration, but only the Edit and Run windows can be zoomed (one way is to press *F5*).

At any time in the menu system you can switch your point of view and reconfigure a window's size and position. You can also permanently change a window so that each time the system is booted, your preferred window layout is used. (Refer to the Save Options/Window/Setup in "The Setup Menu" in Chapter 3.)

To open a window, select **Open** from the **Window** menu and then choose the window you'd like to make active. By pressing *Scroll Lock* (along with the *Shift* and arrow keys), you can move your selected window to any position on the screen. The **Tile** option automatically makes all open windows visible and of equal size (in other words, they take up equal portions of the screen). The **Stack** option lets you stack, or layer, all open windows at the largest possible size. The active window is on top; only a portion of the other open windows are visible. Use the **Next** option to make another window the active window. The **Zoom** option lets you zoom to full screen the Edit or Run windows. The **Close** option makes the selected window invisible. For more information on resizing and moving windows, refer to the section entitled "The Window Command" in Chapter 3.

The End of the Tour

That's it for your introductory tour of Turbo Basic. Let's quickly review the steps involved in creating and testing a program:

- Start up TB.EXE and specify the source program you'll be working with. If necessary, set any needed compiler options. Then edit the work file. Once ready for testing, press *R* or *C* to compile the program. If the compiler spots any syntax errors, you'll be dropped into the editor at the point where the error occurred.
- Once a source file is free of syntax errors (that is, it has compiled successfully), run it. If you get the results you expect, save the source program to disk. If you don't get the results you expect, edit the source program and repeat the cycle. You may also choose to compile a working program to .EXE file form.

On the distribution disk you'll find several sample source programs. You may find it useful to study these programs, since several demonstrate aspects of Turbo Basic that are different from or not present in Interpretive BASIC.

C H A P T E R 3

Turbo Basic: The Program

The Turbo Editor

Turbo Basic's built-in editor is specifically designed for creating program source text. If you are familiar with MicroPro's WordStar program, you already know how to use the editor, since its commands are almost identical to WordStar's.

When you choose **Edit** from Turbo Basic's main menu, the Edit window is brought to the top and highlighted, and you are placed in the editor. To leave the editor and return to the main menu bar, press ***Esc*** (the data in the Edit window remains on screen).

You can enter text pretty much as though you were using a typewriter. To end a line, press the ***Enter*** key. When you've entered enough lines to fill the screen, the top line scrolls off the screen. Don't worry, it isn't lost, and you can move back and forth in your text with the scrolling commands that are described later.

The Turbo Basic editor, unlike WordStar, has an "undo" facility that lets you take back changes if you haven't yet left the line. This command (*Ctrl-QL*) is described in the section entitled "Miscellaneous Editing Commands."

Now, let's take a look at the information the status line of the editor window provides:

```
X:Filename.typ    Line    Col  Insert    Indent  Tab
```

X:Filename.typ
Indicates the drive, name, and extension of the file being edited. If the file name and extension is NONAME.BAS, then you have not yet specified a file name. (NONAME.BAS is Turbo Basic's default file name.)

Line
Indicates which line number contains the cursor (relative to the top of the file, not the top of the screen).

Col
Shows which column number contains the cursor.

Insert
Indicates that you are currently in "Insert mode." In Insert mode, characters entered on the keyboard are inserted at the cursor position. Text in front of the cursor moves to the right as you enter new characters. Use the *Ins* key or *Ctrl-V* to toggle the editor between Insert mode and Overwrite mode, in which text entered at the keyboard overwrites characters under the cursor instead of inserting them before existing text. Note: new text lines cannot be entered when you're in Overwrite mode.

Indent
Indicates the auto-indent feature is on. Turn it off with the auto-indent on/off command, *Ctrl-OI*.

Tab
Indicates whether or not you can insert tabs. Use *Ctrl-OT* to toggle this on or off.

Operating the Editor

The most important thing to learn about any editor is how to move the cursor around. You can move around the screen by using a special group of control characters: pressing the *Ctrl* key while simultaneously pressing any of the keys, *A*, *S*, *D*, *F*, *E*, *R*, *X*, *C*, *W*, and *Z*.

The characters are arranged on the keyboard in a manner that logically indicates their use. For example, in the following display:

```
  E
S   D
  X
```

pressing *Ctrl-E* moves the cursor up, *Ctrl-X* moves it down, *Ctrl-S* moves it to the left, and *Ctrl-D* moves it to the right.

The editor uses approximately 50 commands to move the cursor around, page through text, find and replace strings, and so on. These commands can be grouped into four main categories:

- Cursor movement commands
- Insert and delete commands
- Block commands
- Miscellaneous commands

Each group contains logically related commands that are described in the following sections. (Table 3-1 summarizes the commands.) Each entry consists of a command definition, followed by the default keystrokes used to activate the command.

Table 3-1 *Summary of Editor Commands*

Cursor Movement Commands	
Character left	*Ctrl-S* or *Left arrow*
Character right	*Ctrl-D* or *Right arrow*
Word left	*Ctrl -A*
Word right	*Ctrl-F*
Line up	*Ctrl-E* or *Up arrow*
Line down	*Ctrl-X* or *Down arrow*
Scroll up	*Ctrl-W*
Scroll down	*Ctrl-Z*
Page up	*Ctrl-R* or *PgUp*
Page down	*Ctrl-C* or *PgDn*
Extended Movement Commands	
Beginning of line	*Ctrl-QS* or *Home*
End of line	*Ctrl-QD* or *End*
Top of window	*Ctrl-QE*
Bottom of window	*Ctrl-QX*
Top of file	*Ctrl-QR*
End of file	*Ctrl-QC*
Beginning of block	*Ctrl-QB*
End of block	*Ctrl-QK*
Last cursor position	*Ctrl-QP*

Table 3-1 Summary of Editor Commands, continued

Insert and Delete Commands	
Insert mode on/off	*Ctrl-V* or *Ins*
Insert line	*Ctrl-N*
Delete line	*Ctrl-Y*
Delete to end of line	*Ctrl-QY*
Delete character left of cursor	*Ctrl-H* or *Backspace*
Delete character under cursor	*Ctrl-G* or *Del*
Delete word right	*Ctrl-T*
Block Commands	
Mark block begin	*Ctrl-KB* or *F7*
Mark block end	*Ctrl-KK* or *F8*
Mark single word	*Ctrl-KT*
Copy block	*Ctrl-KC*
Move block	*Ctrl-KV*
Delete block	*Ctrl-KY*
Read block from disk	*Ctrl-KR*
Write block to disk	*Ctrl-KW*
Hide/display block	*Ctrl-KH*
Print block	*Ctrl-KP*
Miscellaneous Commands	
Quit edit, no save	*Ctrl-KD*, *Ctrl-KQ*, or *Esc*
Save and edit	*Ctrl-KS* or *F2*
New file	*F3*
Tab	*Ctrl-I* or *Tab*
Tab mode	*Ctrl-OT*
Auto indent on/off	*Ctrl-OI*
Restore line	*Ctrl-QL*
Set place marker	*Ctrl-KN*
Find place marker	*Ctrl-QN*
Find	*Ctrl-QF*
Find and replace	*Ctrl-QA*
Repeat last find	*Ctrl-L*
Control character prefix	*Ctrl-P*
Abort operation	*Ctrl-U*
Restore error message	*Ctrl-QW*

Basic Movement Commands

Here are some basic commands to start you editing a file right away.

Character left *Ctrl-S* or *Left arrow*
Moves the cursor one character to the left.

Character right *Ctrl-D* or *Right arrow*
Moves the cursor one character to the right.

Word left *Ctrl-A*
Moves the cursor to the beginning of the word to the left. A word is defined as a sequence of characters separated by one of the following:

space < > , ; . ( ) [ ] ^ ' * + − / $

This command works across line breaks.

Word right *Ctrl-F*
Moves the cursor to the beginning of the word to the right (see the definition of a word in "Word left"). This command works across line breaks.

Line up *Ctrl-E* or *Right arrow*
Moves the cursor up one line.

Line down *Ctrl-X* or *Down arrow*
Moves the cursor to the line below.

Scroll up *Ctrl-W*
Scrolls toward the beginning of the file, one line at a time (the entire screen scrolls down).

Scroll down *Ctrl-Z*
Scrolls toward the end of the file, one line at a time (the entire screen scrolls up).

Page up *Ctrl-R* or *PgUp*
Moves the cursor one page up, less one line.

Page down *Ctrl-C* or *PgDn*
Moves the cursor one page down, less one line.

Extended Movement Commands

You may sometimes want to move faster in your documents than the basic movement commands allow. The editor provides six commands to move instantly to the extreme ends of lines, to the beginning and end of the file, and to the last cursor position.

Beginning of line *Ctrl-QS* or *Home*
Moves the cursor to the beginning of the current line (column one).

End of line *Ctrl-QD* or *End*
Moves the cursor to the end of the current line.

Top of screen *Ctrl-QE*
Moves the cursor to the top of the screen.

Bottom of screen *Ctrl-QX*
Moves the cursor to the bottom of the screen.

Top of file *Ctrl-QR*
Moves to the first character in the file.

End of file *Ctrl-QC*
Moves to the last character in the file.

Lastly, the *Ctrl-Q* prefix with a *B*, *K*, or *P* control character allows you to jump to certain special points in a document.

Beginning of block *Ctrl-QB*
Moves the cursor to the block-begin marker set with *Ctrl-KB*. The command works even if the block is not displayed (see "Hide/display block" under "Block Commands") or if the block-end marker is not set.

End of block *Ctrl-QK*
Moves the cursor to the block-end marker set with *Ctrl-KK*. The command works even if the block is not displayed (see "Hide/display block") or the block-begin marker is not set.

Last cursor position *Ctrl-QP*
Moves to the last position of the cursor before the last command. This command is particularly useful after a Find or Find/replace operation has been executed and you'd like to return to the last position before its execution.

Insert and Delete Commands

You can't write a program just by moving the cursor around. You've also got to be able to insert and delete text. The following commands insert and delete characters, words, and lines.

Insert mode on/off *Ctrl-V* or *Ins*
When entering text, you can choose between two basic entry modes: *Insert* and *Overwrite*. You can switch between these modes with the Insert mode toggle, *Ctrl-V* or *Ins*. The current mode is displayed in the status line at the top of the screen.

Insert mode is the editor's default, letting you insert new characters into old text. Text to the right of the cursor simply moves to the right as you enter new text.

Use Overwrite mode to replace old text with new; any characters entered replace existing characters under the cursor. You can't insert new lines of text in Overwrite mode.

Delete character left of cursor *Ctrl-H* or *Backspace*
Moves one character to the left and deletes the character positioned there. Any characters to the right of the cursor move one position to the left. This can also be used to remove line breaks.

Delete character under cursor *Ctrl-G* or *Del*
Deletes the character under the cursor and moves any characters to the right of the cursor one position to the left. This command does not work across line breaks.

Delete word right of cursor *Ctrl-T*
Deletes the word to the right of the cursor. This command works across line breaks, and may be used to remove line breaks.

Insert line *Ctrl-N*
Inserts a line break at the cursor position.

Delete line *Ctrl-Y*
Deletes the line containing the cursor and moves any lines below it one line up. There's no way to restore a deleted line, so use this command with care.

Delete to end of line *Ctrl-QY*
Deletes all text from the cursor position to the end of the line.

Block Commands

The block commands also require a control character command sequence. If you feel dazzled at this point, return to this section when you feel the need to move, delete, or copy whole chunks of text. For the persevering, let's continue.

A block of text is any amount of text, from a single character to hundreds of lines that have been surrounded with special block-marker characters. There can be only one block in a document at a time. A block is marked by placing a block-begin marker before the first character and a block-end marker after the last character of the desired portion of the text. Once marked, the block may be copied, moved, deleted, or written to a file.

Mark block begin *Ctrl-KB* or *F7*
Marks the beginning of a block. The marker itself is not visible, and the block itself only becomes visible when the block-end marker is set. Marked text (a block) is displayed in a different intensity.

Mark block end *Ctrl-KK* or *F8*
Marks the end of a block. The marker itself is invisible, and the block itself becomes visible only when the block-begin marker is also set.

Mark single word *Ctrl-KT*

Marks a single word as a block, replacing the block-begin/block-end sequence, which is a bit clumsy for marking a single word. If the cursor is placed within a word, then this word will be marked. If it is not within a word, then the word to the left of the cursor will be marked.

Hide/display block *Ctrl-KH*

Causes the visual marking of a block to be alternately switched off and on. The block manipulation commands (copy, move, delete, and write to a file) work only when the block is displayed. Block-related cursor movements (jump to beginning/end of block) work whether the block is hidden or displayed.

Copy block *Ctrl-KC*

Copies a previously marked block to the current cursor position. The original block is unchanged, and the markers are placed around the new copy of the block. If no block is marked or the cursor is within the marked block, nothing happens.

Move block *Ctrl-KV*

Moves a previously marked block from its original position to the cursor position. The block disappears from its original position and the markers remain around the block at its new position. If no block is marked, nothing happens.

Delete block *Ctrl-KY*

Deletes a previously marked block. No provision exists to restore a deleted block, so be careful with this command.

Write block to disk *Ctrl-KW*

Writes a previously marked block to a file. The block is left unchanged, and the markers remain in place. When this command is issued, you are prompted for the name of the file to write to. The file can be given any legal name (the default extension is .BAS). (If you prefer to use a file name without an extension, append a period to the end of its name.)

You can use wildcards to select a file to overwrite; a directory is displayed. If the file specified already exists, a warning is issued before the existing file is overwritten. If no block is marked, nothing happens.

Read block from disk *Ctrl-KR*

Reads a disk file into the current text at the cursor position, exactly as if it were a block. The text read is then marked as a block. When this command is issued, you are prompted for the name of the file to read. You can use wildcards to select a file to read; a directory is displayed. The file specified may be any legal file name.

Print block *Ctrl-KP*

Sends the marked block to the printer. If no block has been marked or if the marked block is hidden, the entire file is printed.

Miscellaneous Editing Commands

This section describes commands that do not fall into any of the aforementioned categories.

Quit edit, no save *Ctrl-KD*, *Ctrl-KQ*, or *Esc*

Quits the editor and returns you to the main menu. Saving the edited file on disk is done explicitly with the main menu's **S**ave option under the **F**iles command, automatically via the **A**uto save edit option under **M**iscellaneous in the **S**etup menu, or while in the editor (see the next command).

Save and Edit *Ctrl-KS* or *F2*

Saves the file and remains in the editor.

New file *F3*

Lets you erase text from your current edit file and create a new file; otherwise, it simply creates a new file. When you press *F3*, you are queried whether you want to save the current text file if one exists.

Tab *Ctrl-I* or *Tab*

Tabs are fixed to eight columns apart in the Turbo Basic editor.

Tab mode *Ctrl-OT*

Toggles the tab option on and off. When "Tab" is visible onscreen, you can insert tabs; when toggled off, the tab is automatically set to the beginning of the first word in the previous line. (When Tab is on, auto-indent is disabled.)

Auto indent on/off *Ctrl-OI*

Provides automatic indenting of successive lines. When active, the indentation of the current line is repeated on each following line; that is, when you press *Enter*, the cursor does not return to column one but to the starting column of the line you just terminated. When you want to change the indentation, use the space bar and *Left arrow* key to select the new column. When auto indent is on, the message Indent is displayed in the status line; when off, the message is removed. Auto indent is on by default. (When Tab is on, auto-indent is disabled.)

Restore line *Ctrl-QL*

Lets you undo changes made to a line as long as you have not left the line. The line is restored to its original state regardless of any changes you have made.

Set place marker *Ctrl-KN*

Mark up to four places in text by pressing *Ctrl-K*, followed by a single digit (0–3). After marking your location, you can work elsewhere in the file and then easily return to your marked location by using the *Ctrl-QN* command (being sure to use the same marker number).

Find place marker *Ctrl-QN*

Finds up to four place markers (0–3) in text. Move the cursor to any previously set marker by pressing *Ctrl-QP* and the marker number.

Find *Ctrl-QF*

Lets you search for a string of up to 30 characters. When you enter this command, the status line is cleared, and you are prompted for a search string. Enter the string you are looking for and then press *Enter*. The search string may contain any characters, including control characters. Control characters are entered into the search string with the *Ctrl-P* prefix. For example, enter a *Ctrl-T* by holding down the *Ctrl* key as you press *P* and then *T*. You may include a line break in a search string by specifying *Ctrl-M J* (carriage return/line feed). Notice that *Ctrl-A* has a special meaning: It matches any character and may be used as a wildcard in search strings.

Search strings may be edited with the Character left, Character right, Word left, and Word right commands. Word right recalls the previous search string, which may then be edited. The search operation may be aborted with the Abort command (*Ctrl-U*).

When the search string is specified, you are asked for search options. The following options are available:

B Searches backward from the current cursor position toward the beginning of the text.

G Globally searches the entire text, irrespective of the current cursor position, stopping *only* at the last occurrence of your search string.

n Where *n* equals a number, finds the *n*th occurrence of the search string, counted from the current cursor position.

N Finds the next occurrence of a search string, starting at your current position in your file. Note that the *G* option overrides *N* when both are used at the same time.

U Ignores uppercase/lowercase distinctions.

W Searches for whole words only, skipping matching patterns embedded in other words.

Examples:

W Searches for whole words only. The search string "term" will match "term," for example, but not "terminal."

BU Searches backward and ignores uppercase/lowercase differences. "Block" matches both "blockhead" and "BLOCKADE," and so on.

125 Finds the 125th occurrence of the search string.

You can end the list of find options (if any) by pressing *Enter* and the search starts. If the text contains a target matching the search string, the cursor is positioned at the end of the target, or at the beginning if searching backward. The search operation may be repeated by the Repeat last find command (*Ctrl-L*).

Find and replace *Ctrl-QA*
This operation works identically to the Find command except that you can replace the "found" string with any other string of up to 30 characters. Note that *Ctrl-A* can be used in the Find string as a wildcard but has no special meaning in the Replace string.

When the search string is specified, you are asked to enter the string to replace the search string. Enter up to 30 characters; control character entry and editing is performed as stated in the Find command. If you just press *Enter*, the target is replaced with nothing, and in effect is deleted.

Your choice of options are the same as those in the Find command, with the addition of the following:

N Replaces without asking; does not ask for confirmation of each occurrence of the search string.

n Replaces the next *n* cases of the search string. When also using the *G* option, the search begins at the top of the file; otherwise it starts at the current cursor position.

Examples:

N10 Finds the next ten occurrences of the search string and replaces without asking.

GW Finds and replaces whole words in the entire text, ignoring uppercase/lowercase. It prompts for a replacement string.

GNU Finds throughout the file uppercase and lowercase small, antelope-like creatures (get it?) and replaces them without asking.

Again, you can end the option list (if any) by pressing *Enter*, and the Find and replace starts. When the item is found (and if the *N* option is not specified), the cursor is positioned at the end of the item, and you are asked "Replace (Y/N)?" at the prompt line at the top of the screen. You may abort the Find-and-replace operation at this point with the Abort command (*Ctrl-U*). The Find-and-replace operation may be repeated by the Repeat last find command (*Ctrl-L*).

Repeat last find *Ctrl-L*
Repeats the latest Find or Find-and-replace operation as if all information had been reentered.

Control character prefix *Ctrl-P*
Allows you to enter control characters into the file by prefixing the desired control character with a *Ctrl-P*; that is, first press *Ctrl-P*, then press the desired control character. Control characters will appear as low-intensity capital letters on the screen (or inverse, depending on your screen setup).

Abort operation *Ctrl-U*
Lets you abort any command in process whenever it pauses for input, such as when Find and replace asks "Replace Y/N?", or during entry of a search string or a file name (Block read and write).

Restore error message *Ctrl-QW*
Press these keys to restore the error message once it has disappeared from the Editor window status line.

The Editor Versus WordStar

A few of the Turbo Basic editor's commands are slightly different from WordStar. Note also that although the editor contains only a subset of WordStar's commands, several features not found in WordStar have been added to enhance program source code editing. These differences are discussed here.

Turbo's cursor movement controls, *Ctrl-S*, *Ctrl-D*, *Ctrl-E*, and *Ctrl-X*, move freely around on the screen without jumping to column one on empty lines. This does not mean that the screen is full of blanks—on the contrary, all trailing blanks are automatically removed. This way of moving the cursor is especially useful for program editing; for example, when matching indented FOR/NEXT pairs.

Ctrl-S and *Ctrl-D* do not work across line breaks. To move from one line to another you must use *Ctrl-E*, *Ctrl-X*, *Ctrl-A*, or *Ctrl-F*.

In Turbo Basic, carriage returns cannot be entered at the end of a file in Overwrite mode; that is, if Insert mode is off, pressing *Enter* at the end of a file will not insert a carriage return character or move the cursor to the next line. However, you can either switch to Insert mode or use *Ctrl-N* in Overwrite mode to enter carriage returns.

The WordStar sequence *Ctrl-Q Del*, delete from cursor position to beginning of line, is not supported.

Turbo Basic allows you to mark a single word as a block using *Ctrl-KT*. This is more convenient than WordStar's two-step process of marking the beginning and the end of the word separately.

Since editing in Turbo Basic is done entirely in memory, the *Ctrl-KD* command does not change the file on disk as it does in WordStar. Updating the disk file must be done explicitly with the Save option within the **F**ile menu or automatically via the **A**uto save edit option under **M**iscellaneous in the **S**etup menu. You can also use *F2* or *Ctrl-KS*.

Turbo's *Ctrl-KQ* does not resemble WordStar's *Ctrl-KQ* (quit edit) command. The changed text is not abandoned—it is left in memory, ready to be compiled and saved.

Turbo's ***Ctrl-QL*** command restores a line to its pre-edit contents as long as the cursor has not left the line.

The Turbo editor's ***Ctrl-QI*** command toggles the auto-indent feature on and off.

Last, but not least, Turbo's ***Backspace*** key works like WordStar's ***Del*** key: It deletes the character to the left of the cursor. ***Del*** in Turbo deletes the character *under* the cursor.

The Compiler

Turbo Basic's compiler is an all-assembly language, high-performance compiler. To invoke the compiler, press ***C*** (for **C**ompile) at the main menu. If a **M**ain file has been set, then, if necessary, you are prompted whether you'd like to save the current work file. If so, the current work file is saved, the **M**ain file brought in, and compilation begins.

The compiler writes the compiled program either to memory (the default) or to disk, depending on the current **C**ompile to setting of the compiler **O**ptions menu. As it works, the compiler ticks off in increments of 20 the number of lines and statements processed to that point. The status of the compiler is displayed in the Message window.

If an error is detected, the editor is automatically invoked and the cursor is positioned on the offending statement. The error message is displayed on the top line of the editor. When you move the error, the status line reappears. To restore the error message, press *Ctrl-QW*.

After a successful compilation, the Message window displays the total number of lines and statements in the program, plus the amount of free space left in memory for compilation (see Figure 3-1). Note that the amount of free space left will be greater when you compile to an .EXE or .TBC file than when you're compiling to memory.

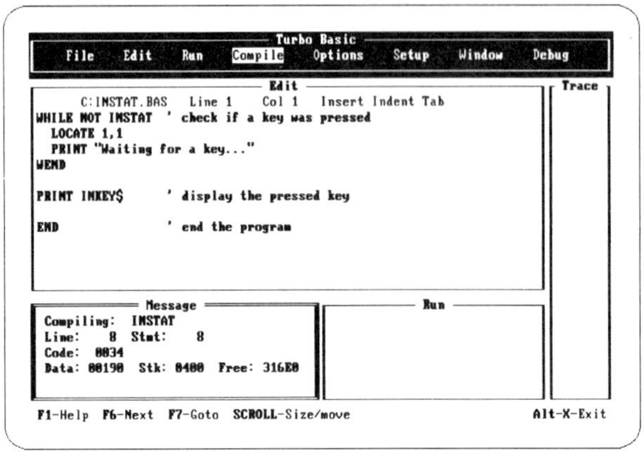

Figure 3-1 Compilation Screen

The three-line object code summary lists in hexadecimal the size of the code segments, the stack, and the data area of the generated program.

The Main Menu

Turbo Basic operates by a series of commands, pull-down menus, and pop-up menus, and offers four windows to the programming environment (shown in Figure 3-2). This section describes the function of each main menu command and their respective pull-down menus and pop-up menu options (if any).

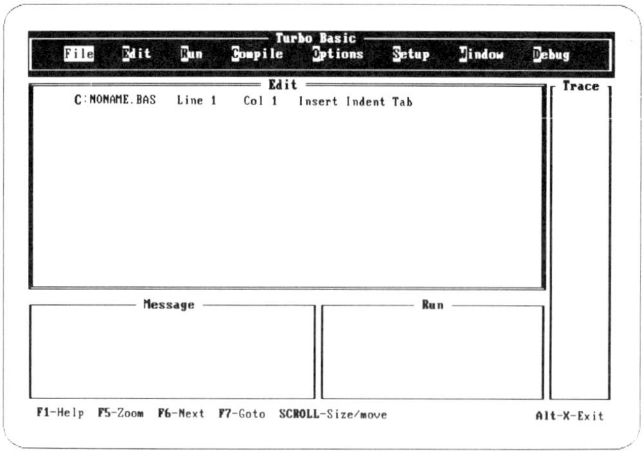

Figure 3-2 Main Menu

To make a selection and invoke a function at the main menu, press the key corresponding to the highlighted, uppercase letter of the desired option or use the arrow keys to move to the desired option and then press *Enter*. For example, pressing *E* (for Edit) starts up the editor. Pressing *Enter* after the selected keystroke is not required. To exit from any of the pull-down menus, simply press *Esc* (more than once if you are in pop-up menus) to return to the main menu.

If you are in the Edit window or any of the pull-down or pop-up menus, pressing *Alt* and the first letter of a menu item will take you to that menu item.

Installation of colors, directories, and other features can be performed via the Setup pull-down menu (described later). Any changes made can be saved in a .TB file or directly to the TB.EXE file in the same directory as the Turbo Basic system (the Turbo directory). The default .TB file is TBCONFIG.TB, but several .TB files can be maintained via the Setup command.

To resize and/or move the active window (the one with the double bars around it), press *Scroll Lock*. Then hold down the *Shift* key and use any of the arrow keys to move and/or size the window to the right, left, up, down, and so on.

Turbo Basic's context-sensitive help provides information relevant to your particular screen, no matter where you are in the menu system. To get help at any level, press *F1*; pressing *Alt-F1* takes you to the previous help screen.

Turbo Basic also has a number of keys ("hotkeys") you can use no matter where you are in the main menu. For example, to exit Turbo Basic from anywhere in the menu system, you can press *Alt-X*. For your convenience, all of the hotkeys are listed in Table 3-2.

***Table 3-2** Turbo Basic Hotkeys*

Keys	Functions
F1	Provides context-sensitive help
F2	Saves your file
F3	Creates new file
F5	Zooms the Run or Edit window
F6	Switches the active window
F7	From within the menu system, goes to the active window
Scroll Lock	Sizes and moves the active window
Esc	Takes you back to the main menu
Alt-C	Compiles the currently loaded program
Alt-E	Edits the currently loaded program
Alt-R	Runs the currently loaded program
Alt-X	Exits the Turbo Basic system
Alt-F	Takes you to the File menu
Alt-O	Takes you to the Options menu
Alt-D	Takes you to the Debug menu
Alt-W	Takes you to the Window menu

The **File** command provides a pull-down menu of several options (see Figure 3-3).

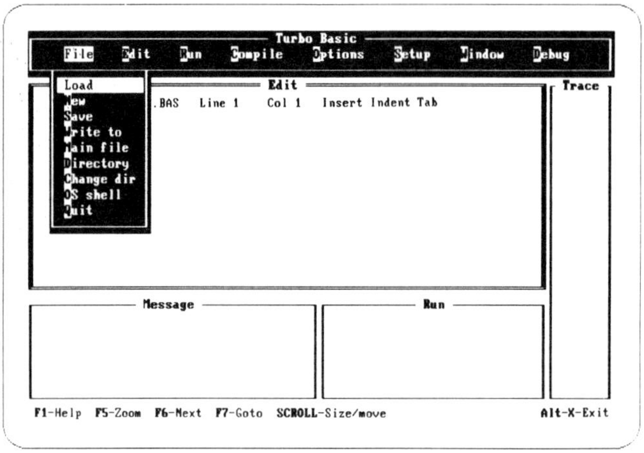

Figure 3-3 File Menu

Load

Load lets you select a work file, which can then be edited, compiled, executed, or saved.

After pressing *L* (for **Load**), you are prompted for a file name. You can enter either of the following:

1. Any legal file name. If the period and file type (extension) are omitted, the .BAS extension is automatically appended. To specify a file name with no extension, enter the name followed by a period.
2. A file name from a directory. The directory facility is consulted when the *File Name* prompt is answered by pressing *Enter* or by typing a file pattern containing wildcards followed by *Enter*. If no file pattern is given, all files are listed. In either case, the cursor can then be moved up and down in the resulting list of file names by using the arrow keys, *Home*, *End*, *PgUp*, and *PgDn*. Choose a file by pressing *Enter*. If you press *Esc*, the cursor returns to the **Load** option.

If you choose to supply your own extensions, avoid those that have special meaning for DOS, such as .EXE, .COM, and .BAT. In addition, don't use .BAK, because the editor creates backups by appending this extension.

Be certain to choose unique file names, whether you use an extension or not. For example, consider files MYPROG.V1 and MYPROG.V2. After editing and saving MYPROG.V1, Turbo Basic renames the original form of the program to MYPROG. BAK. If you were to then edit MYPROG.V2, its original form would also be called MYPROG.BAK, effectively erasing the backup of the first file.

When you press the *Enter* key after entering the name of the work file, Turbo Basic searches the active directory of the logged disk for the file. If it can't find it, a new file is created.

New
This option erases the text currently in the editor and gives the default name NONAME.BAS to the file.

Save
Save saves the current work file to disk. The old version of the named file, if any, is given a .BAK extension. If your work file is named NONAME.BAS and you attempt to save your file, you are given a chance to rename it before the save is executed. If you simply press *Enter*, the file named NONAME.BAS is saved.

Write to
After editing, use the **Write** to option to write the current edit file to disk under a new name. You are prompted to select a new name.

Main file
When working with large programs, you may choose to break the source up into manageable sections. If you exceed the character capacity of the editor, you will have no choice in the matter. The individual parts of a large program are stored and edited as independent "include" files, but when it comes time to compile, they are put together into a single unit.

In tandem with appropriate $INCLUDE metastatements, the **Main** file selection allows you to compile multiple source file programs.

The source module you define as the **Main** file should be the one with the $INCLUDE directives. As always, to edit any module of the program (even the **Main** module), make it the currently loaded file.

Upon receiving a **Compile** command, Turbo Basic checks to see if the current work file is different from the **Main** file. If it isn't different (or if no **Main** file is selected), the work file is compiled. If it is different, you are prompted to save the work file (if it has been changed), and the **Main** file is then loaded into memory. If an error is found during compilation, the file containing the error is automatically loaded so that it may be edited. When the error has been corrected and compilation restarted, you are prompted to save the corrected work file. The **Main** file is then reloaded.

Directory
Press *D* to get a directory listing, to search subdirectories, and to change the mask on the fly.

Change dir
Change dir is used to select another directory. After pressing *C*, you are prompted for a directory path; this becomes your current directory (wherever you go, there you are). Any legal path name can be given. See "The Setup Command" for a description of the other directories used by the system.

OS shell
Pressing *O* calls the DOS operating system; Turbo Basic remains resident in memory. Once DOS has been loaded, any DOS commands can be executed. Control is returned to the resident Turbo Basic system with the EXIT command.

Quit
Quit exits you from the Turbo Basic program to DOS. You are prompted if your current edit file has been modified and has not been saved. (You may also exit Turbo Basic by pressing *Alt-X* from anywhere in the menu system.)

The Edit Command

The **Edit** command invokes the built-in screen editor, passing it the work file for editing. (You name the work file via the **Load** command in the **File** pull-down menu). If a work-file name has not been specified, NONAME.BAS is provided.

To exit the editor and return to the main menu, press *Esc*. Your source text remains displayed on the screen, you need only press *E* to return to it.

The Run Command

The **Run** command executes a program residing in memory. If a compiled program is already in memory, and the source of that program has not been modified in the editor since the last Compile or **Run** and no options have changed, it is executed immediately. If the compiled program is not in memory, the source program in the editor is first compiled, and the resulting program executed.

During program execution, pressing *Ctrl-Break* interrupts program execution if the **Keyboard** break option is set and the running program does I/O. If an error is detected, you are placed in the editor at the point in the program where the error occurred. A description of the error appears on the status line of the editor. Then correct your error and rerun your program (recompilation will occur automatically).

In the Message window, Turbo Basic displays in increments of 20 the number of lines and statements processed. The Run window displays the program output.

Press *Alt-F5* to zoom the Run window while running a program.

The Compile Command

The Compile command compiles the program currently in the editor. Compilation results in a program resident in memory (the default), in an .EXE file, or in a .TBC (chain) file, depending on the current setting of the **C**ompile to switch in the **O**ptions pull-down menu.

Press *C* (or press *Enter* when positioned on this option) to begin compilation. If a **M**ain file is not specified, the loaded file is compiled.

If a **M**ain file has been selected, you are prompted whether you want to save the current work file (if the file in the editor has been modified). The **M**ain file is then loaded and compiled.

As the compilation proceeds, Turbo Basic displays in the Message window the number of lines and statements that have been processed in increments of 20. *Ctrl-Break* aborts the compilation.

If an error is detected, you are placed in the editor at the point in the program where the error occurred. A description of the error appears on the status line of the editor. Correct the offending statement and then recompile.

The Options Command

The **O**ptions command provides a pull-down menu of compiler options (see Figure 3-4). These options are global, controlling the entire compilation unless overridden by internal source program metastatements.

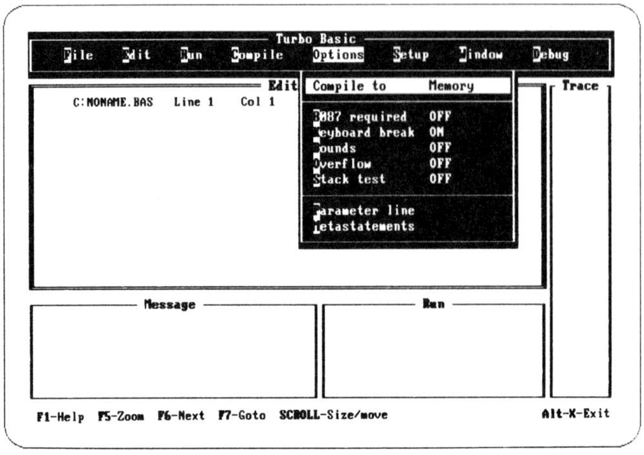

Figure 3-4 Options Menu

Compile to
This setting lets you compile your programs to **Memory**, an **EXE** file, or a **Chain** file. Press *C* and *Enter* (or you can press just *Enter*) to reach the pop-up menu listing these options, then use the arrow keys or press the key that corresponds to the highlighted uppercase letter to make your choice.

The default, **Compile** to **Memory**, is best for program debugging and testing, since it produces the fastest results.

The **EXE**cutable file setting causes the compiler to create programs that can run from the operating system (programs with the .EXE extension). Normally, this mode is selected after a program has been debugged, although certain features of the language (for example, CHAINing) can only be tested from DOS.

The **Chain** file setting produces files (with the .TBC extension) suitable for CHAINing or RUNning from a Turbo Basic-created .EXE file. These files don't include library routines, so they can't be run independently.

Turbo Basic has several code generation switches accessed through the **O**ptions menu. Each switch defaults to off, and produces by default the fastest, smallest, and most versatile programs possible. You may choose to turn on some or all of these switches during your program's development and debugging stages. To reach any option, use the arrow keys or press the highlighted uppercase letter of your choice. These options can be saved to a configuration file via the **S**etup menu.

You can toggle on and off the following options by pressing *Enter* when positioned at the desired item:

- 8087 required
- Keyboard break

- Bounds
- Overflow
- Stack test

8087 required
Turn on this option when you're using an 8087 coprocessor chip for program execution. With this option on, Turbo Basic generates the best possible code for floating-point operations, both fast and compact, using inline 8087 statements. The disadvantage is that a program generated with this option on won't run on a machine without an 8087.

With the 8087 option off (the default), programs can go both ways; that is, if an 8087 is available, the program will use it. If not, the program will use software routines to accomplish the same thing (albeit more slowly).

Note: In some cases, a program will read that your machine has an 8087 chip when it really doesn't; for example, if you've set the switch on for 8087 but have yet to install the chip. This will either cause Turbo Basic to hang when running a program or to generate compile-time errors when compiling. Environment variables solve this problem nicely. Add the following to your AUTOEXEC.BAT file:

```
SET87=no
```

Take a look at Appendix G, "A DOS Primer," for more information on environment variables and AUTOEXEC.BAT files.

Keyboard break
If you want to interrupt a program with *Ctrl-Break*, turn this option on. Note that this applies to *Ctrl-Break* only, not *Ctrl-C*; *Ctrl-C* cannot interrupt a Turbo Basic program. Keep in mind that interrupting a program with *Ctrl-Break* is final—there is no way to continue execution later.

It is also important to note that *Ctrl-Break* doesn't take effect until the program outputs text (not graphics) to the screen or printer or performs keyboard input. This means that you cannot interrupt sequences that don't perform I/O; for example:

```
TightLoop: GOTO TightLoop
```

runs until you reset the system. (However, to save you from this tight loop problem, we have equipped Turbo Basic with an Auto save edit option. In other words, you can set this option on so that if you need to exit from a program by rebooting, you can still manage to save your program. Refer to "The Setup Menu.")

You can use the following options for trapping certain types of run-time errors. Normally, when a program is in the development phase, you'll want all of these options turned on so that you can catch any problems. When your program is debugged, turn these options off to generate a final program version that is faster and requires less memory.

Bounds
If turned on, this option causes the compiler to generate array-subscript-checking code. Subscript-checking code ensures that a subscript is appropriate, given the size of the array it is about to be used on, before reading or writing the indicated element. With **Bounds** checking on, a Subscript range error (error 9) is reported whenever your program attempts to use a subscript too large or too small for a given array.

For example, consider this program:

```
DIM myArray(100)
  x = 114
  y = myArray(x)
```

myArray doesn't have a 114th element, although this blunder won't be caught by the compiler. However, if the program is compiled with **Bounds** testing turned on, a Subscript range error occurs when the third line is executed.

If you run this program with bounds checking turned off, no error is reported, and the value loaded into *y* is whatever is in memory a few bytes beyond the last element of *myArray*. Writing to a nonexistent array element is even worse, since memory used to store who-knows-what is silently overwritten.

Note that the compiler always reports constant out-of-range subscripts. The following program won't compile, regardless of the value of the **Bounds** switch:

```
DIM myArray(100)
  y = myArray(114)
```

Overflow
Overflow results when an arithmetic operation produces a value beyond the storage capacity of integers (−32,768 to +32,767). For example, the code fragment

```
x% = 22555
x% = x% + 19000
```

overflows the +32,767 limit of integer variables. If you compile this program with **O**verflow checking on, an Overflow run-time error is generated. However, with checking off, an erroneous value is assigned to *x%*, and execution continues as if nothing had happened (which the rest of your program probably won't appreciate).

Watch out for intermediate overflow; for example:

```
y% = 20000 : x% = y%
z = (y% + x%) * 2.1
```

Even though the ultimate result of expression (*y%* + *x%*) * 2.1 easily fits into single precision floating-point format, overflow occurs when *y%* and *x%* are added by integer routines before the result is converted to single precision and multiplied by 2.1. Use the CSNG and CDBL functions to force integer operations to be carried out in floating-point form.

Note that **Overflow** checking occurs for integers, long integers, or either of the floating-point types; however, integers have some exceptions (for instance, register calculations).

Stack test

Turning this switch on causes Turbo Basic to generate code that checks for stack collisions upon entry to each subroutine, function, or procedure. If you suspect that your programs are running out of stack space, compile with this switch turned on. To allocate more stack space, use the $STACK metastatement.

The last two entries in the **Options** menu are **Parameter** line and **Metastatements**.

Parameter line

Selecting **P** causes Turbo Basic to prompt for the string that COMMAND$ will return the next time a program is run. This allows you to simulate command line information to assist you in debugging from within Turbo Basic. Pressing *Enter* after entering your string and then pressing *Esc* returns you to the main menu.

Metastatements

The last of the options in the **Options** menu, **Metastatements**, has its own pop-up menu, shown in Figure 3-5. You can select any option by pressing *S* for **Stack**, *M* for **Music**, or *C* for the **Communications** option; otherwise, you can use the arrow keys and press *Enter* when positioned on the desired option. Note that your source program can override these settings.

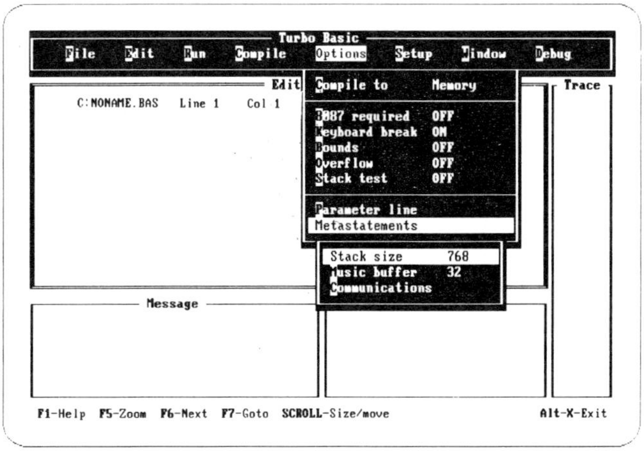

***Figure 3-5** Metastatements Pop-Up Menu*

- Stack size is used to (re)define the stack size. The default is 1024 decimal or 400 Hex bytes (1 paragraph is 16 bytes). When you press *S*, you are prompted for a new stack size in the interval 400 to 7FFE Hex bytes. (See the $STACK metastatement in Chapter 5, "Turbo Basic Reference Directory.")

- **M**usic buffer is the size of the background music buffer. If you're not using SOUND or PLAY, then your resulting code will be smaller if you set this to zero. The minimum is 0; the maximum is 4096 notes. Note that 8 notes equal 1 byte; the default is 32 notes or 256 bytes. (See the $SOUND metastatement in Chapter 5.)
- **C**ommunications refers to the receive buffer for each communications port. (In some programs, you can use the $COM*n* metastatement to change the allocation of either buffer.) The minimum is 0; the maximum is 32767; the default is 256 bytes.

The Setup Command

Select **S**etup when you want to inspect any of the setup parameters, change them, or record the current configuration permanently in a .TB file. The **S**etup menu is shown in Figure 3-6.

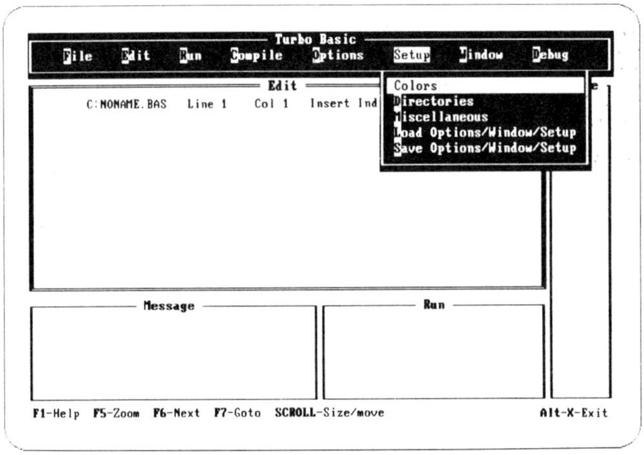

Figure 3-6 *Setup Menu*

Colors
Use this entry to define the colors of one or more system boxes, menus, or windows. Press *C* or *Enter* to bring up the pop-up menu and select **W**indows, **M**enus, or **S**ystem boxes (see Figure 3-7). Three more pop-up menus are available to help you further define changes to the selected window, menu, or box.

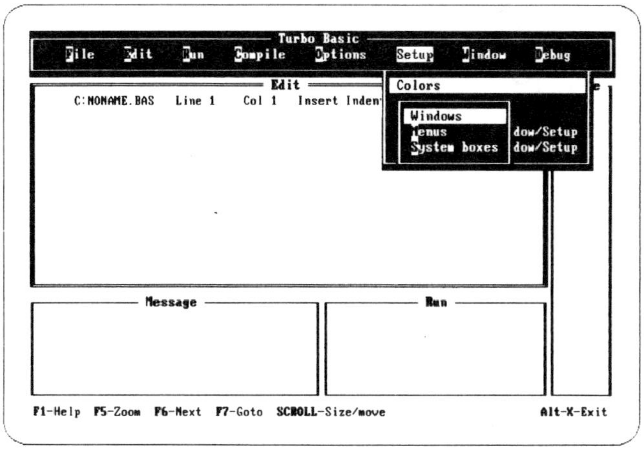

Figure 3-7 Colors' First Pop-Up Menu

As an example, if you select **M**enus from the first pop-up menu, you must choose whether to define the **M**ain/pull-downs, the **F**irst pop-up, **S**econd pop-up, or **T**hird pop-up. If you choose **M**ain/pull-downs, another pop-up appears so you can determine *how* to alter your selection. Your options are **T**itle, **B**order, **N**ormal text, **F**irst letter, **S**election bar, and **R**estore defaults (see Figure 3-8).

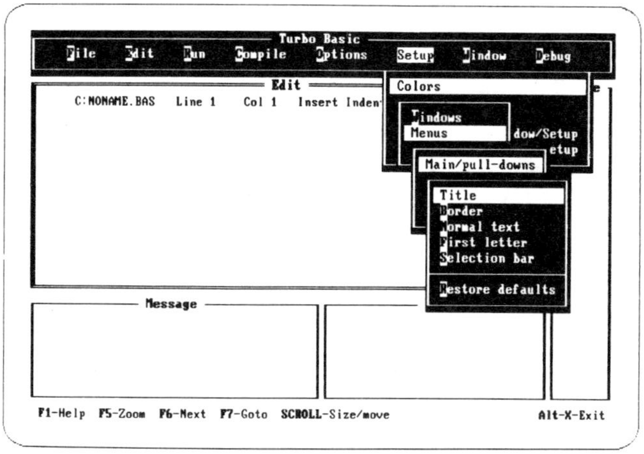

Figure 3-8 Colors' Second Pop-Up Menu

Once you have decided what aspect of the menu to change, say, for example, you choose **S**election bar, a palette selection box appears on your screen. Use the arrow keys to select the desired color from the color palette. Press *Enter* to make your choice and then press *Esc*. The window you have selected reflects the current color value.

Directories
The **Include**, **Executable**, and **Turbo** entries define a drive and path for each of the three directories used by the system. The default directory is wherever you happen to be when you start Turbo Basic.

When selecting a directory, you are prompted for a drive and a path. Type in the drive and/or path, press *Enter*, and Turbo Basic accepts your specification. If you change your mind about which directory you've chosen and want to reselect, you can press *Esc* at any point prior to leaving the system box and before pressing *Enter* and be returned to the directory selections.

The **Include** directories are used for files that contain the Include compiler directive. You can specify multiple directories by separating each one with a semicolon.

The **Executable** directory is used for the .EXE and .TBC files generated by the Turbo Basic system, as well as for compiler-created temporary files. You can only select one directory at a time.

The **Turbo** directory is used for the Turbo Basic system itself; that is, for the system file TB.EXE, the configuration files (.TB), and the help files (TBHELP.TBH). Again, you can only select one directory at a time.

Miscellaneous
Pressing *M* brings up a pop-up menu with two special parameters:

- **Auto save edit.** Toggle this on when you want to automatically save your current work file before running a program.
- **Backup source files.** Toggling this on will automatically back up your files. Toggle it off when you don't want to create a backup file each time you do a save.

All compiler options and setup values are loaded and saved in a configuration file (unless you specify TB.EXE). This is useful for tuning the development environment in different ways. For example, when debugging programs you might want to turn all the compiler options on, as well as enlarge the Trace window and put the global trace flag on. Another sample configuration might be for final production compilations without the Trace or Run windows visible and all option toggles off.

The following options allow you to load and save, respectively, a new configuration setup.

Load Options/Window/Setup
Press *L* to load a .TB file from the Turbo directory and reset the system according to the parameters it contains.

Save Options/Window/Setup
S saves the current setup in a .TB file in the Turbo directory. The configuration can be given any name, but the default (TBCONFIG.TB) is automatically used when Turbo Basic is first started up. You may also save the configuration directory to the TB.EXE file. However, if you do this, you are prompted as to whether you want to alter the original TB.EXE file.

The Window Command

As stated in the main menu section, you can resize and move any active window by pressing *Scroll Lock*, then hold down the *Shift* key and use any of the arrow keys to move the window in the direction desired. By default, all windows are active until you choose to close them.

Press *W* now to activate the **W**indow command's pull-down menu, shown in Figure 3-9.

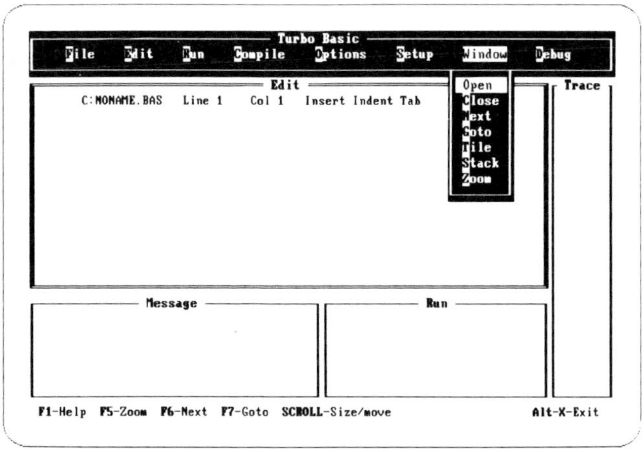

Figure 3-9 Window Menu

Open
Press *O* and select **E**dit, **R**un, **M**essage, or **T**race from the pop-up menu. **O**pen makes the selected window "active." This means if the window had been previously closed, it will be created, and in all cases the "opened" window will be brought to the top of the screen. All other window commands now affect the active window.

Close
Close hides the currently selected window, though it can still be written to.

Next
The **Next** option lets you select another window as the active window without returning to the **Open** option to select a new window. Repeatedly pressing **Next** cycles through the windows. If in a window or main menu, the *F6* key operates the same as the **Next** option.

Goto
After opening a window, use **Goto** to enter that window without returning to the main menu.

Tile
Press *T* to make all active windows occupy an equal portion of the screen. *F6* switches the active window.

Stack
Use the **Stack** option to layer all open windows to the largest possible size. Press *F6* to bring the last screen in the stack to the top of the screen.

Zoom
Selecting the **Zoom** option (or *F5*) makes the selected window fill the screen; however, this option only works on the Run and Edit windows. To regain your original screen setup, toggle **Zoom** again.

The Debug Command

The **Debug** facility offers you two valuable options in its pull-down menu: **Trace** and **Run-time error**.

Trace
Trace lets you globally set program tracing. This switch can be overridden with embedded TRON and TROFF statements. Statement labels, line numbers, and procedure and function names are displayed in this window.

When running in trace mode, use *Alt-F9* to toggle between tracing and executing your program. Pressing *Alt-F10* single-steps to the next line number, label, and so on.

Run-time error
This option is used primarily to find errors that occur in .EXE or .TBC files (standalone programs); no messages are given in these cases. If you are running a program under the Turbo Basic system, all of the following is done automatically.

Invoke this function by pressing *R* or *Enter*. You are then asked to provide the program counter value. Turbo Basic then determines the corresponding point in the source code and puts the cursor on the offending statement.

When a run-time error occurs, Turbo Basic tells you the type of error (always in numeric form, and in words if launched from within Turbo Basic) as well as the value in the processor's program counter at the time of the error.

By recompiling, Turbo Basic is able to calculate the point in a source program corresponding to a run-time address in an object program. For example, consider program TEST.BAS:

```
x = 256
PRINT CHR$(x)
```

Although this program is syntactically correct, and will therefore compile successfully, a run-time error will be generated when the system attempts to print a character with an ASCII value of 256:

```
Error 5 Illegal function call at pgm-ctr: 29
```

The **R**un-time error option uses this program counter value to find the statement that caused the error. **Note:** If an invalid counter value is given, the error message Run-time Error Not Found is generated.

C H A P T E R 4

Turbo Basic: The Language

Program Structure

Turbo Basic programs consist of one or more lines of source text, each of which has the following format:

```
[linenumber] statement [:statement] ... [' comment ]
```

or,

```
label:
```

or,

```
$metastatement
```

linenumber is an integer in the range 0 to 65,535, which may optionally identify program lines. Turbo Basic takes a relaxed stance toward line numbers. They can be freely interspersed with labels, and used in some parts of a program and not in others. In fact, they need not follow in numeric sequence; although no two lines can have the same number, and no line can have both a label and a number. Line numbers are essentially labels.

statements are the building blocks that make up programs. Turbo Basic has approximately 100 statement types (see Chapter 5, "Turbo Basic Reference Directory," for a complete list). A line can contain none, one, or several statements, each separated by a colon.

The following are all valid lines of Turbo Basic:

```
Start:                                  ' label only
10                                      ' line number only
$INCLUDE "CONST.TBS"                    ' metastatement
20  a = a + 1                           ' line number plus statement
a = a + 1 : b = b + 1                   ' two statements
30  a = a + 1 : b = b + 1 : c = a + b   ' line number, three statements
```

The 249 column width of Turbo Basic is the only limit to how many statements can appear on a line. Be aware, however, that some schools of programming thought hold that it is poor practice to put more than one statement on a line, unless you are required to do so by a particular syntactic construction (for example, IF/THEN/ELSE). Unlike Interpretive BASIC, Turbo Basic charges no run-time penalty for spacing and commenting your programs generously—spaces, comments, and blank lines are ignored by the compiler.

All schools of thought hold that it is bad form to write lines wider than the editor window's 80 column width (despite the editor's snazzy horizontal scrolling capability). Go wider than 80 columns and you can't see everything on a line all at once. It won't print out very nicely, either.

In situations where syntax requirements force you to build a line longer than 80 characters (the FIELD statement is notorious for this), put an underscore (_) at the end of the line. This causes Turbo Basic to regard the next line as an extension of the first. This line can be similarly continued. For example:

```
FIELD #1, 30 AS name$, 30 AS address1$, 30 AS address2$,_
          15 AS city$, 2 AS state$, 5 AS zip$,_
          30 AS comments$
```

As far as the compiler is concerned, this is one big line starting with FIELD and ending with *comments$*, without any underscore characters.

comment can be any text added to the end of a line and separated from the program itself by a single quote ('). The single quote (') can be used in place of REM to delimit comments from the statements on that line unless it is at the end of a DATA statement (DATA will think it's part of the string). Unlike REM, it isn't necessary to separate single quoted comments from adjoining statements with a colon. For example, the following are equal in the eyes of the compiler:

```
area = radius^2 * 3.14159     ' calculate the area
area = radius^2 * 3.14159     : REM calculate the area
```

label must appear on a line by itself (though a comment may follow), and serves to identify the statement immediately following it. Labels must begin with a letter, and can contain any number of letters and digits. Case is insignificant: THISLABEL and ThisLabel are equivalent. A label must be followed by a colon; however, statements that refer to the label (for example, GOSUB) must not include the colon.

Examples include:

```
SORTSUBROUTINE:
ExitPoint: a = a + 1       ' illegal; labels must be alone on a line
SortInvoices:
GOSUB SortInvoices         ' referencing a label
```

$metastatements are statements that operate at a different level than standard statements. Called compiler directives, they always begin with a dollar sign ($). Standard statements control the computer at runtime; metastatements, like the selections in the **O**ptions menu, control the compiler at compile time.

An example is the $INCLUDE metastatement, which causes the compiler to introduce the contents of another file at a point indicated in the current file. Note that Turbo Basic metastatements don't appear within REMarks like those of some other BASIC compilers. There can be only one metastatement per line.

Turbo Basic Character Set

Turbo Basic is something like an erector set for building programs. It provides you with a set of fundamental language elements (reserved words and symbols) that can be put together in infinite ways to build any software machine conceivable.

The letters *A* to *Z* or *a* to *z*, and the numbers 0 to 9 can be used in forming identifiers (labels, variables, procedures, and function names).

The numbers 0 to 9; the symbols ., +, and −; and the letters *E, e, D* and *d* can all be used in forming numeric constants.

The following symbols have specific meaning to Turbo Basic:

Symbol	Description/Function
=	Equal sign (assignment operator, relational operator)
+	Plus sign (addition and string concatenation operator)
−	Minus sign (subtraction and negation operator)
*	Asterisk (multiplication operator)
/	Slash (division operator)
\	Backslash (integer division operator)
^	Caret (exponentiation operator)
%	Percent sign (integer-type declaration character)
&	Ampersand (long integer-type declaration character and nondecimal base descriptor)
!	Exclamation point (single-precision type declaration character)
#	Number sign (double-precision type declaration character)
$	Dollar sign (string-type declaration character, metastatement prefix)
( )	Parentheses (function/procedure arguments, arrays, expression prioritizing)
[ ]	Square brackets (valid only for arrays)
	Space (separator)
,	Comma (all-purpose delimiter)
.	Period (decimal point, filename extension separator)
'	Single quote (remark delimiter)
;	Semicolon (all-purpose delimiter)
:	Colon (statement delimiter)
?	Question mark (PRINT substitute)
<	Less than (relational operator)
>	Greater than (relational operator)
"	Double quote (string delimiter)
_	Underscore (line continuation character)

Reserved Words

Turbo Basic reserves the use of certain words for predefined syntactic purposes. These reserved words cannot be used as labels, variables, named constants, or procedure or function names, although your identifiers can contain them (see Table 4-1 on page 64).

For example, END is an invalid variable name, because it conflicts with the reserved word END. However, ENDHERE and FRIEND are acceptable. Starting an identifier with FN is also invalid, because it conflicts with the syntax for user-defined functions.

Attempting to use a reserved word as an identifier produces a compile time syntax error.

Table 4-1 Turbo Basic Reserved Words

$COM1	CLOSE	ERR	LOC	POKE	STRING$
$COM2	CLS	ERROR	LOCAL	POS	SUB
$DEBUG	COLOR	EXIT	LOCATE	PRESET	SWAP
$DYNAMIC	COM	EXP	LOF	PRINT	SYSTEM
$ELSE	COMMAND$	EXP10	LOG	PRINT #	TAB
$ENDIF	COMMON	EXP2	LOG10	PSET	TAN
$EVENT	COS	FIELD	LOG2	PUT	THEN
$IF	CSNG	FILES	LOOP	PUT$	TIME$
$INCLUDE	CSRLIN	FIX	LPOS	RANDOM	TIMER
$INLINE	CVD	FN	LPRINT	RANDOMIZE	TO
$LIST	CVI	FOR	LPRINT #	READ	TROFF
$OPTION	CVL	FRE	LSET	REG	TRON
$SEGMENT	CVMD	GET	MEMSET	REM	UBOUND
$SOUND	CVMS	GET$	MID$	RESET	UCASE$
$STACK	CVS	GOSUB	MKDIR	RESTORE	UNTIL
$STATIC	DATA	GOTO	MKD$	RESUME	USING
ABS	DATE$	HEX$	MKI$	RETURN	USR
ABSOLUTE	DECR	IF	MKL$	RIGHT$	USR0
AND	DEF	IMP	MKMD$	RMDIR	USR1
APPEND	DEFDBL	INCR	MKMS$	RND	USR2
AS	DEFINT	INKEY$	MKS$	RSET	USR3
ASC	DEFLNG	INLINE	MOD	RUN	USR4
AT	DEFSNG	INP	MTIMER	SAVE	USR5
ATN	DEFSTR	INPUT	NAME	SCREEN	USR6
BASE	DELAY	INPUT #	NEXT	SEEK	USR7
BEEP	DIM	INPUT$	NOT	SEG	USR8
BIN$	DO	INSTAT	OCT$	SELECT	USR9
BINARY	DRAW	INSTR	OFF	SERVICE	VAL
BLOAD	DYNAMIC	INT	ON	SGN	VARPTR
BSAVE	ELSE	INTERRUPT	OPEN	SHARED	VARPTR$
CALL	ELSEIF	IOCTL	OPTION	SHELL	VARSEG
CASE	END	IOCTL$	OR	SIN	VIEW
CDBL	ENDMEM	KEY	OUT	SOUND	WAIT
CEIL	ENVIRON	KILL	OUTPUT	SPACE$	WEND
CHAIN	ENVIRON$	LBOUND	PAINT	SPC	WHILE
CHDIR	EOF	LCASE$	PALETTE	SQR	WIDTH
CHR$	EQV	LEFT$	PALETTE USING	STATIC	WINDOW
CINT	ERADR	LEN	PEEK	STEP	WRITE
CIRCLE	ERASE	LET	PEN	STICK	WRITE #
CLEAR	ERDEV	LINE	PLAY	STOP	XOR
CLNG	ERDEV$	LIST	PMAP	STR$	
	ERL		POINT	STRIG	

Numbers in Turbo Basic

The care and feeding of numbers constitutes an important part of every programming system. Turbo Basic, in keeping with the BASIC tradition, has been designed to let you pretty much ignore technical considerations about internal numeric handling. If you never give a thought to such matters as calculation speed, precision, and memory requirement, your programs will still probably work as you expect. However, an understanding of the underlying issues will help you write programs that are faster, more accurate, and require less memory.

For efficiency, Turbo Basic stores and processes numbers in four different forms; that is, it supports four unique numeric "types": *integers, long integers, single-precision floating point*, and *double-precision floating point*.

Integers

The simplest and fastest numbers rattling around inside Turbo Basic programs are *integers*. To Turbo Basic, an integer is a number with no decimal point (what mathematicians call whole numbers) within the range −32,768 to 32,767. These values stem from the underlying 16-bit representation of integers: 32,768 is 2^{15}.

Although this range limits the usefulness of integers, there are almost certainly a few variables in every program you will write (such as the counters in FOR/NEXT loops) that can function within these constraints. If so, using integers produces extremely fast and compact code. Your computer is uniquely comfortable performing integer arithmetic (for example, it does it fast), and each number requires only 2 bytes of memory.

The **O**verflow debugging switch in the **O**ptions menu lets you create programs that automatically check and report incidences of integer variable overflow.

Long Integers

In a significant extension to Interpretive BASIC, Turbo Basic supports a numeric type known as *long integers*. To avoid round-off errors, long integers are the perfect data type for financial applications. Like regular integers, long integers cannot contain decimal points. Unlike integers, however, they span a vast range, from −2,147,483,648 to +2,147,483,647 (-2^{31} to 2^{31}, or −2 billion to +2 billion). The down side of this expanded range is that long integers require 4 bytes of storage, and calculating with them takes longer than with integers.

Long integers are relatively efficient, and are definitely worth a close look, especially in machines that aren't 8087-equipped. Depending on your application, decimal points may be less important than you think. For example, you can define monetary amounts in terms of pennies, and divide by 100 to display dollars. Values as large as $20 million can be expressed this way.

Single-Precision Floating Point

Single-precision floating point (or simply single precision) may be the most versatile numeric type within Turbo Basic. Single-precision values can contain decimal points and have a phenomenal range: from 10^{-38} (a number very close to zero: 0.00000000000000000000000000000000000001) to 10^{38} (a gigantic number: 100,000,000,000,000,000,000,000,000,000,000,000,000), both positive and negative. You would be hard-pressed to dig up a quantity that wouldn't fit into a single-precision number. Calculation speed isn't bad, although not as quick as that for long integers, and 4 bytes are required for each number.

The down side of single precision is that although single precision can represent both enormous and microscopic numbers, it cannot handle beyond six-digit accuracy. In other words, single precision does a good job with figures like $451.21 and $6,411.92, but $671,421.22 can't be represented exactly because it contains too many digits. Neither can 234.56789 or 0.00123456789; a single-precision representation will come as close as it can in six digits: $671,421, or 234.568, or 0.00123457. Depending on your application, this rounding off can be a trivial or crippling deficiency.

Double-Precision Floating Point

Double precision is to single precision what long integers are to integers. They take twice as much space in memory (8 bytes versus 4 bytes), and consequently take longer to calculate and have greater range (10^{308}) and accuracy (16 digits versus 6 digits for single precision).

The storage requirement of double-precision numbers becomes especially significant when dealing with arrays. A double-precision, 5,000-element array requires 40,000 bytes. An integer array with the same number of elements occupies only 10,000 bytes.

Note: Turbo Basic uses the IEEE standard for floating-point arithmetic, not the proprietary Microsoft format used by Interpretive BASIC. You must therefore use the special Microsoft/IEEE translation functions (CVMS, CVMD, MKMS$, and MKMD$) to read and write floating-point data contained in random files created by Interpretive BASIC. (For more information, see the section, "Random Files," later in this chapter.

If you're not sure what floating-point type to use, we suggest double precision. Internally, Turbo Basic's numeric engine runs most efficiently on double-precision gas. Its transcendental functions, such as COS or LOG, return double-precision values. Single precision may still be best for large arrays, however, where its size advantage becomes more pronounced.

Calculation and the 8087

The 8087 coprocessor (80287 on AT-type machines) dramatically closes the calculation speed gap between the numeric types offered. Since the 8087 does all calculations in double precision, regardless of type, it makes double precision even more attractive.

Unlike Interpretive BASIC, Turbo Basic does not always round upward the fractional part of a number. Turbo Basic treats in a special manner any number containing a 5 in its fractional part: The number is rounded toward the *closest* even number. For instance, the number 0.5 would be rounded *down* to 0, the *closest* even number. And the number 9.005 would also be rounded *down* to the *closest* even number, which in this case would be 9.000.

Since the most-typical method of rounding numbers always rounds them upward, Turbo Basic's method actually provides a more even distribution.

Constants

Turbo Basic programs process two distinct classes of data: *constants* and *variables* (discussed after this section). A variable is allowed to change its value as a program runs. A constant's value is fixed at compile time and cannot change during program execution. Turbo Basic supports three types of constants: *string constants, numeric constants*, and in an extension to Interpretive BASIC, a special form of integer constant, *named constants*.

String Constants

String constants are simply groups of characters surrounded by double quotes; for example:

```
"This is a string"
"3.14159"
"Tim Jones, Attorney at Law"
```

If a string constant is the last thing on a line, the closing quotes are optional:

```
PRINT "This is sloppy but legal.
```

Numeric Constants

Numeric constants represent numeric values, and consist primarily of the digits 0 through 9 and a decimal point. Negative constants need a leading minus sign (−); a plus sign (+) is optional for positive constants. The amount of precision you supply determines the internal representation (integer, long integer, single precision, or double precision) Turbo Basic will use in processing that constant.

If the value contains no decimal point and is in the range -32,768 to 32,767, then Turbo Basic uses its integer type.

If the value is an integer in the range -2^{31} to 2^{31-1} inclusive (about −2 billion to +2 billion), yet outside the range for integer constants, Turbo Basic uses its long integer type. (Note: The long integer type is not available in Interpretive BASIC.)

If the value contains a decimal point, and has up to six digits, Turbo Basic uses its single-precision floating-point type.

A numeric constant with a decimal point and more than six digits, or a whole number too large to be a long integer, is stored in double-precision floating-point format. For example:

345.1	Single precision
1.10321	Single precision
1.103213	Double precision
3453212.1234	Double precision

Identifying Integer Constants in Other Bases

It is sometimes convenient to express integers in bases other than decimal. This is particularly true when expressing information that is binary in character; for example, machine addresses. Turbo Basic allows you to specify integer data in hexadecimal (base 16), octal (base 8), and binary (base 2) notation. Note that long integers can't be represented with the alternate notation.

Hexadecimal constants consist of up to four characters, where each character is from the set 0 through 9 and *A* through *F*, and must be preceded by *&H*.

Octal constants contain only the characters 0 through 7, can be up to 6 digits long, and must be preceded by *&O* (or *&Q* or simply *&*).

Binary constants contain only 0s and 1s, can be up to 16 digits long, and must be preceded by *&B*.

Each of the following constants represents the integer, 256 decimal:

```
256
&H100
&O400
&400
&B100000000
```

Named Constants

Turbo Basic allows you to refer to integer constants by name. This is an enhancement to Interpretive BASIC, something like the CONST feature of Pascal. Only integers can be named in this way.

To name an integer constant, *precede* its identifier with the percent sign (%) and assign an integer constant to it. Unlike a variable, you can use a named constant on the left side of an assignment statement exactly once, and only a constant value (not a variable or expression) may be assigned to it. For example:

```
%debug = -1             ' a named constant, value -1
debug% = 12409          ' an integer variable
PRINT %debug, debug%    ' they are separate entities...
```

Use named constants for conditional compilation flags (see the metastatements in Chapter 5) and to increase the readability of your programs. (You can also use named constants to reduce the incidence of "magic numbers" in your programs. Magic numbers are mysterious values that mean something to you when you first write a program, but not when you come back to it six months later.)

Variables

A variable is an identifier that represents a numeric or string value. Unlike a constant, the value of a variable can change during program execution. Like labels, variable names must begin with a letter and can contain any number of letters and digits. Be generous in naming important variables. Unlike Interpretive BASIC, in Turbo Basic long variable names don't steal run-time memory. The variables *EndOfMonthTotals* and *emt* both require exactly 4 bytes of run-time storage.

Turbo Basic supports five variable types: *string, integer, long integer, single precision*, and *double precision*. A variable's name determines its type. Usually, variable typing is accomplished by appending a type declaration character to the variable name.

String variables end with a dollar sign ($):

```
a$ = "Turbo Basic"
```

Integer variables use a percent sign (%):

```
a% = 15
```

Long integers use the ampersand (&) as a type identifier:

```
a& = 7000
```

Single-precision floating-point variables use the exclamation point (!):

```
a! = 1.1
```

Double-precision floating-point variables end with the number sign (#):

```
a# = 1.031
```

If you don't include a type declaration character with a variable, Turbo Basic will use its default type, single precision. To make another type the default, use the DEF*type* statement. For example:

```
a# = 1.031     ' a# is a double precision variable
b = 16.5       ' b is single precision
a% = 3         ' a% is an integer variable; a# is a separate variable
DEFINT m       ' default type for variables beginning with m now integer
m = 16         ' m is an integer...
```

Note that a%, a#, a&, a$, and a! are five separate variables.

Arrays

An array is a group of string or numeric data sharing the same variable name. The individual values that make up an array are called *elements*. An element of an array can be used in a statement or expression wherever you would use a regular string or numeric variable. In other words, each element of an array is itself a variable.

At program startup time, each element of each numeric array is set to zero. String arrays are set to the null string (" "). DIMensioning a dynamic array also clears each element. If a program is later restarted with the RUN statement, this initializing is repeated.

Declaring the name and type of an array, as well as the number and organization of its elements, is performed by the DIMension statement. For example:

```
DIM payments(55)
```

creates an array variable *payments*, consisting of 56 single-precision elements, numbered 0 through 55. Array *payments* and a single-precision variable also named *payments* are separate variables.

Subscripts

Individual array elements are selected with *subscripts*, integer expressions within parentheses to the right of an array variable's name. For example, *payments(3)* and *payments(44)* are two of *payment*'s 56 elements. Normally, the first element of an array is selected with a subscript value of zero, although this can be changed with either the DIM or OPTION BASE statements; for example:

```
' This DIM statement declares a 56-element array
' with subscript bounds of 0 to 55.
DIM payments(55)
------------------
OPTION BASE 1
' This DIM statement declares a 55-element array
' with subscript bounds of 1 to 55 because of the
' OPTION BASE statement.
DIM payments(55)
```

If you use an array in a program without DIMensioning it, Turbo Basic proceeds as though you had declared an eleven-element array (subscript values 0 through 10). However, we strongly recommend that you take the time to explicitly dimension every array your program uses.

In an enhancement to Interpretive BASIC array handling, Turbo Basic allows you to define a *range* of subscript values rather than just an upper limit. For example, the DIM statement

```
DIM b(50:60)
```

creates array *b*, consisting of eleven single-precision elements numbered 50 through 60.

The statement:

```
DIM c(50:60, 25:45)
```

creates the two-dimensional array *c*, containing 231 (11 * 21) elements.

Turbo Basic's subscript range declaration capability allows you to model a program's data structures more closely to the problem at hand.

For example, consider a program tracking 19th century birth statistics. This program's central data structure is a single-precision array of 100 elements that contain the number of babies born in each year of the last century. Ideally, you would create an array that used subscript values equal to the year in which the births occurred (for example, *births*(1851) represents how many babies came into the world in 1851), so that a code passage like

```
DIM births(1899)
.
.
.
FOR n = 1800 TO 1899
  PRINT "There were" births(n) "births in" n
NEXT n
```

would be as straightforward as possible. Unfortunately, DIM *births*(1899) creates a 1,900-element array, of which the first 1,800 are waste. Traditionally, BASIC programmers have tackled this problem by declaring the array as

```
DIM births(99)
```

and by playing games with subscripts:

```
FOR n = 1800 TO 1899
  PRINT "There were" births(n-1800) "births in" n
NEXT n
```

While this sort of thing works, it complicates things and slows programs down, because suddenly there's 100 subtractions to do that weren't there before.

The related OPTION BASE statement can also be used to determine the lowest element of an array, although the range mechanism is more powerful and preferred.

String Arrays

The elements of string arrays hold strings instead of numbers. Each string can be a different length, from 0 to 32,767 characters. The total string space for strings and string arrays is 64K. For example:

```
DIM a$(50)
```

creates a sequence of 51 independent string variables:

```
a$(0) = "A medium length string"   'a 21 character string
a$(1) = ""                         'a null string (the default)
a$(2) = SPACE$(20000)              'a 20,000 character string
.
.
.
a$(50) = "The last one"
```

Multidimensional Arrays

Arrays can have one or more *dimensions*, up to a maximum of 8. A one-dimensional array such as *payments* is a simple list of values. A two-dimensional array represents a table of numbers with rows and columns of information. Multidimensional arrays with no ready analog in the real world are equally possible:

```
DIM a(15)              (a one-dimensional list)
DIM b(15,20)           (a two-dimensional table)
DIM c(5,5,10,20,3)     (a five-dimensional Blurfquatz)
```

The maximum number of elements per dimension is 32,768.

Array Bounds Testing

Turbo Basic tries hard to keep you from getting into trouble with bad subscripts (that is, subscripts that are too large or too small for a given array). And the compiler tells you about bad constant subscripts:

```
DIM a(50)
a(51) = 33
```

This program won't compile, because Turbo Basic won't knowingly generate code to access the 52nd element of a 51-element array. However, if you use variables as subscripts, the compiler won't find the mistake:

```
DIM a(50)
n = 51
a(n) = 33
```

Even though this code compiles without error, you can still trap the out of range reference in line 3 at runtime by compiling with the **B**ounds debugging switch turned on. (See "The Options Command" in Chapter 3 for more information on subscript checking.)

Array Storage Requirements

For technical reasons relating to execution speed and code size efficiency, Turbo Basic limits the size of individual arrays to 64 Kbytes, although a program can have as many 64K arrays as memory permits. The maximum number of elements an array may contain is a function of its type, as shown in the following:

Type	**Storage Requirement**
Integer	2 bytes per element (32,768 per 64K)
Long Integer	4 bytes per element (16,384 per 64K)
Single Precision	4 bytes per element (16,384 per 64K)
Double Precision	8 bytes per element (8,192 per 64K)
String	4 bytes per element (16,384 per 64K)

Note: Only pointer and length information is contained in a string array element. The string data itself is stored in string space, and occupies as many bytes as the string has characters. String space can contain a maximum of 64K characters.

Dynamic Allocation

Turbo Basic supports *dynamic memory allocation*. Dynamic allocation means creating variable-size arrays at runtime, rather than defining fixed-sized (or *static*) structures at compile time.

This allows you to construct arrays that are exactly as large as they need to be to handle data the program is given at runtime. Once their function is complete, memory allocated to dynamic arrays can be given back and used again.

To create a dynamic array, simply use variable arguments in a DIM statement; if the memory is available, the array will be created. When your program is finished using that array, use the ERASE statement to get rid of it so the memory can be used for other purposes.

For example:

```
' figure out how many records are in an inventory file,
' then dimension dynamic arrays and load them up
```

```
OPEN "PARTS.DTA" AS #1 LEN = 56
count = LOF(1) / 56
DIM partNo(count), desc$(count), quan(count), cost(count)
GOSUB LoadArrays
GOSUB UseArrays
ERASE partNo, desc$, quan, cost
```

To take advantage of Turbo Basic's dynamic arrays, you need only make a judgment call about each array in your program: static or dynamic? Is its size fixed according to the design of the program, or is it dependent on some parameter that isn't known until runtime? For example, array *births* from the earlier example is best created as a static structure—it's always going to be exactly 100 elements long.

The pitfall of dynamic arrays is that you may try to DIMension a large array and fail because there isn't enough free memory around at runtime to fulfill your request. If a program contains only static arrays and has enough memory to get started, it can't run out; its arrays are created before the program even begins to run.

A program using dynamic arrays must therefore be aware that there may not be enough memory available at runtime to declare the arrays desired. Before attempting to DIMension a dynamic array, use the FRE(−1) function to see if there's enough room for it.

Declaring Static or Dynamic Arrays

The $DYNAMIC and $STATIC metastatements control the default type of arrays in a program. Usually a program will only contain one of these metastatements. By default, the compiler assumes the $STATIC attribute.

Arrays are considered dynamic in the following cases:

- If declared after the $DYNAMIC metastatement is used, as in

```
10 $DYNAMIC
20 DIM A(10)
```

- If declared as dynamic explicitly, as in

```
10 DYM DYNAMIC A(10)
```

- If a variable is used in the DIM statement, as in

```
10 X% = 10
20 DYM A(X%)
```

- If the array is included in a COMMON statement, as in

```
10 DIM A(10)
20 COMMON A(1)
```

- If there are two or more DIM statements for the same array identifier, as in

```
10 DIM A(10)
20 A(0) = 10
30 DIM A(10)
```

- If an array is declared local to a procedure or function, as in

```
DEF FNTest%
  LOCAL A()
  DIM A(10)
  FNTest% = A(0)
END DEF
```

The storage class of an array can also be set by using the STATIC and DYNAMIC attributes within a DIM statement. In addition, an array is always dynamic if an expression is used in the associated DIM statement. For example:

```
$STATIC              ' from here on, assume arrays are static
DIM a(40), b(20,20)  ' therefore a and b are both static arrays
DIM DYNAMIC c(20)    ' DYNAMIC attribute overrides $STATIC default
DIM d(n)             ' using a variable in DIM also forces DYNAMIC attribute
$DYNAMIC             ' from here down, compiler assumes arrays are dynamic
DIM e(50)            ' therefore e is dynamic
```

Dispose of dynamic arrays with the ERASE statement. ERASEing a static array doesn't reclaim any memory, but does set its elements to zero (for string arrays, to the null string).

Expressions

An expression consists of operators and operands that perform certain operations when an expression is evaluated. There are two fundamental types of expressions in Turbo Basic: *string* and *numeric*.

A *string expression* consists of string constants, string variables, and string functions (those that end with "$"), optionally combined with the concatenation operator, the plus sign (+). String expressions reduce to a string; that is, a sequence of ASCII characters of known length. Examples of string expressions include:

```
"Cats and dogs"
a$
a$ + z$
LEFT$(a$ + z$)
a$ + MID$("Cats and dogs",5,3)
RIGHT$(MID$(a$ + z$,1,6),3)
```

Numeric expressions consist of numeric constants, variables, and functions, optionally separated by numeric operators. Numeric expressions always reduce to a value of one of the four numeric types (integer, long integer, single precision, double precision). Examples of numeric expressions include:

```
37
37/15
a
37/a
SQR (37/a)
SQR ((c + d)/a) * SIN (37/a)
```

In forming numeric expressions, you should be aware that certain operations will be performed first. Following is a list of the order of expression evaluation. Exponentiation has the highest priority; IMP the lowest.

- Exponentiation (^)
- Negation (−)
- Multiplication, Floating-Point Division (*, /)
- Integer Division (\)
- Modulo (MOD)
- Addition, Subtraction (+, −)
- Relational Operators (<, <=, =, >=, >, <>)
- NOT
- AND
- OR, XOR
- EQV
- IMP

For example, the expression 3 + 6 / 3 evaluates to 5, not 3. Because division has a higher priority than addition, the division operation (6 / 3) is performed first.

To handle operations of the same priority, Turbo Basic proceeds from left to right. For example, in the expression 4 − 3 + 6, subtraction (4 − 3) is performed before the addition (3 + 6), producing the intermediate expression 1 + 6.

Operations inside parentheses are of highest priority and are always performed first; within parentheses, standard precedence is used.

Operators

The numeric operators are classified into three major groups: *arithmetic*, *relational*, and *logical*.

Arithmetic Operators

Arithmetic operators perform normal mathematical operations. Table 4-2 lists the Turbo Basic arithmetic operators in precedence order.

Table 4-2 Arithmetic Operators

Operator	Action	Example
^	Exponentiation	10^4
−	Negation	−16
*, /	Multiply, FP divide	45 * 19, 45 / 19
\	Integer division	45 \ 19
MOD	Modulo	45 MOD 19
+, −	Add, Subtract	45 + 19, 45 − 19

A couple of these operators merit a word of explanation. The backslash (\) represents integer division. Integer division rounds its operands to integers and produces a truncated quotient with no remainder; for example, 5 \ 2 evaluates to 2, and 9 \ 10 evaluates to 0.

The remainder of an integer division can be determined with the MOD (*modulo*) operator. (Note that the MOD operator is only valid for short integers.) The MOD operator is like integer division except that it returns the remainder of the division rather than the quotient; for example, 5 MOD 2 equals 1, and 9 MOD 10 equals 9.

Relational Operators

Relational operators allow you to compare the values of two strings or two numbers (but not one of each) to obtain a Boolean result of TRUE or FALSE. The result of the comparison is assigned an integer value of −1 if the relation is TRUE, and 0 if the relation is FALSE. For example:

```
PRINT 5 > 6, 5 < 6, (5 < 6) * 15
```

prints out 0, −1, and −15. Although they can be used in any numeric expression (for example, $a = (b > c) / 13$), the numeric results returned by relational operators are generally used in an IF or other decision statement to make a judgment regarding program flow. Table 4-3 lists the relational operators.

Table 4-3 Relational Operators

Operator	Relation	Example
=	Equality	$x = y$
< >	Inequality	$x <> y$
<	Less than	$x < y$
>	Greater than	$x > y$
< =	Less than or equal to	$x <= y$
> =	Greater than or equal to	$x >= y$

When arithmetic and relational operators are combined in an expression, arithmetic operations are always evaluated first. For example, 4 + 5 < 4 * 3 evaluates to -1 (TRUE), because the arithmetic operations are carried out before the relational operation, which ultimately tests the truth of the assertion: $9 < 12$.

Logical Operators

Logical operators perform logical (Boolean) operations on integers. Used with relational operators, they allow you to set up complex tests like

```
IF day > 29 AND month =  2 THEN PRINT "Error in date"
```

This statement performs a logical AND on the integer results returned by the two relational operators. (The AND operator has a lower priority than the ">" and "=" relational operators, so parentheses aren't needed.) For example, if *day* = 30 and *month* = 2, both relational operators return TRUE (-1). The underlying binary representation of integers is such that -1 has a value of &HFFFF (all bits turned on); 0 is &H0000, all bits turned off.

The AND operator then performs a logical AND on these two TRUE results:

```
    1111 1111 1111 1111 (-1)
AND 1111 1111 1111 1111 (-1)
    ------------------------
    1111 1111 1111 1111 (-1)
```

producing a TRUE (nonzero) result.

The OR (sometimes called *inclusive or*) operation returns TRUE if one or both of its arguments are TRUE, and returns FALSE only if both arguments are FALSE. For example:

```
-1 OR 0 is TRUE
0 OR 0 is FALSE
5 > 6 OR 6 < 7 is TRUE
```

The XOR (*exclusive or*) operation returns TRUE if the values being tested are different, and returns FALSE if they are the same. For example:

```
-1 XOR 0 is TRUE
-1 XOR -1 is FALSE
5 > 6 XOR 6 < 7 is TRUE
```

The EQV (*equivalence*) function is the opposite of XOR. It returns TRUE if the two logical values being tested are the same, and returns FALSE if they are not:

```
-1 EQV 0 is FALSE
-1 EQV -1 is TRUE
5 > 6 EQV 1 > 99 is TRUE
```

The IMP (*implication*) operator returns FALSE only if the first operand is TRUE and the second one FALSE:

```
-1 IMP -1 is TRUE
0 IMP -1 is TRUE
0 IMP 0 is TRUE
-1 IMP 0 is FALSE
```

Note that the logical operators operate on integers, not long integers or floating-point values. If the operands of a logical expression cannot be converted to integers, overflow occurs:

```
x = 500000
IF x OR y THEN GOTO Exit
```

This IF statement results in an overflow error when *x* cannot be successfully converted to an integer.

Bit Manipulations

In addition to creating complex tests, logical operators permit control over the underlying bit patterns of their integer operands. The most common operations are AND, OR, and XOR (exclusive OR) masking.

AND masks are used to clear selected bits of an integer quantity without affecting the other bits of that quantity. For example, to clear the most-significant 2 bits in the integer value &H9700, use AND with a mask of &H3FFF; that is, the mask contains all ones, except for the bit positions you wish to force to zero:

```
    1001 0111 0000 0000 &H9700
AND 0011 1111 1111 1111 &H3FFF   (the mask)
    --------------------------
    0001 0111 0000 0000 &H1700   (the result)
```

An OR mask *sets* selected bits of an integer without affecting the other bits. To set the most-significant 2 bits in &H9700, use OR with a mask of &HC000; that is, the mask contains all zeros, except for the bit positions you wish to force to one:

```
    1001 0111 0000 0000 &H9700
OR  1100 0000 0000 0000 &HC000  (the mask)
    --------------------------
    1101 0111 0000 0000 &HD700  (the result)
```

An XOR mask *complements* (reverses) selected bits of an integer quantity without affecting the other bits of that quantity. For example, to complement the most-significant 2 bits in &H9700, use XORs with a mask of &C0000; that is, all zeros, except for the positions to be complemented:

```
    1001 0111 0000 0000 &H9700
XOR 1100 0000 0000 0000 &HC000  (the mask)
    --------------------------
    0101 0111 0000 0000 &H5700  (the result)
```

XOR operations are common in graphics, since they permit an object to be moved nondestructively against a complex background. XOR the object once to draw it against the background, then XOR the same object in the same place to erase it, restoring the background to its original condition.

Strings and Relational Operators

Turbo Basic allows you to compare string data. String expressions can be tested for equality as well as for "greater than" and "less than" alphabetic ordering.

Two string expressions are equal if and only if they contain exactly the same characters in exactly the same order. For example:

```
a$ = "CAT"
PRINT a$ = "CAT", a$ = "CATS", a$ = "cat"
```

String ordering is based on two criteria and in this order: (1) the underlying ASCII values of the characters they contain, and (2) length. For example, *A* is less than *B* because the ASCII code for *A*, 65, is less than the code for *B*, 66. Note, however, that *B* is less than *a* because the ASCII code for each lowercase letter is greater than the corresponding uppercase character (exactly 32 greater). When sorting mixed uppercase and lowercase information, you may choose to use the UCASE$ or LCASE$ functions to keep case differences from interfering with the sort.

Length figures in only if both strings are identical up to the length of the shorter string, in which case the shorter one evaluates as less than the longer one; for example, "CAT" is less than "CATS."

Subroutines, Functions, and Procedures

Turbo Basic program structure can be simplified by using *subroutines, procedures,* and *functions*. A subroutine is a labeled set of instructions to be executed when a GOSUB is reached. A procedure is like a miniprogram (also referred to as a *subprogram*) that performs some vital part of your main program. A function is a set of routines that return a string or numeric result, usually related to the parameters passed to the function. By placing complex and/or frequently used code into these structures, you can both simplify and shorten your programs.

Turbo Basic's procedures and user-defined functions go beyond the simple structuring offered by subroutines. Although millions of BASIC programs have been written with GOSUB/RETURN as their primary organizational device, we encourage you to use these more advanced structures.

The procedures and functions in Turbo Basic offer true recursion, parameter passing, and access to local, static, and global variables. If you've never experienced the benefits of parameter passing, local variables, and recursion, you owe it to yourself to give these a try.

Procedures and functions are more alike than they are different. The most obvious distinction between them is that functions return a value, and are therefore invoked implicitly by appearing within expressions (with "FN" tacked on the front). Procedures do not return a value, and must be explicitly invoked with the CALL statement. For example:

```
a = b + FNCubeRoot(c)          ' a function call
CALL OutChar(a)                ' a procedure call
```

Subroutines

Subroutines are the traditional method of subdividing BASIC programs, consisting of labeled groups of statements ending with a RETURN. To execute a subroutine, you can use a GOSUB statement to indicate the label associated with the subroutine's first statement. When a RETURN statement is encountered, control returns to the statement immediately after the calling GOSUB. For example:

```
GOSUB AddMonths
PRINT total
END

AddMonths:
  total = 0
  FOR i = 1 TO 12
    total = total + month(i)
  NEXT i
RETURN
```

Functions

There are two types of functions: predefined functions (such as COS and LEFT$), which are defined by the language, and user-defined functions, which can be either single or multiline. (For more detail on predefined functions, see the specific entries in Chapter 5, "Turbo Basic Reference Directory.")

The syntax for defining a single-line function is

```
DEF FNidentifier [(parameter list)] = expression
```

where *identifier* is a user-defined name for a specific expression. *parameter list* is an optional comma-delimited sequence of one or more identifiers that represent data objects to be sent to the function when it is called at runtime. (You are limited to 16 parameters for any function.) *expression* defines the processing to attain the value the function returns.

For example, consider a meteorologic program that must constantly convert between degrees Celsius (which is used internally) and degrees Fahrenheit (which is displayed on the screen and accepted from the keyboard). Single-line functions are a boon to this type of program:

```
DEF FNCtoF(degreesC) = (1.8 * degreesC) + 32
DEF FNFtoC(degreesF) = (degreesF - 32) * .555555
```

To display variable temperature, which by convention always holds Celsius values, use FNCtoF (read as "function *C* to *F*") in any statement that can accept a numeric expression; for example, PRINT:

```
temp = 100
PRINT FNCtoF(temp)
```

To convert your values from Fahrenheit to Celsius, use FNFtoC:

```
INPUT "Enter today's high: ", th
temp = FNFtoC(th)
```

Turbo Basic's multiline functions take on a larger role than that permitted by the simple single-line functions of Interpretive BASIC. Turbo Basic allows a function to spread over many program lines and in effect to be used like a subroutine that also happens to return a value. The formal syntax for declaring a multiline function is

```
DEF FNidentifier [(parameter list)]
  [variable declaration]
  .
  . statements
  .
  [EXIT DEF]
  [FNfunction name = expression]
END DEF
```

where *identifier* declares the function name. *parameter list* is an optional comma-delimited list of formal parameters that represent variables to be passed to the function when it is called.

To illustrate, consider multiline function *Factorial*, a statistician's best friend. (You may recall from a past classroom experience that the factorial of positive integer n, written as $n!$, is the product of the positive integers less than or equal to n. For instance, $6! = 6 * 5 * 4 * 3 * 2 * 1 = 720$.)

Factorials are not included in Turbo Basic's set of built-in math operators, but multiline functions pick up the slack:

```
100 DEF FNFactorial#(x%)
110    LOCAL i%, total#
120    IF x% < 0 OR x% > 170 THEN FNFactorial# = -1 : EXIT DEF
130    total# = 1
140    FOR i% = x% TO 2 STEP -1           ' we could also work up...
150      total# = total# * i%
160    NEXT i%
170    FNFactorial# = total#
180 END DEF
```

FNFactorial demonstrates the structure of a multiline function (the line numbers are included so we can refer to various lines by number in this discussion—they are, of course, optional).

Function definitions are bracketed by the DEF FN and END DEF statements; indenting the statements between DEF FN and END DEF a couple of spaces clarifies this structure.

Line 100 gives the function its name and consequently a type (# equals double precision). FNFactorial has a single integer formal parameter, *x%*.

Line 110 declares a pair of "local" variables, *i%* and ***total#***. Local variables are temporary structures available and visible only within function and procedure definitions (they're discussed in detail in a later section entitled 'Local Variables").

Line 120 performs error checking on the argument passed to FNFactorial. There's no point in trying to figure out the factorial of a negative number (no such animal) or of a value so large that it produces a result beyond the 10^{308} range of double precision (factorials get big in a hurry—170! is a whopping 7.26E + 308). In these cases, you define the function's return value as −1 and EXIT DEF. Programs that use FNFactorial need to recognize that a return value of −1 represents an error condition and behave accordingly. (Incidentally, 0! is defined to be 1.)

EXIT DEF is to functions what RETURN is to subroutines: It returns control to the statement that called the function in the first place. It's tempting to use RETURN for this purpose, but don't. Note that EXIT DEF is not necessary unless you need to return before reaching the end of the function.

Lines 130 through 160 define an algorithm for calculating factorials. This part of a multiline function (the "body") can be as long or as short as necessary.

Line 170 determines the value FNFactorial returns by making an assignment to the function name. Surprisingly, an assignment isn't a syntactic requirement for function definitions. If you don't perform an assignment to the function name, the value returned is undefined.

FNFactorial's definition is terminated by the END DEF statement in line 180. END DEF, like EXIT DEF, returns execution to the statement that called the function in the first place. (The END statement gets a workout in Turbo Basic syntax—it's used to terminate a number of structures.)

Ever wondered how many permutations are possible with a deck of playing cards? FNFactorial knows:

```
PRINT FNFactorial#(52)
```

yields the result of 8.065817517094388E069.

Since FNFactorial is defined as having an integer formal parameter, floating-point arguments are rounded to integers before being passed to it; for example, FNFactorial(2.7) is the same as FNFactorial(3). If you call FNFactorial with a number larger than Turbo Basic's convert-to-integer routine can handle (greater than 32,767 or less than −32,768), you'll get run-time error 6, Overflow.

This same processing is performed on arguments to Turbo Basic's built-in functions that expect integer arguments; for example, LOCATE 2.7,1 puts the cursor on line 3.

Formal Versus Actual Parameters

The variables that appear in a function definition's parameter list are called *formal parameters*. They serve only to define the function, and are entirely separate from other variables in the program with the same name. To illustrate, consider this short program:

```
100 DEF FNArea(x,y) = x * y
110 x = 56
120 PRINT x, FNArea(2,3), x
```

Variable *x* in lines 110 and 120 of this program is unrelated to formal parameter *x* that is defined in function *Area* in the first line. When this program runs, *x* retains its value on either side of the call to FNArea: It prints out as 56 both times.

The values provided at runtime to a function are sometimes called *actual parameters*. In the last example, the numeric constants 2 and 3 were the actual parameters passed to FNArea. The actual parameters could just as easily have been variables:

```
a = 2 : b = 3
PRINT FNArea(a, b)
```

Function Types

Functions can return any of the four numeric types (integer, long integer, single and double precision floating point), as well as string types. A function's type, like a variable's, is controlled by its name. It uses type declaration characters and the DEF*type* statement; for example:

```
DEF FNIntSquareRoot%(x) = INT(SQR(x))
PRINT FNIntSquareRoot%(2)
```

and

```
DEF FNRepeatFirst$(a$) = LEFT$(a$,1) + a$
PRINT FNRepeatFirst$("Hello")
```

Attempting to assign a string function to a numeric variable or a numeric function to a string variable produces what you'd expect—error 13, Type Mismatch.

Procedures

Procedures are code blocks surrounded by the SUB and END SUB statements. The formal syntax for declaring a procedure is

```
SUB procname [(parameter list)] [INLINE]
  [variable declaration]
  .
  . statements
```

```
  .
  [EXIT SUB]
END SUB
```

procname declares the procedure name, which can be up to 31 characters long but whose name cannot be contained within any other SUB statement in the program. *parameter list* is an optional comma-delimited list of formal parameters that represent variables to be passed to the procedure when it is called. (You are limited to 16 parameters for any procedure.) INLINE specifies that the procedure has a variable number of untyped parameters and that the procedure will contain inline assembly code (see Appendix C, "Assembly Language Interface").

As stated earlier, the most obvious difference between functions and procedures is that procedures don't return a value; however, they also are not called from within expressions, don't have a type, and don't include an assignment to the procedure name. Procedures are invoked with the CALL statement, much like GOSUB invokes subroutines.

Consider this program that defines and calls procedure *PrintTotal*:

```
SUB PrintTotal(a,b,c,d)
  LOCAL total
  total = a + b + c + d
  PRINT total
END SUB
w = 1 : x = 2 : y = 0 : z = 3
CALL PrintTotal(w,x,y,z)
```

Passing Arrays to Procedures

Unlike functions, procedures allow you to pass entire arrays as arguments. The procedure definition must declare that it expects an array argument by including an appropriate entry in its formal parameter list. Array arguments are indicated by appending to a formal parameter identifier a set of parentheses enclosing a numeric constant. This value indicates the number of dimensions in the array, not the size of the array. To illustrate,

```
SUB CountZeros(a(1), size, count)
' count returns the number of zero elements in one-dimensional,
' single-precision array a, which has size +1 elements
  LOCAL i
  count = 0
  FOR i = 0 TO size
    IF a(i) = 0 THEN count = count + 1
  NEXT i
END SUB
```

The presence of *a*(1) in the parameter list defines *CountZeros*' first argument as a one-dimensional array. It doesn't tell how large the array will be. That task falls to the second argument, *size*. *count* is used to return the number of zero elements found in array *a*. Calling *CountZeros* goes like this:

```
size = 100 : DIM Primes(size)
GOSUB StrikePrimes              ' all nonprimes get a nonzero value
CALL CountZeros (Primes(), size, primesCount)
PRINT "There are" primesCount "prime numbers <=" size
END
```

Procedure and Function Definitions and Program Flow

The position of procedure and function definitions within a program is immaterial. A function can be defined in line 1 or line 1000 of a program regardless of where it is used. And you need not direct program flow through a procedure or function as an initialization step (which you must do with single-line functions in Interpretive BASIC). The compiler sees your definitions wherever they are positioned.

Also, unlike subroutines, program execution can't accidentally "fall into" a procedure or function. As far as the execution path of a program is concerned, function and procedure definitions are invisible. For example, when this four-line program is executed:

```
CALL PrintSomething
SUB PrintSomething
  PRINT "Printed from within PrintSomething"
END SUB
```

the message appears only once.

Note: You must treat your procedure and function definitions as isolated islands of code. Don't jump into or out of them with GOTO, GOSUB, or RETURN statements—you may get unpredictable and/or disastrous results.

Note that neither procedure nor function definitions may be nested; that is, you cannot define another procedure or function within a procedure or function definition (although a procedure or function can contain calls to other procedures and functions).

Argument Checking

Unlike some other BASIC compilers, Turbo Basic checks to make sure that the number and type of arguments in a program's procedure and function calls agrees with the number and type of formal parameters in the corresponding definitions. For instance, attempting to compile the program

```
DEF FNDummy(a,b)
END DEF
t = FNDummy(3)
```

results in a Parameter Mismatch error in line 3, because FNDummy requires two arguments.

Passing Parameters by Value or Reference

There are some subtle but important differences between functions and procedures, and understanding these differences requires understanding how Turbo Basic processes procedure and function calls at runtime (see Table 4-4).

Table 4-4 Procedure/Function Differences

Action	Functions	Procedures
Return a value	Yes	No
Calling method	Called within expressions	Use CALL statement
Parameter passing	Pass by value	Pass by reference and by value
Default variables	SHARED	STATIC
Array arguments	No	Yes

First, take a look at this short program that defines and calls function *CylVol*:

```
DEF FNCylVol(radius, height) STATIC
  FNCylVol = radius * radius * 3.14159 * height
END DEF
r = 4.7 : h = 12.1
vol = FNCylVol(r,h)
```

Now, imagine the run-time processing necessary to execute this program. First, you assign values to variables *r* and *h*. Then you'll call FNCylVol, passing it the numeric information in *r* and *h*. But wait—just how do you provide this information to the function?

There are two ways: (1) use 4.7 as the radius and 12.1 as the height, or (2) use variable *r* as the radius and variable *h* as the height. The first technique is called *pass-by-value*; the second, *pass-by-reference*.

Pass-by-value means a copy of the arguments in a call are placed in storage temporarily and then transmitted when needed into the called routine. Once the procedure/function has executed, the value in storage vanishes; thus the originals are left unchanged.

Pass-by-reference means a pointer is passed that indicates where (the address) the data is stored. In the example, the addresses of variables *r* and *h* are passed as parameters. The called routine can then get and change the actual values itself.

Turbo Basic uses both passing schemes (their ramifications will become clear in a moment).

The pass-by-value method allows any constant or expression to be used as an argument. At runtime, the expression is evaluated and reduced to a simple value that is passed to the function. For example:

```
v = FNCylVol(r, h*2 + 4.1)
```

The pass-by-value technique has no problem communicating $h * 2 + 4.1$ to *FNCylVol*. The expression is evaluated, and the result sent off to the function.

On the other hand, however, the pass-by-reference method, since it allows the routine to manipulate the value, does not handle constants and expressions (an expression like $h * 2 + 4.1$ has no address in memory—only variables do). The pass-by-reference method only works when an argument to a procedure is a single variable argument.

Law I of parameter passing: Both variables and expressions can be transmitted using the pass-by-value technique: Pass-by-reference permits only variables or arrays to be sent.

The advantage of pass-by-reference is that the called routine can affect the value of variables passed to it, and thereby pass information back to the caller. Since a routine passed data by reference is given an address, it knows where that variable is located and is therefore able to both read and write it. By contrast, a routine that is passed a variable by value cannot affect the original variable, because it doesn't know where the original variable is stored.

Law II of parameter passing: Variables passed by reference can be changed by a called routine; variables passed by value cannot.

To illustrate, consider this program:

```
a = 0 : b = 2 : c = 3
CALL Add(a,b,c,total)
PRINT a, total
END
SUB Add(i,j,k, sum) STATIC
  sum = i + j + k
END SUB
```

When *Add* returns, variable *total* contains the sum of *a*, *b*, and *c*. (*Add* could have been defined to change the value of each of its arguments; however, since it only assigns to its fourth parameter, only *total* is affected by the call to *Add*.)

Law III is the consequence of Laws I and II for Turbo Basic: *Function arguments are passed by value; procedure arguments are passed by reference* and *by value.*

This means that single variable names can appear as arguments in a procedure call and those variables can be altered. If you want to pass by value a single variable to a procedure, enclose the variable in parentheses. This forces Turbo Basic to parse it as an expression. Procedures may also accept constants and expressions as pass by value.

Function calls can accept constants, variables, and expressions but they cannot alter their values.

You are free to assign to a formal parameter within a function definition; in fact, it is often convenient to use a function's formal parameters as temporary variables. Doing so will not, however, change the value of the actual parameter; for example:

```
DEF FNDummy(a,b,c)
  a = a + b + c
  PRINT a
END DEF
x = 1 : y = 2 : z = 3
t = FNDummy(x,y,z)
PRINT x
```

Dummy's assignment to its formal parameter *a* doesn't affect the value of variable *x*.

Since passing a variable to a function causes a copy of that variable's data to be placed into local storage, problems arise if the variable is very large (that is, an array). Therefore, Turbo Basic doesn't permit array variables to be passed by value, although you can pass individual elements of arrays.

Local Variables

In Interpretive BASIC, all variables are global. This means that no matter where a variable appears in a program, at the most important sequence of the main program or the most trivial loop in an obscure subroutine, that variable is available to the entire program. This allows the following sort of bug to creep in:

```
' main program
EmployeeCount = 10
n = 1
GOSUB CalcChecks
n = n + 1
GOSUB PrintChecks

CalcChecks:
GOSUB CalcDeductions
RETURN

CalcDeductions:
  FOR n = 1 TO EmployeeCount
   .
   .
   .
  NEXT n
RETURN

PrintChecks:
   .
   .
   .
RETURN
```

Variable *n* in obscure subroutine *CalcDeductions* and variable *n* in the main program are one and the same. As a result, when control finally returns to the main program, *n* doesn't hold the 1 the main program put there earlier, but holds the value of *EmployeeCount* + 1 as a result of the FOR/NEXT loop in *CalcDeductions*.

In keeping with its informal style, BASIC doesn't require that you "declare" variables (that is, specify in a statement someplace that you are about to use a variable named such-and-such). Even if you religiously track your program's variables, a single slip of a finger can foul things up.

To help prevent this problem, Turbo Basic allows "local" variables within procedures and functions. A local variable, unlike a *global* variable, only exists in the routine in which it is declared. Local variables alone are a sufficiently good reason to swear off subroutines forever. For example, study function *AddReceipts*:

```
DEF FNAddReceipts
  LOCAL x, y, total
  FOR x = 1 TO 12
    FOR y = 1 TO 30
      total = total + receipts(x,y)
    NEXT y
  NEXT x
  FNAddReceipts = total
END DEF
```

Since variables *x* and *y* are declared as local to FNAddReceipts, you can use variable names *x* and *y* elsewhere in this program (programmers with a mathematical bent are wont to use *x* and *y* for *every* variable) without affecting the values of *x* and *y* in FNAddReceipts (or vice versa).

FNAddReceipts' local variables exist only while that function is being called—before and after that function, it's as though they never existed. To illustrate, consider this code segment that calls FNAddReceipts:

```
x = 35
thisYear = FNAddReceipts
PRINT x
```

The fact that the name *x* has been given to other variables in the process of calculating a return value for *FNAddReceipts* doesn't affect the *x* in lines one and three. Through the magic of stack allocation, the *x* in *FNAddReceipts* is a separate variable, one that doesn't exist after the function returns.

Local variables must be declared before any executable statements in a procedure or function. Local variables can be arrays; simply dimension the array after declaring it as local.

```
SUB Dummy
  LOCAL a, locArray()
  DIM DYNAMIC locArray(50)
  .
  .
  .
```

```
  ERASE locArray
END SUB
```

Local arrays are automatically deallocated on exit from a procedure or function.

A quirk of local variables is that they lose their value between each routine that contains them. With each invocation, their storage is freshly created and they are initialized to zero (or null strings). For example:

```
SUB Dummy
  LOCAL c
  PRINT c
  c = c + 1
END SUB
```

You can CALL *Dummy* all day long and it will always print 0.

The Shared Attribute

Procedures and functions can also declare variables with the *shared* attribute. A *shared* variable is the opposite of a local variable: It is visible to and usable by the rest of the program (such variables are often called *global* variables).

```
DEF FNDummy
  SHARED a
  a = 6
  FNDummy = a
END DEF
PRINT FNDummy, a
```

Because of the SHARED declaration, variable *a* in FNDummy and variable *a* in the PRINT statement are one and the same.

Undeclared variables within function definitions default to the shared attribute; for example, in function *AddReceipts* shown earlier, array *receipts* was assumed to be a shared variable. Within procedure definitions, the default is STATIC. We strongly urge you, however, to explicitly declare every variable that appears in a procedure or function definition.

Static Variables

Static variables are a cross between local and shared variables. Like a local variable, a static variable doesn't interfere with other variables in the program that have the same identifier—it is only visible from within the procedure or function that declares it. Like a shared variable, a static variable occupies a permanent spot in memory, and therefore does not lose its value between invocations of the function or procedure. It is initialized to zero or null (in the case of strings) only when the program begins.

```
SUB Dummy STATIC
  STATIC i
  i = i + 1
  PRINT i
END SUB
i = 16
CALL Dummy
CALL Dummy
PRINT i
```

Dummy's static variable *i* is a different variable from variable *i* in the "main program." Unlike a local variable, however, it retains its value between invocations of its enclosing procedure. It starts out as 0, like any variable, and is incremented twice by the two calls to *Dummy*.

With the appropriate use of arguments and local variables, procedures and functions can be made totally independent of the programs in which they appear. Using Turbo Basic's main-file/work-file concept and $INCLUDE metastatement, these procedures and functions can be effortlessly passed into new programs.

Recursion

Turbo Basic supports *recursion*, a process whereby a function or procedure calls itself, either directly or indirectly. Here's a recursive rendition of FNFactorial:

```
DEF FNFactorial#(n%)
  IF n% > 1 AND n% <= 170 THEN
    FNFactorial# = n% * FNFactorial#(n%-1)
  ELSEIF n% = 0 OR n% = 1 THEN
    FNFactorial# = 1
  ELSE
    FNFactorial# = -1
  END IF
END DEF
```

One thing is immediately obvious: The recursive algorithm is shorter than the nonrecursive one. FNFactorial has been reduced to a single IF block with no local variables. Brevity is a characteristic of recursive programs.

Another characteristic of recursive code is deceptive complexity. The best way to understand a recursive algorithm is to work through some test cases with pencil and paper. Let's determine the factorial of 3 by mentally going through the gyrations a Turbo Basic program would if given the statement

```
PRINT FNFactorial#(3)
```

To start off, an argument of 3 is passed by value to the function. The first thing FNFactorial does is check to see if its argument is greater than 1 and less than or equal to 170; 3 passes this test, so the statement controlled by the first THEN clause is executed:

```
FNFactorial# = 3 * FNFactorial#(2)
```

This line assigns the function name the value 3 (so far so good) multiplied by the value of FNFactorial(2), whatever that is. Before the assignment can take place, you must call FNFactorial again, this time with an argument of 2. Put this to-be-continued assignment statement on hold; you'll return to it later.

A second invocation of FNFactorial receives the argument of 2 and proceeds normally. Again, it finds that its argument is greater than 1 and less than or equal to 170, so again you'll find yourself at the recursive statement

```
FNFactorial# = 2 * FNFactorial#(1)
```

Put this assignment statement on hold also, and call FNFactorial a third time, this time with an argument of 1.

FNFactorial(1) is easy to figure out—it's defined as 1 in the second THEN clause. This time, finally, FNFactorial is allowed to return, and it returns the value of 1 to the most recently put-on-hold invocation of FNFactorial. And its assignment statement is allowed to finish:

```
FNFactorial# = 2 * 1
```

With this middle invocation of FNFactorial complete, a value of 2 is returned to the original invocation of FNFactorial and the first to-be-continued statement:

```
FNFactorial# = 3 * 2
```

After this last assignment, control returns to the PRINT statement and a "6" appears on the screen.

There are no black and white answers to when you should use recursion, but in general use it when the problem itself has a recursive flavor. Factorials, for example, are sometimes defined in math textbooks recursively:

For any positive integer *n*,
if $n > 1$ then
  $n! = n * (n-1)!$
else
  $n! = 1$

Using a recursive algorithm will probably require that you increase your program's run-time stack with the $STACK metastatement, since each level of recursion could take 125 bytes (this amount varies). To determine the amount of stack space left, use the FRE(−2) function.

Files

Once you have created a program or a collection of data that you'll need to access again, the next logical step is to save it. In saving your data, you are creating a *file* that can be used for input or output. There are three file types you can create: *sequential, random access*, and *binary*. We'll discuss each of these types here, but first let's look at how to name files and/or *directories* (which contain several files or *subdirectories*).

As a citizen of an MS-DOS world, the files you create and access using Turbo Basic must conform to DOS naming conventions. File names consist of two parts, separated by a period:

```
filename.ext
```

where *filename* can be from one to eight characters, and *ext* is an optional type extension of up to three characters. If a file name is longer than eight characters, Turbo Basic automatically truncates the name and adds a period at its end. For example, if you enter

```
TESTINGDATA
```

it becomes

```
TESTINGD.
```

If a string has a period that separates the file name and its extension but the file name is over eight characters long, Turbo Basic truncates the name to eight characters and then appends the extension, like so:

```
VERYLONGFILENAME.TBS
```

becomes

```
VERYLONG.TBS
```

If you use an extension with more than three characters, the extra characters are truncated; for example:

```
TESTING.DATA
```

becomes

```
TESTING.DAT
```

File names and extensions can contain the following characters:

A–Z 0–9 ( ) { } @ # $ % ^ & ! - _ ' / ~

Note that the space character cannot be used, and lowercase letters are automatically converted into uppercase. Following are examples of valid file names:

```
MYFIRST.TBS
MY1ST.TBS
MY_ABCS.(1)
10-25-51.@@@
```

In addition to statements for creating, reading, and writing files, Turbo Basic has tools to perform certain DOS-like utility functions from within a program. The NAME statement renames files. KILL deletes files. MKDIR creates directories. CHDIR changes the active directory. RMDIR deletes directories. There isn't a COPY command; use binary file techniques instead (or use SHELL to invoke COMMAND.COM).

File names used in Turbo Basic statements (for example, KILL and OPEN) must be in string form; for example:

```
KILL "myfile.bak"
```

or

```
a$ = "myfile.bak" : KILL a$
```

but not

```
KILL myfile.bak
```

For more information about files and directories, consult Appendix G, "A DOS Primer," and your DOS manual.

Directories and Path Names

In MS-DOS 2.0 and above (Turbo Basic and the programs it creates won't run on earlier versions), formatting a floppy or hard disk creates a fixed-sized directory known as the *root*. Entries in the root directory can represent both files and additional directories (called *subdirectories*).

Like ordinary files, subdirectories have standard file names and extensions, and can grow and expand as necessary. Subdirectories can contain subdirectories of their own, resulting in a system of files and directories resembling an upside-down tree (see Figure 4-1).

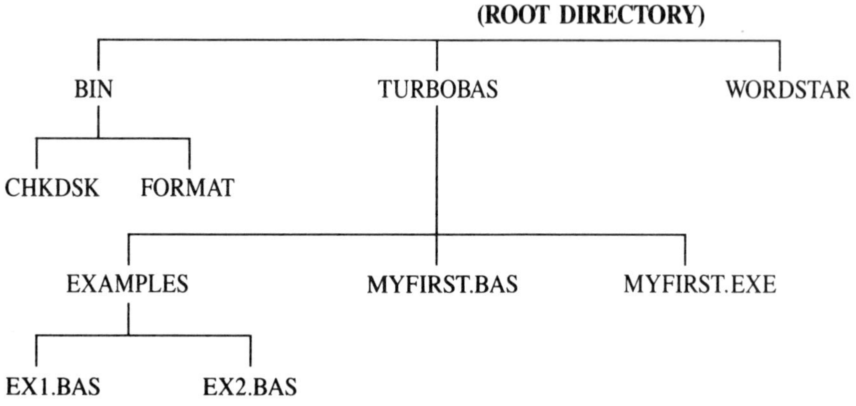

Figure 4-1 *Hierarchy of a File System*

At the top of the file system tree is the root directory, the name of which is predefined as a single backslash: (\). Files in the tree are specified by indicating the directory chain, or path name, that leads to them.

Path names are formed by listing the subdirectories leading to the file, separated by backslashes (\). In other words, the complete description of file CHESS.BAS in directory \TURBO\BASIC\GAMES is

```
disk drive letter and colon
|
C:\TURBO\BASIC\GAMES\CHESS.BAS
  |-----------------||---||--|
           |          |    |
   directory         file  extension
     path            name
```

A leading backslash (\) indicates that a path starts from the root directory, as opposed to the current directory. DOS keeps track of the current directory (also known as the *active* or *default* directory), the one it will search for files when you don't specify a path. If a path name doesn't begin with a backslash, then it describes a path relative to the current directory. For example, if \TURBO\BASIC is the current directory, both of the following accurately describe the location of CHESS.BAS:

```
GAMES\CHESS.BAS
```

or

```
\TURBO\BASIC\GAMES\CHESS.BAS
```

In every subdirectory, a directory listing from either DOS or Turbo Basic (using FILES) lists two special files: . and .. . The single period file name identifies the directory being listed as a subdirectory. The double period file name refers to the parent of this directory. For example, to change the active directory to the parent of the current active directory, use the CHDIR statement with the special double period file name.

```
CHDIR ".."
```

File Storage Techniques

Turbo Basic offers three distinct ways to store and retrieve information from disk: *sequential*, *random*, and *binary* file I/O. Each has advantages and disadvantages, which one works best for you will depend on your application.

Crash Course in Database Management

Traditional programming nomenclature subdivides data files into individual *records*, each of which consists of one or more *fields*. For example, in a mailing list program, each record in the data file represents a person. Within each record are fields containing specific facts about that person. For example, *state* and *zip code* are two fields you might find in a mailing list file. When put on paper, rows represent records, and columns fields:

Name	Address	City	St.	Zip	Class	Contrib.
Cathy Harvey	1010 E. Redwood	Sioux City	IA	51103	73	0.00
Andrew Rich	37 Anderson Rd.	Houston	TX	77018	58	500.00
Larry Irving	3210 Main	Lindsborg	KS	67456	81	0.00

This alumni mailing list file has three records, each with seven fields. For reasons we'll explain shortly, a distinction is usually made between numeric and string fields. In this example, the last three fields are numeric and the rest are string.

Sequential Files

Sequential file techniques are a straightforward way to read and write files. Turbo Basic's sequential file commands create text files: files of ASCII characters with carriage-return/line-feed pairs separating records.

Quite possibly the best reason for using sequential files is their degree of portability to other programs, programming languages, and computers. Because of this, you can often look at sequential files as the common denominator of data processing: They can be read by word processing programs and editors (such as Turbo Basic's), absorbed by other MS-DOS applications such as database managers, and sent through serial ports to alien computers.

The idea behind sequential files is simplicity itself: write to them as though they were the screen, and read from them as though they were the keyboard.

Create a sequential file using the following steps:

1. *OPEN the file in sequential OUTPUT mode.* To create a file in Turbo Basic, you must use the OPEN statement. Sequential files have two options to prepare a file for output:

   OUTPUT: If a file does not exist, a new file is created. If a file already exists, its contents are erased and the file is then treated as a new file.

   APPEND: If a file does not exist, a new file is created. If a file already exists, Turbo Basic appends any data written to that file at its end.

2. *Output data to a file.* Use WRITE#, PRINT #, or PRINT# USING to write data to a sequential file.

3. *CLOSE the file.* The CLOSE statement closes a file variable after the program has completed all I/O operations.

To read a sequential file:

1. *OPEN the file in sequential INPUT mode.* Prepare the file to be read from.

2. *Read data in from the file.* Use Turbo Basic's INPUT #, INPUT$, or LINE INPUT# statements.

3. *CLOSE the file.* The CLOSE statement closes a file variable after the program has completed all I/O operations.

(See Chapter 5, "Turbo Basic Reference Directory," for detailed information about the file operations mentioned here.)

The drawback to sequential files is that you only have sequential access to your data: You access one record at a time, starting with the first record. This means if you want to get to the last record in a sequential file of 23,000 records, you'll have to go through the first 22,999 records.

Sequential files, therefore, are best suited to applications that perform sequential processing (for example, word counting, spelling-checking, printing mailing labels in file order) or in which all the data can be held in memory simultaneously. This allows you to read the entire file in one fell swoop at the start of a program and to write it all back at the end. In between, the information can be accessed through temporary, random access homes in numeric and string arrays.

Sequential files lend themselves to database situations in which the length of individual records is variable. For example, suppose the alumni list had a comments field. Some people may have 100 bytes or more of comments; others, perhaps most, will have none. Sequential files handle this problem without wasting disk space.

Two types of sequential files can be created using Turbo Basic: (1) field-delimited sequential files, where each field on each line in the file is separated (delimited) by special characters, and (2) nondelimited sequential files, where each file looks exactly the same as it would whether its data is displayed on the screen or printed on the printer. These two file types are created using the WRITE # and PRINT # statements, respectively. (Use INPUT #, INPUT$, or LINE INPUT# for reading the information back in from either type of sequential file.)

Field-Delimited Sequential Files

If you look at a sequential file created by Turbo Basic, you can see that the data in the file is separated (delimited) by commas and any strings are enclosed in double quotes—in exactly the form the INPUT # statement expects to find the data. (The double quotes around strings keep you from getting into trouble with embedded commas. Numbers don't need the quotes because they are written without commas.)

Consider the following program and execute it:

```
' This program opens a sequential file for output. It writes a couple lines of
' different types of data to the file using the WRITE # statement.

OPEN "SEQUENTI.BAS" FOR OUTPUT AS #1             ' assign the file variable
                                                 ' to #1

StringVariable$ = "This is a string of text"     ' define some
Integer% = 1000                                  ' variables and
FloatingPoint! = 30000.1234                      ' initialize them

' now write a line of text to the sequential file
WRITE# 1, StringVariable$, Integer%, FloatingPoint!

StringVariable$ = "Another String"
Integer% = -32767
FloatingPoint! = 12345.54321

' write another line of text
WRITE# 1, Integer%, StringVariable$, FloatingPoint!

CLOSE #1                                         ' close the file variable

END                                              ' end the program
```

The contents of the file SEQUENTI.BAS look like this:

```
"This is a string of text",1000,30000.123046875
-32767,"Another String",12345.54296875
```

The most important thing to note here is that the WRITE # statement outputs information to the sequential file exactly as the INPUT # statement expects to find it.

The following program reads in the sequential file that the last example program created:

```
' This program opens a sequential file for input. It reads a
' couple of lines of different types of data from the file using
' the INPUT # statement.

OPEN "SEQUENTI.BAS" FOR INPUT AS #1          ' assign the file variable
                                             ' to #1

StringVariable$ = ""                         ' define some
Integer% = 0                                 ' variables and
FloatingPoint! = 0                           ' initialize them

' now read a line of text from the sequential file
INPUT # 1, StringVariable$, Integer%, FloatingPoint!

PRINT StringVariable$, Integer%, FloatingPoint!

StringVariable$ = ""
Integer% = 0
FloatingPoint! = 0

'read another line of text
INPUT # 1, Integer%, StringVariable$, FloatingPoint!

PRINT Integer%, StringVariable$, FloatingPoint!

CLOSE #1                                     ' close the file variable

END                                          ' end the program
```

The important thing to remember here is that the previous examples would not work correctly if you used the PRINT # statement to create the data file. When creating a file to be read with the INPUT # statement, use the WRITE # statement rather than PRINT #.

Nondelimited Sequential Files

In a nondelimited sequential file, the data looks exactly as it would if it had been displayed to the screen using PRINT or printed on the printer using LPRINT. You may use the USING optional parameter when performing output to a sequential file exactly as you would when doing screen or printer output.

Consider the following program and execute it:

```
' This program opens a sequential file for output. It writes
' a couple lines of different types of data to the file using
' the PRINT # and PRINT# USING statements.

OPEN "SEQUENTI.BAS" FOR OUTPUT AS #1          ' assign the file variable
                                              ' to #1

StringVariable$ = "This is a string of text"  ' define some
Integer% = 1000                               ' variables and
FloatingPoint! = 30000.1234                   ' initialize them

' now write a line of text to the sequential file
PRINT # 1, StringVariable$, Integer%, FloatingPoint!

StringVariable$ = "Another String"
Integer% = -32767
FloatingPoint! = 12345.54321

'write another line of text but format it with USING
PRINT # 1, USING "+##### & ##.##^^^^";Integer%, _
                                  StringVariable$, FloatingPoint!

CLOSE #1                                      ' close the file variable

END                                           ' end the program
```

The contents of the file SEQUENTI.BAS look like this:

```
This is a string of text      1000          30000.123046875
-32767 Another String 12.35E+03
```

As with field-delimited sequential files, the most important thing to note here is the format of the data and how it can be read. If you attempt to use the same INPUT # statement as the one in the second example program, Turbo Basic would return a run-time error. Turbo Basic would read the word "This" in the first line as the string variable and try to read the next two words as the two numeric variables. Instead, you must use the INPUT$ or the LINE INPUT# statements to read in this information.

The following program reads in the sequential file that the last example program created:

```
' This program opens a sequential file for input. It reads a
' couple lines of different types of data from the file using
' the LINE INPUT# and INPUT$ statements.

OPEN "SEQUENTI.BAS" FOR INPUT AS #1     ' assign the file variable
                                        ' to #1

StringVariable$ = ""

' now read a string of 80 characters in from the sequential file
StringVariable$ = INPUT$(80, 1)

PRINT StringVariable$
```

```
' input an entire line of input regardless of its length
LINE INPUT# 1, StringVariable$

PRINT StringVariable$

CLOSE #1                              ' close the file variable

END                                   ' end the program
```

Following are Turbo Basic statements and functions that control sequential file I/O:

Statement/Function	Operation
CLOSE	Terminates operations on a file(s).
EOF	Returns a signal when the end of a file is reached.
INPUT #	Reads a record (line of text) into the indicated variable(s).
INPUT$	Reads *n* characters into a string variable.
LINE INPUT #	Reads an entire line into a single string variable.
OPEN	Opens a file for INPUT, OUTPUT, or APPEND mode and gives it a number.
PRINT #, PRINT # USING	Prints to the file as though it were the printer or screen.
WRITE #	Writes comma-delimited data to a file.

Random Files

Random access files consist of records that can be accessed in any sequence. What this means is that the data is stored exactly as it appears in memory, thus saving processing time (because no translation is necessary) both when the file is written to and when it is read.

Generally speaking, random files are a better solution to database problems than sequential files, although they are not without disadvantages. For one thing, random files aren't especially transportable. You can't peek inside them with an editor or type them in a meaningful way to the screen. In fact, moving a Turbo Basic random file to another computer or language will probably require that you write a translator program to read the random file and output a text (sequential) file. One example of the transportability problem strikes close to home. Since Interpretive BASIC uses Microsoft's nonstandard format for floating-point values, and Turbo Basic uses IEEE standard floating-point conventions, you can't read the floating-point fields of random files created by Interpretive BASIC with a Turbo Basic program, or vice versa, without a bit of extra work.

We've provided four special functions to get around this hurdle: CVMS and CVMD to turn Microsoft-format numeric fields into bona fide Turbo Basic single- and double-precision variables, and MKMS$ and MKMD$ to turn single- and double-precision values into Microsoft-format strings that can then be written to a file.

The major benefit of random files is implied in their name: Every record in the file is available at any time. For example, in a database of 23,000 alumni, a program can go straight to record 22,709 or 11,663 without reading any others. This capability makes it the only reasonable choice for large files, and probably the better choice for small ones, especially those with relatively consistent record lengths.

Random files can be wasteful of disk space, because space is allocated for the longest possible field in every record. For example, including a comment field of 100 bytes makes every record take an extra 100 bytes of disk space, even if only one in a thousand uses it.

On the other extreme, if records are consistent in length, especially if they contain mostly numbers, random files can save space over the equivalent sequential form. In a random file, every number of the same type (integer, long integer, single precision, double precision) occupies the same amount of disk space. For example, the following five single-precision values each require 4 bytes (the same space they occupy in memory):

```
0
1.660565E-27
15000.1
641
623000000
```

By contrast, in a sequential file, numbers require as many bytes as they have ASCII characters when PRINTed, plus one for the delimiting comma. For example:

```
WRITE #1, 0;0
```

takes 3 bytes, and

```
PRINT #1, 0;0
```

takes 6 bytes, and

```
PRINT #1.660565E-27
```

takes 13 bytes.

The modest price you pay for the benefits of random files is a bit of extra processing necessary to get strings and numbers into and out of a form that the random file routines can handle.

You can create, write, and read random files using the following steps:

1. *OPEN the file and specify the length of each record.*

   ```
   OPEN filespec AS [#]filenum LEN = record.size
   ```

The LEN parameter indicates to Turbo Basic that this is a random access file. Unlike sequential files, you don't have to declare whether you're OPENing for input or output, because you can simultaneously read and write a random file.

2. *Execute a FIELD statement to define a mapping between a series of string variables (after this operation they become "field variables") and the "file buffer."*

   ```
   FIELD filenum, width AS string-var [width AS string-var]...
   ```

   This buffer is the loading dock for data to be written to or read from this particular file. The FIELD statement must be executed at least once for a given random file.

3. *To write a record to the file, use LSET and RSET to load the field variables with the data to be written.* Numbers must first be converted to string form with the appropriate "make" function (for example, MKS$ for single precision) before LSET or RSET can be used. Finally, use PUT to write the record to the file at the position you specify.

4. *To read a record from the file, use the GET statement to read the record you want.* Then load your program's string and numeric variables from the appropriate buffer variables. Before you can do anything with it, numeric data must be converted from string form with one of the "convert" functions (for example, CVS for single precision).

5. *When finished, CLOSE the file.*

Following are Turbo Basic statements and functions that control random file reading and writing:

Statement/Function	Operation
CLOSE	Closes the file.
CVI, CVL, CVS, CVD	Converts field variable into the corresponding numeric type.
FIELD	Defines the field variables.
GET	Reads a record.
LOC	Determines the last record number read.
LSET, RSET	Assigns to a field variable.
MKI$, MKL$, MKS$, MKD$	Converts specific numeric types into a form that can be assigned to a field variable.
MKMS$, MKMD$, CVMS, CVMD	Special Microsoft-format translation functions.
OPEN	Opens the file as random.
PUT	Writes a record.

And following is a sample program using random files:

```
' program to read from a mailing list database
' user inputs record number; program displays
' all the fields for that record.
' this program couldn't read the sequential file described before
OPEN "ADDRESS.DTA" AS #1 LEN = 81 ' "LEN = 81" declares file as random

' define the record layout of file #1
' note use of continuation character
FIELD #1, 25 AS FileName$, 25 AS address$,_
         15 AS city$, 2 AS state$,_
          4 AS zip$, 2 AS class$, 8 AS contrib$

' Zip$ is a long integer, class$ an integer, contrib$ a double-precision real.
' all now exist in the file as strings.
' When we read one of these numeric fields, we must
' convert it back into a number before using it.

INPUT "Which record do you want to see: ", recnumber
GET #1, recnumber
' the data is now in the file buffer
PRINT "Data for record" recnumber
PRINT "Name: " FileName$
PRINT "Address: " address$
PRINT "City/State/Zip " city$, state$, CVL(zip$)
PRINT "Class: " CVI(class$)
PRINT "Most recent contrib: " CVL(contrib$)
```

Warning: Don't ever assign to a field variable; that is, don't use a field variable on the left side of an assignment statement. Assigning to a field variable disconnects the variable from its designated buffer. For example, after

```
zip$ = a$
```

field variable *zip$* no longer refers to the buffer it was assigned to in the FIELD statement. And subsequent LSETs and RSETs won't bring it back.

Binary Files

Turbo Basic's binary file technique is an extension to Interpretive BASIC that allows you to treat any file as a numbered sequence of bytes, without regard to ASCII characters, number versus string considerations, record length, carriage returns, or anything else. With the binary approach to a file problem, you read and write a file by specifying which bytes to write and where in the file they should go. This is similar to the services provided by DOS system calls (used in assembly language) for reading and writing files.

Flexibility always comes at a price. BINARY mode files require that you do all the work to decide what goes where. Binary may be the best option when dealing with alien files that aren't in ASCII format; for example, a dBASE® or Lotus® 1-2-3 file. Of course, you'll have to know the precise structure of the file before you even attempt to break it down into numbers and strings agreeable to Turbo Basic.

Every file opened in BINARY mode has an associated position indicator that points to the place in the file that will be read or written to next. Use the SEEK statement to set the position indicator and the LOC function to read it.

Binary files are accessed in the following way:

1. OPEN the file in BINARY mode. You need not specify whether you're reading or writing—you can do either or both.
2. To read the file, use SEEK to position the file pointer at the byte you want to read. Then use GET$ to read a specified number of characters (from 1 to 32,767) into a string variable.
3. To write to the file, load a string variable with the information to be written. Then use PUT$ to specify the string data and the point in the file to which it should be written.
4. When finished, CLOSE the file.

Following are the Turbo Basic statements and functions that control binary file reading and writing:

Statement/Function	Operation
CLOSE	Closes the file
GET$	Reads the specified number of bytes starting at seek position
LOC	Determines the seek position in the file
LOF	Returns the length of file
OPEN	Opens the file and declares it as binary
PUT$	Writes the specified number of bytes starting at seek position
SEEK	Moves the position indicator

Device I/O

Turbo Basic supports so-called device files; that is, it supports hardware devices such as the keyboard, screen, and printer as though they were sequential files. Each supported device has a reserved file name that ends in a colon:

Name	Function
KYBD:	The keyboard can be opened for input. Reading from device file KYBD: is like using INKEY$.
SCRN:	The screen can be opened for output. Writing to the SCRN: device file is like PRINTing.
LPT1-3:	Line printers 1 to 3.
COM1-2:	Communcations ports 1 and 2.

For example:

```
OPEN "SCRN:" FOR OUTPUT AS #1 : PRINT #1, "Hello"
```

has the same effect as

```
PRINT "Hello"
```

and

```
OPEN "KYBD:" FOR INPUT AS #1 : INPUT #1, a$, b$
```

is the same as

```
INPUT a$, b$
```

Graphics

When it comes to displaying information on the screen, a program generated by Turbo Basic must work within the constraints of the display hardware available to it. Turbo Basic supports these classes of video interfaces on PCs and compatibles: the Monochrome Display Adapter, which is only capable of monochrome text; the Color/Graphics Adapter (CGA) and the Enhanced Graphics Adapter (EGA), both of which can produce text and graphics in color and in black and white; the Multi-Color Graphics Array Adapter (MCGA), which runs on IBM's Personal System/2 Model 30; and the Video Graphics Adapter (VGA), which runs on IBM's Personal System/2 Models 30, 50, 60, and 80 (see Table 4-5).

Corresponding to the talents of these video boards, Turbo Basic can select any of the supported text or graphics modes with the SCREEN and/or WIDTH statements.

Table 4-5 Graphics Adapter Characteristics

Adapter	Screen Mode	Text Format	Comments
Monochrome	0	80 column	80 × 25 characters, with 4 attributes (normal, highlight, blinking, underline)
CGA	0, 1, 2	40/80 col.	Up to 16 colors (in text mode only); up to 4 colors in graphics mode. Screen resolution: 640 × 200 pixels.
EGA	0, 1, 2, 7, 8, 9, 10	40/80 col.	Screen resolution: up to 640 × 350 pixels. Up to 16 colors out of a 64-color palette (depending on EGA memory)
MCGA	0, 1, 2, 11	40/80 col.	CGA including a screen resolution of 640 × 480 pixels; black and white in screen mode 11.
VGA	0, 1, 2, 7, 8, 9, 10, 11, 12	40/80 col.	EGA and MCGA including a screen resolution of 640 × 480 pixels; up to 16 colors in screen mode 12.

CGA = Color/Graphics Adapter
EGA = Enhanced Graphics Adapter
MCGA = Multi-Color Graphics Array Adapter
VGA = Video Graphics Adapter

The Text Modes

In 80 column text mode (the only mode available with the Monochrome Display Adapter), the screen consists of 25 lines of 80 character positions each, numbered 1 to 25 (top to bottom) and 1 to 80 (left to right). (See Figure 4-2.) In 40 column text mode (available with the CGA/EGA adapters), the screen consists of 25 lines of 40 characters. Each position on each line can contain any of the characters listed in the character set chart in Appendix F.

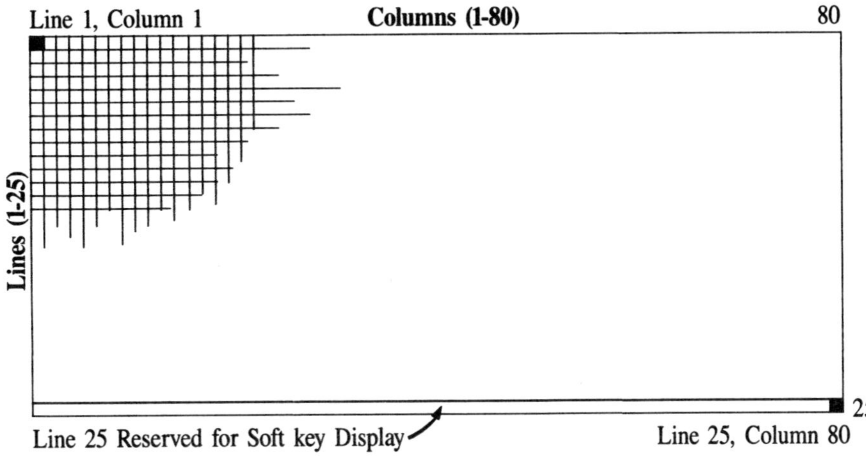

Figure 4-2 *Text Mode Screen*

Generally speaking, you place characters on the screen by moving the cursor to the desired position with the LOCATE statement and then using PRINT. Exotic characters that are difficult to generate at the keyboard can be produced with the CHR$ function (see Appendix F).

The 25th (lowest) line of the screen rates special consideration: The KEY statement loads it with function key descriptions ("soft keys"). To protect these key descriptions, the 25th line is never scrolled or written to unless you turn off the function key display with KEY OFF.

For monochrome adapters, the COLOR statement can be used to create special effects such as inverse and reduced intensity video and underlined and/or blinking text. With a CGA/EGA adapter, the COLOR statement is used to select the actual color to be displayed for output from PRINT statements.

In text mode, the CGA/EGA adapters support up to eight display "pages"; the page being processed and/or displayed is set with the SCREEN statement.

The Graphics Modes

Turbo Basic has a full complement of commands to plot points, lines, and graphic shapes on the screen in various colors. Unless you have appropriate video display hardware, such as the Color/Graphics Adapter or the Enhanced Graphics Adapter or equivalent, these commands won't work as described. (In general, attempting to use a graphics command on text-only hardware produces an Illegal Function Call error.)

In graphics modes, the screen is treated as a grid of small dots, or *pixels*, any one of which can be turned on (white or some color), or off (the background color, usually black). The pixels are identified by their position on an (x,y) grid, the origin of which by default is at the upper left-hand corner of the screen. x values represent horizontal distance from the left edge of the screen, and y values represent vertical distance from the top edge of the screen. Note that this convention for y is reversed from conventional cartesian geometry, in which y values get smaller as you move from high to low.

Depending upon the mode selected (and possibly upon the amount of video memory installed), the horizontal resolution may be 320 or 640 pixels, while the vertical resolution may be 200 or 350 (see Figure 4-3). This combination also determines the number of colors available (2/4/16), as well as the maximum number of video "pages" (1/2/4/8). Pixel numbering is indexed to zero, unlike text row and column counting, which starts at one.

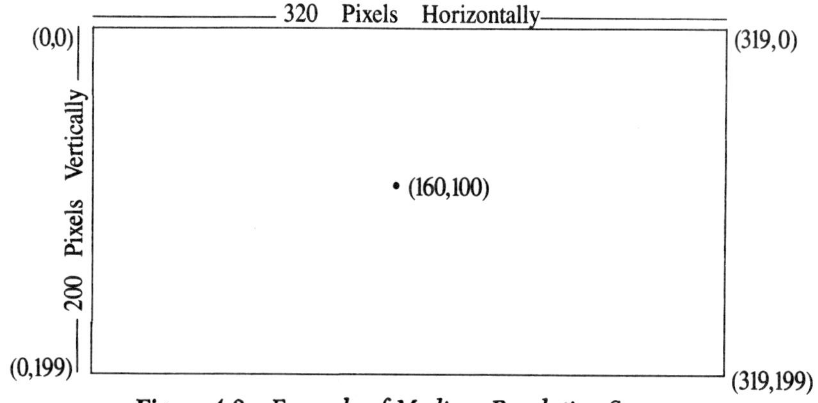

***Figure 4-3** Example of Medium Resolution Screen*

Each pixel has an associated color value (or ***attribute***) ranging from 0 to the maximum for the mode. The color resulting from each value is controlled by the COLOR and PALETTE statements.

Last Point Referenced (LPR)

After most graphic operations, an imaginary pen point is poised at an x,y coordinate on the screen. The position of this pen is called the *last point referenced*, or LPR. When you first invoke a graphics mode with the SCREEN statement, the LPR is set to the center of the screen.

Certain drawing commands are able to accept the LPR as a coordinate argument. For example, if the LINE statement is given only a destination point, the line is drawn between the LPR and the specified destination point. Afterward, the LPR becomes the destination point.

Absolute and Relative Coordinates

Most of Turbo Basic's plotting statements can specify coordinates in both *relative* and *absolute* form.

In absolute form, an (x,y) coordinate pair describes exactly where an operation should occur; for example, PSET (50,75) turns on the pixel 50 pixels from the left of the screen and 75 pixels from the top.

In relative form, a coordinate is specified relative to the LPR and represents the horizontal and vertical displacement from the LPR. This form uses the keyword STEP to differentiate it from standard absolute coordinates. For example, if the LPR is (60,75):

```
PSET (10,20)
```

specifies the point (10,20), and

```
PSET STEP (10,20)
```

specifies the point (70,95), 10 over and 20 down from the LPR. A negative relative coordinate value specifies a point above or to the left of the LPR.

Redefining Screen Coordinates

If you aren't comfortable with this addressing system, use the WINDOW statement to change the mapping between the (x,y) pairs given in plotting statements and the pixels on the screen. For example:

```
WINDOW (-1,1) - (1,-1)
```

redefines screen coordinates to more closely resemble the cartesian plane of analytical geometry, with the origin in the middle, and y values increasing as you move upward. After this WINDOW statement, PSET (0,0) turns on physical pixel (100,160), PSET $(-1,-1)$ turns on the screen's lower left-most pixel, and PSET (.5,.5) turns on physical pixel (220,50) in the middle of the upper right-hand quadrant. Using WINDOW can greatly simplify mathematical charts and graphs.

The VIEW statement allows you to create an active region, or "window," on the graphics screen, and to optionally specify coordinates relative to the window's upper left-hand corner. You cannot manipulate pixels outside of the window.

The graphics commands include the following:

Command	Function
CIRCLE	Draws all or part of a circle.
COLOR	Selects color palette and background color.
DRAW	A mini-drawing language.
GET	Loads numeric array with pixel information from screen.
LINE	Draws a line or a box, given two points.
PAINT	Fills an enclosed area with a solid color or pattern.
PALETTE	Controls and selects one or more colors in the palette.
PALETTE USING	Changes all palette entries with one statement.
PMAP	Performs mapping between physical and world coordinates.
POINT	Returns information about a point or last point referenced.
PRESET	Plots a point (default = attribute 0).
PSET	Plots a point (default = max attribute for current resolution).
PUT	Copies the contents of a numeric array to the screen (see GET).
SCREEN	Selects graphics mode.
VIEW	Declares active area for graphics operations.
WINDOW	Defines window coordinates.

C H A P T E R 5

Turbo Basic Reference Directory

Turbo Basic's 200-odd commands can be grouped according to their syntactical class as *functions*, *statements*, *system variables*, and *metastatements*.

Functions (predefined, as opposed to user-defined) return a value and must therefore be used within expressions. Most require one or more arguments; for example:

```
t = COS(3.1)          ' numeric function w/ 1 numeric argument
t$ = LEFT$("Cat",2) ' string function w/ 1 string and 1 numeric argument
```

Statements are the indivisible building blocks that make up programs. Statements must appear on a line all by themselves or with delimiting colons between adjacent statements; for example:

```
CIRCLE (160,100), 50     ' draw a circle
CALL MySub (x,y,z)       ' call a procedure
a = a + 1                ' do an assignment (see LET statement)
```

System variables are predefined identifiers for accessing and controlling certain system information; for example:

```
a$ = DATE$        ' read system date
TIME$ = "00:00"   ' set system time
```

Metastatements are compiler directives. Strictly speaking they aren't part of the language, but instead operate at a different level, controlling the behavior of the compiler; for example:

```
$INCLUDE "module1.tbs"    ' load and process include file
$STACK &H1000             ' set stack size
```

Metastatements, like the switches in the compiler **Options** submenu, control the compiler at compile time rather than the computer at runtime. Metastatements are preceded by a dollar sign ($) to differentiate them from ordinary statements. There can be only one metastatement per line, and unlike some other compiled BASICs, they are *not* placed inside REMarks.

The Directory Format

Each directory entry contains a description, the syntax, general remarks, and an example using the statement, function, or procedure. Where appropriate, related entries are cross-referenced, any use restrictions are outlined, and any differences between Turbo Basic's and Interpretive BASIC's use of an item are noted.

Following are the syntax description conventions used in the alphabetical command reference.

numeric expression
A numeric constant, numeric function, or numeric variable, or a combination thereof, using arithmetic, logical, and relational operators. Sometimes the type of a numeric expression is specified; for example, *integer expression*. Examples include:

```
16
x
16 * x
SIN(3.14159)
SIN(x /(16 * x))
```

string expression
A string constant, string variable, or string function, or a combination thereof, optionally including the concatenation operator, the plus sign (+). Examples include:

```
"Cat"
a$ + "Cat"
LEFT$(a$ + "Cat",4)
```

filespec
A string expression describing an MS-DOS file name (eight characters with an optional three-character extension preceded by a period, case insignificant), possibly including a drive and/or path specification. Except where noted, file names must be expressed as string variables or enclosed in double quotes; for example:

```
"MYFIRST.BAS"
"turbobas\myfirst.bas"
"a:\turbobas\myfirst.bas"
```

path

A string expression describing a valid subdirectory on the logged drive. Examples include:

```
"\TURBOBAS"
"GAMES"
```

LPR

The "Last Point Referenced" is used as an implicit coordinate value in some plotting operations, and is set by most graphics statements.

label

label represents either an alphanumeric label or line number identifying a program line. Line numbers and labels are more or less interchangeable in Turbo Basic syntax except that labels must appear on a line by themselves.

Typography

Italics indicate areas within commands to be filled in with application-specific information; for example:

```
REG register,value
```

UPPERCASE text denotes part of a command that must be supplied verbatim; for example:

```
RESUME NEXT
```

Brackets ([ ]) mean that the enclosed information is optional; for example:

```
OPEN filespec AS [#] filenum
```

means that you can include a number sign (#) before the file number in an OPEN statement or leave it out, at your option. Therefore both of the following are legal:

```
OPEN "cust.dta" AS 1
OPEN "cust.dta" AS #1
```

Braces ({ }) indicate a choice of two or more options, one of which must be used. The options are separated by vertical bars (|). For example:

```
KEY {ON|OFF}
```

means that both KEY ON and KEY OFF are valid statements, and that KEY by itself is not.

Ellipses (...) indicate that part of a command can be repeated as many times as necessary. For example:

```
READ variable [,variable]...
```

means that multiple variables, separated by commas, can be processed by a single READ statement:

```
READ a$
READ a$, b$, a, b, c
```

Three vertically spaced periods indicate the omission of one or more lines of program text; for example:

```
FOR n = 1 TO 10
   .
   .
   .
NEXT n
```

$COM metastatement

Function — $COM allocates space for the serial port receive buffer.

Syntax — `$COMn size`

Remarks — *n* indicates the communications adapter (1 or 2) and *size* is an integer constant defining the capacity of the buffer for that adapter (0 to 32,767). The default is 256. The default value can be set and saved in the **Options** menu. Default values can be overridden by metastatements in the code.

Restrictions — The size of the buffer specified in the $COM metastatement must be within the range 0 to 32,767. Interpretive BASIC will allocate the same size buffer for both communications ports if they exist. In Turbo Basic, the sizes of these two buffers are set independently.

Differences — This functionality is only available via command-line parameters when invoking Interpretive BASIC.

Example

```
' $COM metastatement is used to alter the
' default space allocated to buffers
' for serial ports

' set up routine to process COM input
$COM1  1024  'set up a 1K input buffer
ON COM(1) GOSUB GetComInput

COM(1) ON    ' turn on COM input handling
OPEN "COM1:" AS #1 ' open file variable as COM1

PRINT "Press any key to terminate the program..."
' while a key hasn't been pressed
WHILE NOT INSTAT
  LOCATE 2,1
  PRINT TIME$          ' display the time
WEND

END                    ' end of program

GetComInput:    ' process COM port interrupt
  ' read input from COM port buffer
  INPUT# 1,ComPortInput$
  RETURN
```

$DYNAMIC metastatement

Function $DYNAMIC declares default array allocation to be dynamic.

Syntax `$DYNAMIC`

Remarks The $DYNAMIC metastatement takes no argument and declares the default array allocation type to be dynamic.

Space for dynamic arrays is allocated at runtime. You can use the ERASE statement to deallocate the array. Dynamic arrays provide more efficient use of memory.

Arrays can also be declared as dynamic by using the DYNAMIC keyword or expression arguments in a DIM statement. Arrays with variable dimensions that are declared common or local to a procedure or function are always dynamic.

See Also DIM
ERASE
FRE
$STATIC

Example

```
$DYNAMIC

' set up error handler
ON ERROR GOTO ErrorHandler

' display memory available in array space
PRINT FRE(-1)

DIM BigArray(10000)  ' declare dynamic array
BigArray(6666) = 66  ' assign data
' display memory available in array space
PRINT FRE(-1)

ERASE BigArray ' deallocate dynamic array
' display memory available in array space
PRINT FRE(-1)

' run-time error returned if run with
' bounds checking on
PRINT BigArray(6666)
END                 ' end program

ErrorHandler:
  PRINT "An error of type " ERR;
  PRINT " has occurred at address" ERADR
  END
```

$EVENT metastatement

Function $EVENT controls generation of event-trapping code.

Syntax `$EVENT{ON|OFF}`

Remarks If your program contains an event trap of some sort (for example, ON KEY, ON COM), then $EVENT defaults to ON, causing the compiler to generate event-checking code between every statement of your program. If your program doesn't do trapping, then $EVENT is OFF and no event-checking code is generated.

$EVENT gives you control over what parts of your program will do event checking. If there's an area where maximum speed is more important than instant event response, then bracket this code with $EVENT OFF and $EVENT ON metastatements.

Example

```
'EVENT example
ON TIMER (1) GOSUB WasteTime
TIMER ON

PRINT "Slow loop"
x = timer
FOR i = 1 TO 10000
  i = i + i - i
NEXT i
y = timer
PRINT "loop time is " y-x

$EVENT OFF

PRINT "Fast loop"
x = timer
FOR i = 1 TO 10000
  i = i + i - i
NEXT i
y = timer
PRINT "loop time is " y-x

END
WasteTime:

FOR j = 1 TO 1000 : j = j + j - j : NEXT j : PRINT
RETURN
```

$IF/$ELSE/$ENDIF metastatements

Function $IF, $ELSE, and $ENDIF define portions of a source program to be compiled or skipped (often referred to as conditional compilation).

Syntax
```
$IF const
.
. statements
.
[$ELSE
.
.   statements ]
.
$ENDIF
```

Remarks *const* is a named constant or constant value. If *const* is nonzero (TRUE), then the statements between $IF and $ELSE are compiled, and the statements between $ELSE and $ENDIF are not. If *const* is zero (FALSE), then the statements between $IF and $ELSE are ignored, and those between $ELSE and $ENDIF are compiled.

The $ELSE clause is optional, but $ENDIF is required.

Conditional compilation statements can be nested to a level of 256 deep.

Example
```
%ColorScreen = 1  ' setting named constant to nonzero value
                  ' indicates operation on color system
' setting zero value indicates operation
' on monochrome system
$IF %ColorScreen
  DEF SEG = &HB800 ' address of graphics
                   ' screen memory
$ELSE
  DEF SEG = &HB000  ' address of monochrome
$ENDIF              ' screen memory

FOR I% = 0 to 4000 STEP 2
  POKE I%,ASC("A")    ' fill screen with A's
NEXT I%

' save all 4000 bytes of video ram
BSAVE "$IF.DTA",0,4000

END                 ' end program
```

$INCLUDE metastatement

Function $INCLUDE includes a text file.

Syntax `$INCLUDE filespec literal`

Remarks Use $INCLUDE to compile the text of another file along with the current file. *filespec literal* is a string constant and the file it represents must follow DOS file name conventions and must represent a Turbo Basic source file. If no file name is specified for the include file, the extension .BAS is assumed.

The $INCLUDE mechanism causes the compiler to treat the included file as though it were physically present in the original text at that point. This allows you to break your source program up into manageable chunks. Turbo Basic's work-file/main-file concept is related to $INCLUDE. To illustrate, consider the files CALCAREA.BAS and CONST.BAS:

```
    File CALCAREA.BAS

PRINT "Circle area calculating program"
PRINT "If you find this program useful"
PRINT "Please send $3,500 to:"
PRINT
PRINT "Frank Borland"
PRINT "4585 Scotts Valley Drive"
PRINT "Scotts Valley, CA 95066"
PRINT "------------------------------"
$INCLUDE "CONST.BAS"
INPUT "Enter radius ", r
PRINT "Area = " pi * r * r
END

    File CONST.BAS

' All purpose constants
pi = ATN(1) * 4
%true = -1
%false = 0
%maxx = 319
%maxy = 199
```

To compile this program, CALCAREA must be made the "main file," since it is the file with the $INCLUDE statement. The work file shifts back and forth between either one, depending on which needs editing (that is, has errors). Regardless of the current work file, a compilation always starts with CALCAREA (the main file). (For more information, see the section in Chapter 3, "The Main Menu.")

When the Turbo Basic compiler encounters the $INCLUDE metastatement in line 7 of CALCAREA, it suspends reading from the code, and loads and begins to read characters from CONST. BAS. When this code is exhausted, the compiler picks up where it left off in the original program.

$INCLUDE metastatements can be nested to 5 deep; that is, an included file may have $INCLUDE metastatements of its own.

Example

```
' Save the following to a file
' called "EXAMPLE.INC"

SUB SayHello      ' procedure prints
  PRINT "Hello"   ' Hello on screen
END SUB

' The following is the main program
$INCLUDE "EXAMPLE.INC"  ' include source file

CALL SayHello      ' call procedure defined
                   ' in the include file

END                ' end program
```

$INLINE metastatement

Function $INLINE declares inline machine code in an inline subprocedure.

Syntax `$INLINE [byte list]|[filespec literal]`

Remarks $INLINE may only occur within the body of an inline subprocedure.

byte list is a sequence of integer values in the range 0 to 255 to be coded directly into the object code at this point.

filespec literal is the name of a file that contains the code to be inserted inline. This code must be relocatable and must preserve and restore the following registers: Stack Segment (SS), Stack Pointer (SP), Base Pointer (BP), and Data Segment (DS). Inline code may reference parameters using BP relative addressing. For more information, refer to Appendix A, "Numeric Considerations," and Appendix C, "Assembly Language Interface."

Example

```
SUB Shriek INLINE
' $INLINE makes the speaker give off a shriek
  $INLINE &HBA, &H00, &H07, &HE4, &H61, &H24
  $INLINE &HFC, &H34, &H02, &HE6, &H61, &HB9
  $INLINE &H40, &H01, &HE2, &HFE, &H4A, &H74
  $INLINE &H02, &HEB, &HF2

END SUB
CALL Shriek
END   'end the program
```

$SEGMENT metastatement

Function $SEGMENT declares a new code segment.

Syntax `$SEGMENT`

Remarks Use the "no-argument" $SEGMENT metastatement to break up your source program when the compiler reports that the 64K code segment limitation has been exceeded:

```
Error 409 Segment Overflow Press <ESC>
```

Everything after the $SEGMENT metastatement will be placed into a new code segment. This makes every flow control statement (GOSUB, GOTO) that passes control across this boundary an *intersegment* (far) move, call, or jump, which requires slightly more time and stack space to complete. This effect can be minimized by placing $SEGMENT statements where natural lines of division occur in your program; for example, between major subroutines or between the main program and initialization or termination code.

There can be up to 16 code segments in a Turbo Basic program. The compilation status data printed after compilation will show the sizes of each segment, separated by slashes (/).

Note: You cannot use a $SEGMENT statement within a structured block; for example, FOR/NEXT, DO/LOOP, WHILE/WEND, IF BLOCK.

Example

```
SUB Proc1
  PRINT "This is a dummy procedure "
END SUB

$SEGMENT  ' define second segment

SUB Proc2
  PRINT "This is another dummy procedure "
END SUB

$SEGMENT  ' define third segment

SUB Proc3
  PRINT "This is another dummy procedure "
END SUB

CALL Proc1
CALL Proc2
CALL Proc3

END       ' end the program
```

$SOUND metastatement

Function $SOUND declares the capacity of the background music buffer.

Syntax `$SOUND buffer size`

Remarks *buffer size* is a numeric constant and indicates the note capacity of the PLAY statement's background buffer, from 1 to 4,096. Increasing the capacity of the buffer to the maximum number of notes you intend to play in a given program makes note-count trapping (and the attendant degradation in performance) unnecessary.

Each note requires 8 bytes of memory; the default capacity is 32 notes or 256 bytes. The default value can be changed and saved using the **M**usic Buffer entry on the **O**ptions menu. Default values are overridden by metastatements embedded in the code.

$STACK metastatement

Function — $STACK declares the size of the run-time stack.

Syntax — `$STACK` *`count`*

Remarks — *count* is a numeric constant from 1024 to 32K. $STACK determines how much run-time memory will be devoted to the stack. The stack is used for return addresses during subroutine calls and within structured statements, and is used for the local variables of multi-line functions. The default (and minimum) size is 1024 (400H) bytes.

You may want to allocate more stack space if your program is abnormally nested, uses large local variables, or performs recursion. If you suspect that a program is running out of stack space, recompile it with the **S**tack test option in the **O**ptions menu. Programs generated with this debugging switch turned on always check the available stack space before entering subroutines, procedures, and functions. Default values are overridden by metastatements embedded in the code.

You can check the amount of free stack space for yourself with the FRE(−2) function.

See Also — FRE

Example

```
' Gives a stack of 4,096 bytes...
$STACK &H1000
PRINT FRE (-2) ' display the amount of stack
               ' space available
```

$STATIC metastatement

Function $STATIC declares the default array allocation to be static.

Syntax `$STATIC`

Remarks The $STATIC metastatement takes no argument and declares the default array allocation type to be static. Space for static arrays is allocated at compile time. Arrays with constant dimensions are always static except if the array is declared local to a procedure or a function or if there's more than one dimension for the same array.

Static arrays cannot be erased. The ERASE statement only initiates each element in the array to zero or to null strings.

Note that the $STATIC metastatement, despite a cosmetic similarity, has nothing whatever to do with the STATIC statement, which declares a special type of local variable within procedures and functions.

The compiler's default is $STATIC.

See Also
DIM
$DYNAMIC
ERASE
FRE

Example

```
$STATIC   ' explicitly declares static arrays

PRINT "Memory available: ",FRE(-1)
' memory remains the same

DIM A(50)   ' A is a static array
PRINT "Memory available: ",FRE(-1)

N = 50

' B is a dynamic array because of the
' expression used as the argument
' in the DIM statement
DIM B(N)
PRINT "Memory available: ",FRE(-1)
' now there is less

ERASE A
PRINT "Memory available: ",FRE(-1)
' no difference because A not deallocated
' just zeroed

ERASE B
PRINT "Memory available: ",FRE(-1)
' more memory because dynamic
' arrays deallocated
END          ' end the program
```

ABS function

Function ABS returns an absolute value.

Syntax `y = ABS(numeric expression)`

Remarks ABS returns the absolute value of a numeric expression. The absolute value of *x* indicates its magnitude without regard to its sign. For example, the absolute value of -3 is 3; the absolute value of $+3$ is 3.

Example

```
' ABS returns the current distance from home by
' taking the absolute value of the distance

' assign a location
Location# = -6.5
' display the current position
PRINT "Current location: ",Location#
' display the distance from home
PRINT "Distance from home: ",ABS(Distance#)(Location#)
```

ASC function

Function ASC returns the ASCII code of a string's first character.

Syntax `y = ASC(`*`string expression`*`)`

Remarks ASC returns the ASCII code (0 to 255) of the first character of *string expression*.

To convert an integer to a character string, use the complementary function CHR$, which produces a one-character string when fed an ASCII value.

Restrictions The string expression passed to ASC may not be a null (empty) string. If it is, run-time error 5 is generated, Illegal Function Call.

See Also CHR$

Example

```
PRINT "The ASCII value of A is ";ASC("A")
```

ATN function

Function ATN returns a trigonometric arctangent.

Syntax `y = ATN(numeric expression);`

Remarks ATN returns the arctangent (inverse tangent) of *numeric expression*; that is, the angle with a tangent of *numeric expression*. ATN returns a double-precision result.

The result, as with all operations involving angles in Turbo Basic, is in radians rather than degrees. Radians are a unit of angle measurement that is mathematically more convenient than degrees. Where angles specified in degrees range from 0 to 360, angles specified in radians range from 0 to 2π, with 0 radians measured along the positive *X* axis and increasing counterclockwise. This puts the positive *Y* axis (90 degrees) at $\pi/2$ radians, the negative *X* axis (180 degrees) at π radians, and the negative *Y* axis (270 degrees) at $3\pi/2$ radians:

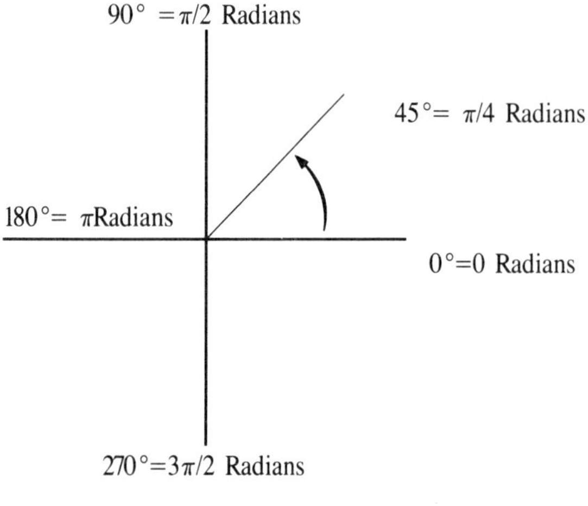

If you (or your application) are more comfortable with degrees, radians can be converted to degrees by multiplying a radian value by 57.2958. For example, the arctangent of 0.23456 is

```
  ATN(.23456) radians
= 0.230395 radians
= (0.230395 * 57.2958) degrees
= 13.2 degrees
```

Convert degrees to radians by multiplying by 0.0174533. For example:

```
  14 degrees
= (0.0174533 * 14) radians
= 0.24435 radians
```

Rather than memorizing the radians/degrees conversion factors, calculate them for yourself by remembering this relationship: 2π radians equals a full circle equals 360 degrees, so 1 radian is $180/\pi$ degrees. Conversely, 1 degree equals $\pi/180$ radians.

For your reference, π to 16-digit accuracy is

```
3.14159 26535 89793
```

This value can be calculated by the expression

```
pi# = 4 * ATN(1)
```

Degrees-to-radians and radians-to-degrees conversions are a good application for single-line functions.

See Also

COS
SIN
TAN

Example

```
' calculate the value of PI using ATN
PI# = 4 * ATN(1)
PRINT PI#
```

BEEP statement

Function BEEP makes the speaker sound.

Syntax `BEEP [count]`

Remarks BEEP plays an 800 Hz tone through the built-in speaker for 0.25 seconds. The optional numeric argument causes *count* BEEPs.

BEEP has the same effect as outputting the ASCII bell character (code 7) to the screen; for example, PRINT CHR$(7). More melodious tones can be created with the SOUND and PLAY statements.

See Also PLAY
SOUND

Example

```
BEEP 2    ' get the user's attention
```

BIN$ function

Function BIN$ returns the binary string equivalent of a number.

Syntax `s$ = BIN$(numeric expression)`

Remarks *numeric expression* is in the range −32,768 to 65,535. Any fractional part is rounded before the string is created. If *numeric expression* is negative, BIN$ returns the two's complement form of the number.

See Also HEX$
OCT$

Example

```
' This example displays both decimal and
' binary values for −5 to 5

FOR I% = −5 TO 5      ' for −5 to 5
  ' display decimal and binary values of I&
PRINT USING "The binary equivalant of -## = &";I%,BIN$(I%)
NEXT I%

END           ' end the program
```

BLOAD statement

Function: BLOAD loads a BSAVEd file into memory.

Syntax: `BLOAD filespec [,address]`

Remarks: *filespec* is a string expression specifying the file to load, and must follow standard DOS naming conventions, optionally including a drive specifier and/or path. *address* is an optional numeric expression from 0 to 65,535 indicating where in the current segment the file should be loaded. If omitted, BLOAD places the file at the address from which it was BSAVEd initially.

If *address* is given, it overrides the address information saved with files produced by the BSAVE statement. Since no checking is done on the address of a BLOAD, it is quite possible to inadvertently load a file on top of DOS and/or your program and crash the system.

Restrictions: BLOAD will not directly load EGA memory.

See Also: BSAVE
DEF SEG

Example:

```
REM LoadGraphicsScreen
DEF SEG &HB800
BLOAD "Picture",0
```

BSAVE statement

Function BSAVE saves a memory range to disk.

Syntax `BSAVE filespec, address, length`

Remarks *filespec* is a string expression specifying the file the data should be written to. *filespec* must follow standard DOS naming conventions, and may optionally include a drive specifier and/or path information. *address* is a numeric expression ranging from 0 to 65,535 and indicates the offset part of the address from which *filespec* will be saved (see DEF SEG statement). *length* is the number of bytes to save, from 0 to 65,535.

BSAVE saves a memory range to disk (in effect saves a digital snapshot of the indicated range at the time of the BSAVE). Files created with BSAVE can then be reloaded with the BLOAD command; optionally, files can be loaded at a different address than where the BSAVE occurred.

BSAVE and BLOAD are often used to save and load screen images by directly reading and writing display memory. The display buffer of the Monochrome Display Adapter is 4,000 bytes long and begins at offset 0 in segment &HB000. The display buffer for the Color/Graphics Adapter is 4,000 bytes long in text mode (SCREEN 0), and 16,384 bytes long in both medium and high resolution graphics modes; both begin at offset 0 in segment &HB800.

Restrictions Before executing a BSAVE statement, the programmer should explicitly set the segment that will be saved to disk using the DEF SEG statement.

See Also BLOAD
DEF SEG

Example

```
' BSAVE fills the screen with A's and saves to disk

FOR I% = 1 to 2000
PRINT "A";  'fills screen with A's
NEXT I%

' define segment for BSAVE
DEF SEG = &HB000

' saves monochrome video ram
BSAVE "TEXT.PIC",0,4000
' twice the number of characters
' because of attributes

END         ' end the program
```

CALL statement

Function CALL invokes a procedure (subprogram).

Syntax `CALL procname [(parameter list)]`

Remarks *procname* is the name of a procedure defined elsewhere in the program with the SUB statement. *parameter list* is an optional, comma-delimited list of variables, expressions, and/or constants to be passed to *procname*.

There are three types of SUB procedures: STATIC, standard procedures, and INLINE. The proceeding discussion applies to all types; however, the way the compiler handles parameter lists is dependent on the type of SUB procedure.

The number and type of arguments passed must agree with the parameter list in *procname*'s definition; otherwise, a compile-time Parameter Mismatch error occurs.

If the SUB procedure is an INLINE procedure, the number of arguments is variable and no type checking is performed on the parameters. It is the responsibility of the SUB INLINE procedure to know or determine the number and type of parameters that are passed to it. (For more on SUB INLINE, refer to Appendix C, "Assembly Language Interface.")

When procedure arguments are passed by reference (that is, variables), they are changeable by the called procedure. When a variable is enclosed in parentheses, it is passed by value and the original value cannot be changed. Note that expressions and constants are always passed by value.

Array arguments are specified by using an empty set of parentheses after the array name. Entire arrays are always passed by reference. For example:

```
CALL SumArray (a())    ' pass array a to SumArray
CALL SumArray (a(3))   ' pass element 3 of a to SumArray
```

See Also $INLINE
SUB

Example

```
DIM Array(1)     ' declare array of 2 numbers

SUB TestProcedure(I%, L&, S!, D#, E, A(1))
' This procedure simply outputs the values
' of each parameter passed to it.
  PRINT I%; L&; S!; D#; E; A(0)
END SUB ' end procedure TestProcedure
```

```
Integer% = 1
LongInt& = 2
SinglePre! = 3
DoublePre# = 4
Array(0) = 5

CALL TestProcedure(Integer%, LongInt&, SinglePre!, _
                   DoublePre#, Integer%^2,Array())

END              ' end the program
```

CALL ABSOLUTE statement

Function CALL ABSOLUTE invokes an assembly language routine.

Syntax `CALL ABSOLUTE address(parameter list)`

Remarks *address* is a numeric scalar containing the offset of the external routine to be invoked. The segment is defined by the most recent DEF SEG statement. *address* must be in the range −32,768 to 65,535. Negative values will be converted by the compiler to positive.

The parameter list form maintains compatibility with Interpretive BASIC by passing short integer parameters onto the stack. This form only allows integers to be passed. (See Appendix C, "The Assembly Language Interface.")

The register buffer is loaded into the processor's registers just before a CALL ABSOLUTE or CALL INTERRUPT and is saved back just after returning. At any given time, the buffer contains the state of the processor as it existed at the completion of the most recent external subroutine.

The register buffer is accessed by the REG statement and function, which uses a numeric argument to reference the corresponding register, as shown in the following:

Register Argument	Register
0	Flags
1	AX
2	BX
3	CX
4	DX
5	SI
6	DI
7	BP
8	DS
9	ES

REG as a statement loads the selected element of the register buffer with the indicated integer value:

```
REG 2,&H1000 ' load 1000H into BX of register buffer
```

REG as a function returns the value of the selected element in the register buffer:

```
PRINT REG(2) ' print value in BX of register buffer.
```

The programmer is responsible for preserving the Data Segment (DS), Base Pointer (BP), Stack Segment (SS), and Stack Pointer (SP) registers.

See Also

CALL INTERRUPT
DEF SEG
REG

Example

```
DEFINT a-z
DIM a(100)
DIM FillRoutine(10)

FillRoutine (0) = &HF2FC
FillRoutine (1) = &HCBAA

REG 1, -1
REG 3, 101 * 2
REG 9, VARSEG(a(0))
REG 6, VARPTR(a(0))

DEF SEG = VARSEG(FillRoutine(0))
PRINT a(1)
WHILE NOT INSTAT : WEND
FillAdr = VARPTR(FillRoutine(0))
CALL ABSOLUTE FillAdr '(REG)

PRINT a(1)
END
```

CALL INTERRUPT statement

Function — CALL INTERRUPT calls a system interrupt.

Syntax — `CALL INTERRUPT n`

Remarks — *n* is an integer expression representing the interrupt to call, from 0 to 255. Just before the interrupt handler receives control, the processor's registers are loaded with the values in the machine register buffer. When the interrupt handler returns, the buffer takes on the values in the processor's registers. At any given time, the buffer contains the state of the processor's registers as they existed at the completion of the most recent external call or REG statement.

The DOS technical reference manual contains complete information on the many functions available through the CALL INTERRUPT mechanism.

The programmer is responsible for preserving the Stack Segment (SS) and Stack Pointer (SP) registers.

Restrictions — Before executing the CALL INTERRUPT statement, the appropriate CPU registers must be initialized through the REG statement. After executing the CALL INTERRUPT statement, the CPU registers' values must be accessed through the REG function.

See Also — CALL ABSOLUTE
REG

Example

```
' CALL INTERRUPT executes a DOS interrupt service

$INCLUDE "REGNAMES.INC"
REG %AX, &H0200
' AH = 02 Hex DOS standard output char function

REG %DX, REG(%DX)AND &HFF02
' DL = 02 Hex DH remains the same
' DL:= character to output

CALL INTERRUPT &H21  ' call interrupt 21
```

CDBL function

Function CDBL converts a number to double-precision format.

Syntax

```
y = CDBL(numeric expression)
```

CDBL converts a numeric variable or expression into double-precision form.

Use CDBL to eliminate the chance of integer overflow in expressions that combine integer and floating-point operands. For example:

```
y# = (z% + x%) / a#
```

This expression will result in overflow if (*z% + x%*) is greater than 32,767. To avoid the possibility, use CDBL to force one of the integer variables to double-precision form. This causes the entire expression to be evaluated in double precision:

```
y# = (CDBL(z%) + x%) / a#
```

Restrictions The range of the expression passed to CDBL must be within the legal range for a double-precision number.

See Also CINT
CLNG
CSNG

Example

```
' CDBL is useful in preventing run-time errors

X% = 2000      ' declare an integer variable
Y% = 2000       ' assign Y% the value of X%
Z# = CDBL(X%) * Y%  ' prevent overflow by converting X%

PRINT X%, Y%, Z#    ' display values of three variables

END
```

CEIL function

Function — CEIL converts a numeric variable or expression to an integer by returning the smallest integer greater than or equal to its argument.

Syntax — `y = CEIL(numeric expression)`

The CEIL function converts a numeric variable or expression to an integer by returning the largest integer that is greater than or equal to its argument.

Differences — This function is not available in Interpretive BASIC.

See Also — CINT
FIX
INT

Example

```
FOR I! = -2.5 to 2.5 STEP 0.5
' display the ceiling for a series of values
PRINT USING "The ceiling of ### is ###.";I!,CEIL(I!).
NEXT I!

END     ' end program
```

CHAIN statement

Function CHAIN invokes a Turbo Basic chain module (created as a .TBC or .EXE file).

Syntax `CHAIN` *`filespec`*

Remarks *filespec* is a string expression that follows standard DOS naming conventions and represents a Turbo Basic chain module (extension .TBC). If the extension is omitted, .TBC is assumed. Therefore, if you want to specify an .EXE file, you must append .EXE to the file name. The variables listed as COMMON in both the current program and the destination program are passed to the destination program.

In the testing phase, the calling program must be compiled to an .EXE file, because you can't chain from within Turbo Basic. The called program must be compiled to disk as a chain module (an .EXE or .TBC file).

If the arguments to the COMMON statements in the calling program and the called program don't match (for example, floating-point variables in one place and integers in another), a run-time error occurs.

Turbo Basic doesn't support Interpretive BASIC's line number-oriented CHAIN options, including DELETE, MERGE, and CHAIN *linenumber*. Since you can't specify a line number within a destination chain module, execution always starts at the beginning.

In translating a CHAINed system of Interpretive BASIC programs to Turbo Basic, you may find that Turbo Basic's expanded use of memory allows consolidating individual modules into a single program, making chaining unnecessary.

Restrictions CHAINing can only be done when a program is being executed from DOS; that is, from an .EXE file. MERGE, DELETE, ALL, and CHAINing to a line number are not supported.

Differences In Turbo Basic, CHAINing is done from one compiled program to another that has been compiled to a .TBC or .EXE file.

See Also COMMON

Example

Consider PROG1 that chains to PROG2:

```
PROG1.BAS
' declare variables to be passed
' to the chained program:
' single precision scalar variables a and b,
' and integer array c%
DIM c%(3000)
a = 65 : b = 13 : c%(2000) = 12
COMMON a, b, c%(1)
' specify # of dimensions in array
CHAIN "PROG2"

PROG2.BAS

' declare variables to be received
' from the invoking program
' they must be in the same order, have the same
' type, but don't need the same name
COMMON x, y, z%(1)
PRINT x, y, z%(2000)
```

When PROG1.EXE is invoked from DOS, it will automatically bring in module PROG2.TBC and execute it, printing out the values assigned in PROG1. When PROG2 ends, it returns to DOS, not to PROG1.

CHDIR statement

Function CHDIR changes the current directory (DOS's CHDIR, or CD, command).

Syntax `CHDIR path`

Remarks *path* is a string expression conforming to DOS path conventions (described in Chapter 4's section entitled "Files"). If *path* does not indicate a valid directory, run-time error 76 occurs, Path Not Found.

The CHDIR statement changes the current (active or default) directory. It is analogous to DOS's CHDIR command except that it can't be abbreviated as CD. Running a program that changes the current directory from within Turbo Basic also changes Turbo Basic's active directory.

Example

```
INPUT "New directory: ",Path$
CHDIR Path$  ' change to user-specified directory

END
```

CHR$ function

Function — CHR$ converts an ASCII code into a one-character string.

Syntax — `s$ = CHR$(integer expression)`

Remarks — CHR$ returns a one-character string whose single character has ASCII code *integer expression*, a value from from 0 to 255. CHR$ complements the ASC function, which returns an ASCII code of a string's first character. CHR$ is handy for creating characters that are difficult to enter at the keyboard, such as graphics characters for screen output and control sequences for printer output.

The value of the integer expression passed to CHR$ must be within 0 to 255. Using an argument out of the range 0 to 255 produces run-time error 5, Illegal Function Call.

See Also — ASC

Example

```
' CHR$ displays the ASCII character set on screen

FOR I% = 0 TO 255
  PRINT USING " !";CHR$(I%);
  ' display ASCII character represented by I%

NEXT I%

END
```

CINT function

Function CINT converts its argument to an integer.

Syntax `y = CINT(numeric expression)`

Remarks The CINT function converts a numeric variable or expression to an integer by rounding the fractional part of *numeric expression*. If *numeric expression* is out of the range −32,768 to +32,767, an Overflow error occurs (run-time error 6).

This conversion is performed implicitly by assigning to an integer variable or calling a procedure or function that takes an integer argument.

Differences Unlike Interpretive BASIC, Turbo Basic does not always round the fractional part of a number up. If the fractional part of a number is equal to .5, it is rounded toward the even number.

See Also CDBL
CEIL
CLNG
CSNG
FIX
INT

Example

```
FOR I! = 0.0 TO 5.0 STEP 0.2
  ' display converting result
  PRINT USING "CINT of #.# = #";I!,CINT(I!)
NEXT I!

END       ' end the program
```

CIRCLE statement

Function CIRCLE draws a circle or part of a circle.

Syntax `CIRCLE (x,y) ,radius [,color [,start, end [,aspect]]]`

Remarks (x,y) is the center of the circle, and can be specified in either absolute or relative form (using STEP). (See Chapter 3's section on graphics for more information about absolute and relative coordinates.)

radius is a numeric expression controlling the size of the circle.

color is an integer expression determining the color of the circle. Acceptable values are 0 to 3 in medium resolution graphics (default is 3), and 0 to 1 in high resolution graphics (default is 1). The default color is the highest possible color for the mode you are in. Using a color argument out of these ranges produces run-time error 5, Illegal Function Call. (See the COLOR statement for more information about color selection.)

start and *end* are optional numeric parameters defining the starting and ending points of the arc to be drawn, specified in radians (see the discussion of radians in the ATN entry). Use them when you want to draw only part of a circle. If *start* and *end* are omitted, the entire circle is drawn. For example:

```
SCREEN 1 : pi = 4 * ATN(1)
CIRCLE (160,100), 50, 3, 0, pi
```

draws a white semicircular arc from 0 radians (0 degrees) to π radians (180 degrees).

Negative *start* and *end* values cause pie-chart-style wedges to be drawn; that is, the edges of the arc are automatically connected to the center point. For example:

```
SCREEN 1 : pi = 4 * ATN(1)
CIRCLE (160,100),50,, -pi/4, -pi/2
```

draws a 45 degree pie slice, from $\pi/4$ radians (45 degrees) to $\pi/2$ radians (90 degrees), which is depicted on page 149. To start a wedge on the positive x axis, use a negative number slightly less than zero (for example, .0001) rather than -0.

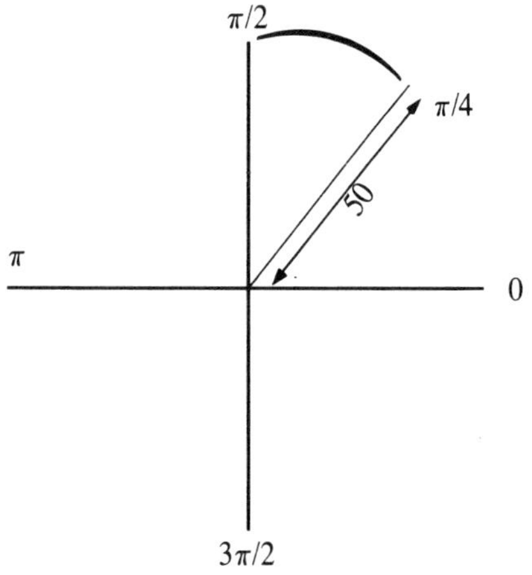

aspect is a numeric expression controlling how oval or round the circle will be. The default is 5/6 (0.833333) in medium resolution, and 5/12 (0.416667) in high resolution. Depending on your particular display board/video monitor combination, you may need to tinker with these values (or adjust your monitor) to get round circles.

The LPR after drawing a circle is its center.

Example

```
' This program demonstrates CIRCLE's capabilities:
' changing the location, the radius, the color,
' and the aspect ratio. CIRCLE can also draw arcs
' and wedges, useful for "pak-man" games.

PI# = 4 * ATN(1)  ' calculate the value of PI
SCREEN 1    ' go into graphics mode

FOR Radius% = 1 TO 20 ' increase the size of the circle
  Colour% = Radius% MOD 4 ' calculate a display color
  CIRCLE(250,150), Radius%, Colour% ' center at 250, 150
NEXT Radius%

CIRCLE(220,60), 50,1,-(PI#*5/4), -(PI#*3/4) 'pak-man body
CIRCLE STEP (-5,-25), 5,1                    ' and eye

Radius% = 50
' ellipses can produce illusions like spheres...
FOR Aspect = 0 TO 2.0 STEP 0.09
  CIRCLE(90,100),Radius%,,,,Aspect
NEXT Aspect
END
```

CLEAR statement

Function — CLEAR clears variable memory.

Syntax — `CLEAR`

Remarks — CLEAR is a parameterless command that sets numeric variables to zero and string variables to null. CLEAR turns off any event trapping that is on (such as music that may be PLAYing), and re-initializes array and string memory.

Note: A CLEAR statement inside a loop will clear the counter causing an endless loop.

Use the ERASE command to selectively free up arrays in memory.

Restrictions — Turbo Basic does not support dynamically setting the stack and data segments; thus, there are no parameters to this statement.

Differences — The differences between Interpretive BASIC's CLEAR statement and Turbo Basic's stem primarily from the differences between compilers and interpreters. Interpretive BASIC allows you to dynamically set the stack and data space, where Turbo Basic's stack and data space is fixed at compile time.

See Also — ERASE
$STACK

Example

```
' This program demonstrates what CLEAR can do

DIM Array$(1)   ' declare an array of strings

PLAY "MB L1 EFGABCDEF"      ' play music in background
ON PEN GOSUB PenHandler     ' set up light pen trapping
ON STRIG(0) GOSUB Button0Handler  ' set up joystick trapping

'initialize the string data
Array$(0) = "This is a string in Array$(0)"
Array$(1) = "This is a string in Array$(1)"

'display the string data
PRINT USING "Array element 1: &";Array$(0)
PRINT USING "Array element 2: &";Array$(1)
PRINT
INPUT "Press <ENTER> to execute CLEAR statement";_Dummy$

CLEAR        ' do a CLEAR
```

```
PRINT
' display no longer existing string data
PRINT USING "Array element 1: &";Array$(0)
PRINT USING "Array element 2: &";Array$(1)
PRINT
PRINT "The string variables are now empty."

END         ' end the program

PenHandler:   ' define a dummy label for the light pen trap
RETURN

Button0Handler:  ' define a dummy label for the joystick
RETURN
```

CLNG function

Function CLNG converts to a long integer.

Syntax `y = CLNG(numeric expression)`

Remarks CLNG converts a numeric variable or expression to a long integer by rounding the fractional part of its argument. If *numeric expression* is out of the range of -2^{31} to $+2^{31} - 1$ (approximately -2 billion to $+2$ billion), run-time error 6 occurs, Overflow.

Restrictions The numeric expression passed to the CLNG function must be within the legal range of a long integer.

Differences This function is not available in most Interpretive BASICs because they do not support long integers.

See Also CDBL
CINT
CSNG
FIX
INT

Example

```
PRINT CLNG(2.0E9), CLNG(33.4), CLNG(-121.9), CLNG(100251.6)

END    ' end the program
```

CLOSE statement

Function CLOSE closes a file or device.

Syntax `CLOSE [[#] filenum [,[#] filenum]...]`

Remarks CLOSE ends the relationship between a file number and a file established in an OPEN statement and concludes I/O to that file. The file buffer is flushed, and if *filenum* represents a file (rather than a device), a DOS CLOSE is performed on it to update the directory.

It's good practice to periodically CLOSE files that a program writes. This ensures that all the information is written and the file's operating system directory entry is properly updated in case of a subsequent power failure or other problem.

A CLOSE with no file number specified closes all open devices and files (so do RESET, END, STOP, and RUN).

See Also END
OPEN
STOP

Example

```
' Open a file assigned to the printer device
OPEN "LPT1:" AS #1

PRINT# 1,"THIS IS A TEST" ' send string to printer

CLOSE# 1        ' close file variable
OPEN "CLOSEFIL.ONE" FOR OUTPUT AS #1    ' open two different files
OPEN "CLOSEFIL.TWO" FOR OUTPUT AS #2

PRINT# 1,"THIS IS A TEST"   ' write string to each file
PRINT# 2,"THIS IS A TEST"

CLOSE             ' close all open files

END
```

CLS statement

Function CLS clears the screen.

Syntax

```
CLS
```

Remarks In text mode, CLS clears the screen to the background color and homes the cursor to the upper left-hand corner (row 1, column 1).

CLS in graphics mode clears the screen to the background color. The LPR becomes the center of the screen, either (160,100) or (320,100), depending on whether the current mode is medium or high resolution, respectively.

If a VIEW statement has been executed, CLS clears only the viewport. To erase the entire display, first use VIEW without arguments to turn off the viewport and then CLS to clear the screen.

See Also COLOR
SCREEN
VIEW

Example

```
' CLS clears the screen to the background color

Print " This is a test of the CLS statement "
INPUT "Press <ENTER> to clear the screen...",Dummy$

Color 10,1   ' set color to Green on Blue

CLS          ' clear the screen to Blue

END
```

COLOR statement (graphics mode)

Function — COLOR sets the colors for graphics operations.

Syntax — For SCREEN 1: `COLOR [background] [,[palette]]`

For SCREENs 7, 8, 9, 10: `COLOR [foreground] [,[background]]`

Remarks — *background* is an integer expression from 0 to 63 specifying background color. *palette* is an integer expression from 0 to 1, selecting one of two color palettes. *foreground* is an integer expression from 1–15.

Arguments to this command determine the screen's background color and the palette of four colors that will be used in subsequent drawing statements. After you've determined the palette and background color with a COLOR statement, the color of individual objects is controlled by arguments to the various plotting commands (CIRCLE, LINE, and so on).

In high resolution mode on a Color/Graphics Adapter, black and white are the only possible colors. Consequently, the COLOR statement has no meaning in this mode, and trying to use it results in run-time error 5, Illegal Function Call.

SCREEN 1
Background 0–255: The actual background color used is background MOD 16. Thus a background of 1 and 16 produces the same result.

Palette 0–255: Select a predefined palette, as shown in the following:

Color	Palette 0	Palette 1
1	Green	Cyan
2	Red	Magenta
3	Brown	White

Even numbers select Palette 0, and odd numbers select Palette 1, the default. Palette 0 gives your program the ability to create objects in green, red, and brown. Palette 1 offers the colors cyan (greenish blue), magenta (reddish purple), and white.

SCREENS 7 and 8

EGA only: Colors are dependent on the current palette.

Foreground 1–15: The selected color is used for both writing characters and drawing graphics.

Background 0–15: Selects background color.

SCREEN 9

Foreground 1–15: The selected color is used for both writing characters and drawing graphics. If your EGA has only 64K of memory, you can only use values in the 1–3 range.

Background 0–63: Selects background color.

SCREEN 10

Foreground 1–3: The selected color is used for writing characters and drawing graphics; 1 = Black, 2 = Blink, 3 = High Intensity. A foreground color of 0 results in an Illegal Function Call.

Use the PALETTE statement to change default attributes:

Background 0–8: The selected color is used for background.

Note: Color value 0 for either palette is the background color specified in this statement, and the foreground color defaults to the maximum attribute.

Restrictions

In screen mode 2, the COLOR statement returns run-time error 5, Illegal Function Call.

Example

```
' This program demonstrates the COLOR statement
' in graphics mode.

' switch to medium resolution graphics mode,
' and set palette 0

SCREEN 1
COLOR ,0

FOR Radius% = 1 TO 20 ' increase the size of the circle
  Colour% = Radius% MOD 4   ' calculate a display color
  CIRCLE(160,100), Radius%, Colour%  ' display a circle
NEXT Radius% ' with center at 250, 150


delay 2

COLOR  ,1    ' change the palette

delay 2

' set the palette and background color,
' and clear the screen

COLOR 6,0 : CLS

' draw a red circle in the middle of the screen
CIRCLE (160,100), 50, 2

delay 2

END
```

COLOR statement (text mode)

Function	COLOR sets text color.
Syntax	`COLOR [foreground] [,[background] [,border]]`

Remarks

foreground is an integer expression from 0 to 31 specifying character color. *background* is an integer expression from 0 to 7 specifying background color. *border* is an integer expression from 0 to 15 and determines border color. If any of these parameters are outside the indicated range, run-time error 5 occurs, Illegal Function Call.

For standard Color/Graphics-type video boards, your foreground choices include the following:

0	Black	8	Gray
1	Blue	9	Light Blue
2	Green	10	Light Green
3	Cyan	11	Light Cyan
4	Red	12	Light Red
5	Magenta	13	Light Magenta
6	Brown	14	Yellow
7	White	15	High Intensity White

Characters can be made to blink by setting *foreground* to the desired color value plus 16. For example, a foreground setting of 22 (6 + 16) produces blinking brown characters.

Monochrome display adapters can't display color, so foreground values are interpreted as follows:

0	Black
1	Underlining
2–7	White
8	Black
9	High intensity underline
10–15	High intensity
16	Black
17	Underline black
18–23	Blink
24	Black
25	High intensity, underline, blink
26–31	High intensity, blink

Background values of 0 through 6 produce a black background. Value 7 results in a white background.

Note: On either adapter, characters become invisible when the *foreground* is equal to the *background.*

Enhanced Graphics Adapters (EGA) and Video Graphics Array Adapters (VGA) with enhanced monitors can display 16 colors from a palette of 64 colors (see PALETTE).

Restrictions

The border parameter has no effect on an EGA or a VGA with an enhanced monitor.

Example

```
' This program demonstrates the COLOR statement
' in both text and graphics modes.

' display a table of attributes
FOR Back% = 0 TO 7
  FOR Fore% = 0 TO 15
    COLOR Fore%, Back%
    PRINT USING " ### ";Back%*16+Fore%;
  NEXT Fore%
  PRINT
NEXT Back%

PRINT

FOR Back% = 0 TO 7 ' display a table of all the attributes
  FOR Fore% = 16 TO 31     ' with blinking
    COLOR Fore%, Back%     ' set display color
    PRINT USING " ### ";Back%*16+Fore%-16;
  NEXT Fore%
  PRINT
NEXT Back%

END
```

COM(n) statement

Function COM(*n*) controls the trapping of serial port events.

Syntax `COM(n) {ON|OFF|STOP}`

Remarks *n* is the number of the communications adapter to be trapped (1 or 2).

A COM(*n*) ON statement allows trapping by the routine specified in a previous ON COM(*n*) statement. After COM(*n*) ON, Turbo Basic checks between the execution of every statement to see if any characters have arrived at the specified serial port. If it finds that such an event has occurred, it calls the subroutine specified in the ON COM(*n*) statement.

If COM(*n*) is OFF, activity at serial port *n* is ignored.

Communications trapping stops after a COM(*n*) STOP statement; however, any activity is remembered so that an immediate trap occurs when a COM(*n*) ON statement is executed.

Use the $COM metastatement to increase or decrease the size of the COM buffer.

See Also ON COM(*n*)

Example

```
' The COM(n) statement demonstrated.  Note: This
' program will not display anything if your COM1
' port is not receiving input

' set up routine to process COM input
ON COM(1) GOSUB GetComInput

' allocate a 5K array to store input
DIM ComPortInput(5 * 1024)
' allocate a pointer to next available buffer space
HeadPtr% = 0
' and the next to print
TailPtr% = 0

' turn COM input handling on
COM(1) ON
' set up 1K input buffer
$COM1 1024
' open a file variable as COM1
OPEN "COM1" AS #1

PRINT "Press any key to terminate the program..."
' while a key hasn't been pressed
WHILE NOT INSTAT
' if the buffer isn't empty
  IF TailPtr% <> HeadPtr% THEN
    ' display input
```

```
    PRINT "COM Port input: ";ComPortInput(TailPtr%)
    ' step to next spot in buffer
    TailPtr% = TailPtr% + 1
  END IF
  LOCATE 2,1
  PRINT TIME$
WEND

END            ' end of program

' process COM port interrupt
GetComInput:
  ' read input from COM port buffer
  INPUT# 1,ComPortInput(HeadPtr%)
  ' point to next buffer space
  HeadPtr% = HeadPtr% + 1
  RETURN

EndOfInput:    ' end of COM port input
  PRINT "Reached the end of input..."
  END          ' end the program
```

COMMAND$ function

Function COMMAND$ returns the command line used to start the program from DOS.

Syntax `s$ = COMMAND$`

Remarks COMMAND$ returns everything that was typed at the DOS prompt in the process of invoking a program, with the exception of the program name itself (some manuals refer to this text as the "trailer").

Use COMMAND$ to collect run-time arguments such as file names and program options. For example, consider the DOS command:

```
FASTSORT cust.dta cust.new
```

where FASTSORT is a Turbo Basic-produced .EXE program. When FASTSORT gets control, COMMAND$ will hold everything that was typed at the DOS prompt after the program name itself, in this case, the string "cust.dta cust.new." It's up to the definition of FASTSORT to decide what to do with this string (maybe it could break COMMAND$ into *filename1* and *filename2*, and sort the contents of *filename1* into new file *filename2*).

To test a program that uses COMMAND$ from within Turbo Basic, use the **P**arameter line option of the **O**ptions menu to set the string that COMMAND$ returns.

Restrictions The maximum length of the DOS command line is 127 characters.

Example

```
' This program demonstrates the COMMAND$ function.

PRINT "The command line parameters passed to this program are"
PRINT COMMAND$
```

Compile this program in memory and run it twice, changing the parameter entry in the **O**ptions menu each time.

COMMON statement

Function — COMMON declares one or more variables to be passed to a chained program.

Syntax — `COMMON variable [,variable]...`

Remarks — *variable* is an array or scalar variable to be made available to the next CHAINed program. Arrays are specified by including the number of dimensions in parentheses after the variable name.

COMMON statements can appear anywhere in a program, and there can be more than one, but a given variable can appear only once.

A matching COMMON statement(s) must appear in the program that is CHAINed to. The names of the variables used in the COMMON statement don't matter, but the number and type does. If the variables declared as common in the invoking program don't match the type and quantity of variables declared as common in the receiving program, a run-time error is generated.

Differences — Turbo Basic does not support the CHAIN ALL parameter provided by Interpretive BASIC. You must explicitly define each variable to be common across the chained programs.

When specifying an array as a common variable in Turbo Basic, you must specify the number of dimensions of the array.

Interpretive BASIC doesn't require matched COMMONs because only the CHAIN from needs a COMMON; CHAIN to needs none. Turbo Basic, on the other hand, requires that the variables in each common statement be correctly ordered. In other words, the names of the variables in the main and chain programs can be different but the types of the variables must correspond. The following COMMON statement is correct:

```
' Main program
COMMON I%, Array(1), J#

' Chained program
COMMON Int%, RealArray(1), DblPre#
```

Restrictions — Turbo Basic does not support Interpretive BASIC's CHAIN ALL COMMON override.

Example

```
' These programs demonstrate the COMMON statement.
' In order to execute these programs, do the following:
' (1) compile the first program to an .EXE file,
' (2) compile the second program to a .TBC file,
' (3) at the DOS prompt, execute the first program.

' Program MASTER. Compile this program to an .EXE file.
DIM OldArray$(1)   ' declare an array of two strings
OldArray$(0) = "This is the first string in the array"
OldArray$(1) = "This is the second string in the array"

OldInteger% = 12345
OldLongInt& = 123450000
OldSinglePre! = 12345.12345
OldDoublePre# = 1.0E+300

' specify the variables that are common to the master
' and slave programs
COMMON OldArray$(1), OldInteger%, OldLongInt&,_
       OldSinglePre!, OldDoublePre#

CHAIN "SLAVE.TBC"  ' chain to slave program

END   ' end program

' Program SLAVE. Compile this program to a .TBC file.
COMMON NewArray$(1), NewInteger%, NewLongInt&,_
       NewSinglePre!, NewDoublePre#

PRINT  NewArray$(0)
PRINT  NewArray$(1)
PRINT  NewInteger%, NewLongInt&, NewSinglePre!,_
       NewDoublePre#
```

COS function

Function COS returns a trigonometric cosine.

Syntax `y = COS(numeric expression)`

Remarks *numeric expression* is an angle specified in radians. To convert radians to degrees, multiply by 180/π. To convert degrees to radians, multiply by π/180. (See the discussion of radians under the ATN function.)

COS returns a double-precision value.

See Also ATN
SIN
TAN

Example

```
' This program demonstrates the COS function

PI# = ATN(1) * 4

FOR I% = 0 TO 360 STEP 45
  PRINT USING "The Cosine of ### degrees = ##.##";_
              I%,COS(PI#/180 * I%)
NEXT I%

END
```

CSNG function

Function — CSNG converts a numeric expression to its single-precision equivalent.

Syntax — `y = CSNG(numeric expression)`

Remarks — CSNG converts a numeric variable or expression into single-precision, floating-point form. CSNG is usually used to prevent intermediate overflow when processing integer operands.

See Also — CDBL
CINT
CLNG

Example

```
PRINT CSNG(&HFFF), CSNG(13241.1324), CSNG(&HF000)
```

CSRLIN function

Function CSRLIN returns the current vertical cursor position (row number).

Syntax

```
y = CSRLIN
```

Remarks CSRLIN returns an integer from 1 to 25, representing the current vertical position (row number) of the cursor. Use the POS function to read the cursor's horizontal position (column number).

The LOCATE statement moves the cursor to a specific line and column.

See Also LOCATE
POS

Example

```
Col=POS    ' save cursor row
Row=CSRLIN 'save cursor column
CLS
LOCATE Row, Col 'restore cursor position
END
```

CVI, CVL, CVS, CVD functions

Function
CVI, CVL, CVS, and CVD convert string data read from random files to numeric form.

Syntax

```
y% = CVI(2-byte string)
y@ = CVL(4-byte string)
y! = CVS(4-byte string)
y# = CVD(8-byte string)
```

Remarks
CVI converts a 2-byte string to an integer. CVL converts a 4-byte string to a long integer. CVS converts a 4-byte string to a single-precision value. CVD converts an 8-byte string to a double-precision value.

Because of the way Turbo Basic handles random files, numeric values must be translated into strings before they can be written to disk, and translated back into numbers when the file is read.

Don't confuse these functions (which are strictly for random file processing) with the VAL function, which takes a string like "3.7" and turns it into a number.

See Also
MKD$
MKI$
MKL$
MKS$

Example

```
' This program creates a random access data
' file and writes some data to it. It then
' reads this data back, converting it to usable
' form using the preceding functions.

' open a random access file
OPEN "R", #1, "CVISLD.DTA" ,18

FIELD #1, 2 AS Integer$, 4 AS LongInt$,_
          4 AS SinglePre$, 8 AS DoublePre$

MaxInt% = 32767

' write data to file, convert it, and assign it
' to the buffer before writing it to the data
' file
FOR I% = 1 TO 5
  LSET Integer$    = MKI$(I%)
  LSET LongInt$ = MKL$(I% + CLNG(MaxInt%))
  LSET SinglePre$ = MKS$(CSNG(I% * CSNG(MaxInt%)))
  LSET DoublePre$ = MKD$(MaxInt%^I%)
  PUT #1,I%
NEXT I%
```

```
FOR I% = 1 TO 5   ' read data from file
  GET #1, I%      ' display it on screen
  PRINT CVI(Integer$), CVL(LongInt$),_
        CVS(SinglePre$), CVD(DoublePre$)
NEXT I%

CLOSE #1     ' close the file

END
```

CVMD, CVMS functions

Function CVMD and CVMS convert string variables read from Microsoft-format random files to numeric form.

Syntax

```
y! = CVMS(4-byte string)
y# = CVMD(8-byte string)
```

Remarks CVMS (**C**on**V**ert **M**icrosoft **S**ingle-precision string) converts a 4-byte string representing a single-precision value in Microsoft format to a single-precision value in Turbo Basic IEEE format.

CVMD (**C**on**V**ert **M**icrosoft **D**ouble-precision string) converts an 8-byte string representing a double-precision value in Microsoft format to a double-precision value in Turbo Basic IEEE format.

These functions are provided solely for compatibility with existing Interpretive BASIC random files.

Example

```
' open a random access file
OPEN "CVMD.DTA" AS #1 LEN = 12

FIELD #1, 4 AS Single$, 8 AS Double$

FOR I = 1 TO 5       ' write some data to the file
  ' convert the data and assign data file
  LSET Single$ = MKMS$(I)
  LSET Double$ = MKMD$(I^I)
  PUT #1,I
NEXT I

FOR I = 1 TO 5       ' read the data from the file
  GET #1, I          ' display data on screen
  PRINT CVMS(Single$), CVMD(Double$)
NEXT I%

PRINT CVS(x$), CVMS(x$)
CLOSE #1              ' close the file

END
```

DATA statement

Function DATA declares constants for READ statements.

Syntax `DATA constant [,constant]...`

Remarks *constant* is a numeric or string constant. Numeric constants can be floating point or integer and can optionally be expressed in hexadecimal or octal. String constants don't have to be enclosed in quotes unless they contain delimiters (commas or colons) or significant leading or trailing blanks, and can be freely mixed with numeric constants. For example:

```
DATA Taco,.79,Chicken Supreme,2.29,"Dr. Pepper, large",.89
```

A program can contain many DATA statements and they need not be on sequential lines. Each can contain as many constants as you can fit on a line.

At runtime, READ statements access the DATA constants from left to right and top to bottom in the order in which they appear in the source program. The most common error associated with DATA statements and READing is getting out of sync and trying to load string data into a numeric variable; this generates a syntax error (run-time error 2). Unfortunately, you won't get an error loading numeric constants into string variables, even though that is probably not what you intended.

The RESTORE command lets you reread constants from the first statement or any specified DATA statement.

If you try to READ more times than your program has constants, run-time error 4 results, Out of Data.

Restrictions You cannot use underscore continuation characters in DATA statements.

Don't use the single quote (') to comment a DATA statement because Turbo Basic will think that the last entry and your comment are part of a single, long string constant. For example:

```
DATA cats,dogs,pigs ' list the animals
```

is interpreted as containing three string constants:

```
"cats," "dogs," and "pigs ' list the animals.";
```

You can, however, safely use :REM for this purpose:

```
DATA cats,dogs,pigs : REM list the animals
```

See Also READ
RESTORE

Example

```
' This  program demonstrates use of
' the DATA statement

SUB ProcessResults(StudentName$, StudentAverage%)
LOCAL Total%, Value%, I%
  Total% = 0
  READ StudentName$
  FOR I% = 1 TO 10
    READ Value%
    Total% = Total% + Value%
  NEXT I%
  StudentAverage% = Total%\10
END SUB


FOR Student% = 1 TO 3
  CALL ProcessResults(SName$, Average%)
  PRINT USING "&'s average is ###";SName$, Average%
NEXT Student%

END  ' end program

DATA W. Perry,  78, 65, 35, 79, 86, 93, 79, 85, 99, 96
DATA P. Watson, 98, 94, 70, 88, 99, 100, 75, 96, 100, 95
DATA M. Ciccone, 65, 59, 75, 82, 56, 79, 82, 76, 69, 89
```

DATE$ system variable

Function DATE$ sets and retrieves the system date.

Syntax

```
DATE$ = s$ (set date according to information in s$)
s$ = DATE$   (s$ now contains date information)
```

Remarks Assigning a properly formatted string value to DATE$ sets the system date.

Assigning DATE$ to a string variable makes the system date available for processing. DATE$ returns a 10-character string in the form *mm-dd-yyyy*, where *mm* represents the month, *dd* the day, and *yyyy* the year.

To change the date, your string must format the date in one of the following ways:

```
mm-dd-yy
mm/dd/yy
mm-dd-yyyy
mm/dd/yyyy
```

For example:

```
DATE$ = "10-25-86"
```

sets the system date to October 25, 1986.

Restrictions The year assigned to the DATE$ system variable must be within the range 1980 to 2099.

See Also TIME$

Example

```
' display the current system date
PRINT "The current system date is " DATE$
INPUT "Please enter the new date in the form MM-DD-YY"; NewDate$
DATE$ = NewDate$
  PRINT "The system date is now set to " DATE$

END  ' end the program
```

DECR statement

Function — DECR decrements a variable.

Syntax — `DECR` *`variable`* `[`*`,size`*`]`

Remarks — *variable* is a numeric variable, and *size* is an optional numeric expression that indicates the value to be subtracted from *variable*. If *size* is omitted, 1 is used.

DECR is a handy way to decrement a variable. Use the INCR statement to increment a variable.

See Also — INCR

Example

```
I% = 15          ' initialize counter variables
J% = 500

WHILE I% > 0
  PRINT I%, J%   ' display the value
  DECR I%        ' decrement the value by 1
  DECR J%, 5     ' decrement the value by 5
WEND

END              ' end the program
```

DEF FN/END DEF statement

Function DEF FN/END DEF define a function.

Syntax Single line:

```
DEF FNidentifier [(argument list)] = expression
```

Multiline:

```
DEF FNidentifier [(argument list)]
  [LOCAL variable list]
  [STATIC variable list]
  [SHARED variable list]
    .
    . statements
    .
    [EXIT DEF]
    [FNidentifier = expression]
  END DEF
```

Remarks *identifier* is the unique name to be associated with the function, and must follow the naming conventions for labels and variables (that is, a letter followed by any number of letters and/or digits). *argument list* is an optional, comma-delimited sequence of formal parameters. The parameters used in the argument list serve only to define the function: They have no relationship to other variables in the program with the same name.

DEF FN and END DEF bracket and name a subroutine-like group of statements called a *function*. A function may be optionally passed one or more arguments by value. Functions return a value (the type of which is controlled by the function's name, as though it were a variable) and may therefore be called from any statement that can accept a value of the appropriate type.

Function Definitions and Program Flow

The position of function definitions is immaterial. A function can be defined in line 1 or line 1,000 of a program without regard for where it is used; and you need not direct program flow through a function as an initialization step (as you must do with single-line functions in Interpretive BASIC). The compiler sees your definitions wherever they might be.

Also, unlike subroutines, execution can't accidentally "fall into" a function. As far as the execution path of a program is concerned, function and procedure definitions are invisible.

For example:

```
t = FNPrintStuff
DEF FNPrintStuff
  PRINT "Printed from within FNPrintStuff"
END DEF
```

When this four-line program is executed, the message appears only once, since *PrintStuff* is called in the first line.

Function definitions should be treated as isolated islands of code; don't jump into or out of them with GOTO, GOSUB, or RETURN statements. Within definitions, however, such statements are legal.

Note that function and procedure definitions may not be nested; that is, it is illegal to define a procedure or function within a procedure or function (although a procedure or function definition can contain calls to other procedures and functions).

Declaring Local Variables (Multiline Functions Only)

To declare local variables within a function, use the LOCAL statement before any executable statements in the definition. For example:

```
LOCAL a%, b#, bigArray%()
```

creates three local variables: *a%* and *b#* (integer and double precision, respectively), and integer array *bigArray*. The array must then be dimensioned appropriately:

```
DIM DYNAMIC bigArray%(1000)
```

Static and Shared Variables

By default, variables that appear within function definitions have the SHARED attribute; that is, they are global to the rest of the program. Since this default is subject to change, you should make an effort to declare every variable used in a function.

Declare variables with the STATIC attribute if it is important that a variable not lose its value with every invocation, and yet it may only be altered within the function.

A multiline function definition usually includes an assignment to the function identifier and must be terminated with END DEF. If you choose not to include an assignment to the function identifier, then the value returned by the function is undefined.

Use the EXIT DEF statement to return from a function that is someplace other than at the end.

See Also LOCAL
SHARED
STATIC

Example

```
$STACK &H7FFF
Total = 1

DEF FNFactorial%(I%)
' This function calculates the factorial of the
' parameter I%

  Total = Total * I%

  IF I% > 1 THEN
    Subb% = FNFactorial%(I% - 1)
  END IF

  FNFactorial% = Total

END DEF       ' end function FNFactorial

PRINT "Input the number you wish to calculate the ";
INPUT "factorial of: ",J%

PRINT FNFactorial%(J%)

END           ' end the program
```

DEFINT, DEFLNG, DEFSNG, DEFDBL, DEFSTR statements

Function — DEFINT, DEFLNG, DEFSNG, DEFDBL, and DEFSTR declare the default type of variable identifiers.

Syntax — `DEFtype letter range [,letter range]...`

Remarks — *type* represents one of the five Turbo Basic variable types: INT, LNG, SNG, DBL, and STR. *letter range* is either a single alphabetic character (*A* through *Z*, case insignificant), or a range of letters (two letters separated by a dash; for example, *A-M*).

The DEF*type* statement tells the compiler that variables and user-defined functions beginning with the specified letter or range of letters will be a certain type. This allows you to use variables other than single precision floating point in your program without including type identifiers (for example, %, #).

By default, when the compiler finds a variable name without a type identifier, it assumes the variable to be single precision floating point. For example, in this statement, both *n* and *m* are assumed to be single precision:

```
n = m + 16
```

If, however, this statement were preceded by

```
DEFINT n, m
```

then *n* and *m* would both be integer variables, as would any other variable whose name started with *n* or *m* in uppercase or lowercase.

Turbo Basic's execution of DEF*type* is subtly different from Interpretive BASIC's. The interpreter makes typing judgments according to where the DEF*type* statement occurs in program execution order. Turbo Basic, as a compiler, considers DEF*type*'s position in the source file. For example, in executing this program

```
10 GOTO 30
20 DEFINT A-M
30 j = 45.3 : PRINT j
```

Interpretive BASIC never sees the typing statement in line 20. When it encounters *j* in line 30, *j* becomes a single-precision variable and is printed as 45.3. Turbo Basic, by contrast, makes decisions about variable typing at compile time, without regard for the execution path (which, at compile time, it knows nothing about). It only cares that a DEFINT statement appeared physically before variable *j*'s first appearance, so it makes *j* an integer variable and prints out 45.

Restrictions A DEF*type* statement will redefine the type of any corresponding variables that are already being used in the program. The example program demonstrates this rather subtle point.

Example

```
' assign a value to a single-precision number
I = 35567.999
PRINT "Single Precision number",I
' display the value

' explicitly declare a variable of the
' same name and type
DEFSNG I

PRINT "Single Precision number",I

' explicitly declare a variable of the same name,
' but different type
DEFINT I

' print the value of the new variable
PRINT "Integer number:",I

' All identifiers starting with the letters
' A to C are double-precision type until
' another DEF statement
DEFDBL A-C

' all identifiers starting with the letters
' J to Z are Long Integer type until another
' DEF statement
DEFLNG J-Z

' assign a value to a double-precision variable
A = 32767.1
' assign a value to a Long Integer
Z = -1
' assign a value to the previously defined
' integer variable
I = &H8FFF

PRINT "Three different types: ",A,Z,I

END                ' end the program
```

DEF SEG statement

Function — DEF SEG defines the data segment to be used by BLOAD, BSAVE, CALL ABSOLUTE, PEEK, and POKE statements.

Syntax — `DEF SEG [=`*`numeric expression`*`]`

Remarks — *numeric expression* can range from 0 to 65,535.

DEF SEG defines the memory segment into which subsequent BLOAD, BSAVE, CALL ABSOLUTE, PEEK, and POKE statements will specify offsets. A segment is an addressing construct used by Intel 86 family processors. Addresses must be specified with two integers: a segment and an offset into the segment.

DEF SEG with no argument returns the segment value to its start-up default value. The first 256 bytes of the default segment contains information used by your program's run-time support system. One interesting address is at offset &HF4E in this segment. POKEing values into this address changes the color of text written to the screen in any graphics mode. The color depends on what mode you're in. Another useful address in the default data segment is at location 0 and 1. This word contains the segment of Turbo Basic's strings.

See Also — COLOR

Example

```
'This program fills the screen with A's,
' poking directly into video ram.

'Define a function that determines the
' address of video memory

' get the type of video board from user
DEF FN VideoScreen%
' LOCAL ScreenType%    ' declare a local variable
  PRINT "Please enter the type of screen you are using "
  INPUT "[1 for Mono, 2 for Color] : ";ScreenType%
  SELECT CASE ScreenType%    ' assign function's result
    CASE 1            ' based on user's input
      ' monochrome video ram location
      FN VideoScreen% = &HB000
    CASE 2
      ' color video ram location
      FN VideoScreen% = &HB800
  END SELECT
END DEF            ' end the function
```

```
' define segment for POKE and BSAVE
DEF SEG = FN VideoScreen%

FOR I% = 0 to 4000 STEP 2
  POKE I%,ASC("A")  ' fill screen with A's
NEXT I%

END
```

DELAY statement

Function DELAY inserts a pause.

Syntax `DELAY` *seconds*

Remarks *seconds* is a numeric expression indicating the number of seconds Turbo Basic should pause before executing the next statement. **Note:** DELAY accepts floating-point arguments, and fractional delays with a resolution of approximately 0.054 seconds may be specified.

Using DELAY rather than software do-nothing loops results in programs that run appropriately on machines of differing processing speeds (that is, 8088-based versus 80286-based, or 6 MHz versus 8 MHz).

Example

```
PRINT "Press any key to terminate the program..."

WHILE NOT INSTAT  ' while a key has not been pressed
  LOCATE 10,30
  PRINT TIME$      ' display the time
  DELAY 5  ' delay for 5 seconds
WEND

END   ' end the program
```

DIM statement

Function DIM declares arrays.

Syntax

```
DIM {STATIC|DYNAMIC} var (subscripts) [,var(subscripts)]...
DIM {STATIC|DYNAMIC} var (min:max [,min:max]...)[,var [,min:max]]...
```

Remarks *var* is an identifier used for the array.

subscripts is a comma-delimited list of one or more integer expressions defining the dimensions of the array.

DIM declares array variables and defines their size and number of dimensions.

In an enhancement to Interpretive BASIC syntax, Turbo Basic allows you to define a *range* of subscript values (*min:max*) rather than just an upper limit. For example:

```
DIM b(50:60)
```

creates an array of 11 single-precision elements, numbered 50 through 60. The statement

```
DIM c(50:60, 25:45)
```

creates a two-dimensional array of 11 × 21 total elements.

The range syntax can be extended for multidimensional arrays:

```
DIM births(1800:1899,1:12)
```

The related OPTION BASE statement can also be used to determine the lowest element in an array, although the range mechanism is more powerful and is preferred.

Turbo Basic sets each element of a numeric array to 0 when a program is first executed, and sets string arrays to the null string (length = 0). If a program is restarted again with the RUN statement, numeric arrays are reset to 0 and string arrays to the null string.

If an array variable is used without a preceding DIM statement, the maximum value of its subscripts defaults to 10, as though you had included (10) in your DIM statement. It is good practice, however, to explicitly declare every array.

The minimum value that can be used as an array subscript is 0, unless specified otherwise with the OPTION BASE command.

The optional STATIC and DYNAMIC arguments control, respectively, whether space for the array will be pre-allocated by the compiler or allocated dynamically. If omitted, arrays default to static allocation unless the $DYNAMIC metastatement has been given, an expression is used in the DIMension statement, the array name appears in two DIM statements, or the array is declared local to a procedure or a function.

The bounds-checking switch accessed through the **O**ptions menu causes the compiler to create code that checks subscripts for appropriateness whenever an array is referenced.

Differences Turbo Basic allows the programmer to specify both the starting and ending indices of an array. Interpretive BASIC allocates all arrays dynamically, but Turbo Basic will try to allocate arrays statically (at compile time), which makes them faster. You may explicitly override the type of allocation used.

See Also $DYNAMIC
FRE
$STATIC

Example

```
DIM declares an array

' named constant specifying array's upper dimension
%MaxDim = 20
' named constant specifying array's lower dimension
%MinDim = 1

' allocate array of %MaxDim integer elements
DIM Array%(%MinDim:%MaxDim)

' initialize array with random numbers
FOR Count1% = %MinDim to %MaxDim
  Array%(Count1%) = INT(RND * 10)
NEXT Count1%

END
```

DO/LOOP statement

Function DO/LOOP is a loop with a test for TRUE or FALSE at the top and/or bottom of the loop.

Syntax

```
DO [{WHILE|UNTIL} expression]
.
. statements [EXIT LOOP]
.
[LOOP|WEND] [{WHILE|UNTIL} expression]
```

Remarks *expression* is a numeric expression, in which nonzero values represent TRUE, and zero values FALSE.

DO and LOOP are loop builders for all seasons. They allow you to create loops with the test for the terminating condition at the top of the loop, the bottom, both places, or neither. A DO statement must always be paired with a matching LOOP statement at the bottom of the loop. Failure to match DO and LOOP results in compile-time errors.

Use WHILE and UNTIL to add a test to a DO/LOOP. Use the WHILE reserved word if the loop should be repeated if *expression* is TRUE, and terminated if *expression* is FALSE. UNTIL causes the opposite effect; that is, the loop will be terminated if the condition is TRUE, and repeated if FALSE.

For example:

```
DO WHILE a = 13
  .
  . statements
  .
 LOOP
```

executes the statements between DO and LOOP as long as *a* is 13.

```
DO UNTIL a = 13
  .
  . statements
  .
LOOP
```

executes the statements between DO and LOOP as long as *a* is *not* 13.

At any point in a DO/LOOP you may include an EXIT/LOOP statement. This is equivalent to performing a GOTO to the statement after the terminating LOOP. (For more information, see the EXIT statement.)

Note that this DO/LOOP:

```
DO WHILE a < b
  .
  .
  .
LOOP
```

has the same effect as this WHILE/WEND loop:

```
WHILE a < b
  .
  .
  .
WEND
```

Although the compiler doesn't care about such things, indent the statements between DO and LOOP a couple of spaces. This helps to clarify the structure of the loop.

Example

```
' This program waits until a key is pressed.
DO
LOOP UNTIL INSTAT

END
```

DRAW statement

Function DRAW draws shapes onto the graphics screen.

Syntax `DRAW string expression`

Remarks DRAW plots objects onto the graphics screen according to commands embedded in the string argument passed to it. In effect, *string expression* is a program for an interpretive DRAW "language." DRAW executes command strings to produce images on the screen, much as PLAY executes command strings to create music.

Movement	Commands
U*n*	Move up
D*n*	Move down
L*n*	Move left
R*n*	Move right
E*n*	Move up and right
F*n*	Move down and right
G*n*	Move down and left
H*n*	Move up and left

n is the distance to move (see **S*n***, the scaling factor that follows). Movement always begins at the LPR, and adjusts the LPR accordingly. (LPR stands for "last point referenced," and refers to the last point referred to by certain drawing statements. For more information, see the graphics section in Chapter 4.)

For example:

```
DRAW "D10R5"
```

draws an *L* shape (down 10, right 5) starting with the LPR. It leaves the LPR set to the last pixel plotted.

M *x,y* moves to coordinate *x,y*. If *x* has a leading plus or minus sign, the move is relative; otherwise it is absolute. For example:

```
DRAW "D10 R5 M30,50"
```

draws the *L* from before, and then finishes it off with a line to pixel (30,50).

The following prefixes can precede any movement command:

B moves, but doesn't plot.

N moves, but returns to the original position when finished.

For example:

```
DRAW "BM 180,20 NU10 ND10 NL10 NR10"
```

moves without drawing to pixel (180,20), and then draws a plus sign.

Other Commands

An sets angle *n*. The value of *n* can range from 0 to 3, where 0 equals 0 degrees, 1 equals 90 degrees, 2 equals 180 degrees, and 3 equals 270 degrees.

TA*n* turns angle *n*. The value of *n* can range from −360 to +360 degrees. If *n* is positive, the angle turns counterclockwise. If it is negative, then the angle turns clockwise. Values outside the valid range cause run-time error 5, Illegal Function Call. Note that **TA*n*** is *not* cumulative.

C*n* draws in color *n*. Check the PALETTE statement for the range of *n* in each display mode. The default color is the highest legal attribute.

S*n* sets scale factor to *n*/4, where *n* can range from 1 to 255. For example, if *n* = 8, the scale factor is 2. DRAW multiplies the scale factor by arguments to the *U*, *D*, *L*, *R*, *E*, *F*, *G*, *H*, and relative *M* commands to determine the ultimate size of objects. The default for *n* is 4, which results in a unity scaling factor (that is, no scaling).

The aspect ratio of the display you are using determines the relationship between *X* and *Y*. On an ideal (nonexistent) display with an aspect ratio of 1/1, a dot in the *X* is the same length as a dot in the *Y* direction. However, the displays for IBM computers have the following aspect ratios:

Monitor/Adapter	Screen 1	Screen 2	Screen 7/8/9	Screen 10
Color	5/6	5/12	N/A	N/A
Enhanced	5/6	5/12	8.76/12	N/A
Enhanced Mono	N/A	N/A	N/A	9.52/12

X VARPTR$(*variable*); executes substring; that is, it executes a second command string from within a primary DRAW string. The X command is something like a GOSUB; for example:

```
DRAW "X" + VARPTR$(X$)
```

P *color,boundary* starts at the current (*x*,*y*) coordinate and fills with color *color*, stopping at areas of color *boundary*.

In each instance, the *n*, *x*, or *y* argument can be either a constant (as has been shown thus far in examples) or a variable in the form

=VARPTR$(*variable*);

For example:

```
DRAW "e15"
```

is the same as

```
a = 15
DRAW "e=" + VARPTR$(a)
```

DRAW ignores spaces in its command string—you may want to use them to make your DRAW programs more readable.

Restrictions

Turbo Basic does not recognize variable names in DRAW strings. Thus, you must use VARPTR$(*n*) to access the contents of variables at runtime within the DRAW string. Instead of

```
DRAW "U = I%;"
```

use

```
DRAW "U =" +VARPTR$(I%)
```

Example

```
' switch into medium resolution graphics mode
SCREEN 1

House$ = "U20 G5 E20 F20 H5 D20 L30"
DRAW House$

DRAW "BE3"
DRAW "P1,3"
FOR I% = 1 TO 280 STEP 40
  DRAW "BM= " +VARPTR$(I%) + ",40"
  DRAW House$
NEXT I%

END   ' end the program
```

END statement

Function
: END terminates execution of a program or defines the end of a structured block.

Syntax
: `END [{DEF|IF|SELECT|SUB}]`

Remarks
: END without arguments terminates program execution. END statements can be placed anywhere in a program, and there can be more than one. Encountering an END causes a program to close all open files and return to DOS (or to Turbo Basic, depending on where the program was launched).

An END isn't strictly required by the compiler, although using it is good practice. If a program simply runs out of statements to execute, the same effect is generated.

END followed by the DEF, IF, SUB, or SELECT reserved words defines the end of a structured block.

See Also
: DEF
IF
SELECT
STOP
SUB

Example

```
SUB DummyProc
  PRINT "Hello"
END SUB         ' end definition of procedure

DEF FN DummyFunc$
  FN DummyFunc$ =  "Hello again"
END DEF         ' end function definition

INPUT "Execute the procedure or the function [1 or 2]";Which%
IF Which% > 0 THEN
  SELECT CASE Which%
    CASE 1
      CALL DummyProc
      END       ' end the program
    CASE 2
      PRINT FN DummyFunc$
      END       ' end the program
    CASE ELSE
      PRINT "An illegal choice was made..."
  END SELECT    ' end case statement
END IF          ' end if then block

END             ' end the program
```

ENDMEM function

Function ENDMEM returns the address of the end of physical memory.

Syntax

```
y = ENDMEM
```

Remarks ENDMEM returns a long integer representing the address of the last byte of physical memory. ENDMEM, in conjunction with the MEMSET statement, can be used to allocate space in high memory for assembly language subroutines.

While executing a program in memory, ENDMEM actually returns the end of physical memory minus the size of the symbol table. When Turbo Basic is compiling in memory, it stores the symbol table at the highest address in memory.

See Also MEMSET

Example

```
'display the result
PRINT "The end of addressable memory is: ",ENDMEM

END          ' end the program
```

ENVIRON statement

Function — ENVIRON modifies information in the environment table.

Syntax

```
ENVIRON string expression
```

Remarks — *string expression* defines both the name of parameter to be changed, added, or deleted, and the new parameter information itself. The two must be separated by an equal sign (=).

ENVIRON and the related function ENVIRON$ are used to configure the environment to be passed to programs executed via the SHELL statement. (For more information, see the SHELL statement in this manual and the SET command in the DOS reference manual.)

For example:

```
ENVIRON "PATH=\TURBOBAS"
```

sets DOS's PATH parameter to "\TURBOBAS." A subsequently SHELLed copy of COMMAND.COM will automatically search directory \TURBOBAS to find files that aren't in the current directory.

To delete a parameter from the environment table, include only a semicolon (;) after the equal sign:

```
ENVIRON "PATH=;"
```

deletes the path parameter from the environment table.

Restrictions — You may not expand the environment space. To add new entries, you must free up space by deleting existing entries.

See Also — ENVIRON$
SHELL

Example

```
' Display and change the PATH
' environment variable
PRINT ENVIRON$("PATH")
ENVIRON "PATH=\"
```

ENVIRON$ function

Function ENVIRON$ retrieves environment table parameters.

Syntax

```
s$ = ENVIRON$(parameter string)
s$ = ENVIRON$(n)
```

Remarks *parameter string* is a string expression containing the parameter to be retrieved. *n* is an integer expression in the range 1 to 255.

ENVIRON$ and the related statement ENVIRON are used to configure the environment to be passed to programs executed via the SHELL statement. (For more information, see the SHELL statement in this manual and the SET command in the DOS reference manual.)

If a string argument is used, ENVIRON$ returns the text that follows *parameter string* in the environment table. Note that ENVIRON$ distinguishes between uppercase and lowercase letters. If *parameter string* is not found or no text follows the equal sign, the null string is returned.

If the numeric form is used, ENVIRON$ returns a string containing the *n*th parameter from the start of the table. If there is no *n*th parameter, a null string is returned.

Example See the example in the ENVIRON entry.

EOF function

Function
EOF returns end-of-file status.

Syntax
`y = EOF(filenum)`

Remarks
filenum is the value specified when the file was OPENed.

EOF returns TRUE (−1) if end-of-file has been reached on the specified file; otherwise, FALSE (0) is returned.

EOF is only valid for disk files opened for sequential input and for communications files. An EOF return of −1 for a communications file means the buffer is empty.

Example
The following example reads information from sequential file TEXT.DTA until the end of the file is reached:

```
OPEN "TEXT.DTA" FOR INPUT AS #1
top:
  IF EOF(1) THEN
    PRINT c "records (lines) in file TEXT.DTA"
  END IF
  INPUT #1, dummy$
  c = c + 1
GOTO top
```

or, stated more elegantly:

```
OPEN "TEXT.DTA" FOR INPUT AS #1
WHILE NOT EOF(1)
  INPUT #1, dummy$
  INCR c

WEND
PRINT c "records (lines) in file TEXT.DTA" : END
```

ERADR function

Function ERADR returns the address of the most recent error.

Syntax

```
y = ERADR
```

Remarks ERADR returns a long integer value representing the position of the most recent error. ERADR is the same program counter value that would have been printed had error trapping not been turned on (that is, it can be used by the **R**un-time error selection of the **O**ptions menu to find the position in the source program of the statement generating the error).

ERADR is intended as a last resort in error-handling routines. If an error routine has no plan for handling a particular error, the least you can do is print the error code (ERR) and ERADR to the screen and tell your users to report the occurrence.

See Also ERL
ERR
ERROR
ON ERROR

Example

```
ON ERROR GOTO Trap ' set up run-time error handling

DIM X%(10)
FOR I% = 1 TO 10
  READ X%(I%)     ' Read X ten times
  PRINT X%(I%);   ' with only seven data items
NEXT I%           ' returns out-of-data error

' an insufficient number of data
' elements are available
DATA 1,2,3,4,5, 6, 7

END               ' end the program

' The following error handler prints
' the ERRor number and ADRess.
Trap:
  LOCATE 10,15
  ' Print message in middle of screen
  PRINT "An error of type " ERR " has occurred at address" ERADR
  LOCATE 11,15
  PRINT "Please note these values and check your manual"
  END             ' end the program
```

ERASE statement

Function ERASE deletes dynamic arrays and resets static arrays.

Syntax `ERASE array name [,array name] ...`

Remarks *array name* is the name of an array(s) you want to reset or deallocate. Note that empty parentheses should not be included with *array name*.

If *array name* is dynamic, its space in memory is released and *array name* can later be redimensioned with another DIM statement.

If *array name* is static, ERASEing it simply clears its elements to 0 (or the null string for string arrays).

Restrictions You cannot ERASE an array that never existed or, in the case of dynamic arrays, has already been erased.

Differences Turbo Basic allows static arrays that are faster than dynamic arrays. Interpretive BASIC only allows dynamic arrays.

See Also CLEAR
DIM
$DYNAMIC
FRE
$STATIC

Example

```
ON ERROR GOTO ErrorHandler  ' set up error handler
PRINT FRE(-1)    ' display array space available

' declare dynamic array, assign data to it,
' and display array space available
DIM DYNAMIC BigArray(10000)
BigArray(6666) = 66
PRINT FRE(-1)

ERASE BigArray   ' deallocate dynamic array
PRINT FRE(-1)    ' display array space available

' This statement will return a run-time error
' if the program is run with bounds checking on
PRINT BigArray(6666)
END              ' end the program

ErrorHandler:
PRINT "An error of type " ERR;
PRINT " has occurred at address" ERADR
END
```

ERDEV, ERDEV$ functions

Function ERDEV and ERDEV$ return device driver information.

Syntax

```
y = ERDEV
y$ = ERDEV$
```

Remarks When a device error occurs, integer function ERDEV returns error information in its least-significant byte. This byte represents the INT 24 error code. The most-significant byte contains bits 15, 14, 13, 3, 2, 1, and 0 of the device attribute word.

ERDEV$ contains the name of the device: 8 bytes for character devices and 2 for block devices. (See the *IBM DOS Technical Reference Manual* for more information.)

Example

```
' set up an error handler
ON ERROR GOTO ErrorHandler

PRINT "Open the door to drive A and press any key..."
WHILE NOT INSTAT : WEND  ' wait for a key

' try to get a directory
FILES "A:\*.*"

END                         ' end the program

ErrorHandler:               ' critical error handler

' display an error message indicating
' problem and source
PRINT USING "Critical error ## occurred with &";
             ERDEV,ERDEV$
RESUME NEXT
```

ERL, ERR functions

Function ERL and ERR return the line and error code of the most recent error.

Syntax

```
y = ERL
y = ERR
```

Remarks ERL returns the line number of the most recent error. If the error occurs in a statement without a line number, ERL returns the number of the nearest numbered line, working backward toward the beginning of the program. If there are no numbered lines between the point of the error and the start of the program, ERL returns 0.

ERR returns the number of the most recent run-time error. Test it in error-trapping subroutines to execute code appropriate to the type of error that occurred.

Note: The ERL, RESUME, and RESUME NEXT statements cause the compiler to generate a 4-byte pointer for each statement in a program. Therefore, programmers concerned with the size of their generated code should take note. Using RESUME [*Line #*] generates a single jump instruction. ERL is normally used for debugging purposes so it is probably of little concern.

Differences The rules concerning which side of a relational operator a line number compared to ERL should be on are not applicable to Turbo Basic. This is because Turbo Basic does not have a RENUM instruction. Also, the result of Interpretive BASIC's ERL when an error occurs during the execution of a DIRECT MODE statement is not applicable in Turbo Basic.

See Also ERADR
ERROR
ON ERROR

Example

```
' set up a run-time error handling
ON ERROR GOTO Trap

DIM X%(10)

FOR I% = 1 TO 10
40 READ X%(I%)      ' Read X ten times
  PRINT X%(I%);   ' with only 7 data items,
NEXT I%           ' returns out-of-data error
```

```
' an insufficient number of data
' elements are available
 70 DATA 1,2,3,4,5, 6, 7

 80 END                ' end the program

 90 Trap:
IF ERL=40 THEN
  RESTORE
  RESUME
ELSE
  PRINT "Unknown Error" : END
END IF
```

ERROR statement

Function ERROR forces a run-time error.

Syntax `ERROR` *`errcode`*

Remarks *errcode* is an integer expression from 0 to 255.

If *errcode* is a predefined run-time error code (see Appendix E), then ERROR causes your program to behave as though that error had occurred. This is intended as an aid in debugging error-trapping routines.

To define your own error codes, use values for *errcode* that aren't used by Turbo Basic. If you don't define an error-handling procedure for these new custom error codes, then Turbo Basic displays the message:

```
Error n at pgm-ctr: address,
```

where *n* is the error code and *address* is the value in the processor's program counter at the time the error was encountered.

Example

```
' Force illegal function call error for bad input

DEF FN func%=(X%)
  IF X% > 65 THEN
    ERROR 5 ' Raise illegal function call error
  ELSE
    FNfunc%= X%*1000
  END IF
END DEF

PRINT FN func(66) ' cause illegal function call error
```

EXIT statement

Function EXIT leaves a structure prematurely.

Syntax `EXIT {SELECT|DEF|FOR|IF|LOOP|SUB}`

Remarks The EXIT statement lets you leave a structured statement or procedure or function definition someplace other than at its end. The type of structure being EXITed must be included as part of the EXIT statement, according to the following:

EXIT Option	**Structure Exited**
SELECT	SELECT statement
DEF	Function definition
FOR	FOR/NEXT loop
IF	IF Block
LOOP	DO/LOOP or WHILE/WEND loop
SUB	Procedure definition

Using EXIT can save messy GOTOs.

Restrictions When using EXIT to exit from a function, you must assign the function a result before the EXIT is executed.

Example

```
' This program demonstrates all the EXIT
' statements. Both a procedure and function
' are used to terminate execution.
' Subroutines also demonstrate different
' available EXIT statements by implementing
' LOOP constructs along with SELECT CASE
' and IF THEN ELSE.

SUB Controls(Sel%, Dummy%)

' EXIT statements can be used to terminate
' SELECT CASE and IF THEN ELSE constructs.
' EXIT also terminates the procedure's
' execution.

  SELECT CASE Sel%
    CASE 1
      ' use case statement to tell the user
      ' something about the number entered
      SELECT CASE Dummy%
        CASE < 0
          PRINT "Number is less than zero"
          ' exit select case statement
          EXIT SELECT
        CASE > 0
          PRINT "Number is greater than zero"
        ' exit select case statement
```

```
          EXIT SELECT
        CASE ELSE
          PRINT "Number is 0"
      END SELECT
      EXIT SUB                    ' exit the procedure
    CASE 2
      ' use IF THEN ELSE to do what SELECT
      ' CASE does
      IF Dummy% < 0 THEN
        PRINT "Number is less than zero"
        EXIT IF
      ELSEIF Dummy% > 0 THEN
        PRINT "Number is greater than zero"
        EXIT IF    ' exit if then
      ELSE
        PRINT "Number is 0"
      END IF
  END SELECT
  PRINT "You selected number 2"
END SUB

DEF FN Loops(Sel%)

' A parameter passed to the function indicates
' which EXIT will be executed. Each loop
' structure does the same thing to demonstrate
' how EXIT can be used to terminate the
' execution of the loop.

' We are also demonstrating how EXIT
' can be used to exit out of a function.
' EXIT DEF is used to EXIT from the first
' two selections.  This prevents the
' print statement from being executed.

  ' assign a value to the function result
  FN Loops = -1
  SELECT CASE Sel%
    CASE 1
      ' use EXIT to leave this loop instead
      ' of letting it terminate normally
      FOR I% = 1 TO 32767
        PRINT RND(Dummy%)
        EXIT FOR                  ' exit the for loop
      NEXT I%
      EXIT DEF                    ' exit entire function
    CASE 2
      ' use EXIT to leave this infinite loop
      ' instead of letting it terminate normally
      DO
        PRINT RND(Dummy%)
        EXIT LOOP                 ' exit the loop
      LOOP
      EXIT DEF                    ' exit entire function
    CASE 3
      ' use EXIT to leave this infinite loop
      ' instead of letting it terminate normally
      WHILE 1
```

```
        PRINT RND(Dummy%)
        ' this is the same as exiting
        EXIT LOOP
      WEND                          ' a DO loop
  END SELECT
  PRINT "You executed selection 3"
END DEF                             ' end function definition

' start Main program

' make three calls to Loops selecting each
' of the different loops available
PRINT FN Loops(1)
PRINT FN Loops(2)
PRINT FN Loops(3)

INPUT "Enter a number: ";Dummy%  ' get user's input
' execute Controls selecting each
' control structure
FOR Count% = 1 TO 2
  CALL Controls(Count%, Dummy%)
  CALL Controls(Count%, Dummy%)
NEXT Count%

END                                 ' end the program
```

EXP, EXP2, EXP10 functions

Function EXP returns e^x; EXP10 returns 10^x; EXP2 returns 2^x.

Syntax EXP:

```
y = EXP(x)
```

EXP2:

```
y = EXP2(x)
```

EXP10:

```
y = EXP10(x)
```

Remarks EXP returns *e* to the *x*th power, where *x* is a numeric expression and *e* is the base for natural logarithms, approximately 2.718282. You'd get the same result with the statement *e^x*. One thing you can do with EXP is calculate *e* itself:

```
e = EXP(1)
```

EXP2(*x*) returns 2 to the *x*th power, where *x* is a numeric variable or expression. You'd get the same result with the expression *2^x*.

EXP10(*x*) returns 10 to the *x*th power, where *x* is a numeric variable or expression. You'd get the same result with the expression: *10^x*.

EXP, EXP2, and EXP10 return double-precision results.

Example

```
FOR I = 1 TO 10
  PRINT USING "EXP of ## = ####^^^^";I,EXP(I)
NEXT I
END
```

FIELD statement

Function FIELD defines field variables of a random file buffer.

Syntax
```
FIELD [#]filenum, width AS string-var
      [,width AS string-var]...
```

Remarks *filenum* is the number used when the file was opened, *width* is the number of bytes allocated to the field variable, and *string-var* is the field variable itself.

FIELD defines a mapping between string variables and the I/O buffer of a random access file. Once used in a FIELD statement, these string variables gain a special status as "field variables." They should only be assigned using RSET and LSET in preparation for writing to the indicated random access file.

Restrictions An identifier used in a FIELD statement must never be used on the left side of an assignment statement. Doing this causes the identifier to no longer be identified with the random access file's field definitions.

See Also LSET
RSET

Example
```
' open a random access file
OPEN "R", #1, "CVISLD.DTA" ,18
' OPEN "FIELD.DTA" FOR OUTPUT AS #1 LEN = 18

' make two field definitions for each field
FIELD #1, 2 AS Integer$, 4 AS LongInt$,_
          4 AS SinglePre$, 8 AS DoublePre$
FIELD #1, 2 AS A$, 4 AS B$, 4 AS C$, 8 AS D$

MaxInt% = 32767

' write some data to the file
FOR I% = 1 TO 5
  ' convert the data and assign it to the
  ' buffer before writing it to the data file
  LSET Integer$   = MKI$(I%)
  LSET LongInt$ = MKL$(I% + CLNG(MaxInt%))
  LSET SinglePre$ = MKS$(CSNG(I% * CSNG(MaxInt%)))
  LSET DoublePre$ = MKD$(MaxInt%^I%)
  PUT #1,I%
NEXT I%

' read the data from the file
FOR I% = 1 TO 5
  ' and display it on screen
  GET #1, I%
  PRINT CVI(A$), CVL(B$), CVS(C$), CVD(D$)
NEXT I%

CLOSE #1' close the file

END     ' end the program
```

FILES statement

Function FILES displays the directory contents (like DOS's DIR command).

Syntax `FILES [filespec]`

Remarks *filespec* is a string expression following DOS naming conventions, and may optionally include a drive specifier and path information. If *filespec* is omitted, all the files in the current directory are displayed.

filespec can contain wildcard characters; for example, ? and *, à la DOS's DIR command:

```
FILES "*.*"
```

lists all the files in the current directory.

```
FILES "*.BAS"
```

lists only Turbo Basic source files.

At the end of the FILES listing, Turbo Basic displays the number of free bytes on the device containing the current directory. Subdirectory files are indicated by the DIR suffix.

Restrictions Specifying a nonexistent drive or directory in the FILES statement will cause a run-time error.

Example

```
INPUT "Enter the drive and directory you would like to list ";_Dir$

' display the directory specified
FILES Dir$

END ' end the program
```

FIX function

Function FIX truncates to integer.

Syntax `y = FIX(numeric expression)`

Remarks FIX strips off the fractional part of its argument and returns the integer part (unlike CINT and INT, which perform rounding).

See Also CEIL
CINT
INT

Example

```
FOR I = 50 TO 52 STEP RND
  PRINT USING "The integer part of ##.## is ##";I,FIX(I)
NEXT I

END  ' end the program
```

FOR/NEXT statements

Function FOR and NEXT define an automatically incrementing (or decrementing) loop.

Syntax

```
FOR variable = x TO y [STEP z]
.
. statements
.
NEXT [variable [,variable]...]
```

Remarks *variable* is a numeric variable serving as the loop counter, and *x*, *y*, and *z* are numeric expressions defining the starting and stopping conditions of the loop. *x* is the initial value of the counter, *y* is the final value of the counter, and *z* is an optional incrementing value.

The statements between FOR and NEXT are executed repeatedly. With each pass through the loop, *variable* is incremented by *z*. If *z* is omitted, the stepping value defaults to 1. The loop terminates when the counter variable is greater than or equal to *y* (or, for a negative *z*, less than or equal to *y*).

FOR/NEXT loops run fastest with integer variables as the counter variable and constants for *x*, *y*, and *z*.

The body of the loop is skipped altogether if the initial value of *x* is greater than *y* or if *z* is negative and *x* is less than *y*.

FOR/NEXT loops can be nested within other FOR/NEXT loops. Be sure to use unique counter variables and to make sure that the inner loop's NEXT statement occurs before the outer loop's NEXT.

This code has crossed loops and won't compile:

```
FOR n = 1 TO 10
FOR m = 1 TO 20
   .
   .
   .
NEXT n
NEXT m
```

If multiple loops end at the same point, a single NEXT statement containing each counter variable suffices:

```
FOR n = 1 TO 10
FOR m = 1 TO 20
   .
   .
   .
NEXT m,n
```

The counter variable in the NEXT statement can be omitted altogether, but if you include it, it must be the right variable. For example:

```
FOR n = 1 TO 10
   .
   .
   .
NEXT    ' NEXT n would work too, but not NEXT m
```

Although the compiler doesn't care about such things, indent the statements between FOR and NEXT by two or three spaces to set off the structure of the loop.

Use the EXIT FOR statement to leave a FOR/NEXT loop before it has completed.

If a NEXT is encountered without a corresponding FOR, run-time error 1 occurs, NEXT Without FOR.

Example

```
FOR I% = 1 TO 10
  PRINT "For loop iteration " I%
  ' display iterations
NEXT I%

PRINT "Press any key..."    ' pause
WHILE NOT INSTAT
WEND

' use STEP to decrement FOR loop
FOR I% = 50 to 1 STEP -5
  PRINT "For loop iteration " (45-I%)\ 5
  ' notice the lack of parameter for NEXT
NEXT

END
```

FRE function

Function FRE returns the amount of free memory available to your program.

Syntax `y = FRE({string expression|-1|-2})`

Remarks FRE with a string argument returns a long integer representing the number of bytes of free RAM in string memory. FRE(−1) returns the free RAM in your program's array space. FRE(−2) tells how much room is left on the stack.

Differences Turbo Basic's FRE function provides more information than that of Interpretive BASIC. The FRE statement in Interpretive BASIC returns the amount of available memory in the BASIC data segment; thus a call to FRE(S$) and FRE(0) return the same number.

However, since Turbo Basic provides more memory to work with, its FRE statement has more functions. Turbo Basic has a separate string segment; thus, FRE(S$) returns available string space. Turbo Basic has a large (>64K) array space so FRE(−1) returns available array memory. And Turbo Basic supports procedure and recursion so FRE(−2) returns available stack space.

Example

```
ON ERROR GOTO ErrorHandler  ' set up error handler

' display memory available in string,
' data, and stack segments
PRINT FRE("String Space"),FRE(-1),FRE(-2)

DIM DYNAMIC BigArray(10000)  ' declare dynamic array
BigArray(6666) = 66          ' assign some data to it
' display memory available in string,
' data, and stack segments
S$="abc..z"
PRINT FRE("String Space"),FRE(-1),FRE(-2)


ERASE BigArray ' deallocate dynamic array
' display memory available in string,
' data, and stack segments
S$=""
PRINT FRE("String Space"),FRE(-1),FRE(-2)

' This statement returns a run-time error if
' the program is run with bounds checking on
PRINT BigArray(6666)
END            ' end program

ErrorHandler:
  PRINT "An error of type " ERR " has occurred at address" ERADR
  END
```

GET statement (files)

Function GET reads a record from a random file.

Syntax `GET [#] filenum [,recnum]`

Remarks *filenum* is the number the file was opened under, and *recnum* is the record to be read, from 1 to 16,777,215 ($2^{24} - 1$). If *recnum* is omitted, then the next record in sequence (following the one specified by the most recent GET or PUT) is read.

Example

```
' open a random access file
OPEN "GET.DTA" AS #1 LEN = 18

' make two field definitions for each field element
FIELD #1, 2 AS Integer$, 4 AS LongInt$,_
          4 AS SinglePre$, 8 AS DoublePre$
FIELD #1, 2 AS A$, 4 AS B$, 4 AS C$, 8 AS D$

MaxInt% = 32767

FOR I% = 1 TO 5    ' write some data to the file
  ' convert data and assign to buffer
  ' before writing to data file
  LSET Integer$    = MKI$(I%)
  LSET LongInt$    = MKL$(I% + CLNG(MaxInt%))
  LSET SinglePre$ = MKS$(CSNG(I% * CSNG(MaxInt%)))
  LSET DoublePre$ = MKD$(MaxInt%^I%)
  PUT #1,I%
NEXT I%

FOR I% = 1 TO 5    ' read data from file
GET #1, I%         ' display it on screen
  PRINT CVI(A$), CVL(B$), CVS(C$), CVD(D$)
NEXT I%

CLOSE #1           ' close the file

END                ' end the program
```

GET statement (graphics)

Function — GET reads all or part of the graphics screen into an array.

Syntax — `GET (x1,y1)-(x2,y2), array`

Remarks — (*x1*, *y1*) and (*x2*, *y2*) specify the upper left and lower right boundaries, respectively, of the area on the graphics screen to GET. *array* is a numeric array.

GET and its complementary command PUT are used to first read and then write graphic images onto the screen. The only constraint on the numeric array used to hold the data read from the screen is that it must be large enough to hold it. Use this formula to calculate the size of an array necessary to hold a given range of the screen:

```
BytesNecessary = 4 + INT((x *bitsPerPixel + 7) / 8) * y
```

where *x* and *y* are the horizontal and vertical dimensions, respectively, of the area to be captured. *bitsPerPixel* is a constant related to graphics mode: 2 for medium resolution and 1 for high resolution.

Screen	Bits per pixel
1	2
2	1
7	4
8	4
9	4
10	2

For example, to store a medium resolution image 35 pixels wide by 45 pixels high, you'll need an array of

```
4 + INT((35 * 2 + 7) / 8) * 45 bytes
```

or 409 bytes.

The 409 bytes represent an integer array of 205 elements, thus a dimension statement of DIM *buffer%*(204) gets the job done. (Remember that by default every array has a zeroth element; so array *buffer%* has 205 two-byte elements, 0 to 204, for a total of 410 bytes.)

Turbo Basic stores the graphics data in the buffer array in the following format:

```
buffer%(0):   The number of bits horizontally
buffer%(1):   The number of bits vertically
buffer%(2)
.
.             The graphic information itself
.
buffer%(204)
```

Because of the organization of display memory, animations based on GET and PUT are faster if you choose screen regions aligned on byte boundaries. For medium resolution, use *x* values evenly divisible by 4; for high resolution, use *x* values evenly divisible by 8.

The basic strategy in using GET and PUT to animate an object from point *A* to point *B* is as follows:

```
Draw the object
GET the object into an array
position = old location = point A
DO UNTIL position = point B
  PUT XOR the object at old location     ' erase/draw
  position = position + increment
  PUT XOR the object at position
  Delay if necessary
  old location = position
LOOP
```

Example

```
' allocate a buffer to store graphics image
DIM Buffer%(143)

' switch to medium resolution graphics mode
SCREEN 1

CIRCLE (16,16),8,2             ' draw a circle

GET (0,0) - (31,31), Buffer%  ' get the circle

' copy it all over the screen
FOR I% = 0 TO 9
  PUT(I% * 32,100), Buffer%
NEXT I%

END                            ' end the program
```

GET$ function

Function GET$ reads a string from a file opened in BINARY mode.

Syntax `GET$ [#] filenum, count, string variable`

Remarks *count* is an integer expression ranging from 0 to 32,767.

GET$ reads *count* bytes, beginning from the current file position (which can be set by SEEK), from file number *filenum* and assigns it to *string variable*. File *filenum* must have been opened in BINARY mode. After the GET$, the current file position will have been advanced by *count* bytes.

GET$, PUT$, and SEEK provide a low-level alternative to sequential and random file-processing techniques that allows you to deal with files on a byte-by-byte basis.

See Also OPEN
PUT$
SEEK

Example

```
SUB CreateFile
' GET$ opens a file and writes
' 256 characters to it.

LOCAL I%

  ' open file for BINARY I/O
  OPEN "GET$.DTA" FOR BINARY AS #1

  ' write some data to it
  FOR I% = 0 TO 255
    PUT$ #1, I%, CHR$(I%)
  NEXT I%
END SUB   ' end procedure CreateFile

DEF FNReadIt$(Start%, Size%)
' GET$ reads in the indicated amount of data
' from the file.

LOCAL TempStr$, Char$, I%

  ' seek to correct position in file
  SEEK 1, Start%

  ' read in Size% bytes
  GET$#1, Size%, TempStr$

  FNReadIt$ = TempStr$
END DEF       ' end function ReadIt
```

```
CALL CreateFile     ' create data file

' get user's input
PRINT "Enter the starting point[0..255] and how many "
PRINT "bytes of data[0..255] you wish to "
INPUT "read from the file: ",St%, Sz%

PRINT FNReadIt$(St%, Sz%) ' read the data

END   ' end the program
```

GOSUB statement

Function GOSUB invokes a subroutine.

Syntax `GOSUB label`

Remarks The GOSUB statement causes Turbo Basic to jump to the statement prefaced by *label*, after first saving its current address on the stack. Executing a RETURN returns control to the statement immediately following the GOSUB.

Turbo Basic's procedures and functions can do the work of subroutines with the added benefits of recursion, parameter passing, and local and static variables.

See Also DEF FN
SUB
RETURN

Example

```
PI# = ATN(1) * 4  ' calculate value of Pi

Radius! = 55       ' declare single-precision variable
GOSUB CalcArea     ' jump to subroutine

Radius! = 13
GOSUB CalcArea     ' jump to subroutine

END   ' end the program

' calculate and display the area of a circle
CalcArea:
  Area = PI# * Radius^2  ' calculate area
  PRINT Area        ' display result
  RETURN            ' return from subroutine
```

GOTO statement

Function GOTO sends program flow to the statement identified by *label*.

Syntax `GOTO label`

Remarks GOTO causes program flow to shift unconditionally to the code identified by *label*.

Used in moderation, GOTOs are a fast and effective programming device. Used carelessly, they can choke a program with kudzu-like strands of code that can be almost impossible to puzzle out (especially months and years after they are written). Modern programming practice minimizes GOTO usage with subroutines, procedures, and functions and structured statements such as FOR/NEXT, WHILE/WEND, DO/LOOP, IF BLOCK, and SELECT. The EXIT statement can also assist in GOTO reduction.

See Also EXIT

Example

```
X = 0

Start:          ' define a label
  X = X + 1     ' increment X
  IF X < 20 THEN ' if X < 20 then jump the PrintOut
    GOTO PrintOut
  END IF

END

PrintOut:       ' display the value of X
  PRINT "Variable X = " X
  GOTO Start    ' jump back to Start
```

HEX$ function

Function HEX$ converts a number into its hex string equivalent.

Syntax `s$ = HEX$(numeric expression)`

Remarks *numeric expression* can range from from −32,768 to 65,535. Any fractional part of *numeric expression* is rounded before the string is created. If the argument to HEX$ is negative, HEX$ returns the two's complement form of the number.

See Also BIN$
OCT$

Example

```
PRINT HEX$(65535)
PRINT HEX$(-1)
```

IF statement

Function — IF tests a condition and alters program flow if the condition is met.

Syntax — `IF integer expression [,] THEN statement(s) [ELSE statement(s)]`

Remarks — If *integer expression* is TRUE (evaluates to a nonzero result), the statement(s) following THEN and before any optional ELSE is executed. If *expression* is FALSE (zero result), then the statement(s) following the ELSE is executed. If the optional ELSE clause is omitted, execution continues with the next line of the program.

Usually, *integer expression* will be a result returned by a relational operator, although not always, as shown here:

```
IF printerOn THEN LPRINT answer$
```

Here, the LPRINT statement is executed if "flag" variable *printerOn* has a nonzero value.

A colon must not appear before the ELSE keyword; for example, the following statement will not compile:

```
IF a < b THEN c = d : ELSE e = f
```

The IF statement and all its associated statements, including those after an ELSE, must appear on the same logical line. The following is therefore illegal:

```
IF a < b THEN t = 15 : u = 16 : v = 17
ELSE t = 17 : u = 16 : v = 15
```

because the compiler treats the second line as a brand-new statement unrelated to the one above it. If you have more statements to squeeze in than can fit on one line, you can use the line continuation character, the underscore (_), to spread a single logical line over several physical lines. For example, following is a legal way of restating the last example:

```
IF a < b THEN t = 15 : u = 16 : v = 17_
ELSE t = 17 : u = 16 : v = 15
```

However, a better alternative is to use the block IF statement. You can also use the block IF statement to form a multiline series of IF statements.

Differences — Turbo Basic has extended the IF THEN ELSE statement to enable multiple lines of code in an IF THEN ELSE construct. Turbo Basic also provides the ELSEIF and END IF statements for the block IF statement.

See Also IF block
SELECT

Example

```
' single line IF
INPUT "Enter a number", X
IF X > 100 THEN PRINT "BigNumber" ELSE PRINT "SmallNumber"
END
```

IF block statement

Function IF block creates a series of IF statements.

Syntax

```
IF integer expression [,] THEN
.
. statement(s)
.
[ELSEIF integer expression [,] THEN
.
.statement(s)]
.
[ELSE
.
. statement(s)]
.
END IF
```

Remarks IF block is an extension to Interpretive BASIC, allowing multiple tests over multiple lines.

In executing IF block statements, the truth of the expression in the IF statement is checked first. If FALSE (zero result), each of the following ELSEIF statements are examined in order (there can be as many ELSEIF statements as desired). As soon as one is found to be TRUE, Turbo Basic executes the statement(s) following the associated THEN and jumps to the statement just after the terminating END IF without making any further tests. The statement(s) after the optional ELSE clause are executed if none of the earlier tests are successful.

Note that there can be nothing on the first line of an IF block after the THEN keyword; that's how the compiler can tell an IF block from a conventional IF statement. Also note that nothing follows the ELSE.

IF block statements can be nested; that is, any of the statements after any of the THENs may contain IF blocks.

(It is useful to indent the statements controlled by each test a couple of spaces, as shown in the example section.)

IF block statements must be terminated with END IF. Note that END IF has a space and ELSEIF does not.

See Also SELECT

Example

```
RANDOMIZE TIMER
bankroll = 100 : bet = 5 : delayVal = .5
WHILE NOT INSTAT  ' press a key to stop
  roll = INT(RND(1) * 6) + INT(RND(1) * 6) + 2
  PRINT STRING$(30,"-")
  PRINT "Bankroll =" bankroll
  PRINT roll : DELAY delayVal
  IF roll = 2 OR roll = 3 OR roll = 12 THEN
    PRINT "You lose"
    bankroll = bankroll - bet
  ELSEIF roll = 7 OR roll = 11 THEN
    PRINT "You win!"
    bankroll = bankroll + bet
  ELSE
    PRINT "Your point is" roll
    noPoint = -1
    WHILE noPoint
      nextRoll = INT(RND(1) * 6) + INT(RND(1) * 6) + 2
      PRINT nextRoll : DELAY delayVal
      IF roll = nextRoll THEN   ' nested IF block
        PRINT "You win!"
        bankroll = bankroll + bet
        noPoint = 0
      ELSEIF nextRoll = 7 THEN
        PRINT "You lose"
        bankroll = bankroll - bet
        noPoint = 0
      ' ends the IF roll = nextRoll block
      END IF
    WEND          ' ends noPoint WHILE loop
  END IF          ' ends first IF block
WEND              ' ends WHILE NOT INSTAT loop
```

INCR statement

Function INCR increments a variable.

Syntax `INCR numeric variable [,size]`

Remarks *size* is an optional numeric expression that indicates the value to be added to the specified variable. If *size* is omitted, 1 is used.

INCR is simply a quick way to increment a variable without using an assignment statement.

Differences This statement is not available in Interpretive BASIC.

See Also DECR

Example

```
I% = -15          ' initialize counter variables
J% = -500

WHILE I% < 0
  PRINT I%, J%    ' display the value
  INCR I%         ' increment value by 1
  INCR J%, 5      ' increment value by 5
WEND

END               ' end the program
```

INKEY$ function

Function: INKEY$ reads the keyboard without echoing the character.

Syntax:

```
s$ = INKEY$
```

Remarks: INKEY$ returns a string of 0, 1, or 2 characters reflecting the status of the keyboard buffer.

A null string (LEN(s$) = 0) means that the buffer is empty.

A string of length (LEN(S$) = 1) means the string contains the ASCII value of the most recently pressed key; for example, 13 for *Enter* (also known as carriage return), 65 for *A*.

A two-character string (LEN(S$) = 2) means a non-ASCII key was pressed. The first character in the string has a value of 0 and the second, an extended keyboard code, represents one of the keyboard's non-ASCII keys, such as *Home*, *PgDn*, or the arrow keys. (See the extended keyboard code chart in Appendix F to determine the key pressed.)

If a defined function key is pressed (see the KEY statement), INKEY$ returns the sequence of characters (one per invocation of INKEY$) that would have resulted had the characters in the definition been typed independently.

INKEY$ is designed as a bulletproof mechanism for getting user input into your program without the restrictions of the INPUT statement. Since INKEY$ doesn't wait for a character to be pressed before returning a result, you will usually use it within a loop in a low-level subroutine, continuously checking it and building an input string to be checked by higher level routines.

INKEY$ passes all keystrokes, including control keys such as *Tab*, *Enter*, and *Backspace*, to your program without displaying or processing them, with the following exceptions:

- *Ctrl-Break* terminates the program unless the Keyboard break option was turned off when the program was compiled.
- *Ctrl-Alt-Del* causes a system reset.
- *Shift-PrtSc* performs a screen dump.

See Also: INSTAT

Example

```
PRINT "Enter some characters followed by <ENTER>:"

' read some keys and display them
WHILE Char$ <> CHR$(13)
  Char$ = INKEY$
  InputString$ = InputString$ + Char$
WEND

PRINT InputString$

END        ' end the program
```

INP function

Function INP reads from an I/O port.

Syntax `y = INP(portno)`

Remarks INP returns the byte read from I/O port *portno*, where *portno* indicates a hardware input port and must be in the range 0 to 65,535.

INP is useful for reading status information presented by various hardware subsystems, such as a communications port. (See your computer's technical reference manual for port assignments.)

Use the OUT statement to write to an I/O port.

See Also OUT

Example

```
' The program makes the speaker shriek
' by reading the status register and
' toggling (on and off) the bits
' that control the speaker.

' read value in port 61 Hex
StatusReg% = INP(&H61)
StatusReg% = StatusReg% AND &H00FC
' mask the value read in

' make the tone long enough to hear
FOR J = 1 to 1000
  StatusReg% = StatusReg% XOR 2  ' toggle speaker
  OUT &H61,StatusReg%            ' output new status
  delay .001
NEXT J

END
```

INPUT statement

Function

INPUT prompts the user for values to assign to one or more variables.

Syntax

`INPUT [;] [prompt string {;|,}] variable list`

Remarks

prompt string is an optional string constant. *variable list* is a comma-delimited sequence of one or more string or numeric variables.

INPUT waits for the user to enter data from the keyboard and assigns this data to one or more variables.

If you include a semicolon after *prompt string*, Turbo Basic outputs a question mark after the string. Use a comma instead to suppress the question mark.

Your entry must match the variable type in the INPUT statement; that is, nonnumeric characters are unacceptable for numeric variables. If your entry doesn't match, Turbo Basic will make you reenter the information. For example, entering nonnumeric characters into a numeric variable produces the message

```
?Redo from start
```

If more than one variable is prompted for in a single INPUT statement, then your response for each variable must be separated by commas.

If a semicolon appears immediately after the INPUT keyword, the cursor will remain on the same line when you press ***Enter*** to terminate the response. Otherwise, a carriage-return/line-feed pair is sent to the display.

Differences

Turbo Basic allows information entered in response to an input statement to be separated either by spaces or commas. Interpretive BASIC requires that all input be separated by commas.

Example

```
INPUT "Enter your age and weight: ",Age, Weight

PRINT USING "You are a ### year old & and weigh ###";_
           Age, Weight

END     ' end the program
```

INPUT # statement

Function — INPUT # loads variables with data from a sequential file.

Syntax — `INPUT #filenum, variable list`

Remarks — *filenum* is the number given when the file was opened, and *variable list* is a comma-delimited sequence of one or more string or numeric variables.

The file can be either a disk file, a serial port (COM*n*:), or the keyboard (KYBD:).

The data in the file must match the type(s) of the variable(s) defined in the INPUT # statement. The variable should appear just as if it were being typed by you in response to an INPUT statement; that is, it should be separated by commas with a carriage return at the end. This is the way the WRITE # statement creates files.

See Also — WRITE #

Example

```
SUB MakeFile

' INPUT # opens a sequential file for output.
' Using WRITE #, it writes lines of different
' types of data to the file.

' assign the file variable to #1
OPEN "INPUT#.DTA" FOR OUTPUT AS #1

' define some variables and initialize them
StringVariable$ = "I'll be back."
Integer% = 1000
FloatingPoint! = 30000.1234

' write a line of text to the sequential file
WRITE# 1, StringVariable$, Integer%, FloatingPoint!

CLOSE 1          ' close file variable

END SUB          ' end procedure MakeFile

SUB ReadFile
' This procedure opens a sequential file
' for input. Using INPUT #, it reads
' lines of different types of data
' from the file.

' assign the file variable to #1
OPEN "INPUT#.DTA" FOR INPUT AS #1

StringVariable$ = ""   ' define some
Integer% = 0           ' variables and
FloatingPoint! = 0     ' initialize them
```

```
' read a line of text from the
' sequential file
INPUT# 1, StringVariable$, Integer%, FloatingPoint!

PRINT StringVariable$, Integer%, FloatingPoint!

CLOSE #1    ' close file variable

END SUB       ' end procedure ReadFile

CALL MakeFile
CALL ReadFile

END           ' end the program
```

INPUT$ function

Function INPUT$ reads a specific number of characters from the keyboard or a file.

Syntax `s$ = INPUT$(n [, [#] filenum])`

Remarks *n* is the number of characters to be read and *filenum* is the file to read from. If *filenum* is omitted, the keyboard is read.

If the keyboard is used, no characters appear on the screen, and all characters are passed to the destination string. INPUT$'s main virtue, relative to other techniques for reading files or the keyboard, is that it allows you to accept all characters including control characters.

The BINARY file mode offers this attribute in a more flexible way.

Note: Certain keys and key combinations (for example, the function and cursor control keys) do not return ASCII values. When such keys are pressed, INPUT$ substitutes CHR$(0); INKEY$ doesn't have this limitation.

See Also INKEY$

Example

```
OPEN "INPUT#.DTA" FOR INPUT AS #1
S$ = INPUT$(15, #1);
PRINT S$
CLOSE #1
END
```

INSTAT function

Function INSTAT returns keyboard status.

Syntax `y = INSTAT`

Remarks INSTAT returns keyboard status information. If a key has been pressed, INSTAT returns −1; otherwise it returns 0. INSTAT doesn't remove a keystroke from the buffer, so if it ever returns TRUE (−1), it will continue to return TRUE until the keystroke is removed by INKEY$ or another keyboard-reading command.

See Also INKEY$

Example

```
WHILE NOT INSTAT    ' check if a key was pressed
  LOCATE 1,1
  PRINT "Waiting for a key..."
WEND

PRINT INKEY$         ' display the pressed key

END                  ' end the program
```

INSTR function

Function INSTR searches a string for a pattern.

Syntax `y = INSTR([n,] target string,pattern string)`

Remarks *n* is an integer expression ranging from 1 to 32,767, and *target string* and *pattern string* are any string variables, expressions, or constants.

INSTR returns the position of *pattern string* in *target string*. If *pattern string* isn't in *target string*, INSTR returns 0. If the optional *n* parameter is included, the search begins at position *n* in *target string*.

If *pattern string* is null (length 0), INSTR returns 1 (or *n* if *n* is specified).

INSTR is case sensitive.

Example

```
' get user's input
LINE INPUT "Please input a string: ";DummyStr$
PRINT "Now input a substring that exists in the ";
INPUT "first string: ";SubStr$

' display the location of substring
PRINT USING "The string ' & ' exists starting at ";_
            SubStr$;
PRINT USING " location ### in &";_
            INSTR(1,DummyStr$,SubStr$), DummyStr$

END           ' end the program
```

INT function

Function INT converts a numeric expression to an integer.

Syntax `y = INT(numeric expression)`

Remarks INT returns the largest integer less than or equal to *numeric expression*.

See Also CEIL
CINT
FIX

Example

```
PRINT "X", "INT(X)"
PRINT
FOR N = 1 TO 6
  READ X#
  PRINT X#, INT(X#)
NEXT N

DATA 3.1, -3.1, 3.5, -3.5, 3.9, -3.9

END
```

IOCTL statement, IOCTL$ function

Function IOCTL and IOCTL$ communicate with a device driver.

Syntax Statement:

```
IOCTL [#]filenum,string expression
```

Function:

```
s$ = IOCTL$ [#] filenum
```

Remarks *filenum* is the file number of the desired device driver. *string expression* contains information to be sent to the driver. The format of the string information sent to or received from a device driver is a function of the driver itself.

IOCTL sends data to a device driver. IOCTL$ reads data from a device driver.

For more information, consult the device driver section of the *IBM DOS Technical Reference Manual.*

KEY statement

Function KEY sets and displays function key contents and defines key trap values.

Syntax

```
KEY {ON|OFF|LIST}
KEY n, string expression
KEY n, CHR$(shiftstatus)+CHR$(scancode)
```

Remarks KEY ON and KEY OFF turn on and off the function key display at the bottom of the screen. Note that turning off the display doesn't affect function key definitions. KEY LIST sends the current function key definitions to the screen. When function keys are displayed, the 25th line of the screen is never scrolled, and attempting to LOCATE the cursor on that line results in an Illegal Function Call (run-time error 5).

KEY *n*, *string expression* sets function key *n* to *string expression*, where *string expression* has a length of 15 characters or less (only the first 6 appear on the status line). To disable a function key, assign it the null string. A carriage return in the string (CHR$(13)) is displayed as a small left arrow.

KEY *n*, CHR$(*shiftstatus*) + CHR$(*scancode*) associates a key (or combination of keys) with a number (*n*, from 15–20) for key trapping with subsequent ON KEY and KEY(*n*) ON statements. The format is as follows:

- *shiftstatus* is an integer expression ranging from 0 to 255 that controls the response of the trap to the state of the *Ctrl*, *Caps Lock*, *Num Lock*, *Alt*, and both *Shift* keys.
- *scancode* is a numeric value from 1 to 83 that defines the key to trap, according to the Scan Code Table in Appendix F. Note that keys 59 through 68, 72, 75, 77, and 80 are trapped already (they're the function and cursor control keys), so defining them has no effect.

Use the following to build a value for *shiftstatus*:

Modifier Key	Binary Value	Hex Value
Right Shift	0000 0001	01
Left Shift	0000 0010	02
Ctrl	0000 0100	04
Alt	0000 1000	08
Num Lock	0010 0000	20
Caps Lock	0100 0000	40

As an example, suppose we want to trap "shift-escape"; that is, we want a certain subroutine to get control whenever the **Esc** key is pressed along with either ***Shift*** key. First, you must build the *shiftstatus* mask. You want both ***Shift*** keys to be recognized, so you must add the masks for each: 01H + 02H = 03H. Next you can consult the scan code table in Appendix F and discover that the **Esc** key has scan code 1. The following statement tells Turbo Basic about your plan:

```
KEY 15,CHR$(&03) + CHR$(1)
```

You must use key value 15 because the first 14 are predefined to represent the function and cursor control keys. Next you define a trap subroutine to be called whenever ***Shift-Esc*** is pressed:

```
ON KEY(15) GOSUB ShiftEscape
```

where *ShiftEscape* is a label at the start of the trap subroutine. Finally you turn on trapping for key 15 with the KEY(*n*) statement:

```
KEY(15) ON
```

See Also

KEY(*n*)
ON KEY

Example

```
' This program shows the KEY ON/OFF and
' KEY N string expressions

' turn off function key display
KEY OFF

' assign string expressions to the function keys
FOR N% = 1 TO 10
  READ A$
  KEY N%, A$ + CHR$(13)
NEXT N%
KEY LIST  'Display function key definitions
' turn on function key display
KEY ON

' wait for user to press a key
WHILE NOT INSTAT
WEND

' data statements used by READ
DATA Help, Enter, Edit, Change, Report, Print, Setup
DATA DOS, Copy, Quit

END          ' end the program
```

KEY(n) statement

Function KEY(*n*) turns trapping on or off for a specific key.

Syntax `KEY(n) {ON|OFF|STOP}`

Remarks *n* is the trapped key, an integer expression from 1 to 25, 30, or 31, according to the following:

n	Key
1–10	Function keys F1–F10
11	Cursor Up
12	Cursor Left
13	Cursor Right
14	Cursor Down
15–25	Keys defined by KEY statement
30	Function key F11
31	Function key F12

KEY(*n*) ON turns on trapping of key *n*. This means that a check is made between every statement to see if key *n* has been pressed; and if it has, program execution is diverted to the routine specified in an ON KEY statement for that key.

KEY(*n*) OFF disables trapping of key *n*.

KEY(*n*) STOP also disables key trapping but remembers the occurrence of KEY (*n*) pressing, so that if a KEY ON statement is subsequently executed, a trap occurs immediately.

See Also $EVENT
ON KEY

Example

```
' turn on key checking
KEY ON

' assign strings to keys
KEY 1, "Hello" + CHR$(13)
KEY 2, "GoodBye" + CHR$(13)
KEY 10, CHR$(13)

' set up a key trap for F10
' assign a string to it.
ON KEY(10) GOSUB GoodBye

' turn on F10 trapping
KEY(10) ON

' get user's input
INPUT "Press F1: ";Dummy$
INPUT "Press F2: ";Dummy$
```

```
PRINT "Press F10 now ..."

' now, the GoodBye subroutine will be called
WHILE NOT INSTAT : WEND ' wait for the F10 key

END           ' end the program

GoodBye:
  KEY(10) OFF ' turn off trapping

  ' now, the character string assigned
  ' to F10 will be played back
  PRINT "Press F10 now to quit the program..."
  RETURN
```

KILL statement

Function KILL deletes a file (like the DOS DEL command).

Syntax `KILL filespec`

Remarks *filespec* is a string expression and represents the file or files to be deleted, and can optionally include a path name and/or wildcard characters. KILL is analogous to DOS's DEL (ERASE) command.

Like DEL, KILL cannot delete a directory. Use RMDIR instead, after first deleting all the files in the directory.

Example

```
' set some simple error handling
ON ERROR GOTO FileError

' get the file's name
INPUT "Please enter the file to delete: ", FileName$

' delete the file
IF FileName$ <> "" THEN
  KILL FileName$
END IF

END          ' end the program

FileError:   ' tell about the error
  PRINT "Error ";
  PRINT  Err " occurred when deleting the file"
  END
```

LBOUND function

Function LBOUND returns the lowest bound possible (the smallest subscript) for an array's specified dimension.

Syntax `LBOUND(`*`array(dimension)`*`)`

Remarks *array* is the name of the array being dimensioned. *dimension* represents an integer from 1 up to the number of dimensions in *array*. You can determine an array's size by using LBOUND with UBOUND. To determine the upper limit of an array dimension, use UBOUND.

If you don't specify a subscript range (see DIM), then the default lower bound is 0. You can override the default lower bound using the OPTION BASE statement.

See Also DIM
OPTION BASE
UBOUND

Example

```
' dimension array with lower and upper bounds
DIM Array%(1900:2000,10:20)

' print out the lower array bound
PRINT "Lower Array Bound of Dimension 2 is ";LBOUND(Array%(2))
END
```

LCASE$ function

Function	LCASE$ returns a lowercase-only string.
Syntax	`s$ = LCASE$(`*`string expression`*`)`
Remarks	LCASE$ returns a string equal to *string expression* except that all the uppercase letters in *string expression* will have been converted to lowercase.
See Also	UCASE$
Example	`PRINT LCASE$("What's that WATERMELON for?");`

LEFT$ function

Function LEFT$ returns the left-most *n* characters of a string.

Syntax `s$ = LEFT$(string expression,n)`

Remarks *n* is an integer expression and specifies the number of characters in *string expression* to be returned. *n* must be in the range 0 to 32,767.

LEFT$ returns a string consisting of the left-most *n* characters of its string argument. If *n* is greater than or equal to the length of *string expression*, all of *string expression* is returned. If *n* is 0, LEFT$ returns the null string.

See Also MID$
RIGHT$

Example

```
PRINT LEFT$("Hello out there in the universe!", 5)
```

LEN function

Function: LEN returns the length of a string.

Syntax: `y = LEN(string expression)`

Remarks: LEN returns a value from 0 to 32,767, representing the number of characters in *string expression*. Note that this range is vastly expanded over Interpretive BASIC's maximum string length of 255.

Example:

```
INPUT "Enter a string: ",DummyStr$

PRINT USING "The length of the string = ### ";_
            LEN(DummyStr$)

END      ' end the main program
```

LET statement

Function LET assigns a value to a variable.

Syntax `[LET] variable = expression`

Remarks *variable* is a string or numeric variable, and *expression* is of a suitable type (that is, string for string variables and numeric for numeric variables).

LET is optional in assignment statements and in practice is usually omitted.

Example

```
INPUT "Enter a string: ",DummyStr$

' assign TempStr$ a value using LET
LET TempStr$ = DummyStr$

PRINT TempStr$, DummyStr$

END
```

LINE statement

Function: LINE draws a straight line or an optionally filled box.

Syntax: `LINE [(x1,y1)] - (x2,y2) [,[color] [,B[F]] [,pattern]]`

Remarks: (*x1*,*y1*) and (*x2*,*y2*) are the coordinates of two points on the graphics screen and can be specified in either absolute or relative form. (See Chapter 4 for more information about absolute and relative coordinates.) *color* is an integer expression describing the color in which the line or box should be drawn. *pattern* is an integer mask controlling how the line or box is drawn.

To draw a line to point (*x*,*y*) from the LPR in the default color, type

```
LINE -(x,y)
```

To draw that same line in a different color, type

```
LINE -(x,y), 2
```

To draw a line from point (*x1*,*y1*) to point (*x2*,*y2*), type

```
LINE (x1,y1) - (x2,y2)
```

To draw a box with upper left corner (*x1*,*y1*) and lower right corner (*x2*,*y2*), type

```
LINE (x1,y1) - (x2,y2),,B
```

To fill a box with attribute 2, type

```
LINE (x1,y1) - (x2,y2),2,BF
```

To draw a nonsolid line, include the *pattern* argument. For example, to create a dotted line, use a *pattern* value of &HAAAA (1010 1010 1010 1010 binary). Note that *pattern* does not affect filled boxes.

```
LINE (x1,y1) - (x2,y2),,,maskword
```

After a LINE statement, the LPR becomes the second of the two points in the LINE statement.

See Also: FILL

Example

```
' draw a diagonal line across the screen
SCREEN 1,0
LINE (0,0) - (319,199)

' draw a horizontal dashed line
LINE (0,100) - (319,100),,,&HCCCC

' draw a 50 pixel square filled with color 2
' and the upper left-hand corner at (10,20)
LINE (10,20) - (60,70), 2, BF

' play connect the dots
READ X,Y
PSET (X,Y)  ' set the LPR
FOR N = 1 TO 11
  READ X,Y
  LINE -(X,Y)
NEXT N

LOCATE 9,9
PRINT "ORLAND"

END          ' end the program

DATA 10,20, 50,20, 55,25, 55,40, 50,45, 10,45
DATA 50,45, 55,50, 55,65, 50,70, 10,70, 10,20
```

LINE INPUT statement

Function LINE INPUT reads a line from the keyboard into a string variable, ignoring delimiters.

Syntax `LINE INPUT [;] [prompt string;] string variable`

Remarks *prompt string* is an optional string constant to be sent to the screen prior to waiting for your response. *string variable* is the variable that will be loaded with the data you enter at the keyboard. Use LINE INPUT instead of INPUT when you have to enter string information that contains delimiters (that is, commas) that would otherwise confuse an INPUT statement. For example:

```
INPUT "Enter patient address: "; a$
```

will fail if the address contains a comma:

```
Enter patient address: 101 Main Street, Apt 2
? Redo from start
```

LINE INPUT accepts commas without a problem.

If a semicolon follows the LINE INPUT statement, then when *Enter* is pressed to end the input sequence, a carriage return won't be sent to the display (that is, the cursor will stay on the same line).

Example

```
PRINT "Enter several fields of input, you needn't "
LINE INPUT "worry about delimiting them in any way:"_
         DummyStr$

PRINT DummyStr$

END   ' end the main program
```

LINE INPUT # statement

Function LINE INPUT # reads a line from a sequential file into a string variable, ignoring delimiters.

Syntax `LINE INPUT #filenum, string variable`

Remarks *filenum* is the number of the file to read and *string variable* is the string variable to be loaded.

LINE INPUT # is like LINE INPUT except that the data is read from a sequential file rather than from the keyboard. The current record in the file is read and loaded into *string variable*. As with LINE INPUT, use LINE INPUT # to collect data that has delimiter characters (commas) mixed in with data.

If the data in the file was written with the WRITE # statement, it is already correctly delimited and INPUT # is the best way to read it.

Example

```
SUB MakeFile
' LINE INPUT # opens a sequential file
' for output. Using PRINT # and PRINT # USING,
' it writes different types of data
' to the file

  ' assign a file variable to #1
  OPEN "LINEINP#.DTA" FOR OUTPUT AS #1

  ' define some variables and initialize them
  StringVariable$ = "There's trouble in River City."
  Integer% = 1000
  FloatingPoint! = 30000.1234

  ' write a line of text to the sequential file
  PRINT # 1, StringVariable$, Integer%, FloatingPoint!

  CLOSE #1     ' close the file variable

END SUB        ' end procedure MakeFile

SUB ReadFile
' Opens a sequential file for input
' uses LINE INPUT # and INPUT$ to read
' lines of different types of data
' from the file.

  ' assign the file variable to #1
  OPEN "LINEINP#.DTA" FOR INPUT AS #1

  StringVariable$ = ""
```

```
  ' input an entire line regardless of length
  LINE INPUT # 1, StringVariable$

  PRINT StringVariable$

  CLOSE #1      ' close the file variable

  END SUB       ' end procedure ReadFile

CALL MakeFile
CALL ReadFile

END     ' end the program
```

LOC function

Function — LOC returns the current file position.

Syntax

```
y = LOC(filenum)
```

Remarks — *filenum* is the value under which the file was OPENed. The behavior of LOC depends on the mode in which the file was OPENed.

If *filenum* is a random file, LOC returns the number of the last record written or read.

If *filenum* is a sequential file, LOC returns the number of 128-byte blocks written or read since opening the file. By convention, LOC returns one block for files that have been opened but have not yet been written or read.

If *filenum* is a binary file, LOC returns the SEEK file position.

For a communications file, LOC returns the number of characters in the input buffer.

Example

```
OPEN "LOC.DTA" FOR BINARY AS #1
PUT$ #1, "TurboBasic"
PRINT LOC(1)
CLOSE
END
```

LOCAL statement

Function LOCAL declares local variables in a procedure or function.

Syntax `LOCAL variable list`

Remarks The LOCAL statement is legal only in function and procedure definitions, and must appear before any executable statements in the associated definition. LOCAL defines one or more variables as "local" to the enclosing procedure or function. A local variable can have the same name as other variables in other parts of the program and can also have the same name as other local variables in other function and procedure definitions without conflict; they are separate variables.

To declare a local array, include its identifier and an empty set of parentheses in the variable list, then DIMension the array in a subsequent statement.

Local variables are allocated on the stack and are initialized to zero (for string variables, use the null string) with every invocation of the enclosing function or procedure.

Undeclared variables in procedures are given the static attribute by default; nonetheless, we recommend that you explicitly declare each variable.

See Also DIM
SHARED
STATIC

Example

```
SUB Locals
LOCAL a(), i%
DIM DYNAMIC a(10:20)
  FOR i% = 10 TO 20
    a(i%) = i%
  NEXT i%
END SUB
```

LOCATE statement

Function: LOCATE positions the cursor and/or defines the cursor's shape.

Syntax: `LOCATE [row][,[column][,[cursor][,start][,stop]]]`

Remarks: *row* is an integer expression defining the screen line on which the cursor should be positioned (1–25). *column* specifies the column (1–80). *cursor* is a numeric value that controls whether or not the cursor will be visible (0 means invisible; 1 means visible). The 25th line is not available unless the function key display is inactive (see the KEY OFF statement).

start and *stop* are integer expressions that control the size of the cursor and represent how many scan lines the cursor will consist of. The top scan line is line 0; the bottom is 7 for Color/Graphics Adapters and 13 for Monochrome Adapters.

LOCATE is used most often before a PRINT statement to control where on the screen the output will go.

See Also: KEY OFF
PRINT

Example:

```
CLS
CRSLIN and POS
INPUT "Input X and Y coordinates: ",X%, Y%

' position cursor and change its shape
LOCATE X%,Y%,1,4,5
PRINT "Hi";
WHILE NOT INSTAT : WEND  ' wait for a key

END     ' end the program
```

LOF function

Function LOF returns the length of a file.

Syntax `y = LOF(filenum)`

Remarks *filenum* is the number under which the file was opened.

LOF returns the length of the indicated file in bytes. For communications files, LOF represents the size of the available space in the communications buffer.

Example

```
OPEN "TB.EXE" FOR BINARY AS #1
PRINT "The size of Turbo Basic is";LOF(1)
CLOSE #1
END
```

LOG, LOG2, and LOG10 functions

Function LOG returns the natural (base *e*) logarithm; LOG2 returns the logarithm of base 2; LOG10 returns the logarithm of base 10.

Syntax LOG:

```
y = LOG(numeric expression)
```

LOG2:

```
y = LOG2(numeric expression)
```

LOG10:

```
y = LOG10(numeric expression)
```

Remarks LOG returns the natural logarithm (base *e*, where *e* = 2.718282...) of its argument. If *numeric expression* is less than or equal to zero, run-time error 5 results, Illegal Function Call.

The natural logarithm of *x* is the power to which *e* would have to be raised to equal *x*.

LOG, LOG2, and LOG10 return double-precision results.

Example

```
FOR I! = 1 TO 50 STEP 2.5
  PRINT USING "The natural log of ## = ##^^^^"; _
              I!, LOG(I!)
NEXT I!

END          ' end the program
```

LPOS function

Function LPOS returns the "cursor position" of the printer buffer.

Syntax `y = LPOS(printer)`

Remarks *printer* is an integer expression from 0 to 3, selecting the printer from the following:

```
0, 1      LPT1:
2         LPT2:
3         LPT3:
```

LPOS reports how many characters have been sent to the printer since the last carriage return character was output.

See Also POS

Example

```
' assign width of printer to a named constant
%Wid = 80

' display ASCII and extended ASCII characters
' on the screen and to the printer.
FOR I% = 0 TO 255
  IF (I% > 32) THEN
    PRINT USING  " !";CHR$(I%);
    LPRINT USING " !";CHR$(I%);
  END IF

  ' advance to next line if running out of room
  IF LPOS(0) = %Wid THEN
    LPRINT CHR$(13) + CHR$(10)
  END IF
NEXT I%

END        ' end the program
```

LPRINT, LPRINT USING statements

Function: LPRINT and LPRINT USING send data to the printer (LPT1:).

Syntax:

```
LPRINT [expression list [;]]
LPRINT USING format string; expression list
```

Remarks: *expression list* is a comma- or semicolon-delimited series of numeric and/or string expressions. *format string* contains formatting information.

LPRINT and LPRINT USING perform the same actions as PRINT and PRINT USING except that *expression list* is sent to the printer (LPT1) rather than to the screen.

Note: By default, Turbo Basic inserts a carriage-return/line-feed pair after printing 80 characters on a line. This characteristic can be changed with the WIDTH statement.

See Also: LPOS
PRINT
PRINT USING
WIDTH

Examples:

```
LPRINT USING ## is my lucky number.";7
END
```

LSET statement

Function — LSET moves string data into the random file buffer.

Syntax — `LSET` *`field variable`* `=` *`string expression`*

Remarks — LSET and its sister statement RSET move string information into field variables defined as belonging to the buffer of a random file.

If the length of *string expression* is less than the size of *field variable* specified in a FIELD statement, LSET left-justifies this field by padding it with spaces. This means spaces are appended after the last character of *string expression* such that after the LSET assignment, LEN(*field variable*) still equals the width defined in the associated FIELD statement.

RSET does right-justification with space padding (spaces are added before the first character of *string expression*).

LSET and RSET can also be used to format output to the screen or printer:

```
a$ = space$(20)
RSET a$ = "Right-just"
PRINT a$
```

See Also — FIELD
LEN
RSET

Example

```
OPEN "LSET.DTA" AS #1 LEN = 18

' define the field names and sizes of files
FIELD 1,2 AS FileInt$, 4 AS FileLong$,_
      4 AS FileSngl$,8 AS FileDbl$

' assign values to the fields and write
' the record to the random access file
FOR Count% = 1 TO 5
  LSET FileInt$  = MKI$(Count%)
  LSET FileLong$ = MKL$(Count%^2)
  LSET FileSngl$ = MKS$(Count%^2.1)
  LSET FileDbl$  = MKD$(Count%^4.4)
  PUT 1,Count%
NEXT Count%

CLOSE 1        ' close the file

END            ' end main program
```

MEMSET statement

Function MEMSET declares the upper memory limit.

Syntax `MEMSET address`

Remarks *address* is a long integer expression defining the absolute address of Turbo Basic's upper memory limit. *address* must be less than the amount of memory installed in the system. In practice, *address* is usually calculated by subtracting a constant from the value returned by the ENDMEM function.

MEMSET is designed to set aside memory for assembly language subroutines. If Turbo Basic cannot accommodate this request because of either an inappropriate argument or insufficient memory, then run-time error 7 results, Out of Memory.

See Also ENDMEM

Example

```
PRINT FRE(-1)  ' display available array space

' save 128 bytes at the top of memory
MEMSET ENDMEM - &H80
PRINT FRE(-1)   ' display available memory

END             ' end the program
```

MID$ function

Function — MID$ returns a character string.

Syntax — `s$ = MID$(string expression,n [,m])`

Remarks — *n* and *m* are numeric variables or expressions, and can range from 1 to 32,767 and 0 to 32,767, respectively.

MID$ as a function returns an *m*-character string beginning with the *n*th character of *string expression*. If *m* is omitted or there are fewer than *m* characters to the right of the *n*th character of *string expression*, the remaining characters of *string expression*, up to and including the *n*th character, are returned. If *n* is greater than the length of *string expression*, MID$ returns a null string.

See Also — LEFT$
MID$ statement
RIGHT$

Example

```
INPUT "Input a string: ",DummyStr$

TempStr$ = DummyStr$
PRINT DummyStr$
' Reverse the order of characters using MID$
' function and statement simultaneously.
FOR I% = 1 TO LEN(DummyStr$)
  MID$(DummyStr$,I%,1) = MID$(TempStr$,_
      (LEN(TempStr$) - I%) + 1, 1)
NEXT I%

PRINT DummyStr$

END            ' end the program
```

MID$ statement

Function MID$ replaces string characters.

Syntax `MID$(string variable,n [,m]) = replacement string`

Remarks *n* and *m* are numeric variables or expressions, and can range from 1 to 32,767 and 0 to 32,767, respectively.

As a statement, MID$ replaces *m* characters of *string variable*, beginning at character position *n* with the contents of *replacement string*. If *m* is included, it determines how many characters of *replacement string* are inserted into *string variable*. If omitted, all of *replacement string* is used. MID$ will never alter the length of a string.

See Also LEFT$
MID$ function
RIGHT$

Example

```
' MID$, the statement
b$ = "Hurricane Camille"
MID$(b$,11)  = "Carla  "  ' Omitted optional m parameter
PRINT b$
```

MKDIR statement

Function MKDIR creates a subdirectory (like DOS's MKDIR command).

Syntax `MKDIR path`

Remarks *path* is a string expression describing the directory to be created. (See Chapter 4 for information about file names and paths.)

MKDIR (make directory) creates the subdirectory specified by *path*.

If you try to create a directory that already exists, run-time error 5 occurs, Illegal Function Call.

Example

```
' set up an error handler
ON ERROR GOTO DirError

PRINT "Please enter the directory you would like to ";
INPUT "create: ",DirName$

MKDIR DirName$       ' create directory

END                  ' end the program

DirError:
  PRINT "There is a problem in creating the directory."
  END
```

MKI$, MKL$, MKS$, MKD$ functions

Function MKI$, MKL$, MKS$, and MKD$ convert numeric data into strings (for random file output).

Syntax
```
s$ = MKI$(integer expression)
s$ = MKL$(long integer expression)
s$ = MKS$(single-precision expression)
s$ = MKD$(double-precision expression)
```

Remarks The *Make* functions are part of the process of getting numeric values into random access files. Since the statements that write information to the buffer of a random file (LSET and RSET) operate only on strings, numeric data must be translated into string form before it can be PUT into a random file.

MKI$(*i*) returns a two-character string consisting of the two 8-bit values that Turbo Basic uses to internally represent integer variable *i*. MKL$ returns a 4-byte string equivalent of a long integer. MKS$ returns a 4-byte string equivalent of a single-precision value. MKD$ returns an 8-byte string equivalent of a double-precision value. The complementary functions CVI, CVL, CVS, and CVD are used when *reading* random files.

Don't confuse these functions with STR$ and VAL, which respectively turn a numeric expression into printable form and vice versa:

```
i = 123.45
a$ = STR$(i) : b$ = MKS$(i)
' a$ contains something worth putting
' on the screen; b$ doesn't
PRINT a$, b$
```

See Also CVD
CVI
CVL
CVS

Example

```
OPEN "MKILSD.DTA" AS #1 LEN = 18

' define the field names and sizes
' of the fields
FIELD 1,2 AS FileInt$, 4 AS FileLong$,_
      4 AS FileSngl$, 8 AS FileDbl$

' assign values to the fields and write
' the record to the random access file
FOR Count% = 1 TO 5
  LSET FileInt$  = MKI$(Count%)
  LSET FileLong$ = MKL$(Count%^2)
  LSET FileSngl$ = MKS$(Count%^2.1)
  LSET FileDbl$  = MKD$(Count%^4.4)
  PUT 1,Count%
NEXT Count%

CLOSE 1        ' close the file

END            ' end main program
```

MKMD$, MKMS$ functions

Function MKMD$ and MKMS$ convert numeric data into Microsoft-format strings (for random file output).

Syntax

```
s$ = MKMS$(single-precision expression)
s$ = MKMD$(double-precision expression)
```

Remarks The "Make Microsoft" functions are provided solely for compatibility with existing random files that contain floating-point values in Microsoft format.

MKMS$ creates a Microsoft-format 4-byte string from a single-precision value; MKMD$ makes an 8-byte Microsoft string given a double-precision value.

See Also CVMD
CVMS

Example

```
' open a random access file
OPEN "CVMD.DTA" AS #1 LEN = 12

FIELD #1, 4 AS Single$, 8 AS Double$

MaxInt% = 32767

FOR I% = 1 TO 5   ' write data to file
  LSET Double$ = MKMD$(I% + MaxInt%)
  PUT #1,I%
NEXT I%

FOR I% = 1 TO 5   ' read data from file
  GET #1, I%      ' display on screen
  PRINT CVMS(Single$), CVMD(Double$)
NEXT I%

CLOSE #1          ' close the file

END               ' end the program
```

MTIMER function and statement

Function MTIMER reads or resets the microtimer.

Syntax Function:

```
y = MTIMER
```

Statement:

```
MTIMER
```

Remarks MTIMER is designed to measure elasped time, primarily for very short operations. It offers greatly improved resolution; however, the accuracy drops off sharply after approximately 54 milliseconds.

As a function, MTIMER returns the number of microseconds that have elapsed since the most recent MTIMER statement. MTIMER is accurate to within about two microseconds.

As a statement, MTIMER resets the microtimer to zero.

Restrictions The MTIMER statement and function are used in pairs. You must issue the MTIMER statement and then call the function to get the result. Subsequent references to the function will yield a value of zero if you haven't restarted the microtimer with the MTIMER statement.

MTIMER and SOUND/PLAY each use channel 2 of the 8255 timer chip, and are mutually exclusive. Therefore, execution of SOUND or PLAY statements between the MTIMER statement and MTIMER function forces the microtimer to be reset to zero elapsed time.

Example

```
' initialize the timer
MTIMER

PI# = ATN(1) * 4  ' calculate PI

' get the value of the timer
ElapsedTime! = MTIMER

PRINT USING "It took ##### milliseconds ";ElapsedTime!;
PRINT " to calculate the value of PI."

END               ' end the program
```

NAME statement

Function NAME renames a file (like DOS's REN function).

Syntax `NAME` *filespec1* `AS` *filespec2*

Remarks *filespec1* and *filespec2* are string expressions conforming to DOS path and file name conventions. The NAME operation gives the data represented by *filespec1* the name *filespec2*. Since *filespec2* can contain a path name, it is possible to move the data from one directory to another, as long as you don't try to rename from one disk to another.

Example

```
INPUT "Enter the name of the file to rename: ",OldName$
INPUT "Enter the new name of the file: ",NewName$

print oldname$,newname$
NAME OldName$ AS NewName$

END          ' end of program
```

OCT$ function

Function	OCT$ returns a string representing the octal (base 8) form of a numeric expression.
Syntax	`s$ = OCT$(numeric expression)`
Remarks	*numeric expression* is in the range −32,768 to 65,535. OCT$ returns a string representing the octal form of its integer argument. If *numeric expression* has a fractional portion, it is rounded before the conversion takes place. Use the HEX$ and BIN$ functions to convert values to hexadecimal and binary strings, respectively.
See Also	BIN$ HEX$
Example	`PRINT OCT$(-1)` `PRINT OCT$(65535)`

ON COM(n) statement

Function ON COM(*n*) declares the trap subroutine for serial port events.

Syntax `ON COM(n) GOSUB label`

Remarks *n* is the number (1 or 2) of the communications adapter (serial port) to be read. *label* identifies the trap subroutine. If *label* is the special line number 0, then trapping is disabled.

The ON COM(*n*) statement has no effect until communications events are enabled for a given serial port by an appropriate COM ON statement. Once the COM ON statement has been executed, checking occurs between the execution of every subsequent statement to see if a character has arrived at the specified serial port. If one has, a GOSUB is performed to the designated subroutine.

See Also Appendix B, "Event Trapping"

ON ERROR statement

Function ON ERROR specifies an error-handling routine and turns on error trapping.

Syntax `ON ERROR GOTO label`

Remarks *label* identifies the first line of the error-trapping routine.

Once error handling has been turned on with this statement, instead of displaying an error message and terminating execution, all run-time errors result in a jump to your error-handling code. Use the RESUME statement to continue execution.

To disable error trapping, use ON ERROR GOTO 0. You could use this technique if an error occurs for which you have not defined a recovery path; you may also choose to display the contents of ERL at this time.

If you're running an .EXE program from DOS with error trapping turned off, any run-time errors that occur cause a message to be printed and the program to terminate. The message is in the form

```
Error errnum at pgm-ctr = address
```

If the program is launched from within Turbo Basic and an error occurs, you are placed in the editor at the location of the error. On the status line will be a brief description of the run-time error:

```
Error errnum: error message
```

See Also ERADR
ERL
ERR
ERROR
RESUME

Example

```
' Set up the error handler
ON ERROR GOTO ErrorHandler

WHILE 1       ' this loop ends with an error
  I = 10/0    ' this causes a run-time error
WEND

ErrorHandler:
  PRINT "Handler caught run-time error ";
  PRINT ERR," at line " ERL
END
```

ON/GOSUB statement

Function ON/GOSUB calls one of several possible subroutines according to the value of a numeric expression.

Syntax `ON n GOSUB label [,label] ...`

Remarks *n* is a numeric expression ranging from 0 to 255, and *label* identifies a statement to branch to.

n determines which label is jumped to (for example, if *n* = *4*, the fourth label in the list receives control). If *n* is 0 or greater than the number of labels in the list, Turbo Basic continues execution with the next statement in sequence.

Each subroutine should end with RETURN to resume execution with the statement immediately following the ON/GOSUB statement.

The SELECT and IF block statements can also perform multiway branching and are more flexible than ON/GOSUB.

Example

```
FOR I% = 1 TO 3
  ON I% GOSUB OneHandler, TwoHandler, ThreeHandler
NEXT I%

END          ' end main program

OneHandler:
  PRINT "Handler number",I%
  RETURN

TwoHandler:
  PRINT "Handler number",I%
  RETURN

ThreeHandler:
  PRINT "Handler number",I%
  RETURN
```

ON/GOTO statement

Function ON/GOTO sends program flow to one of several possible destinations based on the value of a numeric expression.

Syntax `ON n GOTO label [,label] ...`

Remarks *n* is a numeric expression ranging from 0 to 255, and *label* identifies a statement in the program to branch to.

n determines which label is jumped to (for example, if $n = 4$, the fourth label in the list receives control). If *n* is 0 or greater than the number of labels in the list, Turbo Basic continues execution with the next statement in sequence.

The SELECT and IF block statements can perform multi-way branching with greater flexibility.

Example

```
FOR I% = 1 TO 3
  ON I% GOTO OneHandler, TwoHandler, ThreeHandler
Back:

NEXT I%

END          ' end main program

OneHandler:
  PRINT "Handler number",I%
  GOTO Back:

TwoHandler:
  PRINT "Handler number",I%
  GOTO Back:

ThreeHandler:
  PRINT "Handler number",I%
  GOTO Back:
```

ON KEY(n) statement

Function — ON KEY(*n*) declares the trap subroutine to get control if a specific key is pressed.

Synax — `ON KEY(n) GOSUB label`

Remarks — *label* identifies the first statement of the trap subroutine, and *n* is the trapped key, an integer expression from 1 to 25, 30, or 31, according to the following:

n	Key
1–10	Function keys F1–F10
11	Cursor Up
12	Cursor Left
13	Cursor Right
14	Cursor Down
15–25	Keys defined by KEY statement
30	Function key F11
31	Function key F12

The ON KEY statement has no effect until key events are enabled by a KEY ON statement. Once a KEY ON statement has been executed, Turbo Basic checks between the execution of every subsequent statement to see if the specified key was pressed. If it was, Turbo Basic performs a GOSUB to the designated subroutine.

The KEY(*n*) OFF statement turns off checking for key *n*. Use the KEY statement to define a key for trapping that isn't a function or cursor control key.

Use the $EVENT metastatement for fine control over Turbo Basic's generation of event-checking code.

See Also — $EVENT
KEY(*n*)

Example

```
' This program demonstrates the KEY(n) statement.

' turn key checking on
KEY ON

' assign strings to keys
KEY 1, "Hello" + CHR$(13)
KEY 2, "GoodBye" + CHR$(13)
KEY 10, CHR$(13)

' set up a key trap for F10 in addition
' to assigning a string to it.
```

```
ON KEY(10) GOSUB GoodBye

'  turn F10 trapping on
KEY(10) ON

' get user input
INPUT "Press F1: ";Dummy$
INPUT "Press F2: ";Dummy$

PRINT "Press F10 now ..."

' when user presses F10 now, the GoodBye
' subroutine will be called
WHILE NOT INSTAT : WEND ' wait for the F10 key

END ' end the program

GoodBye:
  KEY LIST    ' list the current defined keys
  KEY(10) OFF    ' turn trapping off

  ' now when the user presses F10, the character
  ' string assigned to the key will be played back
  PRINT "Press F10 now to quit the program..."
  RETURN
```

ON PEN statement

Function ON PEN declares the trap subroutine to get control if light-pen activity occurs.

Syntax `ON PEN GOSUB label`

Remarks *label* identifies the first statement in the light-pen-handling subroutine.

The ON PEN statement has no effect until light-pen events are enabled by a PEN ON statement. Once a PEN ON statement has been executed, a check is made between the execution of every subsequent statement to see if the light pen was activated. If so, the designated subroutine is called.

The PEN OFF statement turns off light-pen checking.

After a light-pen trap, an implicit PEN STOP statement is executed to keep from calling the trap subroutine repetitively from within itself (and filling up the stack). The closing RETURN of the handling subroutine automatically performs a PEN ON unless the routine executes an explicit PEN OFF statement.

Use the $EVENT metastatement for finer control over Turbo Basic's generation of event-checking code.

See Also $EVENT
PEN

Example

```
ON PEN GOSUB PenHandler    ' set event handler

PEN ON          ' turn on event trapping

PRINT "Press any key to stop..."
WHILE NOT INSTAT
WEND

END             ' end the program

PenHandler:
  FOR I% = 1 TO 9
    PRINT PEN(I%)
  NEXT I%
  RETURN
```

ON PLAY statement

Function — ON PLAY declares the trap subroutine to get control if the background music buffer contains less than the specified number of notes.

Syntax — `ON PLAY(notecount) GOSUB label`

Remarks — *notecount* is an integer expression, and *label* identifies the first statement in the music-playing subroutine.

The ON PLAY statement has no effect until note checking is enabled by a PLAY ON statement. Once PLAY ON has been executed, Turbo Basic checks between the execution of every subsequent statement to see if the number of notes remaining to be played in the music buffer is less than *notecount*. If it is, Turbo Basic performs a GOSUB to the designated subroutine.

The PLAY OFF statement turns off music buffer checking.

After a music trap, an implicit PLAY STOP statement is executed to keep from calling the trap subroutine repetitively from within itself (and filling up the stack). The closing RETURN of the handling subroutine automatically performs a PLAY ON statement unless the routine has previously executed an explicit PLAY OFF statement.

A PLAY event is not trapped if the buffer is already empty when PLAY ON is executed.

Use the $EVENT metastatement to control the generation of event-checking code. Use the $SOUND metastatement to set the size of the background music buffer.

See Also — $EVENT
PLAY (statement)
$SOUND

Example

```
' This program demonstrates ON PLAY(n)


' allocate 30 bytes of sound buffer space
$SOUND 100

' turn sound event checking on
PLAY ON

' set up play buffer checking
ON PLAY(5) GOSUB FillPlayBuffer
```

```
Notes$ = "GEAGFDGFECFEDGGG"
' play octaves 2 through 4

PlayStr$ = "MB"
FOR Octave% = 2 TO 4
  Octave$ = "O" + STR$(Octave%)
  PlayStr$ = PlayStr$ + Octave$ + Notes$
NEXT Octave%

PLAY PlayStr$
DO
LOOP UNTIL INSTAT
CLEAR

END ' end the program

FillPlayBuffer:

  PRINT PlayStr$
  PLAY PlayStr$
  RETURN
```

ON STRIG statement

Function ON STRIG declares the trap subroutine for the joystick button.

Syntax `ON STRIG(n) GOSUB label`

Remarks *label* identifies the first statement in the "button-pressed" handling subroutine, and *n* is an integer expression indicating the button to be trapped, according to the following:

n	Button
0	Button 1, Joystick A
2	Button 1, Joystick B
4	Button 2, Joystick A
6	Button 2, Joystick B

The ON STRIG statement has no effect until joystick button events are enabled by a STRIG ON statement. Once STRIG ON has been executed, a check is made between the execution of every subsequent statement to see if the indicated button was pressed. If so, the designated subroutine is called.

STRIG OFF turns off checking for the indicated joystick button.

After a trap, an implicit STRIG STOP statement is executed to keep from calling the trap subroutine repetitively from within itself (and filling up the stack). The closing RETURN of the handling subroutine automatically performs a STRIG ON statement unless the routine has previously executed an explicit STRIG OFF statement.

Use the $EVENT metastatement to fine-tune the compiler's generation of event-checking code.

See Also $EVENT
STRIG(*n*)

Example

```
ZeroX = 1
ZeroY = 1
One2
TwoY = 1
FourX = 3
FourY = 1
SixX = 4
SixY = 1

' set event handlers
ON STRIG(0) GOSUB TriggerZero
ON STRIG(2) GOSUB TriggerTwo
ON STRIG(4) GOSUB TriggerFour
```

```
ON STRIG(6) GOSUB TriggerSix

' turn on event checking
STRIG(0) ON
STRIG(2) ON
STRIG(4) ON
STRIG(6) ON

' while a button isn't being pressed, display
' joystick's current coordinates
WHILE NOT INSTAT
  LOCATE 15,15,0
  PRINT STICK(0), STICK(1);
WEND

END     ' end the program

TriggerZero:
  LOCATE ZeroX, ZeroY
  PRINT "Button 1"
  LOCATE 15,15,0
  RETURN

TriggerTwo:
  LOCATE TwoX, TwoY
  PRINT "Button 2"
  LOCATE 15,15,0
  RETURN

TriggerFour:
  LOCATE FourX, FourY
  PRINT "Button 4"
  LOCATE 15,15,0
  RETURN

 TriggerSix:
   LOCATE SixX, SixY
   PRINT "Button 4"
   LOCATE 15,15,0
   RETURN
```

ON TIMER statement

Function ON TIMER declares the trap subroutine to get control every *n* seconds.

Syntax `ON TIMER(n) GOSUB label`

Remarks *label* identifies the first statement of the "time-elapsed" handling subroutine, and *n* is an integer expression indicating the number of seconds to wait, from 1 to 86,400 (24 hours).

The ON TIMER statement has no effect until time-checking is enabled by a TIMER ON statement. Once a TIMER ON statement has been executed, an internal seconds count begins and a check is made between the execution of every statement to see if the indicated number of seconds have elapsed. If so, the designated subroutine is called.

The TIMER OFF statement turns off time-checking.

After a trap, an implicit TIMER STOP statement is executed to keep from calling the trap subroutine repetitively from within itself (and filling up the stack). The closing RETURN of the handling subroutine automatically performs a TIMER ON statement unless the routine has previously executed an explicit TIMER OFF statement. This means that the seconds count is reset to zero after a timer trap.

Use the $EVENT metastatement to control the generation of event-checking code.

See Also $EVENT
TIMER

Example

```
ON TIMER(1) GOSUB DisplayTime ' set timer trap

' turn on timer event-checking
TIMER ON

' wait for a key to be pressed
WHILE NOT INSTAT : WEND

END ' end the program

DisplayTime:
  LOCATE 1,70
  PRINT TIME$;
  RETURN
```

OPEN statement

Function	OPEN prepares a file or device for reading or writing.
Syntax	`OPEN filespec [FOR mode] AS [#]filenum [LEN=record size]`

or

`OPEN mode string, [#]filenum,filespec [,record size]`

Remarks

mode is one of the following:

OUTPUT	Specifies a sequential file to be written to
INPUT	Specifies a sequential file to be read from
APPEND	Specifies a sequential file to be appended to
RANDOM	Specifies a random file for reading or writing
BINARY	Specifies a binary file for reading or writing

mode string is a string expression whose first (and usually only) character is one of the following:

O	Specifies sequential output mode
I	Specifies sequential input mode
A	Specifies sequential output mode at end of file
R	Specifies random input/output mode
B	Specifies binary input/output mode

filenum can be any integer value. Use DOS's FILES statement in a CONFIG.SYS file to increase or decrease this value. (See the DOS reference manual for more information.)

filespec is a string expression specifying the name of the file to be opened and, optionally, a drive and/or path specification.

record size is an integer expression ranging from 1 to 32,767, specifying the length in bytes of each record in a random access file. The default record size is 128 bytes.

The main function of OPEN is to associate a number (*filenum*) with a file or physical device and to prepare that device for reading and/or writing. This number is used, rather than its name, in every statement that refers to the file. Contained in the OPEN statement is information indicating the "mode" of the file; that is, the methods by which the file will be accessed: sequential (for input, output to a new file, or output to an existing file), random access, and binary. An OPEN statement is usually balanced by a matching CLOSE.

The two forms of the command differ only in the level of verbosity:

```
OPEN "myfile.dta" FOR OUTPUT AS #1
```

has the same effect as:

```
OPEN "O",#1,"myfile.dta"
```

OPEN Errors

Attempting to OPEN a file for INPUT that doesn't exist causes run-time error 53, File Not Found. If you try to OPEN a nonexistent file for OUTPUT, APPEND, random access, or BINARY operations, then it is created.

See Also OPEN COM

Example

```
' This program is divided into five procedures. The
' difference between each procedure is the mode
' in which the file is opened and the way the
' data in the file is manipulated.

DEF FN PForKey$(Msg$)
  PRINT Msg$, "Press any key to continue..."
  WHILE NOT INSTAT : WEND
  FN PForKey$ = INKEY$
END DEF    ' end procedure PForKey

SUB SequentialOutput
' The file is opened for sequential
' output and some data is written to it.

  KeyP$ = FNPForKey$("Now for some sequential output")

  ' open a sequential file for output
  OPEN "OPEN.DTA" FOR OUTPUT AS #1

  Integer% = 12345
  TempStr$ = "History is made at night."

  ' write the data to the sequential file
  WRITE# 1,TempStr$, Integer% * 2, TempStr$, Integer% \ 2

  CLOSE 1 ' close the file
END SUB    ' end procedure SequentialOutput

SUB SequentialAppend
' The file is opened for sequential
' output. However, the data in this case
' is added to the end of the file.

  KeyP$ = FNPForKey$("Now to append some more stuff")

  ' open a sequential file to append data to it
  OPEN "OPEN.DTA" FOR APPEND AS #1
```

```
  Integer% = 32123
  TempStr$ = "The best vision is insight--M.Forbes"

  ' append data
  WRITE# 1,TempStr$, Integer% * 0.2, TempStr$, Integer% \ 2

  CLOSE 1         ' close the file
  END SUB         ' end procedure SequentialAppend

SUB SequentialInput
' The file is opened for sequential input,
' and data that is read in is displayed
' to the screen.

  KeyP$ = FNPForKey$("Now to read it back")

  ' open a sequential file and read from it
  OPEN "OPEN.DTA" FOR INPUT AS #1

  ' read first line using LINE INPUT#
  LINE INPUT# 1,TempStr$
  PRINT TempStr$

  ' use INPUT$ to read the rest of the file
  ' a character at a time.
  TempStr$ = ""
  WHILE NOT EOF(1)  ' check if at end of file
   TempStr$ = TempStr$ + INPUT$(1,1)
  WEND
  PRINT TempStr$

  CLOSE 1                 ' close the file

  KeyP$ = FNPForKey$("")

END SUB   ' end procedure SequentialInput

SUB BinaryIO
' The file is opened for binary I/O.
' Data is read using GET$.
' SEEK explicitly moves the file pointer
' to the end of the file and you write
' the same data back to the file.

  KeyP$ = FNPForKey$("Now for binary input AND output")

  ' open a sequential file, read from it
  OPEN "OPEN.DTA" FOR BINARY AS #1

  TempStr$ = ""

  ' use GET$ to read data in and store
  ' it in a string
  WHILE NOT EOF(1)
    GET$ 1, 1, Char$
    TempStr$ = TempStr$ + Char$
  WEND

  PRINT TempStr$
```

```
  ' move the file pointer to the end of the file
  SEEK 1, LOF(1)

  ' PUT$ copies the data back into the binary file
  FOR I% = 1 TO LEN(TempStr$)
    PUT$ 1,MID$(TempStr$,I%,1)
  NEXT I%

  CLOSE 1     ' close the file

  KeyP$ = FNPForKey$("")

END SUB    ' end procedure BinaryIO

SUB RandomIO
' Open a file for random I/O. Use FIELD
' to declare a buffer to hold the data that
' is written and read. GET and PUT read and
' write the data. Note that before GET
' is performed, LSET or RSET are used to
' store the data in the file's buffer.

  KeyP$ = FNPForKey$("Now for some random I/O")

  ' open a random access file
  OPEN "OPEN.DTA" AS #1 LEN = 1

  FIELD 1, 1 AS Char$     ' define a 1-byte buffer

  TempStr$ = ""
  TempSize% = LOF(1)      ' save file size

  ' using GET, read in the entire file
  FOR I% = 1 TO TempSize%
    GET 1,I%
    TempStr$ = TempStr$ + Char$ ' store data
  NEXT I%

  ' PUT copies the data in reverse into
  ' the random file
  FOR I% = LEN(TempStr$) TO 1 STEP -1
    LSET Char$ = MID$(TempStr$,I%,1)
    PUT 1,LOF(1)  ' put at end of file
  NEXT I%

  CLOSE 1     ' close the file

END SUB       ' end procedure RandomIO

' begin body of the main program

CALL SequentialOutput
CALL SequentialAppend
CALL SequentialInput
CALL BinaryIO
CALL RandomIO

END       ' end the program
```

OPEN COM statement

Function OPEN COM opens and configures a communications port.

Syntax

```
OPEN "COMn: [baud] [,parity][,data][,stop][options]"
AS [#]filenum [LEN=num]
```

Remarks *n* indicates the serial port to be opened. *baud* is an integer constant specifying the communications rate: Valid rates are 75, 110, 150, 300, 600, 1200, 1800, 2400, 4800, and 9600 (the default is 300).

parity is a single character specifying parity status according to the following:

S	Space parity (parity bit always 0)
O	Odd parity
M	Mark parity (parity bit always 1)
E	Even parity
N	No parity (ignored on received characters and omitted on transmitted characters)

The default is even parity.

data is an integer constant from 5 to 8 specifying the number of stop bits. The default is 7.

stop is an integer constant from 1 to 2 specifying the number of data bits. The default is a 1-stop bit (for baud rates 75 and 110, it is 2).

filenum is an integer expression and specifies the numeric handle through which you access the communications port.

num is the maximum number of bytes that can be read from or written to the communications port; the default is 128. This value cannot be greater than the size of the buffer for that port, which is set with the $COM metastatement.

The OPEN COM statement includes an option block that controls status-line handling, parity, and carriage-return/line-feed processing.

```
options = [,RS] [,CS[msec]] [,DS[msec]] [,CD[msec]] [,LF] [,PE]
```

RS suppresses the RTS line. CS[*msec*] controls CTS. DS[*msec*] controls DSR. CD[*msec*] controls CD. LF causes a line-feed character to be appended to every carriage-return character. PE turns on parity checking.

The *msec* argument of the CS, DS, and CD options can range from 0 to 65,535 and specifies how many milliseconds Turbo Basic will wait before returning a Device Timeout error. If it is 0 or omitted, then no line-status checking is performed. The default for *msec* is 1,000 for CS and DS, and 0 for CD.

See Also

COM
$COM
ON COM

Example

```
' allocate a string array to store input
DIM ComPortInput$(1)

$COM1 1024     ' set up a 1K input buffer

OPEN "COM1:300,n,8,1,DS,RS,CS,CD" AS #1 LEN = 1

PRINT "Press any key to terminate the program..."
WHILE NOT INSTAT ' while a key hasn't been pressed
  ' if there is any input available
  IF LOF(1) > 0 THEN
    ' read any info available in the com port buffer
    ComPortInput$(0) = INPUT$(LOF(1), #1)
    ' display input
    PRINT "COM Port input: "; ComPortInput$(0)
  END IF
WEND

END          ' end of program
```

OPTION BASE statement

Function OPTION BASE sets minimum value for array subscripts.

Syntax `OPTION BASE` *`integer expression`*

Remarks *integer expression* can range from 0 to 32,767.

OPTION BASE controls what subscript value references the first element of array variables. For example, after OPTION BASE 1, declaring array *x* with the statement

```
DIM x(20)
```

sets aside memory for 20 elements (1 through 20), rather than the default 21 (0 through 20).

Although you can use OPTION BASE to control subscript ranges, Turbo Basic offers a more powerful method via the DIM statement.

See Also DIM

Example

```
' allocate an array of three integers
DIM FirstArray%(2)

' set the starting index of any declared arrays
OPTION BASE 1

' allocate an array of two integers
DIM SecndArray%(2)

FOR I% = 0 TO 2
  ' no zero index; check for zero
  IF I% > 0 THEN
    SecndArray%(I%) = I%
  END IF
    FirstArray%(I%) = I%
NEXT I%

FOR I% = 0 TO 2
  ' no zero index; check for zero
  IF I% > 0 THEN
    PRINT SecndArray%(I%)
  END IF
  PRINT FirstArray%(I%)
NEXT I%

END     ' end the program
```

OUT statement

Function OUT writes to an I/O port.

Syntax `OUT portno,integer expression`

Remarks OUT sends a byte value (0 to 255) to hardware output port *portno*, where *portno* is an integer expression from 0 to 65,535.

OUT is necessary for controlling various hardware subsystems, such as a communications or video adapter. Used improperly, OUT can easily crash a system.

Example

```
' The program makes the speaker shriek
' by reading the status register and
' toggling (on and off) the bits
' that control the speaker.

' read value in port 61 Hex
StatusReg% = INP(&H61)
StatusReg% = StatusReg% AND &H00FC
' mask the value read in

' make the tone long enough to hear
FOR J = 1 to 1000
  StatusReg% = StatusReg% XOR 2  ' toggle speaker
  OUT &H61,StatusReg%            ' output new status
  delay .001
NEXT J

END
```

PAINT statement

Function PAINT fills an enclosed area on the graphics screen with a selected color.

Syntax `PAINT (x,y) [[,color] [,boundary] [,background]]`

Remarks (*x*,*y*) specify a seed point in an enclosed area to be filled. If the seed point is within the enclosed area, then the inside will be filled. If the seed is outside the enclosed area, then the exterior will be filled.

color can be either a numeric or string expression. If it is numeric, it specifies the attribute (color) to fill with. If it is string, then it contains mask information that causes the area to be filled with a pattern rather than a solid color. If you do not specify color, then the foreground color is used.

boundary is the border color of the figure you are filling. PAINT stops the filling whenever it encounters the boundary color.

background is an optional string mask used when you want to repaint areas. The background mask is a tile slice to skip when checking for already filled areas.

The PAINT statement can fill any enclosed shape, no matter how complex. Turbo Basic chooses a byte to be plotted using the formula

y mod tile length

Make sure the region to be filled is fully enclosed, because if the fill "leaks," your entire picture may be ruined.

If argument *color* is numeric, then PAINT fills the shape with the indicated color, stopping at pixels of attribute *boundary* or attribute *color*.

If *color* is a string expression, then *tiling* is used to define a pattern the area is to be filled with. The pattern represented by string *color* arguments is 1-byte wide (representing 4 pixels in medium resolution and 8 pixels in high resolution mode), and from 1 to 64 bytes long (representing 1 to 64 scan lines vertically).

When tiling, *color* must be formatted like so:

```
CHR$(&Hnn) + CHR$(&Hnn)...
```

The mask is based on the underlying bit values of *color*, with the first character representing the first line of the pattern, the second character the second line of the pattern, and so on.

For example, the following pattern represents a checkerboard pattern (50 percent gray scale) in high resolution mode:

```
10101010  (first byte)
01010101  (second byte)
```

To fill an area with this checkerboard, build a string with the appropriate mask information. First convert the binary form to hex:

```
10101010 = &HAA
01010101 = &H55
```

Now construct a two-character string using CHR$:

```
pattern$ = CHR$(&HAA) + CHR$(&H55)
```

Now the statement

```
PAINT (50,50),pattern$
```

fills with gray (checkerboard) paint.

Background is used to define the stop condition when filling an already patterned area. If the fill operation hits a pixel that agrees with the corresponding bit in *background*, then the fill doesn't stop, even if that pixel has color *boundary*.

When tiling, the number of color attributes in each screen mode determines how a screen's pattern is designed. Remember that the number of bits per pixel correlates to the number of color attributes in any given screen mode. You can use the following formula to calculate the number of bits per pixel:

$$LOG_2(X) = Y$$

where X equals the total color attributes of your screen and Y equals the number of bits per pixel.

Tiling SCREEN 1

In medium resolution, using the preceding formula, X equals 4 pixels (which are represented by 1 medium resolution tile byte) and thus Y equals 2 bits per pixel. Since each pixel has a corresponding color attribute, it will take 2 bits of the tile byte to describe 1 out of the 4 attributes.

The following table shows the decimal and hexadecimal values that correspond to each attribute:

Color Palette	Attribute in binary	Pattern in binary	Pattern in hex
0			
green	01	01010101	&H55
red	10	10101010	&HAA
brown	11	11111111	&HFF
1			
cyan	01	01010101	&H55
magenta	10	10101010	&HAA
white	11	11111111	&HFF

Tiling SCREEN 2

There is 1 bit per pixel in high resolution, allowing each tile to represent 8 pixels onscreen. Wherever the mask is valued at 1, a point is plotted. The string can contain up to 64 bytes.

The pattern is depicted in a consistent manner throughout the area defined by *boundary*. When *boundary* is undefined, the entire screen becomes patterned.

Tiling SCREENs 7, 8, 9, 10, 11, and 12

For these enhanced screen modes, the tile pattern is devised by a technique that stores and interprets the string as a stack of 8-bit units known collectively as a *bit plane*. Each screen mode needs 4 bit planes to define 1 tile byte, except mode 10, which requires 2 bit planes.

Example

```
' Here's how to use tile patterns
SCREEN 1: CLS
' define tile pattern for diagonal lines
TIL$=CHR$(&H40)+CHR$(&H40)+CHR$(&H10)+CHR$(&H10)+
    CHR$(4)+CHR$(4)+CHR$(1)+CHR$(1)
CIRCLE (100,100),50
PAINT (100,100),TIL$
' define checkerboard tile pattern
TIL2$=CHR$(&HAA)+CHR$(&HAA)+CHR$(&H80)+CHR$(&H80)+
     CHR$(&H80)+CHR$(&H80)+CHR$(&H80)+CHR$(&H80)
CIRCLE (225,100),50
PAINT (225,100),TIL2$
```

PALETTE, PALETTE USING statements

Function PALETTE and PALETTE USING allow you to change one or more colors in the palette. (To use these statements you must have an Enhanced Graphics Adapter (EGA) or a Video Graphics Array Adapter (VGA).)

Syntax

```
PALETTE[attribute,color]
PALETTE USING integer array name(array index)
```

Remarks *attribute* represents a color in the palette. *color* is an actual display color that replaces the *attribute* in the palette. The *color* displayed on your screen depends on the screen mode setting and hardware display (see the SCREEN statement).

The PALETTE statement allows you to change text or graphics with a color currently on the screen and that change also affects any subsequent text and graphics. This is a handy feature that saves you from redrawing text or graphics if you just want to change a color (see the example section).

PALETTE also lets you map color numbers greater than 15 into the palette. You can even display text invisibly against a background color, and then change the palette for the text color to make it suddenly become visible.

If no arguments are specified in the PALETTE statement, the palette is set to the predefined default colors.

The PALETTE USING statement lets you modify all of your palette entries in a single statement. *integer array name* names the array. When setting your palette, use *array index* to indicate the index of the first array element in the array. (The majority of the time you will specify 0 as the array index.) Make sure you dimension the integer array large enough to fit all sixteen palette entries after *array index*. Any *attribute* in the palette is paired with a *color* from the integer array.

Using a color argument of −1 in an array entry effects no change in the paired *attribute*; however, all other negative values for color are illegal.

Following is a list of attribute and color ranges for different screen modes and monitors:

Table 5-1 Color and Attribute Ranges

Mode	Monitor	Attribute Range	Color Range
0	Mono/EGA	0–15	0–2
	Color/EGA	0–31	0–15
1	Color/EGA	0–3	0–15
2	Color/EGA	0–1	0–15
7	Color/EGA	0–15	0–15
8	Color/EGA	0–15	0–15
9	EGA (64K)	0–3	0–15
	EGA (>64K)	0–15	0–63
10	Mono/EGA	0–3	0–8
11	MCGA/VGA	0–1	0–1
12	VGA	0–15	0–15

Mono = Monochrome
EGA = IBM Enhanced Graphics Adapter
VGA = Video Graphics Array Adapter
MCGA = Multi-Color Graphics Array Adapter

Restrictions

The PALETTE and PALETTE USING statements require an Enhanced Graphics Adapter.

See Also

COLOR
DRAW
SCREEN

Example

```
' the following shows how to use PALETTE
' to change the color of graphics (and text)
' without having to redraw or redisplay the graphics

SCREEN 8       ' set EGA 640x200 16 color mode
PALETTE        ' set default EGA palette colors
LINE (10,10)-(630,190),1,BF  ' draw a box, fill it with blue
DO
  FOR I% = 2 TO 14
    PALETTE 1,I%   ' change the box color from blue
    DELAY .2       ' delay, so you can see the change
  NEXT I%
LOOP UNTIL INSTAT  ' do it until a key is pressed
END
```

PEEK function

Function PEEK returns the byte stored at the specified memory location.

Syntax

```
y = PEEK(offset)
```

Remarks *offset* is a numeric expression from 0 to 65,535, representing the 16-bit offset into the current segment set by the most recent DEF SEG statement. The value returned can range from 0 to 255.

PEEK and the complementary POKE statement are low-level escapes from Turbo Basic's defined uses for memory. One application for PEEK and POKE is in forming byte arrays for applications that don't require the full −32,768 to 32,767 range of integer arrays.

See Also DEF SEG
POKE

Example

```
DIM Array%(5)   ' allocate an array of 6 integers

DEF SEG = VARSEG(Array%(0))

' using POKE, initialize the array
FOR I% = 0 TO 11
  POKE I%, &HFF
NEXT I%

' using PEEK, display the contents of the array
FOR I% = 0 TO 11
  PRINT HEX$(PEEK(I%))
NEXT I%

END       ' end the program
```

PEN function

Function PEN reads light-pen status.

Syntax `y = PEN(option)`

Remarks *option* is a numeric option that controls the information returned by PEN, according to the following:

Option	Effect
0	Pen down since last check? (−1 = yes; 0 = no)
1	*x* coordinate where pen last activated
2	*y* coordinate where pen last activated
3	Current switch value (−1 = down; 0 = up)
4	Most recent *x* coordinate
5	Most recent *y* coordinate
6	Row where pen last activated (1–24)
7	Column where pen last activated (1–80)
8	Most recent row (1–24)
9	Most recent column (1–80)

The light pen must be turned on with PEN ON before performing any PEN function requests.

Example

```
ON PEN GOSUB PenHandler   ' set up the event handler

PEN ON        ' turn on event trapping

PRINT "Press any key to stop..."
WHILE NOT INSTAT
WEND

END          ' end the program

PenHandler:
  FOR I% = 1 TO 9
    PRINT PEN(I%)
  NEXT I%
  RETURN
```

PEN statement

Function — PEN controls the checking of light-pen events.

Syntax — `PEN {ON|OFF|STOP}`

Remarks — The PEN statement controls the checking of light-pen events. The light pen must be turned on with PEN ON before performing any PEN function requests. Executing PEN ON also enables trapping of light-pen events by the routine indicated in an ON PEN statement.

PEN OFF disables the PEN function and turns off pen-event checking.

PEN STOP turns off pen-event trapping, but remembers pen events so that if PEN ON is later issued, a trap occurs immediately.

See Also — ON PEN

Example

```
' This program demonstrates
' the PEN ON statement

ON PEN GOSUB PenHandler
' set up event handler

PEN ON     ' turn on event trapping

PRINT "Press any key to stop..."
WHILE NOT INSTAT
WEND

END        ' end the program

PenHandler:
  FOR I% = 1 TO 9
    PRINT PEN(I%)
  NEXT I%
  RETURN
```

PLAY function

Function — PLAY returns the number of notes in the background music buffer.

Syntax — `y = PLAY(x)`

Remarks — *x* is a dummy numeric argument.

PLAY returns the number of notes in the background music buffer waiting to be played. If music is being played in the foreground or not at all, PLAY returns 0.

See Also — $SOUND

Example

```
' Play do-re-mi-fa-sol
' and count notes remaining
PLAY "MB CDEFG"
Again:
  n = PLAY(1)  ' could be PLAY(anything)
  PRINT n "notes left in buffer"
  IF n = 0 THEN PRINT "Buffer Empty" : END
GOTO Again
```

PLAY statement

Function PLAY creates music.

Syntax `PLAY string expression`

Remarks PLAY is an interpretive mini-language that does for music what DRAW does for graphics. PLAY allows you to define musical passages as a sequence of characters in a string expression and to play them through the computer's speaker.

There are 84 notes available, corresponding to most of the keys on a piano from three octaves below middle *C* to one note less than four octaves above middle *C*. A note may be represented by its numeric value (1–84), or by a written description (that is, *A* through *G* with sharps and flats and octave information).

For example, PLAY "N44" plays note 44, *G* above middle *C*. PLAY "O3G" plays *G* in octave 3 (the same note).

Music definition statements may be grouped into lengthy command sequences:

```
PLAY "O3FGA"
```

plays three notes (*F*, *G*, and *A*) in octave 3. Spaces are ignored by the music interpreter, and should be used to clarify the structure of the command string.

The Commands

The following one- and two-character commands make up the PLAY language:

note-letter [{#|+|−}]

Plays note *note-letter*; *note-letter* is a letter from *A* through *G* (case is insignificant). Including an optional sharp (# or +) or flat (−) modifier after *note-letter* selects the equivalent of a black key on a piano. You cannot sharp or flat a note to obtain a white key result; for example, "*F*−" is invalid.

Nn

Plays note *n*, where *n* is the numeric representation of a note from 1 to 84. Note 1 is the lowest *C* on a piano; 84 the highest *B*. Middle *C* is note 37. Note 0 produces no sound, and can be used as a rest.

On

Selects octave *n*, where *n* is 0 to 6. Each octave begins with *C* and ends with *B*. Middle *C* is the first note of octave 3. The default is octave 4.

>n

Advances the current octave by 1 and plays note *n*. If the octave is 6 (the highest octave), it stays at 6.

<n

Decrements the current octave and plays note *n*. If the octave is 0 (the lowest octave), it stays at 0.

Ln

Sets the duration of notes to follow, according to the following:

L1	Whole note
L2	Half note
L4	Quarter note
L8	Eighth note
L16	Sixteenth note
.	
.	
.	
L64	Sixty-fourth note

In-between values are acceptable (L5 is a valid duration statement). The largest permissible value for *n* is 64.

Pn

Pauses for *n* beats (where *n* represents the period of time specified in the most recent *L* command).

Placing a period after a note causes that note to play for one and a half times its normal value. For example, a dotted quarter note has the combined duration of a quarter note and an eighth note. More than one dot can be used. A second dot acts on the note-dot pair as a whole; for example, a double dotted quarter note plays for 1.5 * (1.5 * 1/4) beat. Dots can also adjust the length of a pause.

Tn

Sets the tempo, where *n* is the number of quarter notes in a minute, and can range from 32 to 255. The default is 120.

MF

"Music Foreground" causes music created by PLAY to run in the foreground (that is, the next statement in your program will not be executed until this one is finished).

MB

"Music Background" causes music to keep playing even while your program is off doing something else. By default, Turbo Basic has a 32-note buffer for background playing, and this can be expanded by the $SOUND metastatement. Also look at the PLAY ON and ON PLAY statements, which are able to periodically inspect the progress of a Music Background song and add new notes as needed.

MN/ML/MS

Depending on this setting, notes can last either three-fourths of the time specified by *L* (MS: "Music Staccato"), seven-eighths of the time specified by *L* (MN: "Music Normal"), or all of the time specified by *L* (ML: "Music Legato").

X VARPTR$(string variable) (execute substring)

The *X* (execute) command allows you to insert a substring into a PLAY statement as a musical subroutine; for example:

```
a$ = "C D E" : PLAY "E D E X" + VARPTR$(a$)
```

plays notes *E*, *D*, *E*, *C*, *D*, and *E*, in that order.

Variable Arguments

In each PLAY command, the argument can be a constant value or it can be specified in the form =VARPTR$(*variable*), where *variable* is a numeric variable. **Note:** Interpretive BASIC allows you to specify variable names within the play string. For example, PLAY "T=x;" sets the tempo to the contents of variable *x*. Although it would be nice if it did, this doesn't work in Turbo Basic because the name information associated with variable *x* isn't around at run-time. Instead, you must use the VARPTR$ technique described earlier.

See Also

ON PLAY
PLAY ON
$SOUND

Example

```
firstline$ = "O3 L4 C L2 E E L8 E L4 E E D C F L1 <A"
secondline$ = "O3 L8 C C C L4 E D L2 <A L4 A L1 >C"
thirdline$ = "L4 C L10 F F. F L1 E"
PLAY "T150"          ' speed up tempo
FOR n = 1 TO 4
  PLAY firstline$
NEXT n
PLAY secondline$ + thirdline$
```

PMAP function

Function PMAP translates physical coordinates to world coordinates and vice versa.

Syntax `y = PMAP(x,option)`

Remarks *x* is the coordinate of the point to be mapped, and *option* is an integer expression from 0 to 3 that controls the PMAP function according to the following:

Option	Effect
0	Map world coordinate *x* to physical coordinate *x*.
1	Map world coordinate *y* to physical coordinate *y*.
2	Map physical coordinate *x* to world coordinate *x*.
3	Map physical coordinate *y* to world coordinate *y*.

PMAP does the scaling specified by the most recent WINDOW statement without putting anything on the screen.

See Also WINDOW

Example

```
' switch to medium resolution graphics mode
SCREEN 1

' define a cartesian origin-in-the-middle kind
' of screen with a generous range of x
' and y values that get larger as you move up
' instead of down.

 WINDOW (-1000,1000) - (1000, -1000)

' PMAP can now do "plot-free" scaling between
' the cartesian screen and physical pixels

PSET (PMAP(0,0), PMAP(0,1)), 2
PSET (PMAP(50,2), PMAP(50,3)), 2
PRINT PMAP(0,0), PMAP(0,1), PMAP(50,2), PMAP(50,3)

END             ' end the program
```

POINT function

Function POINT returns the color of a pixel or LPR information.

Syntax First form:

```
color = POINT (x,y)
```

Second Form:

```
y = POINT (option)
```

Remarks In the first form, (*x*,*y*) specify the coordinates of a medium or high resolution graphics pixel. POINT returns the attribute value (color) of the pixel at (*x*,*y*). If either *x* or *y* is out of range, POINT returns −1.

In the second form, *option* is a numeric variable or expression and controls the effect of POINT, according to the following:

Option	Effect
0	Returns current physical *x* coordinate
1	Returns current physical *y* coordinate
2	Returns current world *x* coordinate
3	Returns current world *y* coordinate

The first form of POINT is useful for simple pixel-at-a-time animation. Use POINT to read the color of a background pixel about to be overwritten into a temporary variable. Then PSET the point to the color of the moving object. Finally, to erase the point, return it to its initial color.

See Also PSET

Example

```
' switch to medium resolution graphics mode
SCREEN 1

CIRCLE (160, 100), 50, 2  ' display a circle

' put a dot in the middle of the circle
PSET (160, 100), 1

' display the dot's color and position
PRINT POINT(160, 100)
PRINT POINT(0), POINT(1)

END           ' end the program
```

POKE statement

Function POKE writes a byte to a specified address.

Syntax `POKE offset,value`

Remarks *offset* is the address, a numeric value ranging from 0 to 65,535. *value* is the byte value to be written to that address, ranging from 0 to 255. *offset* is relative to the segment defined by the most recent DEF SEG statement.

POKE writes byte-sized values to the indicated address, and is a low-level escape from Turbo Basic's normal use of memory. Since POKE performs no error checking, it isn't difficult to crash DOS and/or your program by improper use of this command.

See Also PEEK

Example

```
DIM Array%(5)   ' allocate array of 6 integers

DEF SEG = VARSEG(Array%(0))

' using POKE initialize the array
FOR I% = 0 TO 11
  POKE I%, &HFF
NEXT I%

' using PEEK display array contents
FOR I% = 0 TO 11
  PRINT HEX$(PEEK(I%))
NEXT I%

END             ' end the program
```

POS function

Function POS returns the cursor horizontal position (column number).

Syntax `y = POS(x)`

Remarks *x* is a dummy numeric argument. The value returned by POS ranges from 1 to 80 and represents the horizontal position (column number) of the cursor. Use the CSRLIN function to get the vertical position (row number).

Use the LOCATE statement to move and hide the cursor.

See Also CSRLIN
LOCATE
LPOS

Example

```
' set up the event handler
ON TIMER(1) GOSUB DisplayClock

' turn on event trapping
TIMER ON

' while a key has not been pressed
PRINT "Press any key to stop..."
WHILE NOT INSTAT
WEND

END                ' end the program

DisplayCLock:
  OldX% = POS
  OldY% = CSRLIN
  LOCATE 1,72, 1
  PRINT TIME$
  LOCATE OldY%, OldX%, 1
  RETURN
```

PRESET statement

Function PRESET plots a point on the graphics screen.

Syntax `PRESET (x,y) [,color]`

Remarks (*x*,*y*) are the coordinates of the point to plot on the graphics screen and can be given in either absolute or relative form. *color* is an integer expression defining the color the point should have. Normal mode restrictions apply for the color attribute. Refer to the PALETTE statement for valid attribute ranges in each screen mode.

If a color is specified, PRESET and its complementary command PSET operate identically. The difference between the two is that PRESET has a default color value of 0 (the background color), while PSET defaults to the maximum allowable attribute value for the mode you are in. In other words, without color arguments, PSET turns on pixels and PRESET turns them off.

See Also PSET

Example

```
' switch to medium resolution graphics mode
SCREEN 1

FOR I% = 0 TO 359
  FOR J% = 0 TO 199
    DELAY 0.01
    PSET (I%, J%)
  NEXT J%
NEXT I%

FOR I% = 0 TO 359
  FOR J% = 0 TO 199
    DELAY 0.01
    PRESET (I%, J%)
  NEXT J%
NEXT I%

END          ' end the program
```

PRINT statement

Function PRINT sends data to the screen.

Syntax `PRINT [expression list] [;]`

Remarks *expression list* is a series of numeric and/or string expressions separated by semicolons, blanks, or commas. If *expression list* doesn't end with a semicolon, Turbo Basic outputs a carriage return after the information in *expression list*. If *expression list* is omitted, PRINT outputs only the carriage return.

PRINT uses the punctuation separating the items in its *expression list* to determine where to put things on the screen.

Print Zones

For quick and tidy output, Turbo Basic divides the screen into "print zones" of 14 columns each. Using a comma between items in the *expression list* causes each to be printed at the beginning of the next zone.

A semicolon or space between elements causes each item to be printed next to the previous one, without regard for print zones.

If a PRINT statement is terminated with a comma, semicolon, or SPC or TAB function, the next PRINT statement will output to the same line. Otherwise, the next PRINT statement starts at the left-most column of the next line.

Numeric values are always followed by a space. Positive numbers are also preceded by a space; negative numbers by a minus sign.

The PRINT statement can be abbreviated as a question mark (a typing aid of dubious merit dating from interpretive days of yore):

```
? "Hello"
```

is the same as

```
PRINT "Hello"
```

See Also LPRINT
LPRINT USING
PRINT USING
SPC
TAB

Example

```
N = 2
PRINT "Strings and numbers are" N " of the";
PRINT "things you can PRINT"

' commas as delimiters put data into
' 14-column print zones
A = 1
B = 2
C = 3
PRINT A, B, C, "Text"

' spaces or semicolons as delimiters
' print data flush
PRINT A; B; C; "Text"

END            ' end the program
```

PRINT # and PRINT # USING statements

Function — PRINT # and PRINT # USING write formatted information to a file.

Syntax — `PRINT #filenum, [USING format string;] expression list [;]`

Remarks — *filenum* is the value under which the file was opened. *format string* is an optional sequence of formatting characters (described in the PRINT USING statement). *expression list* is a series of numeric and/or string expressions to be output to the file.

PRINT # sends data to a file exactly like PRINT sends it to the screen. So if you're not careful, you can waste a lot of disk space with unnecessary spaces, or worse, put fields so close together that you can't tell them apart when they are later INPUT #. For example:

```
PRINT #1 1,2,3
```

sends

```
1             2             3
```

to file #1. Because of the 14-column print zones between characters, superfluous spaces are sent to the file. On the other hand,

```
PRINT #1 1;2;3
```

sends

```
1  2  3
```

to the file, and you can't read the separate numeric values from this record because INPUT # requires commas as delimiters. The surest way to delimit fields is to put a comma between each field, like so:

```
PRINT #1, 1 "," 2 "," 3
```

writes

```
1 , 2 , 3
```

to the file, a packet that wastes the least possible space and is easy to read with an INPUT # statement. The WRITE # statement delimits fields with commas automatically.

Example

```
SUB MakeFile

' INPUT # opens a sequential file for output.
' Using WRITE #, it writes lines of different
' types of data to the file.

' assign the file variable to #1
OPEN "INPUT#.DTA" FOR OUTPUT AS #1

' define some variables and initialize them
StringVariable$ = "I'll be back."
Integer% = 1000
FloatingPoint! = 30000.1234

' write a line of text to the sequential file
WRITE# 1, StringVariable$, Integer%, FloatingPoint!

CLOSE 1          ' close file variable

END SUB           ' end procedure MakeFile

SUB ReadFile
' This procedure opens a sequential file
' for input. Using INPUT #, it reads
' lines of different types of data
' from the file.

' assign the file variable to #1
OPEN "INPUT#.DTA" FOR INPUT AS #1

StringVariable$ = ""  ' define some
Integer% = 0          ' variables and
FloatingPoint! = 0    ' initialize them

' read a line of text from the
' sequential file
INPUT# 1, StringVariable$, Integer%, FloatingPoint!

PRINT StringVariable$, Integer%, FloatingPoint!

CLOSE #1   ' close file variable

END SUB      ' end procedure ReadFile

CALL MakeFile
CALL ReadFile

END          ' end the program
```

PRINT USING statement

Function PRINT USING sends formatted information to the screen.

Syntax `PRINT USING` *`format string; expression list`* `[;]`

Remarks *format string* is a string constant or variable that describes how to format the information in *expression list*. *expression list* is the string or numeric information to be printed, separated by commas, spaces, or semicolons. PRINT USING ignores the punctuation in *expression list*.

Formatting String Fields

To print the first *n* characters of a string: If the format string consists of backslashes (\) enclosing zero or more spaces, then Turbo Basic prints as many characters of the output string as the format string is long (including the backslashes). For example, if the format string is "\\" (no spaces, length = 2), then two characters are printed; for "\ \" (two spaces, length = 4), four characters are printed.

```
a$ = "cats and dogs"
PRINT USING "\ \"; a$ : PRINT USING "\\"; a$
```

A format string of "!" causes PRINT USING to output exactly one character of an output string:

```
a$ = "cats and dogs"
PRINT USING "!"; a$
```

To print all of a string, use an ampersand (&) as the format string:

```
a$ = "cats and dogs"
PRINT USING "&"; a$
```

Formatting Numbers

Number signs (#) in the format string represent the digits of a number. Decimal points and other special characters (for example, dollar signs) are then placed appropriately to indicate the formatting, such as the number of digits to the right of the decimal point. For example:

```
PRINT USING "##.##"; 3.14159, .01032

PRINT USING "+##.##"; 12.0101, -6.2
(include sign before number)

PRINT USING "##.##-";  12.0101, -6.2
(include minus sign after number if negative)

PRINT USING "$$##.##"; 12.0101
(print a dollar sign flush with number)
```

```
PRINT USING "**##.##"; 12.0101
(fill leading spaces w/asterisks)

PRINT USING "**$##.##"; 12.0101
(combine the above)

PRINT USING "#####,.##"; 6666.66
(comma before decimal point means group by 3s)

PRINT USING "#.####^^^^"; 34567.12
(4 carets means use scientific notation)

PRINT USING "_###.##"; 12.1010
(underscore preceding a predefined formatting
character causes that character to be output
verbatim rather than be used for formatting
purposes)
```

If a value is too large to be printed in the specified format, a percent sign (%) is printed in front of it:

```
PRINT USING "#.#"; 27.4
```

PSET statement

Function PSET plots a point on the graphics screen.

Syntax `PSET (x,y) [,color]`

Remarks (*x*,*y*) are the coordinates of the point to plot on the graphics screen and can be given in either absolute or relative form. *color* is an integer expression that defines the color the point should have. Normal mode restrictions apply for the *color* attribute. In medium resolution, color values 0 through 3 are acceptable; in high resolution, 0 and 1 are the only possible color values.

If a color is specified, PSET and its complementary command PRESET operate identically. The difference between the two is that PRESET has a default color value of 0 (the background color), while PSET defaults to the maximum allowable attribute value (that is, 3 for medium resolution, 1 for high resolution). In other words, without color arguments, PSET turns on pixels and PRESET turns them off.

See Also POINT
PRESET

Example

```
' switch to medium resolution graphics mode
SCREEN 1

FOR I% = 0 TO 359
  FOR J% = 0 TO 199
    DELAY 0.01
    PSET (I%, J%)
  NEXT J%
NEXT I%

FOR I% = 0 TO 359
  FOR J% = 0 TO 199
    DELAY 0.01
    PRESET (I%, J%)
  NEXT J%
NEXT I%

END          ' end the program
```

PUT statement (files)

Function PUT writes a record to a random file.

Syntax `PUT [#] filenum [,record number]`

Remarks *filenum* is the value specified when the file was OPENed. *record number* is a numeric expression describing the record to be written, and can range from 1 to 16,777,216.

PUT is complementary to GET and writes one record to a random access file. *record number* is optional. If it is omitted, Turbo Basic uses the value used in the last PUT or GET statement plus 1.

Example

```
' open a random access file
OPEN "GET.DTA" AS #1 LEN = 18

' make two field definitions for each field element
FIELD #1, 2 AS Integer$, 4 AS LongInt$,_
          4 AS SinglePre$, 8 AS DoublePre$
FIELD #1, 2 AS A$, 4 AS B$, 4 AS C$, 8 AS D$

MaxInt% = 32767

FOR I% = 1 TO 5   ' write some data to the file
  ' convert data and assign to buffer
  ' before writing to data file
  LSET Integer$   = MKI$(I%)
  LSET LongInt$   = MKL$(I% + CLNG(MaxInt%))
  LSET SinglePre$ = MKS$(CSNG(I% * CSNG(MaxInt%)))
  LSET DoublePre$ = MKD$(MaxInt%^I%)
  PUT #1,I%
NEXT I%

FOR I% = 1 TO 5   ' read data from file
GET #1, I%        ' display it on screen
  PRINT CVI(A$), CVL(B$), CVS(C$), CVD(D$)
NEXT I%

CLOSE #1          ' close the file

END               ' end the program
```

PUT statement (graphics)

Function PUT plots the contents of a numeric array to the graphics screen.

Syntax `PUT (x,y), array [,option]`

Remarks (*x*,*y*) are the coordinates of the top left corner of the rectangle to which the array will be transferred; they can be specified in either absolute or relative form. *array* is a numeric array that contains the graphic data to place on the screen. *option* is one of the reserved words that follow, and controls how the information in *array* will be applied to what's already on the screen:

PUT Options	Effect
PSET	Map exact copy of image in array
PRESET	Map complementary copy of image in array
XOR	Perform XOR operation between array image and screen
OR	Perform OR operation between array image and screen
AND	Perform AND operation between array image and screen

The PSET option causes the data in the array to be put on the screen exactly as GET found it originally, without regard for what is there currently. PRESET maps a complementary image to the screen. For example, if the original data had attribute 3 at some pixel, the copy PUT to the screen with the PRESET attribute will have attribute 0 for that pixel and vice versa. Similarly, attribute 1 will be converted to attribute 2 and vice versa.

The AND, OR, and XOR options perform a logical operation between each pixel in the destination region and before the PUT and the data in the buffer array. When moving objects across complex backgrounds, the XOR option is especially useful; in fact, it is the default. The first PUT XOR draws the object to the screen; a second application in the same place restores the background to its previous condition.

The basic strategy behind animations based on GET and PUT is to

```
DRAW an object into a rectangular area
GET the object into an array
DO
  ERASE the object at its old location
  PUT the object at a new location
LOOP
```

Example

```
' allocate a buffer to store graphics' image
DIM Buffer%(143)

' switch to medium resolution graphics mode
SCREEN 1

CIRCLE (16,16),8,2              ' draw a circle

GET (0,0) - (31,31), Buffer%   ' get the circle

' copy it all over the screen
FOR I% = 0 TO 9
  PUT(I% * 32,100), Buffer%
NEXT I%

END                             ' end the program
```

PUT$ function

Function PUT$ writes a string to a binary mode file.

Syntax `PUT$ [#]filenum, string expression`

Remarks PUT$ writes the contents of *string expression* to file *filenum* at the SEEK file position for this file. File *filenum* must have been opened in BINARY mode.

See Also GET$
OPEN
SEEK

Example

```
OPEN "BASIC.DOC" FOR BINARY A$ 1
PUT$ #1, "BASIC compilers are 99% perspiration"
PUT$ #1, "and 1% inspiration."
CLOSE #1

END
```

RANDOMIZE statement

Function RANDOMIZE seeds the random number generator.

Syntax `RANDOMIZE [numeric expression]`

Remarks If *numeric expression* is omitted, program execution stops and the user is prompted for a seed value upon encountering the RANDOMIZE statement:

```
Random Number Seed?
```

About Random Numbers

Without reseeding, the values returned by the RND function aren't random at all; for a given seed value, the RND function always returns the same sequence of values. Without reseeding, a craps simulation will play out exactly the same way each time the program runs.

A convenient way to assure a unique run each time (assuming your program isn't run at exactly the same time every day) is to use the TIMER function to provide the seed value:

```
RANDOMIZE TIMER
```

Another technique uses the fine-resolution MTIMER (microtimer) statement to time the delay associated with a keypress at the start of the program. It then uses that value to seed the random number generator:

```
MTIMER
PRINT "Press any key to begin..."
WHILE NOT INSTAT : WEND
RANDOMIZE MTIMER
```

See Also RND

Example

```
' initialize the microtimer
MTIMER

PRINT "Press any key to begin..."

WHILE NOT INSTAT
WEND

Dummy$ = INKEY$
' seed the random number generator
RANDOMIZE MTIMER

FOR I% = 1 TO 5 STEP RND(1.5)
  PRINT I%
  IF INSTAT THEN STOP
NEXT I%
END    ' end the program
```

READ statement

Function: READ loads variables from DATA statement constants.

Syntax: `READ variable [,variable]...`

Remarks: *variable* is a numeric or string variable.

READ loads the indicated variable(s) from constants appearing after DATA statements.

At runtime, READ accesses DATA statement constants in the order in which they appear. The most common error associated with DATA statements and READing them is getting out of sync and attempting to load a string into a numeric variable. If this happens, a syntax error (run-time error 2) is issued.

You won't get an error if your program errs in the other direction; that is, if your program loads a numeric constant into a string variable.

If you try to READ more times than your program has constants, Turbo Basic produces run-time error 4, Out of Data.

The RESTORE statement lets you reread constants from the first or any specified DATA statement.

See Also: RESTORE

Example:

```
' This  program demonstrates
' the READ statement

SUB ProcessResults(StudentName$, StudentAverage%)
LOCAL Total%, Value%, I%
  Total% = 0
  READ StudentName$
  FOR I% = 1 TO 10
    READ Value%
    Total% = Total% + Value%
  NEXT I%
  StudentAverage% = Total%\10
END SUB

FOR Student% = 1 TO 3
  CALL ProcessResults(SName$, Average%)
  PRINT USING "&'s average is ###";SName$, Average%
NEXT Student%

END  ' end program

DATA W. Perry, 78, 65, 35, 79, 86, 93, 79, 85, 99, 96
DATA P. Watson, 98, 94, 70, 88, 99, 100, 75, 96, 100, 95
DATA M. Ciccone, 65, 59, 75, 82, 56, 79, 82, 76, 69, 89
```

REG function and statement

Function REG sets or returns a value in the register buffer.

Syntax Function:

```
y = REG(register)
```

Statement:

```
REG register,value
```

Remarks *register* indicates a processor register according to the following:

Number	Register
0	Flags
1	AX
2	BX
3	CX
4	DX
5	SI
6	DI
7	BP
8	DS
9	ES

If *register* is not in the range 0 through 9, run-time error 5 is generated, Illegal Function Call.

value is a numeric variable or expression in the range 0 to 65,535.

REG as a function returns the value of the selected element in the "register buffer." REG as a statement causes the selected element in the register buffer to be loaded with the indicated integer value.

Use REG to pass information to and from assembly language subroutines. The register buffer is loaded into the processor's registers just before an ABSOLUTE or an INTERRUPT call; it is saved back just after returning. At any given time, the buffer contains the state of the processor's registers as they existed at the completion of the most recent external subroutine.

Example

```
DEFINT a-z
DIM a(100)
DIM FillRoutine(10)

FillRoutine (0) = &HF2FC
FillRoutine (1) = &HCBAA

REG 1, -1
REG 3, 101 * 2
REG 9, VARSEG(a(0))
REG 6, VARPTR(a(0))

DEF SEG = VARSEG(FillRoutine(0))
PRINT a(1)
WHILE NOT INSTAT : WEND
FillAdr = VARPTR(FillRoutine(0))
CALL ABSOLUTE FillAdr '(REG)

PRINT a(1)
END
```

REM statement

Function REM delimits the programmer's remarks (comments).

Syntax

```
REM comment
```

Remarks *comment* is any sequence of characters. Unlike Interpretive BASIC's treatment of comments, Turbo Basic REMarks appear only in the source version of a program and consequently don't affect execution in any way.

Note: A comment can appear on a line with other statements, but it must be the last thing on that line. For example, the following won't work:

```
REM now add the numbers : a = b + c
```

because the compiler can't tell where the comment ends and the statement begins. This is right:

```
a = b + c : REM now add the numbers...
```

The single quotation mark (') is an alternative comment delimiter. When a single quote is used, a colon isn't necessary to separate the remark from the other statements on the same line.

Don't use a single quote to delimit comments after a DATA statement. Use :REM instead.

Comments are ignored by the compiler and take no space in object programs, so use them copiously.

Example

```
REM This program demonstrates the REM statement

PRINT "This program demonstrates the REM statement."

REM "END"

END

DATA 1, 2, 3, I'll be back! : REM comment
' Note that the single quote is not treated
' as a comment.
```

RESET statement

Function	RESET closes and flushes all disk files.
Syntax	`RESET`
Remarks	RESET is the same as a CLOSE statement with no arguments.

RESTORE statement

Function RESTORE allows DATA statement constants to be read again.

Syntax `RESTORE [label]`

Remarks *label* is optional and identifies the DATA statement that the next READ will access.

RESTORE causes Turbo Basic to reset its DATA statement counter so that when the next READ statement is encountered, the first item of the first (or indicated) statement is used again.

See Also READ

Example

```
' read some data and restore
' the data pointer
READ A$, B$
RESTORE

' read some more data
READ C$, D$

' display the data
PRINT A$, B$, C$, D$

' point the data pointer at first
' data after label
RESTORE MoreData

' read and display the data
READ A$, B$
PRINT A$, B$

END           ' end the program

' define some data
DATA CAT, DOG

MoreData:
  DATA MONKEY, GNU
```

RESUME statement

Function RESUME restarts execution after error handling.

Syntax `RESUME [{0|NEXT|label}]`

Remarks RESUME and RESUME 0 cause execution to resume at the statement that caused the error.

RESUME NEXT causes execution to resume with the statement directly following the one that caused the error.

RESUME *label* causes execution to resume at the code identified by *label*.

If a RESUME statement is encountered when the program isn't in an error-trapping routine, then run-time error 20 results, Resume Without Error.

Note: The ERL, RESUME, and RESUME NEXT statements cause the compiler to generate a 4-byte pointer for each statement in a program. Therefore, programmers concerned with the size of their generated code should take note. Using RESUME [Line #] generates a single jump instruction. ERL is normally used for debugging purposes so it is probably of little concern.

Example

```
' set the error trap
ON ERROR GOTO ErrorHandler

' this statement causes a run-time error
I# = LOG(-1)

PRINT "The error was trapped ..."

END

ErrorHandler:
  PRINT "Error" ERR " at " ERL
  RESUME NEXT
```

RETURN statement

Function — RETURN returns from the subroutine to the calling program.

Syntax — `RETURN [label]`

Remarks — *label* identifies a line you may optionally direct the flow to.

RETURN terminates the execution of a subroutine and passes control to the statement directly after the calling GOSUB.

The optional *label* is designed to facilitate returning from trap- and error-handling routines. RETURN *label* throws away the address at the top of the stack and performs a GOTO to the statement identified by *label*. In some versions of BASIC, this operation is performed by a POP and a GOTO.

Doing a RETURN without doing a GOSUB first will cause unexpected and difficult-to-track errors. We suggest that you turn Stack test on in the **O**ptions pull-down to catch these errors.

See Also — GOSUB
GOTO

Example — See GOSUB's example.

RIGHT$ function

Function	RIGHT$ returns the right-most *n* characters of the target string.
Syntax	`s$ = RIGHT$(string expression,n)`
Remarks	*n* is an integer expression specifying the number of characters in *string expression* to be returned; it must be in the range 0 to 32,767. RIGHT$ returns the indicated number of characters from its string argument, starting from the right and working left. If *n* is greater than the length of *string expression*, all of *string expression* is returned. If *n* is 0, RIGHT$ returns the null string.
See Also	LEFT$ MID$
Example	`RIGHT$("JOHN JONES",5)`

RMDIR statement

Function RMDIR removes the directory (like DOS's RMDIR command).

Syntax `RMDIR path`

Remarks *path* is a standard path description string.

RMDIR removes the directory indicated by *path*. This statement is the equivalent of DOS's RMDIR command (except that it can't be abbreviated). The same restrictions apply, namely that *path* specify a valid, empty directory. If the directory isn't empty, then run-time error 75 occurs, Path/File Access Error.

Example

```
' set up an error handler
ON ERROR GOTO ErrorHandler

INPUT "Enter the name of the directory to remove: ", D$

RMDIR D$        ' removes directory

END             ' end the program

ErrorHandler:
  PRINT "Error " ERR " at " ERADR
  RESUME NEXT
```

RND function

Function RND returns a random number.

Syntax

```
y = RND [(numeric expression)]
```

Remarks RND returns a random double-precision value between 0 and 1.

Numbers generated by RND aren't really random, but are the result of applying a pseudorandom transformation algorithm to a starting, or seed, value. Given the same seed, Turbo Basic's RND algorithm always produces the same chain of "random" numbers.

The performance of RND depends on the optional numeric value you supply as the argument. With no argument or with a positive argument, RND generates the next number in sequence based on its initial seed value.

With an argument of 0, RND repeats the last number generated.

A negative argument causes the random number generator to be reseeded, so that subsequent uses of RND with no argument or with a positive argument result in a new sequence of values.

In general, use RANDOMIZE TIMER once at the start of your program to produce a new sequence of values with the RND statement. Don't use 0 or negative value arguments with RND unless you are looking for the special effects caused by those values.

To produce random integers between 1 and *n*, inclusive, use this technique:

```
randomNo% = INT(RND * n) + 1
```

Better yet, create it as a function:

```
DEF FNRndInt% (x%) = INT(RND * x%) + 1
```

See Also RANDOMIZE

Example

```
FOR I! = 1 TO 10 STEP 1.34
  PRINT USING "###.##^^^^";RND(I!)
NEXT I!
END
```

RSET statement

Function RSET moves string data into the random file buffer.

Syntax `RSET` *`field variable = string expression`*

Remarks RSET and LSET both move string data into "field variables" that have been defined in a previous FIELD statement as belonging to the buffer of a random file.

If the length of *string expression* is less than the size of *field variable* specified in a FIELD statement, RSET right-justifies this field by padding it with spaces. This means that spaces are inserted before the first character of *string expression* so that after the RSET operation LEN(*field variable*) still equals the width defined in the associated FIELD statement.

LSET does left-justification with space padding (spaces are appended after the last character of *string expression*).

RSET can also be used to format output to the screen or printer:

```
a$ = space$(20)
RSET a$ = "Right-just"
PRINT a$
```

See Also LSET

Example

```
OPEN "RSET.DTA" AS #1 LEN = 18

' define files' field names and sizes
FIELD 1,2 AS FileInt$, 4 AS FileLong$,_
        4 AS FileSngl$, 8 AS FileDbl$

' assign some values to the fields and
' write the record to the random access file
FOR Count% = 1 TO 5
  RSET FileInt$  = MKI$(Count%)
  RSET FileLong$ = MKL$(Count%^2)
  RSET FileSngl$ = MKS$(Count%^2.1)
  RSET FileDbl$  = MKD$(Count%^4.4)
  PUT 1,Count%
NEXT Count%

CLOSE 1       ' close the file

END           ' end main program
```

RUN statement

Function RUN restarts the program.

Syntax `RUN [filespec]`

Remarks RUN with no argument causes a Turbo Basic program to restart itself. All numeric variables (including the elements of arrays) are reset to 0, and string variables are set to the null string.

If *filespec* is included, it is a string expression representing a .TBC or an .EXE file (produced with the compiler **O**ptions menu's Chain or EXE **C**ompile to setting). If *filespec* has no extension, .TBC is assumed; if it does have an extension, then it is used. If running or chaining to an .EXE file, you must explicitly append the .EXE extension to your file name.

Example

```
' Compile this program to a file called:
' MASTER.EXE

' input the name SLAVE in response
' to this prompt
INPUT "Enter the name of the program to RUN: ",N$

RUN N$        ' run the indicated program

END           ' end the program

' compile this program to SLAVE.TBC with the
' Compile to Chain entry in the Options menu
PRINT "We are now in the SLAVE program"

END ' end the program
```

SCREEN function

Function SCREEN returns the ASCII code of the character at the specified row and column.

Syntax `y = SCREEN(row, column [, option])`

Remarks *row* and *column* are integer expressions and can range from 1 to 25 and 1 to 80, respectively.

The SCREEN function is text mode's counterpart to the POINT function of graphics modes. It returns information about the character at the specified row and column; for example, SCREEN 1,1 returns the ASCII code of the character at row 1, column 1.

If the optional *option* parameter is set to 1, it will cause SCREEN to return the attribute stored at (*row,column*) rather than the character.

Example

```
LOCATE 10, 10
PRINT "ASCII"

' The ASCII code for "A" is 65; the default
' display attribute (white on black) is 7
PRINT SCREEN(10,10), SCREEN(10,10,1)

END          ' end the program
```

SCREEN statement

Function SCREEN sets the screen display mode.

Syntax `SCREEN [mode] [,[colorflag]] [,[apage]] [,[vpage]]`

Remarks *mode* is an integer expression ranging from 0 to 10, and has the following effect:

Mode	Effect
0	Sets text mode without changing width
1	Sets medium resolution graphics mode; changes width to 40
2	Sets high resolution graphics mode; changes width to 80
7	Sets medium resolution mode on an EGA, allowing 16 colors and 640 × 200 pixels
8	Sets high resolution mode on an EGA, allowing 16 colors and 640 × 200 pixels
9	Sets enhanced high resolution mode on an EGA with an enhanced display; allows 4 or 16 colors (depending on EGA memory) out of a palette of 64, and 640 × 350 pixels
10	Sets high resolution mode on an EGA with a monochrome monitor; allows 4 attributes and 640 × 350 pixels
11	Sets higher resolution mode on a VGA or MCGA; black and white, 640 × 480 pixels.
12	Sets higher resolution mode on a VGA; allows 16 colors out of a palette of 64, and 640 × 480 pixels.

colorflag controls whether color information will be passed to composite monitors that are connected to the composite video port of Color/Graphics Adapters. In text mode, a FALSE (0) value turns color off. In medium resolution graphics mode, a FALSE value turns color on.

apage is an integer expression ranging from 0 to 7 that controls the text page to be written when PRINT and other output commands write to the screen. This argument is only valid on Color/Graphics Adapters and Enhanced Graphics Adapters and screen modes 0, 7, 8, 9, and 10. (See Chapter 4's section on graphics.)

vpage selects which of the possible screens (0–7) is actually displayed. This argument is only valid on Color/Graphics Adapters and Enhanced Graphics Adapters and screen modes 0, 7, 8, 9, and 10.

Executing the SCREEN statement causes the new mode to be started and the screen to be cleared. The foreground color is set to white and background and border colors to black.

If the mode specified in the SCREEN statement is the same as the current mode, nothing happens.

If the mode is text and only *apage* and *vpage* arguments are included, then the display pages are adjusted as requested.

Example

```
' switch to medium resolution graphics
' with color disabled
SCREEN 1,0
CIRCLE (160,100),50, 2

WHILE NOT INSTAT : WEND
A$ = INKEY$

' switch to text mode with color disabled and
' both active and visual pages set to page 0
SCREEN 0,0,0,0
PRINT "Active page is page 0"

WHILE NOT INSTAT : WEND
A$ = INKEY$

' change the active page to page 2
SCREEN ,,2
PRINT "Active page is page 2"

WHILE NOT INSTAT : WEND
A$ = INKEY$

' now switch to HIRES graphics mode
SCREEN 2
CIRCLE (320,100), 100, 1

END
```

SEEK statement

Function SEEK sets the position in a binary file for GET$ and PUT$.

Syntax `SEEK [#] filenum, position`

Remarks SEEK declares that the next GET$ or PUT$ performed on file *filenum* will occur *position* bytes deep into the file. File *filenum* must have been opened in BINARY mode.

Use the LOC function to return a binary file's current SEEK position.

See Also LOC

Example

```
SUB CreateFile
' SEEK opens a file and writes 256
' characters to it.

LOCAL I%

  ' open a file for BINARY I/O
  OPEN "SEEK.DTA" FOR BINARY AS #1

  ' write some data to it
  FOR I% = 1 TO 256
    PUT$ 1, CHR$(I% - 1)
  NEXT I%
END SUB      ' end procedure CreateFile

DEF FNReadIt$(Start%, Size%)
' This function reads in the indicated
' data from the file.

LOCAL TempStr$, Char$, I%

  ' seek to the correct position
  ' in the file
  SEEK 1, Start%

  I% = 1
  TempStr$ = ""

  ' read in the indicated data--don't
  ' read past end of file
  WHILE (NOT EOF(1)) AND (I% <= Size%)
    GET$ 1, I%, Char$
    TempStr$ = TempStr$ + Char$
    INCR I%
  WEND

  ' assign the function's result
  FNReadIt$ = TempStr$
END DEF      ' end function ReadIt
```

```
' create a data file
CALL CreateFile

' get user's input
PRINT "Enter the starting point[1..256] and how many "
PRINT "bytes of data(256 - Staring Point) you wish to "
INPUT "read from the file: ",St%, Sz%

' read the data
PRINT FNReadIt$(St%, Sz%)

END          ' end the program
```

SELECT statement

Function SELECT returns a general purpose testing statement.

Syntax

```
SELECT CASE expression
  CASE test list
    statements
 [CASE test list
    statements]
 [CASE ELSE
    statements]
END SELECT
```

Remarks *test list* is one or more tests, separated by commas, to be performed on *expression*. *expression* can be either string or numeric, but all *test lists* in a SELECT block must be of the same type.

The tests that may be performed by a CASE clause include equality, inequality, greater than, less than, and range ("from to") testing. Examples of CASE clause tests include:

```
CASE < b            ' relational
CASE 14             ' equality ("=" is assumed)
CASE b TO 99        ' range
CASE 14, b          ' two equality tests
CASE b TO 99, 14    ' combinations (implicitly ORed)
```

There's an implied OR between multiple tests in the same CASE clause. If one or more of the tests in a clause are found to be TRUE, then all the statements up till the next CASE clause are executed. After the last statement, control passes to the statement after END SELECT.

The SELECT statement is a powerful tool for comparing a variable against a number of possible values and then proceeding accordingly. Using it may produce a clearer source program than you could achieve with multiple IFs.

See Also END SELECT
EXIT CASE

Example

```
INPUT "Enter a number", x
SELECT CASE x
CASE < 10
  PRINT "small number"
CASE < 1000
  PRINT "medium number"
CASE 1111, 2222, 3333, 4444
  PRINT "boring number"
CASE ELSE
  PRINT "just another big number"
END SELECT
```

SGN function

Function SGN returns the sign of a numeric expression.

Syntax `y = SGN(numeric expression)`

Remarks If *numeric expression* is positive, SGN returns +1. If *numeric expression* is zero, SGN returns 0. If *numeric expression* is negative, SGN returns −1.

In conjunction with the ON/GOTO and ON/GOSUB statements, the SGN function can produce a FORTRAN-like three-way branch:

```
ON SGN(balance) + 2 GOTO InTheRed, BreakingEven, InTheMoney
```

See Also ON/GOSUB
ON/GOTO

Example

```
' set x and y to 0
x = 0 : y = 0

' user defines x and y
INPUT "Please input a value for x "; x
INPUT "Please input a value for y "; y

' ON the SGN value of x * y
' GOSUB the appropriate subroutine
ON SGN (x * y) +2 GOSUB Minus, Zero, Plus

END       ' end the program

Minus:
  PRINT "Minus Value Entry" : RETURN

Zero:
  PRINT "Zero Value Entry" : RETURN

Plus:
  PRINT "Positive Value Entry" : RETURN
```

SHARED statement

Function SHARED declares shared (global) variables in a procedure or function.

Syntax `SHARED` *`variable list`*

Remarks SHARED defines the variables in its comma-delimited variable list as global to the entire program, rather than limited in scope to the enclosing procedure or function definition. This gives a procedure or function access to variable(s) without having to pass them as parameters. The SHARED statement may appear only in function and procedure definitions, and must come before any executable statements in the associated definition.

To declare an array as a *shared* variable belonging to a procedure or function, include its identifier and an empty set of parentheses in the variable list—you need not, and shouldn't, dimension it again.

Undeclared variables in function definitions default to the shared attribute, but you shouldn't rely on this default in future versions of the compiler. You should explicitly declare all variables that appear in a function or procedure according to their class (LOCAL, STATIC, or SHARED).

See Also LOCAL
STATIC

Example

```
DIM Array$(5)

DEF FNDummy$
SHARED Array$()
  FNDummy$ = Array$(0)
END DEF     ' end the function FNDummy$

Array$(0) = "It works for me."

PRINT FNDummy$

END         ' end the program
```

SHELL statement

Function SHELL loads and executes child process.

Syntax `SHELL [parameter string]`

Remarks *parameter string* is a string expression that contains the name of the .COM, .EXE, or .BAT program ("child process") to run, and optionally contains the parameters you may wish to pass to the child process.

If *parameter string* is omitted, no program is loaded. Instead, the DOS prompt appears and you may enter standard DOS commands; for example, DIR, COPY. You can return to your program by typing EXIT at the DOS prompt.

If *parameter string* is included, then the specified program is executed. When it terminates, your program continues with the next statement.

See Also ENVIRON
ENVIRON$
SHELL in DOS manual

Example

```
PRINT " We will now use the Turbo Basic SHELL "
PRINT " statement to issue the DOS DIR/W command "
PRINT " to see what files are on your drive."
DELAY 3            ' wait 3 seconds

' Use SHELL to leave Turbo Basic and
' issue DIR with /w option
SHELL "DIR/W"

' Print at bottom of display
LOCATE 21,1
PRINT "Now back in Turbo Basic "

END            ' end the program
```

SIN function

Function: SIN returns a trigonometric sine.

Syntax: `y =SIN(numeric expression)`

Remarks: *numeric expression* is an angle specified in radians. To convert radians to degrees, multiply by 57.296. To convert degrees to radians, divide by 0.17453. (See the discussion of radians under the ATN statement.)

SIN returns a double-precision result.

See Also: ATN

Example:

```
' Choose a value for b$ to print in sample
b$ = " Turbo Basic from Borland "

' find the center
center = (79 - LEN(b$)) / 2

' SIN(theta) returns a repeating sequence
' of values ranging smoothly from -1 to 1,
' so tabValue is always between -center
' and +center
  tabValue = center * SIN(theta)
  PRINT TAB(center + tabValue +1) b$
  theta = theta + .1

WEND

END          ' end the program
```

SOUND statement

Function: SOUND generates a tone of specified frequency and duration.

Syntax: `SOUND frequency, duration`

Remarks: *frequency* is an integer expression representing the desired pitch in the range 37 to 32,767 Hertz. *duration* is a floating-point expression that controls the length of the tone as measured in "clock ticks." Clock ticks occur at the rate of 18.2 times per second, so a duration value of 36 lasts just under two seconds. *duration* can range from 0.0015 to 65,535 (one hour).

The SOUND statement doesn't hold up program execution. When one is encountered, the requested tone is begun and execution proceeds normally. If another SOUND is encountered and the duration parameter of the new SOUND statement is zero, then the previous SOUND is turned off. Otherwise, Turbo Basic waits until the first sound completes before executing the new SOUND statement.

SOUND is better at creating special effects (for example, sirens, clicks, and slide whistles) than music.

Restrictions: Note that the SOUND statement will re-initialize the MTIMER microtimer.

See Also: PLAY

Example:

```
' Set music buffer to 800 bytes
$SOUND 100 ' 8 bytes per note

' Use SOUND to produce sound effects
' Following is a motorcycle changing gears.

' first gear
FOR i = 150 TO 175
 SOUND i, 2
NEXT i

' second gear
FOR j = 125 TO 152
 SOUND j, 1.5
NEXT j

' third gear
FOR k = 100 TO 127
 SOUND k, 1.25
NEXT k
```

SPACE$ function

Function SPACE$ returns a string consisting of all spaces.

Syntax

```
s$  = SPACE$(count)
```

Remarks *count* is a positive integer expression ranging from 0 to 32,767 that specifies how many spaces the function is to return.

SPACE$ is one of many text formatting aids available within Turbo Basic.

See Also

LSET
PRINT USING
RSET
SPC
STRING$
TAB

Example

```
' reserve 46 spaces for a$
a$ = SPACE$(46)

' make up a string 46 characters long.
b$ = "This is a string 46 characters long"

' do the same as a$ using the space bar
c$ = "                                              "

' print the LENgth of a$, b$, and c$
PRINT LEN(a$), LEN(b$), LEN(c$)
PRINT
PRINT "As you can see, by using the Space$ I can "
PRINT "Give a$ same value as b$ and c$."

END      ' end the program
```

SPC function

Function SPC skips *n* spaces (used in PRINT statement).

Syntax `PRINT SPC(n)`

Remarks *n* is an integer expression in the range 0 to 255.

Like its sister function TAB, SPC can only be used within the expression list of a PRINT, LPRINT, or PRINT # statement. SPC(*n*) causes *n* spaces to be printed. Don't confuse SPC with the SPACE$ function.

If *n* is larger than the line width defined by the WIDTH statement, then SPC inserts (*n* MOD *width*) spaces.

If SPC appears at the end of the expression list with or without a following semicolon, a carriage return is not output.

See Also TAB
WIDTH

Example

```
' Using SPC, print the words boy and girl
' 40 spaces apart and underline using
' the STRING$ function.
PRINT SPC(5)"Boys" SPC(40) "Girls"
PRINT SPC(5) STRING$(4,61) SPC(40) STRING$(5,61)

FOR i = 1 TO 5

 READ boy$
 READ girl$
' print the names of each boy and
' girl under the proper column.
 PRINT SPC(5) boy$ SPC(40) girl$

NEXT i

END       ' ends the program

DATA "John","Ann"
DATA "Mark","Eve"
DATA "Mike","Kathy"
DATA "Paul","Elizabeth"
DATA "Tony","Sue"
```

SQR function

Function SQR returns a square root function.

Syntax `y=SQR(`*`numeric expression`*`)`

Remarks *numeric expression* is greater than or equal to zero.

SQR calculates square roots using an algorithm faster than the power-of-0.5 method of calculating square roots (that is, $y = SQR(x)$ takes less time to execute than $y = x\hat{}.5$).

Attempting to take the square root of a negative number results in run-time error 5, Illegal Function Call.

SQR returns a double-precision result.

Example

```
' Square Root Table

' label two columns
PRINT "NUMBER" TAB (10) "SQUARE ROOT VALUE"
PRINT

FOR N = 1 TO 10

' use TAB to print square root under
' correct column, use SQR to get square root
PRINT N, TAB(15) SQR(N)

NEXT N

END     ' end the program
```

STATIC statement

Function STATIC declares the static variables in a procedure or function.

Syntax `STATIC` *`variable list`*

Remarks The STATIC statement, which is legal only in procedure and function definitions, defines the variables in its comma-delimited variable list as having a fixed address in memory rather than being stack-based. The identifier associated with a static variable is known only to the enclosing procedure or function; that is, other variables in other parts of the program and other local variables in other definitions can have the same name.

STATIC must appear before any executable statements in the associated definition. To declare an array as a *static* variable belonging to a procedure or function, include its identifier and an empty set of parentheses in the variable list, then DIMension the array in a subsequent statement.

Unlike local variables, static variables do not change their value between invocations of a procedure or function. They are initialized only at the start of a program.

See Also LOCAL
SHARED

Example

```
' declare STATIC procedure with
' a STATIC local

SUB Dummy STATIC     ' variable
STATIC I%
  INCR I
  PRINT I
END SUB       ' end procedure Dummy

I = 16

' call the procedure twice
CALL Dummy
CALL Dummy

PRINT I

END           ' end the program
```

STICK function

Function STICK returns joystick position information.

Syntax `y = STICK(option)`

Remarks *option* is an integer expression ranging from 0 to 3 and has the following effect:

Option	Effect
0	Returns x coordinate for joystick *A*
1	Returns y coordinate for joystick *A*
2	Returns x coordinate for joystick *B*
3	Returns y coordinate for joystick *B*

Note: Because of the design of the joystick interface, you must first execute STICK(0) to trigger the reading process before you can read either dimension of either joystick.

See Also STRIG (statement)

Example

```
' poll the joysticks to determine
' their current position
WHILE NOT INSTAT
  LOCATE 15,15
  PRINT STICK(0), STICK(1), STICK(2), STICK(3);
WEND

END     ' end the program
```

STOP statement

Function STOP halts the program.

Syntax `STOP`

Remarks STOP terminates a program and returns control to the operating system (or to Turbo Basic, depending on where it was launched from). The END statement does the same thing, and is preferred.

Differences Unlike Interpretive BASIC, once Turbo Basic programs are STOPped, they cannot be CONTinued.

See Also END

Example

```
' set up an infinite loop
DO
  ' stop if a key was pressed
  IF INSTAT THEN STOP
LOOP

END          ' end the program
```

STR$ function

Function STR$ returns the string equivalent of a number.

Syntax `s$ = STR$(numeric expression)`

Remarks STR$ returns the string form of a numeric variable or expression; that is, it returns what you would see on the screen were you to PRINT *numeric expression*. If *numeric expression* is greater than zero, STR$ adds a leading space; for example, STR$(14) returns a three-character string, of which the first character is a space.

The complementary function is VAL, which takes a string argument and returns a number.

See Also VAL

Example

```
' set a% to a number
a% = 56.789

' use STR$ to return a$'s numeric value
a$ = STR$(a%)

PRINT a%, a$

' test to see that a% has the same value as a$
IF a% = VAL(a$) THEN
  PRINT " STR$ and VAL appear to work "
END IF

END     ' end the program
```

STRIG function

Function STRIG returns the status of the joystick buttons.

Syntax `y = STRIG(option)`

Remarks The STRIG function returns joyStick TRIGger information according to the value of *option*. *option* is an integer expression that controls the action performed by the STRIG function, according to the following:

Option	Action
0	If button 1 on joystick *A* has been pressed since the last STRIG(1) call, STRIG returns −1; otherwise, STRIG returns 0.
1	STRIG returns −1 if button 1 on joystick *A* is currently down; if not, it returns 0.
2	If button 1 on joystick *B* has been pressed since the last STRIG(2) call, STRIG returns −1; otherwise, STRIG returns 0.
3	STRIG returns −1 if button 1 on joystick *B* is currently down; otherwise, it returns 0.
4	If button 2 on joystick *A* has been pressed since the last STRIG(4) call, STRIG returns −1; otherwise, STRIG returns 0.
5	STRIG returns −1 if button 2 on joystick *A* is currently down; otherwise, it returns 0.
6	If button 2 on joystick *B* has been pressed since the last STRIG(6) call, STRIG returns −1; otherwise, STRIG returns 0.
7	STRIG returns −1 if button 2 on joystick *B* is currently down; otherwise, it returns 0.

Before making any STRIG function calls, you must enable joystick button checking with the STRIG ON statement.

Use the STICK function to read the position of the joystick itself.

See Also STICK

Example See the example under the STRIG statement.

STRIG statement

Function STRIG controls the joystick button event checking.

Syntax `STRIG {ON|OFF|STOP}`

Remarks The STRIG statement controls joystick button checking.

STRIG ON turns on trigger-event checking so that STRIG function requests can be made and trapping performed by the routine specified in an ON STRIG statement.

STRIG OFF turns off trigger-event checking. STRIG STOP keeps a program from responding to a trigger event, but retains a memory of such an event so that if STRIG ON is later executed, an immediate trap occurs.

See Also ON STRIG

Example

```
' turn on event checking
STRIG(0) ON
STRIG(2) ON
STRIG(4) ON
STRIG(6) ON

' poll event status to see if a
' button was pressed
WHILE NOT INSTAT
  LOCATE 1,1
  PRINT STRIG(0), STRIG(1), STRIG(2), STRIG(3)
  PRINT STRIG(4), STRIG(5), STRIG(6), STRIG(7)
WEND

END    ' end the program
```

STRING$ function

Function — STRING$ returns a string consisting of multiple copies of the indicated character.

Syntax — `s$ = STRING$(count,{value|string expression})`

Remarks — *count* and *value* are integer expressions. *count* can range from 1 to 32,767; *value* from 0 to 255.

STRING$ with a numeric argument returns a string of *count* copies of the character with ASCII code *value*. STRING$ with a string argument returns a string of *count* copies of *string expression's* first character.

STRING$(*n*,32), STRING$(*n*," "), and SPACE$(*n*) all do the same thing—produce a string of *n* spaces.

Example

```
' STRING$ and TAB builds a box

' Use 40 equals (=) characters to build
' the top of the box, then print
top$ = STRING$(40,61)
PRINT top$

' use a 1-second delay so you
' can see the box being built.
DELAY 1

' use a loop to build the sides
FOR i = 1 TO 5
PRINT TAB(1) "=" TAB(40) "="
DELAY 1
NEXT i
DELAY 1

' use the top string for the bottom
PRINT top$
DELAY 1

' find the middle of the box and
' print some text
LOCATE 4,15
PRINT " THE MIDDLE "
DELAY 1

' put the cursor out of the way
LOCATE 20,1
END     ' end the program
```

SUB/END SUB, SUB INLINE statements

Function SUB/END SUB and SUB INLINE define a procedure (subprogram).

Syntax

```
SUB identifier [(parameter list)]
  [LOCAL variable list]
  [STATIC variable list]
  [SHARED variable list]
  .
  . statements
  .
  [EXIT SUB]
END SUB
```

For SUB INLINE:

```
SUB procname INLINE
```

Remarks *identifier* is the unique name to be associated with the procedure, and must follow the naming conventions for labels and variables. *parameter list* is an optional, comma-delimited sequence of formal parameters. The parameters used in the argument list serve only to define the procedure; they have no relationship to other variables in the program with the same name.

SUB and END SUB delimit and name a subroutine-like statement group called a *procedure* (or subprogram), which is invoked with the CALL statement and optionally passed parameters by value or by reference.

Inline assembly language programming uses the same calling sequence used with regular procedures. For example:

```
CALL procname[(parameter list)]

SUB procname INLINE
  $INLINE byte list
  $INLINE "COM File Name"
END SUB
```

Any number of $INLINE statements can be specified in any order. A maximum of 16 COM files in any one procedure is the only limitation.

Note that you do not specify the parameter list in the SUB definition.

byte lists are made up of constants or expressions equal to an integer between 0 and 255, and are separated by commas. (Normally, you'll use hex constants for bytes.)

Returns are not necessary in your assembly language code, nor at the end of SUB. The compiler sees to that. (For more information, refer to Appendix C, "Assembly Language Interface.")

Procedure Definitions and Program Flow

The position of procedure definitions is immaterial. A procedure can be defined in line 1 or line 1,000 of a program without regard for where it is used. And you need not direct program flow through a procedure as an initialization step — the compiler sees your definitions wherever they might be.

Also, unlike subroutines, execution can't accidentally "fall into" a procedure. As far as the execution path of a program is concerned, function and procedure definitions are invisible. For example:

```
CALL PrintStuff
SUB PrintStuff
  PRINT "Printed from within PrintStuff"
END SUB
```

When this four-line program is executed, the message appears only once because *PrintStuff* is called in the first line.

Procedure definitions should be treated as isolated islands of code; don't jump into or out of them with GOTO, GOSUB, or RETURN statements. Within definitions, however, such statements are legal.

Note that function and procedure definitions may not be nested; that is, you cannot define a procedure or function within another procedure or function (although a procedure or function definition can contain *calls* to other procedures and functions).

Array Parameters

Array parameters are declared by enclosing in parentheses the number of dimensions (*not* elements) of the array parameter. For example:

```
SUB CalcArray (a(2),sizDim1,sizdim2)
```

declares that *CalcArray* expects three arguments: a two-dimensional, single-precision array, and two single-precision scalar variables. Typically, these scalar arguments would be used to pass the size of array *a*'s two dimensions.

Declaring Local Variables

To declare local variables within a procedure, use the LOCAL statement before any executable statements in the definition. For example:

```
LOCAL a%, b#, bigArray%()
```

creates three local variables: scalar variables *a%* and *b#* (integer and double precision, respectively), and integer array *bigArray%*. The array must then be dimensioned appropriately:

```
DIM DYNAMIC bigArray%(1000)
```

Local array variables must be dynamic. They are automatically deallocated when the procedure terminates.

Static and Shared Variables

By default, variables that appear within procedure definitions have the local attribute. However, since this default is subject to change, you should make an effort to declare every variable used in a procedure.

Use the SHARED statement to declare variables that are global to the rest of the program.

Declare variables with the STATIC statement if it is important that a variable not lose its value with every invocation.

A procedure definition must be terminated with END DEF, which logically returns control to the statement directly after the invoking CALL. Use the EXIT SUB statement to return from a procedure definition from someplace other than at its end.

See Also

$INLINE
CALL
EXIT SUB
LOCAL
SHARED
STATIC

Example

```
DIM Array(1)   ' declare array of numbers

SUB TestProcedure(I%, L&, S!, D#, E, A(1))
  ' SUB/END SUB outputs the values of
  ' each parameter passed to it
  PRINT I%; L&; S!; D#; E; A(0)
END SUB   ' end procedure TestProcedure

Integer% = 1
LongInt& = 2
SinglePre! = 3
DoublePre# = 4
Array(0) = 5

CALL TestProcedure(Integer%, LongInt&, SinglePre!,_
                   DoublePre#, Integer% ^2,Array())

END      ' end the program
```

SWAP statement

Function SWAP exchanges the values of two variables.

Syntax `SWAP var1, var2`

Remarks *var1* and *var2* are two variables of the same type. If you try to swap variables of differing types (for example, string and integer or single precision and double precision), compiler error 475 occurs, Type Mismatch.

SWAP is handy, because a simple trading of values in two consecutive assignment statements doesn't get the job done:

```
a = b : b = a
```

By the time you make the second assignment, variable *a* doesn't contain the value it used to. To do this without SWAP requires a temporary variable and a third assignment:

```
temp = a : a = b : b = temp
```

Example

```
' set a value to a% and b%
a% = 15 : b% = 17

' print the values of each on the same line
PRINT TAB(6)"The value of 'a%' is:"; a% _
            TAB(42) " The value of 'b%' is:"; b%
PRINT

' use SWAP to exchange their values
SWAP a%,b%

' print the new values below the old values.
PRINT " The value of 'a%' is now:"; a%_
        TAB(38) " The value of 'b%' is now:";b%

End  ' end the program
```

SYSTEM statement

Function SYSTEM terminates a program.

Syntax `SYSTEM`

Remarks SYSTEM terminates a program and returns control to the operating system (or to Turbo Basic, depending on where it was launched from). The END statement does the same thing, and is preferred.

See Also END
STOP

Example

```
'  the answer is 5
ans% = 5

' total turns to guess number
FOR i = 1 to 10

INPUT " Please enter a number between 1 and 10 "; x%

' if user gets answer then leave loop and reward
IF x% = ans% THEN GOTO reward

' ask user if he/she wants to go again
INPUT " Do you want to try another number ( Y/N) "; x$

' if user wants to quit then leave program
IF UCASE$(x$) <> CHR$(89) THEN SYSTEM

NEXT i

reward:
PRINT
PRINT " You got it ! "

END                ' end the program
```

TAB function

Function TAB tabs to a specified print position *n* (PRINT statement only).

Syntax `PRINT TAB(n)`

Remarks *n* is an integer expression in the range 1 to 255.

Like SPC, TAB can only be used in the expression list of a PRINT, LPRINT, or PRINT # statement. Use TAB to line up columns of information. TAB causes Turbo Basic's print routines to output to the *n*th position of the current line. If the current cursor position is already past *n* (for example, PRINT TAB(20) with the cursor at column 30), then Turbo Basic skips down to the *n*th position of the next line.

If TAB appears at the end of a PRINT statement's *expression list* with or without a following semicolon, Turbo Basic does not output a carriage return; that is, there is an implied semicolon after TAB.

See Also LPRINT
PRINT
PRINT #
SPC

Example

```
' This program reads list of friends and phone numbers
' then prints to screen using PRINT and TAB

' DIMension two arrays
DIM friend$(1),phone$(1)

' print an empty line then print the words
' name and phone at 5th and 40th position
PRINT
PRINT TAB(5) "NAME" TAB(40) "PHONE"
PRINT

FOR i = 1 TO 5

  READ friend$
  READ phone$

  ' print data at the same location as labels
  PRINT TAB(5) friend$ TAB(40) phone$

NEXT i

END            ' end the program

DATA "John Blaze","423-4598"
DATA "Ann Span","335-2343"
DATA "Bill Write","668-9834"
DATA "Mark Jones","425-5593"
DATA "Dan Moore","438-4593"
```

TAN function

Function TAN returns a trigonometric tangent.

Syntax `y = TAN(numeric expression)`

Remarks *numeric expression* is an angle specified in radians. To convert radians to degrees, multiply by $180/\pi$. To convert degrees to radians, multiply by $\pi/180$. (See the discussion of radians under the ATN statement.)

TAN returns a double-precision result.

See Also ATN
COS
SIN

Example

```
DEFDBL a-z
' using the arctangent function ATN,
' set the value of pi#
pi = ATN(1) * 4

' print the value of pi#
PRINT pi

' pi divided by 4 radians equals 45 degrees
' using the trigonometric tangent function,
' return the number of radians
PRINT TAN(pi / 4)

END            ' end the program
```

TIME$ system variable

Function TIME$ reads or sets system time.

Syntax To read the time:

```
s$ = TIME$
```

To set the time:

```
TIME$ = string expression
```

Remarks System variable TIME$ contains an eight-character string that represents the time of the system clock in the form *hh:mm:ss*, where *hh* is hours (in military form, 0–23), *mm* is minutes, and *ss* is seconds. TIME$ won't be accurate unless DOS's clock was set correctly when the computer was last booted up.

Assigning to TIME$ sets the system clock. Build a string expression containing time information in military (24 hour) format and then assign it to TIME$. Minute and second information can be omitted. For example:

```
TIME$ = "12"         ' set clock to 12 noon
TIME$ = "13:01"      ' set clock to 1:01 P.M.
TIME$ = "13:01:30"   ' set clock to 30 seconds after 1:01 P.M.
TIME$ = "0:01"       ' set clock to one minute after midnight
```

If the hour, minutes, or seconds parameter is out of range (for example, a minutes value of 61), run-time error 5 occurs, Illegal Function Call.

Use the TIMER function to return the number of seconds that have elapsed since the system was booted.

Example

```
'  turn timer checking on
TIMER ON

' print time from the system clock
PRINT " The time is now "; TIME$

' reset the time
INPUT " Please set a new time ( 0 to 23 )"; ANS$

' set new value
TIME$ = ANS$

' print the new time value
PRINT " The new time is "; TIME$

END      ' end the program
```

TIMER function

Function TIMER returns the number of seconds since midnight.

Syntax

```
y = TIMER
```

Remarks TIMER takes no arguments and returns the number of seconds since midnight as a single-precision, floating-point value with a resolution of about one tenth of a second. If the system time hasn't been set since the last boot (with either DOS's TIME command or Turbo Basic's TIME$ system variable), TIMER returns the number of seconds since the system was booted.

See Also MTIMER

Example

```
TIME$ = "12"
PRINT USING "Noon is ##### seconds past midnight";TIMER

END      ' end the program
```

TIMER statement

Function TIMER controls the checking of timer events.

Syntax `TIMER {ON|OFF|STOP}`

Remarks TIMER controls the checking of timer events; that is, it decides whether or not to pass control to the routine specified in an ON TIMER statement after the designated number of seconds have elapsed.

TIMER ON turns on timer event checking. TIMER OFF turns it off. TIMER STOP turns off timer event trapping, but remembers timer events so that if TIMER ON is later issued, a trap occurs immediately.

See Also ON TIMER

Example

```
' set up event handler
ON TIMER(2) GOSUB UpdateClock

' turn on event checking
TIMER ON

WHILE NOT INSTAT : WEND

END       ' end the program

UpdateClock:
  SaveX% = CSRLIN    ' save cursor position
  SaveY% = POS(0)
  LOCATE 24, 36
  PRINT TIME$;
  LOCATE SaveX%, SaveY%  ' restore cursor
  RETURN
```

TRON and TROFF commands

Function TRON and TROFF turn on and off execution trace.

Syntax `TRON` (trace on)

`TROFF` (trace off)

Remarks TRON puts your program into a debugging mode in which source line numbers, statement labels, and procedure and function names are sent to the Trace window as each statement is executed; TROFF turns this debugging mode off.

When running in text mode under Turbo Basic, the trace line numbers, labels, and procedure and function names are sent to the Trace window.

While tracing, press *Alt-F9* to alternate between tracing and executing. Use *Alt-F10* to single-step to the next line number, label, or procedure or function name.

Differences Unlike Interpretive BASIC, in Turbo Basic the physical position of TRON and TROFF in your source program controls their effect rather than their position in the run-time execution path. For example, consider this program:

```
10 GOTO 30
20 TRON
30 x = y + z
40 TROFF
50 END
```

When executing this program, Interpretive BASIC will never turn on the trace, because as far as it's concerned the TRON statement in line 20 doesn't exist. Turbo Basic, on the other hand, makes trace/no trace decisions at compile time and considers all statements after the appearance of TRON as being turned on for tracing. Therefore, a Turbo Basic-produced program will output:

```
[30] [40]
```

when the preceding program runs.

Example

```
' set values for X, Y, and Z
10 X = 0 : Y = 1 : Z = 2

20 goto 40

30 TRON

' when run, displays line numbers 20, 30,
' and 40, not their contents
40 X = Y + Z

' after trace is turned off, value of
' X will print
50 PRINT X

60 TROFF

70 END         ' end the program
```

UBOUND function

Function — UBOUND returns the highest bound possible (largest subscript) for an array's specified dimension.

Syntax — `UBOUND (array(dimension))`

Remarks — *array* is the array being dimensioned. *dimension* is an integer from 1 up to the number of dimensions in *array*.

To find the lower limit of an array, use the LBOUND function.

See Also — LBOUND
OPTION BASE

Example

```
' dimension an array with lower and upper bounds
DIM Array%(1900:2000)

' print out the values of the array
FOR index% = LBOUND(Array%(1)) TO UBOUND(Array%(1))
  PRINT "Array Element (";Index%;") is =";Array%(Indent5)
NEXT Index%

END
```

UCASE$ function

Function UCASE$ returns an all uppercase string.

Syntax `s$ = UCASE$(`*`string expression`*`)`

Remarks UCASE$ returns a string equal to *string expression* except that all the lowercase alphabetic characters in *string expression* are converted to uppercase.

See Also LCASE$

Example

```
PRINT UCASE$ ("TB or not TB...");
```

VAL function

Function VAL returns the numeric equivalent of a string.

Syntax `y = VAL(string expression)`

Remarks The VAL function turns its string argument into a number. If *string expression* begins with numeric characters (0 − 9, +, −, ., *E*, *D*) but also contains nonnumeric characters, then VAL returns the number up to the point of the nonnumeric character. If *string expression* doesn't begin with a numeric character, VAL returns 0. Leading white-space characters (space, tab) are ignored.

VAL is often part of entry routines, since it allows a program to prompt a user for string data. It then turns the data into numeric information as needed, without the risk of your entering nonnumeric data into numeric variables and producing messy ?Redo From Start errors.

See Also STR$

Example

```
' an address-type string
a$ = "34 N. Main St."

' a string without numbers
b$ = "that's right, thirty four"

' numbers with symbols
c$ = "+3.4e1"

' numbers with a leading space
d$ = " 123  go "

' print each VAL from the strings
PRINT VAL(a$), VAL(b$), VAL(c$), VAL(d$)

END           ' end the program
```

VARPTR function

Function VARPTR returns the address of a variable.

Syntax `y = VARPTR(variable)`

Remarks *variable* is any numeric or string variable or element of an array.

VARPTR returns the offset part of the address in memory where *variable* is stored. Such address information is sometimes called a "pointer"; for example, VARPTR(*x*) is said to return a "pointer to *x*."

Because of the expanded memory model used by Turbo Basic programs, VARSEG is also required to fully define the address of a variable. (VARSEG returns the segment part of the address.)

VARPTR is used most often to provide an assembly language subroutine with the location of a variable in memory.

When you use VARPTR to get the offset of a string or an array, keep in mind that the value being returned is the offset of the string or array descriptor, not the data for the string or array. Refer to Appendix C, "Assembly Language Interface," for descriptions of the formats of the string and array descriptors, and a run-time memory map.

See Also VARSEG

Example

```
B% = 55
DEF SEG = VARSEG(B%)

Address% = VARPTR(B%)

PRINT PEEK(Address%)

END  'end the program
```

VARPTR$ function

Function VARPTR$ returns a pointer to a variable in string form.

Syntax `s$ = VARPTR$(variable)`

Remarks *variable* is any numeric or string variable or element of an array.

VARPTR$ returns a pointer to a variable in string form, and is used primarily in the PLAY and DRAW statements to include variable names within command strings.

See Also DRAW
PLAY
VARSEG

Example

```
' switch into medium resolution graphics mode
SCREEN 1

House$ = "U20 G5 E20 F20 H5 D20 L30"
DRAW House$

DRAW "BE3"
DRAW "P1,3"
FOR I% = 1 TO 280 STEP 40
  DRAW "M = " + VARPTR$(I%) + ",40"
  DRAW House$
NEXT I%

END   ' end the program
```

VARSEG function

Function VARSEG returns the segment address of a variable.

Syntax `y = VARSEG(variable)`

Remarks *variable* is any numeric or string variable or element of an array. Because of Turbo Basic's expanded memory model, VARSEG is required along with VARPTR to fully define the address of a variable.

VARSEG returns a numeric value in the range 0 to 65,535. Use VARSEG in conjunction with VARPTR to get the address of a variable, so that a CALL can tell an assembly language routine where the argument it should process is located in memory.

Turbo Basic programs put all nonarray variables in a single segment that can be up to 64K in length. Therefore, using VARSEG on all the nonarray variables in a given program always returns the same value. In fact, this segment value is the default for statements that rely on DEF SEG (for example, PEEK, POKE).

When you use VARSEG to get the offset of a string or an array, keep in mind that the value being returned is the segment of the string or array descriptor, not the data for the string or array. Refer to Appendix C, "Assembly Language Interface," for descriptions of the formats of the string and array descriptors, and a run-time memory map.

See Also VARPTR

Example

```
' B% = 55
DEF SEG = VARSEG(B%)

Address% = VARPTR(B%)

PRINT PEEK(Address%)

END 'end the program
```

VIEW statement

Function VIEW defines the active area (viewport) of the graphics screen.

Syntax `VIEW [ [SCREEN] [(x1,y1) - (x2, y2) [,[color [boundary]]]] ]`

Remarks (*x1, y1*) and (*x2, y2*) are the upper left-hand and lower right-hand corners, respectively, of the viewport being defined. *color* is an optional numeric argument; if included, the new viewport is filled with this color. *boundary* is an optional numeric argument, which when included causes Turbo Basic to draw a border around the new viewport in the specified color. If omitted, no border is drawn.

VIEW defines an area on the graphics screen that can be written to or, conversely, an area that may not be written to. Attempts to set pixels outside of the viewport fail; this is called *clipping*.

SCREEN Option

If the SCREEN keyword is omitted, future point references are taken relative to the top left corner of the viewport, rather than the top left corner of the screen. For example, after

```
VIEW (100,50) - (300,180)
```

then

```
PSET (0,0)
```

turns on the pixel at (100,50).

If SCREEN is included, points are specified in the normal way; that is, relative to the upper left-hand corner of the display. For example, PSET(0,0) refers to the pixel in the extreme upper left-hand corner of the display. However, only those points that fall within the specified viewport are visible (points outside the viewport are clipped).

VIEW with no arguments defines the entire screen as the viewport. Using the SCREEN statement to change screen modes (for example, to go from medium resolution to high resolution), cancels any VIEW setting that may have existed previously.

When a viewport has been defined, CLS clears only the viewport.

See Also CLS
SCREEN
WINDOW

Example

```
SCREEN 1

FOR I = 0 TO 6
  ' set up a view port
  VIEW  (10 * (I + 1), 10 * (I + 1)) - _
        (25 * (I + 1),25 * (I + 1)), I, 3 - I

  ' display a circle in the view port
  CIRCLE (10, 10), I + 1, 3 - I
NEXT I

END        ' end the program
```

WAIT statement

Function WAIT waits for the indicated hardware status condition.

Syntax `WAIT port, n [,m]`

Remarks *port* is an integer expression (in the range 0 to 65,535) specifying a hardware input port. *n* and *m* are integer expressions in the range 0 to 255.

WAIT halts program execution until the specified port presents the specified bit pattern. The byte read from the port is Exclusive ORed with *m* and ANDed with *n*. If the resulting value is zero, the process repeats. If nonzero, Turbo Basic proceeds with the next statement.

If *m* is omitted, WAIT uses a 0 for its value.

Example

```
wait &H60,1

PRINT "hi"

END
```

WHILE/WEND statements

Function WHILE and WEND build a loop with the test at the top.

Syntax

```
WHILE integer expression
.
. [statements]
.
WEND
```

Remarks If *integer expression* is TRUE (evaluates to a nonzero value), all the statements between the WHILE and the terminating WEND are executed. Turbo Basic then jumps to the WHILE statement and repeats the test, and if still nonzero, executes the enclosed statements again. This process is repeated until the test expression finally evaluates to zero, at which time execution passes to the statement after WEND.

If *integer expression* evaluates FALSE (zero) on the first pass, then none of the statements in the loop are executed.

Loops built with WHILE/WEND can be nested (enclosed within each other). Each WEND matches the closest WHILE. If Turbo Basic encounters a WEND statement without a pending WHILE, run-time error 30 occurs, WEND Without WHILE. A WHILE without a matching WEND generates run-time error 29, WHILE Without WEND.

Although the compiler couldn't care less, indent the statements between WHILE and WEND by a couple of spaces to clarify the structure of the loop you've constructed.

Note: WHILE −1 ... WEND creates an infinite loop.

To exit a WHILE/WEND loop prematurely, use the EXIT WHILE statement.

See Also DO/LOOP
EXIT

Example

```
' set the value of I to 0
' and the value of X to 10
I = 0
X = 10

' do this loop until I = 10
WHILE I < X

' add 1 to the value of I
I = I + 1

' see the value of I
PRINT " I = ";I

' wait one second
DELAY 1

' END loop when WHILE condition is met
WEND

PRINT
PRINT " The value of I and X both = 10 "
PRINT  I
PRINT  X

END        ' end the program
```

WIDTH statement

Function WIDTH sets the logical line size.

Syntax `WIDTH [{device name| #filenum},] size`

Remarks *size* is an integer expression from 0 to 255 that specifies the new logical line size.

device name is a string expression optionally describing the device whose WIDTH should be set. Options for *device* are SCRN:, LPT1:, LPT2:, LPT3:, COM1:, and COM2:. If omitted, WIDTH refers to the display (SCRN:). *filenum* is an integer expression representing a file opened for output.

In general, WIDTH determines how many characters can be "printed" to a given device before a carriage return is output, although its exact effect varies according to the device it is applied to.

WIDTH *size* or WIDTH "SCRN:", *size* sets the screen width. The only valid values for size are 40 and 80, and 40 is invalid for a monochrome display.

If the screen is in a graphics mode, changing the width has the effect of changing the graphics mode. For example, if the current mode is high resolution, then WIDTH 40 turns on medium resolution graphics.

WIDTH *device, size* determines the logical line size of the specified device when it is next opened. If the device has already been opened, its width setting is not changed.

Note: LPRINT implicitly OPENs the printer; thus, the effect of WIDTH "LPT1:", *size* is seen immediately.

WIDTH *#filenum, size* changes the width of the device represented by *filenum* immediately. The only devices for which this statement means anything are LPT1:, LPT2:, LPT3:, COM1:, and COM2:.

The WIDTH of each printer defaults to 80. Specifying a WIDTH of 255 effectively disables logical line width counting so that no carriage returns are ever inserted.

Example

```
' set to medium resolution graphics mode
SCREEN 1,0
PRINT " This is a sample of medium res graphics mode."
DELAY 3          ' wait 3 seconds

' using WIDTH, set to high resolution graphics
WIDTH 80
PRINT " This is sample of Hi-res graphics mode "
DELAY 3

' set back to medium resolution graphics mode
WIDTH 40
PRINT " Note, the letters are bigger in medium graphics mode "
DELAY 3

SCREEN 0,1          ' text mode
WIDTH 80
PRINT " This is 80-character text mode "
DELAY 3

' forty-character text mode
WIDTH 40
PRINT " This is 40-character text mode "

' eighty-character text mode
WIDTH 80

' Ask if user's printer can continue the example
INPUT " Are EPSON printer codes supported? (Y or N)"; ans$

' END if your printer does not support Epson codes
IF UCASE$(ans$) <> CHR$(89) THEN END

LPRINT CHR$(15)    ' set physical WIDTH

WIDTH "LPT1:",130       ' set logical WIDTH
LPRINT "Testing in compressed mode set to 130 columns.";
LPRINT " The same line continued to the end of the page."

LPRINT CHR$(18)         ' Reset
WIDTH "LPT1:",80

END                     ' end the program
```

WINDOW statement

Function WINDOW defines the graphics coordinate system.

Syntax `WINDOW [[SCREEN] (x1,y1) - (x2,y2)]`

Remarks ($x1$,$y1$) and ($x2$,$y2$) are two single-precision coordinate pairs. ($x1$,$y1$) represent the lower left-hand portion of the screen, while ($x2$,$y2$) represent the upper right-hand portion of the screen.

If you don't like Turbo Basic's standard 0 to 319 (or 0 to 639), 0 to 199, origin-at-top-left method of addressing the graphics screen, the WINDOW statement allows you to do it your way.

The WINDOW statement translates arbitrary "world" coordinates (which may be a more natural way for your program to express locations) into "physical" coordinates (the addresses of the display's pixels).

One application for WINDOW is to remap the display to correspond to the screen coordinates used by a different computer system. For example, the Apple II graphic display consists of 280 pixels horizontally by 192 pixels vertically. This WINDOW statement

```
WINDOW SCREEN (0,0) - (279,191)
```

causes the PC's display to use the same addressing scheme. After executing this statement, a program migrated from an Apple II that attempts to plot the lower right-most pixel on the Apple II screen it was written for. For example, PSET(279,191) turns on physical pixel 319,199 (the PC's lower right-hand corner).

As another example, suppose you are working with an application in which it is convenient to describe lines and other objects in terms of coordinates much larger than the 0 to 199 and 0 to 639 allowed by standard screen addressing. In this sample application, suppose it would also be useful to have the origin in the center of the display, and to have positive y values become larger as you move up from the origin, as they do in analytical geometry.

The WINDOW statement allows you to treat the medium or high resolution graphics screen as though it were really arranged this way. WINDOW allows you to map the full range of single-precision numbers to the display; for example:

```
WINDOW (-1E6,1E6) - (1E6,-1E6)
```

creates a 4 trillion point (2 million by 2 million) coordinate system. (– 1000000,1000000) is mapped to the upper left-hand pixel, (0,0) to the center of the screen, and (1000000, – 1000000) to the lower right-most pixel. This approximates the standard cartesian plane of coordinate geometry: The origin is in the middle, positive *x* values are right of the origin, and positive *y* values are above the origin.

After executing this statement, any operation that writes to the screen (CIRCLE, LINE, and so forth) will use this new coordinate system.

```
PSET (0,0)
```

turns on the pixel in the center of the screen.

```
PSET (25000,25000)
```

turns on a pixel slightly up and to the right of the center of the screen. The arguments to WINDOW are single-precision floating point, allowing the screen map to make a huge area (millions of pixels in both dimensions), or a tiny fractional area with coordinates between 0 and 1.

If the optional SCREEN keyword is included, it will cause the new coordinate system to retain the default quality that *y* coordinates get larger as you move downward. For example:

```
WINDOW SCREEN (1,-1) - (-1,1)
```

creates a coordinate system in which the top of the screen is represented by *y* coordinates of –1 and the bottom of the screen by *y* coordinates of 1.

Any active WINDOW mapping is turned off by the execution of RUN, SCREEN, or WINDOW with no arguments. The PMAP function performs scaling according to the current WINDOW setting but without putting anything on the screen.

See Also COS
PMAP

Example

```
' set medium resolution graphics mode
SCREEN 1

pi= ATN(1) * 4      ' define a constant

val1 = 5 : val2 = 6: steps=400    ' choose some values

WINDOW (-1,1) - (1,-1)    ' origin at middle

' go around the circle once
FOR  theta = 0 to 2 * pi STEP 2 * pi/steps

  ' circles with unity radius
  radius = COS(2 * theta)

  ' translate to cartesian
  x = radius * cos(val1 * theta)

  ' coordinates with a twist
  y = radius * sin(val2 * theta)

  PSET(x,y)          ' set a pixel

NEXT theta           ' repeat

' press any key to return to editor
WHILE NOT INSTAT : WEND

END                  ' end the program
```

WRITE statement

Function WRITE sends comma-delimited data to the screen.

Syntax `WRITE [expression list]`

Remarks *expression list* is a sequence of numeric and/or string expressions separated by commas or semicolons.

If *expression list* is omitted, a blank line is output.

WRITE is like PRINT except that WRITE inserts commas between items in the *expression list*, puts string data inside double quote marks, and doesn't output a space before positive numbers.

See Also PRINT

Example

```
' This loop reads a piece of data and prints it
' using PRINT statement. Then it prints
' the same data using the WRITE statement.

  FOR i = 1 TO 3

    READ words$, number%
    PRINT words$
    PRINT number%
    WRITE words$,number%

  NEXT i

DATA " HELLO ",10 ," HOW ARE ",20 ," YOU ",30

END                   ' end the program
```

WRITE # statement

Function WRITE # outputs data to a sequential file.

Syntax `WRITE #filenum, expression list`

Remarks *filenum* is the number associated with a device or file when the file was OPENed.

expression list is a sequence of numeric and/or string expressions separated by commas or semicolons.

WRITE # is similar to PRINT # except that WRITE # inserts commas between items in the *expression list*, puts string data inside double quote marks, and doesn't output a space before positive numbers.

WRITE # is the preferred method of writing data fields to a sequential file, since it automatically delimits variables with commas and puts quotes around strings. This makes it easy to INPUT# what you've written out.

See Also PRINT #

Example

```
' open a sequential output file
OPEN "FILE.PRN" FOR OUTPUT AS #1

' read information from DATA statements
' and output to the file
FOR I = 1 TO 6
  READ info$
  WRITE # 1,info$
NEXT I

CLOSE 1        ' close the file

END            ' end the program

' define some data
DATA "Mike","Smith","12 Main St.","Paris","Ca","95066"
```

A P P E N D I X **A**

Numeric Considerations

During the execution of a program, Turbo Basic must sometimes convert numbers from one internal representation to another; for example, from single precision to integer:

```
a = 14.1
b% = a
```

In such cases, Turbo Basic decides what to do with the excess (or missing) precision. The following rules govern numeric type conversion:

- In an assignment statement, the number is stored in the precision of the variable being assigned (that is, on the left side of the equal sign). For example:

  ```
  b = 1.1
  a% = b
  PRINT a%
  ```

- Whenever a more precise representation is assigned to a less precise representation, rounding occurs. For example:

  ```
  a% = 1.5
  b = 123.456789
  PRINT a%, b
  ```

  Note, however, that Turbo Basic treats in a special manner any number containing a 5 in its fractional part: The number is always rounded toward the *closest* even number. For example, 0.5 would be rounded *down* to 0; 9.005 would be rounded *down* to 9.000.

- When a less precise number is converted into a more precise number, the resulting value cannot be any more accurate than the original lower precision value. After this assignment, for example, only the first six digits of *b#* are significant:

```
a = 123.456
b# = a
PRINT b#
```

- In evaluating a numeric expression, Turbo Basic converts all operands in the expression to the precision of the most precise operand in the expression. For example:

```
a = 1.1 : b# = 1.123456
c = a * b#
PRINT a * b#, c
```

Note: When an expression contains both single- and double-precision operands, the result's accuracy is only single precision.

Random Files with Floating-Point Data

Because Interpretive BASIC uses Microsoft's non-standard floating-point formats, Turbo Basic programs must perform a special translation to read and write floating-point data in random files created by Interpretive BASIC. The MKMS$ and MKMD$ ("make Microsoft") functions create Microsoft-format numeric strings; CVMS and CVMD ("convert Microsoft") take Microsoft-format numeric strings and return Turbo Basic-format numeric data.

Internal Representation of the Four Numeric Types

Integers are represented by 16-bit (2 byte) signed numbers, with negative values stored in two's complement form. The least-significant byte is stored at the lowest memory address. For example, 531 decimal equals 213H, and is stored as the 2-byte sequence 13H 02H (13H at lowest address):

	byte 0	byte 1
Hex	13H	02H
Binary	00010011	00000010

And −531 decimal equals two's complement of 213H equals FDEDH, and is stored as the 2-byte sequence ED FD (ED at lowest address):

	byte 0	byte 1
Hex	EDH	FDH
Binary	11101101	11111101

Two's complement means all the bits are flipped and added.

Long integers are represented by 32-bit (4 byte) signed numbers. Negative values are stored in two's complement form. The least-significant word is stored first (in the lowest address), and the least-significant byte of each word comes before the most significant byte. For example, 79033 decimal equals 000134B9H, and is stored as the byte sequence B9H 34H 01H 00H:

	byte 0	byte 1	byte 2	byte 3
Hex	B9	34	01	00
Binary	10111001	00110100	00000001	00000000

And −79033 decimal equals two's complement of 00013469H = FFFECB47H, and is stored as the byte sequence 47 CB FE FF.

Computers and the Real Number System

The real number system is both infinitely long and infinitely dense. In addition to stretching from negative to positive infinity, between any two points on the number line, there are an infinity of points (numbers). For example, between 17.1 and 17.11 are the points 17.101, 17.104, 17.1041, and so on.

Finite machines that they are, computers cannot exactly represent this transcendent system of numbers, although they can be made to approximate it. Compromises between the quality of the approximation on one hand (that is, accuracy) and calculation speed and memory requirement on the other have resulted in two popular models of the real number system: single-precision reals and double-precision reals.

Both of these models map a finite, but usably large, set of discrete values onto a useful length of the real number line. There are gaps between adjacent representable values. When a calculation produces a result in one of the gaps, rounding occurs to the nearest representable point.

The density of representable values is not distributed evenly along the number line. An equal number of representable values exists between successive powers of two. For example, there are as many representable values between 1 and 2 as there are between 131,072 and 262,144. In other words, the gaps between representable values get larger as you move farther from zero in either direction on the number line. Eventually, you get so far away from zero that there are no representable points left. Producing numbers beyond the last representable value in either direction is called *overflow*.

Overflow and Underflow

Floating-point overflow occurs when a result is calculated greater than the maximum positive representable value or less than the most negative representable value. Because of the wide range of values permitted by Turbo Basic, floating-point overflow is a relatively unusual occurrence. Unlike integer overflow, floating-point overflow is always detected.

Floating-point *underflow* occurs when a result falls within the tiny gap between 0 and the first representable points on either the positive or negative arms of the number line. Turbo Basic's math routines handle underflow by inserting a 0 in place of the underflow result, and then continue execution without producing an error message.

Single-Precision Floating Point

Turbo Basic single-precision values are IEEE standard short reals. This format requires 4 bytes of memory, and results in a precision of 6 to 7 decimal digits and a range of approximately

$$8.43 \times 10^{-37} \leq |x| \leq 3.37 \times 10^{38}$$

Single-precision values consist of a 23-bit normalized mantissa, an 8-bit exponent with a *bias* of 7FH, and a sign bit, arranged as shown in Figure A-1. (Bias refers to the difference between the unsigned integer within the exponent field of a floating-point number and the exponent it represents.)

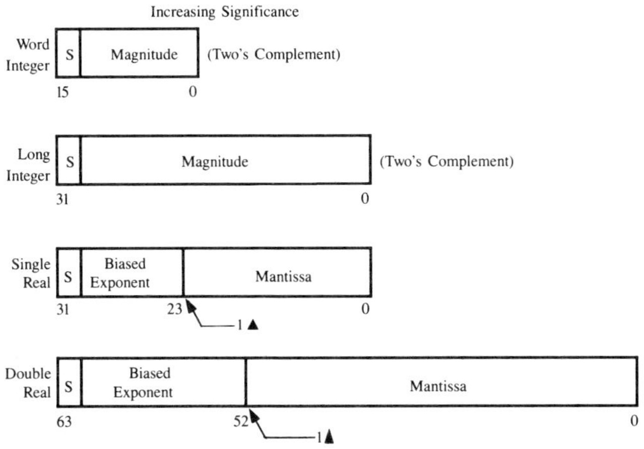

NOTES:
S Sign bit (0 = positive, 1 = negative)
d_n Decimal digit (2 per byte)
X Bits have no significance: 80287 ignores when loading, zeros when storing.
Position of implicit binary point
1 Integer bit of significant: stored in temporary real, implicit (always 1) in short and long real
Exponent bias (normalized values):
Short Real: 127 (7FH) Long Real: 1023 (3FFH) Temporary Real: 16383 (3FFFH)

Figure A-1 Data Formats

Double-Precision Floating Point

Turbo Basic double-precision values are IEEE standard long reals. This format requires 8 bytes of memory, and results in a precision of 15 to 16 decimal digits, and a range of approximately

$$4.19 \times 10^{-307} \leq |x| \leq 1.67 \times 10^{308}$$

Double-precision values consist of a 52-bit normalized mantissa, an 11-bit exponent with a bias of 3FFH, and a sign bit, arranged as shown in Figure A-1.

Following is a program that demonstrates Turbo Basic's internal single-precision format.

```
a! = 167.25
address = VARPTR(a!)          ' address1 points to a!
FOR n = 0 TO 3                ' default segment is okay
  byteval = PEEK(address+n)
  PRINT HEX$(byteval)
NEXT n
```

Let's decode these 4-byte values that supposedly represent 167.25 into single-precision form. First, rearrange them so that the most-significant byte comes first:

```
43 27 40 00
```

Now break them into binary:

Hex	4	3	2	7	4	0	0	0
Binary	0100	0010	0010	0111	0100	0000	0000	0000

Now break it into sign bit, exponent, and normalized mantissa:

	sign	exponent	mantissa
Binary	0	10000110	01001110100000000000000

Subtract the 7FH bias from the exponent:

```
86H - 7FH = true binary exponent of 7
```

A normalized mantissa has an assumed 1 and a binary point at the extreme left, so the mantissa is really

```
1.01001110100000000000000
```

Shifting the binary point right seven places to adjust for the exponent results in

```
10100111.0100000000000000  = 167.25
```

A P P E N D I X **B**

Event Trapping

Turbo Basic supports a background processing capability known as *event trapping*, which can at once simplify and speed up certain operations. Event trapping means getting Turbo Basic to check for various "events," such as a specific key being pressed, rather than having to write statements to do it yourself. Turbo Basic is able to do this checking between every statement in your program, guaranteeing the fastest possible response. If and when the event occurs, the subroutine you defined for handling the event is called automatically.

The following event types can be checked:

- Keystrokes: Has *F10* been pressed? Or the space bar? Or *Shift-Alt-K*? You can have traps for 20 different keys, all running at the same time.
- The status of a countdown timer—control is given to a trap subroutine when *n* seconds have elapsed; for example, to update an on-screen clock every 60 seconds.
- Joystick button pressing.
- Light-pen activity.
- Characters arriving at a serial port (for communications applications).
- The status of the background music buffer (check to see if it needs more notes loaded into it).

You can get a thumbnail sketch of what's trappable and what's not by glancing through the *O* section of Chapter 5, "Turbo Basic Reference Directory," of this manual. Most of the ON *something* GOSUB statements are related to event trapping.

You need not specify to Turbo Basic that you want event-trapping code to be generated. Event-trapping code is automatically generated whenever the compiler encounters any trappable instructions.

An Example

Imagine an accounting program with dozens of menus to choose from and screens to fill out. As the author of this complex application, you want to include a help screen that provides basic information about using it; for example, the keystrokes necessary to edit data fields or to abort a menu selection. For the sake of simplicity, the help system we're about to describe isn't context-sensitive; that is, the same text always appears without regard to where you are in the program when you're asking for help.

Let's make *F1* the help key. In other words, whenever *F1* is pressed, *whatever the context,* help text will be put on the screen.

The event-trapping capability of Turbo Basic allows you to code a "display help text" feature in one place, and call it from all over the program with no further effort. Without event trapping, you'd have to check the status of *F1* (with a GOSUB to the help routine) every place in the program where a user might spend some time.

First, since this is a key you're trapping (not a joystick button or a light pen), you should use the ON KEY(*n*) statement to define the subroutine to get control whenever *F1* is pressed. *n* is an integer expression defining the key to be trapped; it so happens that 1 is the name by which ON KEY knows function key 1.

```
ON KEY(1) GOSUB DispHelpText
```

This line says: When the key trap is turned on, check between every statement to see if *F1* has been pressed. If it has been pressed, call subroutine *DispHelpText*; if it hasn't, execute the next statement.

Subroutine *DispHelpText* itself isn't much more than a series of PRINT statements. Since it doesn't want to disturb the part of the program that was interrupted, it saves the current cursor position before doing anything, and restores it afterward. It prints the help text on the bottom four lines of the screen, where by convention no other part of the program writes.

```
DispHelpText:
  oldcsrx = POS(0) : oldcsry = CSRLIN
  LOCATE 22,1
  PRINT "This program was shipped with a fantastic manual"
  PRINT "carefully prepared by professional writers at great expense."
  PRINT "It contains more information than you will ever need."
  INPUT "Use it. Press Enter to proceed.", dummy$
  LOCATE 22,1 : PRINT SPACE$(320)
  LOCATE oldcsrx, oldcsry
RETURN
```

Now that the trap subroutine has been declared (the code that will get control when *F1* is pressed), turn on trapping with the KEY(*n*) statement:

```
KEY(10) ON
```

After executing this statement, Turbo Basic goes into event-checking mode. Between executing every subsequent statement, it does a quick check to see if *F1* has been pressed. If not, execution continues normally with the next statement. If it finds *F1* pressed, subroutine *DispHelpText* is called. When it RETURNs, control passes to the next statement in the interrupted sequence.

When an event trap occurs, an implicit "trap stop" statement is executed to keep the trap subroutine from being called repetitively from within itself (and filling up the stack). The closing RETURN of the handling subroutine automatically performs an implicit "trap on" statement unless the subroutine, in its body, executes an explicit "trap off." You can substitute the words PEN, PLAY, KEY, STRIG, TIMER, and COM for the word "trap."

Fine-Tuning Event Trapping

Event trapping is a powerful tool, but at a price. Since your program must check between the execution of every statement for the indicated event(s), processing slows down, which, depending on the application, may produce an unacceptable speed penalty. In addition, a program that does event trapping causes the compiler to generate more code (exactly 1 byte more per statement) than it would for a program with no event-trapping statements.

You can control Turbo Basic's generation of event-checking code with the $EVENT metastatement. Use $EVENT in programs that need to do event trapping, but not everywhere. $EVENT OFF prevents event-trapping code from being generated until the appearance of an $EVENT ON metastatement.

To illustrate, consider a sort routine in the accounting program described earlier. Sorts are slow enough already without being interrupted between every statement to see if *F1* has been pressed. Furthermore, since the sort doesn't require any user input, what's the point in putting a help message on the screen?

The solution is to bracket the sort subroutine with $EVENT metastatements:

```
ON KEY(1) GOSUB DispHelpText
KEY(1) ON
.
. main program stuff...
.
$EVENT OFF
SortRoutine:
.
. in here, event-checking code isn't generated...
. this saves time and code size
.
EndSortRoutine:
$EVENT ON
.
. the rest of the program...
.
END
```

There's an important difference between $EVENT and simply turning off the trap with KEY(10) OFF, as you would in Interpretive BASIC. KEY(10) OFF is a dynamic statement (that is, it's executed at runtime) that keeps your program from *responding* to *F1* being pressed, but not from making the test and wasting some time in the process. It goes through the motions because the code to make the check is embedded throughout the program between every statement. $EVENT is a compile-time statement that controls whether the compiler generates event-trapping code.

If $EVENT OFF has been used to defeat the generation of event-checking code in an area, then doing a KEY(1) ON statement in that area has no effect.

A P P E N D I X **C**

Assembly Language Interface

In designing an application, a task may arise that is performed too slowly by Turbo Basic or for some reason can't be performed at all. To address these needs for greater speed and flexibility, Turbo Basic allows your program to call assembly language subroutines and to make DOS and BIOS function requests.

Three forms of the CALL statement are provided in Turbo Basic:

1. CALL to a procedure. This procedure can be either a Turbo Basic or an INLINE assembly language procedure. INLINE assembly is the most powerful form of assembly language interface.
2. CALL ABSOLUTE to the address of an assembly language routine already loaded in memory. This is provided for minimal compatibility with Interpretive BASIC.
3. CALL INTERRUPT to a software interrupt vector number that will take you to an assembly language routine for software interrupt handling. CALL INTERRUPT is generally used to call DOS and BIOS services.

Chapter 5, "Turbo Basic Reference Directory," discusses in detail the CALL and SUB statements for Turbo Basic statements. In this appendix, we will concentrate on the assembly language aspects of the CALL and SUB statements.

Note that the techniques of interfacing with assembly language subroutines are by their nature somewhat complicated. You should become reasonably familiar with assembly language concepts before tackling the information in this appendix.

The CALL ABSOLUTE Statement

Using the CALL ABSOLUTE statement in your Turbo Basic programs invokes an assembly language subroutine that has been previously loaded with the BLOAD statement or is a part of the program's data space.

As an example:

```
DEF SEG = $H5000
MyAsmSub% = &H4000
CALL ABSOLUTE MyAsmSub%
```

invokes the assembly language procedure at offset 4000 Hex (16,384 decimal) into segment 5000 Hex (20,480 decimal). This address is more commonly specified in segment:offset form as 5000:4000.

Syntax of CALL ABSOLUTE:

```
CALL ABSOLUTE <numeric identifier> [(parameter list)]
```

where *numeric identifier* is a numeric scalar variable and evaluates to the range −32768 to +65535. If it is negative, it is forced to positive via two's complement arithmetic. This offset is used in conjunction with the most recently declared DEF SEG to form a callable 32-bit absolute address. If you want to use an expression for the address, you must assign it to *numeric identifier* and then use the identifier in the CALL statement.

Optional parameters are limited to only short integer scalar variables. Parameters are passed by reference with the 16-bit pointers pushed on the stack in order from left to right. All parameters are located in the main data segment pointed to by Data Segment (DS).

This CALL method allows minimal compatibility with Interpretive BASIC. Turbo Basic provides the more powerful SUB INLINE procedures to give you full access to its data storage extensions.

After completing the desired function, the assembly language procedure must perform a intersegment (far) RETURN to Turbo Basic. Execution then proceeds with the statement following the CALL.

The programmer is responsible for preserving the Data Segment (DS), Base Pointer (BP), Stack Segment (SS) and Stack Pointer (SP) registers.

The CALL INTERRUPT Statement

The CALL INTERRUPT statement uses an interrupt vector number to get to an assembly language routine. This call is normally used to call DOS and BIOS interrupt handlers, but can also be used for user-defined software interrupt handlers.

CALL INTERRUPT's syntax follows:

```
CALL INTERRUPT <integer expression>
```

where *integer expression* must evaluate to a value between 0 and 255.

Prior to making the interrupt call, you must set up the appropriate registers using the REG statement. Results returned in registers are stored internally by the compiler and may be accessed with the REG function.

After completing the desired function, the assembly language procedure must perform a RETURN from Interrupt (IRET) to Turbo Basic. Execution then proceeds with the statement following the CALL.

The programmer is responsible for preserving the Stack Segment (SS) and Stack Pointer (SP) registers.

The Register Buffer

The CALL INTERRUPT statement uses the *register buffer* for passing data to and from assembly language subroutines. This is a numbered sequence of 16-bit integers that are mapped to the processor's registers immediately before and after a CALL INTERRUPT.

REG as a statement stores the 16-bit contents of an integer variable into the specified register, according to the numeric argument (0 to 9) specified.

REG as a function returns the 16-bit contents of the specified register, according to the numeric argument (0 to 9) passed to it. The relationship between REG arguments and actual processor registers are depicted in the following table:

Number	Register
0	Flags
1	AX
2	BX
3	CX
4	DX
5	SI
6	DI
7	BP
8	DS
9	ES

To set an element in the register buffer, use REG as a statement; for example:

```
REG 5,&H8000
```

loads 8000 Hex into the buffer's SI register.

Note that REG does not immediately cause a processor register to be loaded or read—it reads and writes the intermediate buffer.

To read an element in the register buffer, use REG as a function; for example:

```
y% = REG(1)
```

loads the integer variable *y%* with the register buffer's counterpart to the AX register.

Again, note that the register buffer is loaded into the processor at the inception of a CALL INTERRUPT statement, and copied from the processor after returning from a CALL INTERRUPT statement.

About DOS and BIOS Function Calls

Interrupts 10H through 1FH are BIOS calls that perform various utility functions. (For more information about BIOS calls, consult the *IBM DOS Technical Reference Manual.*)

Interrupt 21H (33 decimal) is an especially interesting interrupt value, since it is the general calling mechanism for DOS. The request value is put into the most-significant byte of the AX register (AH) and additional parameters are put into other registers as needed. DOS provides scores of useful functions that can be easily accessed through this mechanism. (For more information, consult the DOS reference manual.)

As an example, function *FNFreeSpace* returns the amount of free disk space:

```
DEF FNFreeSpace(drive%) ' DOS function 36H returns the number of
                        ' free clusters on selected drive
                        ' 0 = default drive, 1 = A:, 2 = B:, etc.
REG 4,drive%            ' pass drive number in DX
REG 1,&H3600            ' AH = function number
CALL INTERRUPT &H21
' space = available clusters * bytes/sector * sectors/cluster
'       = BX*CX*AX
FNFreeSpace = CSNG(REG(2)) * REG(3) * REG(1)
END DEF
```

Once defined, *FNFreeSpace* can be called like any other function:

```
' How much room on default drive?
PRINT FNFreeSpace(0)
```

Using CALL with INLINE

INLINE assembly language programming and normal Turbo Basic procedures use the same calling sequence. The definition for the SUB procedure is changed to specify the INLINE assembly language program. This is the most powerful mode of assembly language programming in Turbo Basic.

Syntax:

```
CALL <procname> [(parameter list)]
```

Syntax:

```
SUB <procname> INLINE
  $INLINE <byte list>
  $INLINE "COM File Name"
END SUB
```

Any number of $INLINE statements can be specified in any order. The only limitation is a maximum of 16 COM files in any one procedure.

Byte lists are made up of constants or expressions that evaluate to an integer between 0 and 255 and are separated by commas. Normally, you will use Hex constants for bytes (&H4C,&H90).

Returns are not allowed in your assembly language code, nor at the end of the SUB. The compiler automatically sees to that. If you wish to exit the procedure early, just jump to an assembly language label at the end of your inline code.

Notice that you do not specify the parameter list in the SUB definition.

The programmer is responsible for preserving the Data Segment (DS), Base Pointer (BP), Stack Segment (SS), and Stack Pointer (SP) registers.

Parameters are pushed on the stack as 32-bit pointers to the data items (except for full arrays). Parameters are pushed on the stack in order from left to right.

Passing Numeric Variables

For numeric variables (integer, floating point), you get a 32-bit pointer to the data. (See Appendix A, "Numeric Considerations," for the numeric formats.)

Passing Strings

For string parameters (other than full string arrays), you get a 32-bit pointer to the 4-byte string descriptor. The first 2 bytes contain the length of the string. The next 2 bytes contain the offset of the string data in the string segment.

Note: You must ignore the upper bit on the string length bytes, since it is reserved and may be set. You must AND off this bit before using the length, but the value in memory must never be altered.

Note: You can modify bytes in the string but you can't modify the string's length. To get the string segment pointer, use the first word of the default data segment (word at DS:0). The format of a string descriptor follows:

Bytes 0,1:	Length of string (upper bit is reserved)
2,3:	Offset of data within the string segment

Passing Arrays

For array parameters, the array descriptor (60 bytes long) is pushed on the stack. The format of an array descriptor follows:

Bytes 0,1: Segment address of the array data. The first element always starts at offset 0. For dynamic arrays, it contains zero until the array is dimensioned.

2: Type of the array elements
- 0 = integer
- 2 = long integer
- 4 = single-precision floating-point
- 6 = double-precision floating-point
- 8 = reserved
- 10 = string

3: Number of subscripts

4,5:	Number of elements in the array
6,7:	Array item length 2 bytes = integer 4 bytes = long integer 4 bytes = single-precision floating-point 8 bytes = double-precision floating-point 4 bytes = string descriptor
8,9:	Lower bound for the first subscript of the array
10,11:	Upper bound for the first subscript of the array

The next 6 bytes repeat for up to 8 dimensions (or subscripts).

Bytes 12,13:	Reserved
14,15:	Lower bound for the next subscript of the array
16,17:	Upper bound for the next subscript of the array

Warning: Some parts of the array descriptor are reserved and subject to change in future versions of the compiler. We strongly suggest that you pass the number of elements and the first and last items of an array, and use the resulting pointers.

Array elements are always stored in contiguous memory locations (row major order).

Passing Expression Results

You can pass the result of an expression to assembly language routines but you cannot guarantee the numeric data type that might result. We suggest that you assign the expression to a variable and pass the variable.

Passing Constants

You can pass constants to assembly language routines but you need to identify the resulting type. To do so, use the identifier definition character (%,&,!,or #) after the constant.

Creating an INLINE.COM file

You can create an INLINE.COM file using a debugger (like the DEBUG that comes with your DOS disk) or a macroassembler (purchased separately).

Using DEBUG to create a .COM file

In DEBUG, you can use the *A* (assemble) command to key in the assembly language statements, *N* (name) to give the code a file name with the extension .COM, and *W* (write) to write out the .COM file to disk. Check out the DEBUG section of your DOS manual.

Using a Macroassembler to create a .COM file

When you're using a macroassembler, you actually need four programs: an editor (like SideKick's notepad), the macroassembler, a linker, and a program called EXE2BIN.

First key in your assembly language program with the editor. Next run the macroassembler to create an object file. Then use the linker (LINK on your DOS disk or a linker supplied with your macroassembler) to create an executable (.EXE) file. Finally use EXE2BIN (included on your DOS disk) to convert the executable file to a .COM file.

You can use the following batch file to automate the process:

```
MASM   %1;
LINK   %1;
EXE2BIN %1 %1.COM
```

Here are some guidelines for converting an assembly language program from an .EXE file to a .COM file to be used by Turbo Basic:

- Do not include a stack segment (the linker will report an error message for No Stack Segment, but ignore it).
- All instructions must use only relative addressing for both data and code references.
- It's advisable to keep all local data on the stack, and address it with stack-relative adressing.
- Use an ORG 100H statement at the beginning of the program.
- Preserve the Data Segment (DS), Base Pointer (BP), Stack Segment (SS), and Stack Pointer (SP) registers.

Suppose you come up with an algorithm that requires some nonzero value, say 100, to be quickly loaded into each element of a 200-element integer array. This could be done within a loop like this:

```
DEFINT a-n
DIM a(199)
FOR n = 0 TO 19999
a(n) = 100
NEXT n
```

Unfortunately, for your particular application this "element-at-a-time" scheme is just too slow. So you look for an assembly language solution to the problem of setting every member of an array to a value as close to instantly as possible.

As mentioned earlier, in Turbo Basic you call an assembly language procedure just like you call a regular BASIC procedure. The definition of the procedure specifies that you are using INLINE assembly language code. Look at the following example program:

```
DEFINT A-Z
DIM ARRAY(200)
CALL FILL(ARRAY(0))
FOR I = 0 TO 199
  PRINT A(I)
NEXT I
END

SUB FILL INLINE
  $INLINE &H55             ' push BP         save the Base Pointer
  $INLINE &H89,&HE5        ' mov  BP,SP      move stack pointer to BP
  $INLINE &HC4,&H7E,&H06   ' les  DI,[BP+6]  offset address of parm
  $INLINE &HB8,&H64,&H00   ' mov  AX,64H     constant to FILL
  $INLINE &HB9,&HC8,&H00   ' mov  CX,C8H     length of FILL
  $INLINE &HFC             ' cld             clear the direction flag
  $INLINE &HF3             ' rep             fill the words
  $INLINE &HAB             ' stosw
  $INLINE &H5D             ' pop BP          restore Base Pointer
END SUB
```

The INLINE assembly language procedure FILL doesn't care about arrays. It only knows that it is to load a constant value a number of times into memory, given a specific starting point. Passing the first element in array *A* will accomplish this.

A simple run-time map is depicted in Figure C-1.

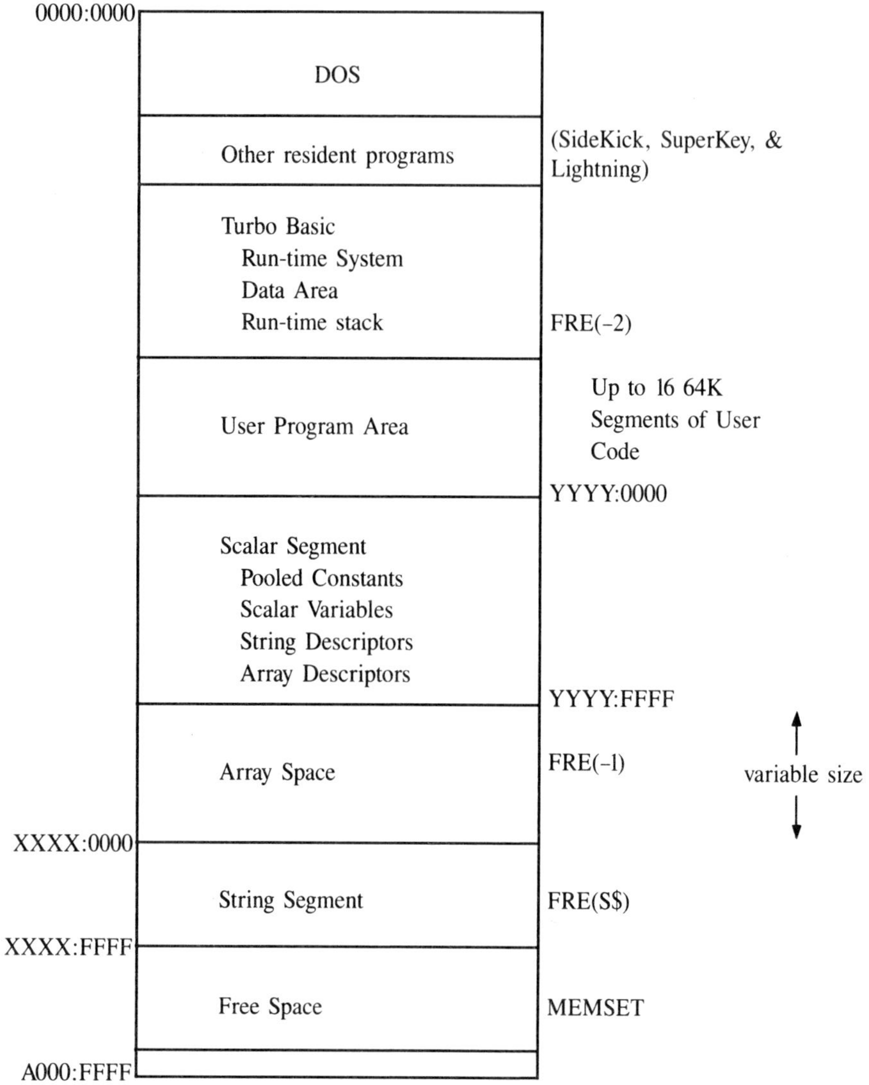

Figure C-1 *Run-time Map*

A P P E N D I X **D**

Comparing Turbo Basic and Interpretive BASIC

There are three principal differences between Turbo Basic and Interpretive BASIC:

1. The Compiler versus the Interpreter
2. Turbo Basic's extensions to the BASIC language
3. Compiler implementation

Each of these items points to many other underlying distinctions between the two BASIC implementations, which we will detail here.

The Compiler Versus the Interpreter

Interpreters tend to blur the distinction between commands for *creating* programs and those actually *used* in programs; in other words, between the program development system and the language itself. For example, EDIT and AUTO aren't part of the language in the sense that GOSUB and PRINT are.

Interpreters execute program code in order. Compilers, on the other hand, first scan all source statements, then generate executable code for the source statements. This latter attribute causes Turbo Basic, as a compiler, to catch errors for program code that would never be executed by Interpretive BASIC.

In the following example using Interpretive BASIC:

```
10 X = 5
20 IF X = 3 THEN GOTO 30 : X = 10 : Z = "AAA"
```

if *X* never equals 3 in the first place, then the statements following THEN will never be executed, and the syntax error of trying to assign a string to a numeric variable will never be found. Secondly, the *X* = 10 and Z = "AAA" statements will never be executed if *X* = 3 because of the GOTO line 30. The compiler will flag any "dead code" as an error at compile-time.

Unsupported Commands

Turbo Basic, because of its true full-screen editor and menu-driven commands for auxiliary functions, has no need for any statements related to loading, saving, and editing source programs; therefore they have been omitted. The corresponding Interpretive BASIC commands are usually used in DIRECT mode and include the following:

AUTO	LOAD
DELETE	NEW
EDIT	RENUM
LIST	SAVE

Turbo Basic lets you create and modify your programs with a text editor, so you have no need for commands to change or erase programs lines (such as EDIT or DELETE). If you want to erase a line, just move the cursor to the specified line and press *Ctrl-Y*. Similarly, there's no need for LIST—instead, you execute the appropriate keystrokes to get the desired portion of the program on the screen.

Turbo Basic's main menu functions perform the same tasks (and more) as that of Interpretive BASIC's SAVE, LOAD, and NEW. And since you don't need line numbers in Turbo Basic, you don't need AUTO and RENUM.

The following commands are also not supported in Turbo Basic:

CONT
Turbo Basic doesn't permit an interrupted program to be restarted. Interrupting a program with STOP or *Ctrl-Break* is the same as executing an END statement.

MERGE
Turbo Basic compiles programs into executable code, therefore it's not possible to merge source program lines at execution time.

MOTOR
The cassette port has not proven to be the most popular attribute of the PC.

USR
The CALL statement does USR's job and more.

Statements Requiring Modification

CALL ABSOLUTE

CALL ABSOLUTE only accepts integer parameters and has been included for minimal compatibility with Interpretive Basic. Turbo Basic provides more powerful CALL INTERRUPT and INLINE assembly procedures for complete assembly language programming. (For more information, see Appendix C, "Assembly Language Interface.")

CHAIN

CHAINed programs must be compiled as either .EXE or .TBC files by selecting the **C**ompile to **E**XE or Compile to **C**hain switch in the compiler **O**ptions menu. COMMON statements in both the originating and chained-to programs must list common variables in the right order (although not necessarily with the same name). You cannot execute a CHAIN statement when running from within Turbo Basic's environment. You can only use CHAIN when running from DOS. The MERGE and DELETE line-number-range options are not supported.

DEF*type*, TRON, TROFF, OPTION BASE

The performance of these statements differ subtly from Interpretive BASIC. Turbo Basic considers each statement's physical position in the source program rather than its position in the execution path of the object program. In other words, it is the position of these statements at compile-time rather than runtime that controls their effect. Using DEF*type* as an example, consider this simple program:

```
10 GOTO 30
20 DEFINT X
30 x = 2.3
40 PRINT x
```

When Interpretive BASIC executes this program, it never sees the typing statement in line 20. Thus, it uses its default variable type (single precision) when it encounters variable *x* in line 30, and then prints out 2.3.

Turbo Basic, on the other hand, gets typing considerations out of the way at compile-time. Since the DEFINT statement physically precedes the first occurrence of *x*, *x* becomes an integer variable, and the PRINT statement outputs 2.

DRAW, PLAY

Both of these statements execute complex instruction strings that cause graphics to be drawn or music to be played, respectively. In Interpretive BASIC, the string information that drives these commands can contain the names of string or numeric variables embedded within the instruction string. For example, in Interpretive BASIC, the statements

```
n = 50
PLAY "T=n; C"
```

set the tempo of PLAYed music to 50 quarter notes per minute and play note *C*. Turbo Basic cannot understand this construction, because after compiling, all information about the identifier associated with variable *n* is lost. However, you can get the same effect by using the VARPTR$ function:

```
n = 50
PLAY "T="+ VARPTR$(n) + "C"
```

Function Parameters
For function parameters, Interpretive BASIC allows you to use the same parameter variable name. Turbo Basic gives a duplicate, local variable error message.

RUN
A Turbo Basic program can use RUN to load and execute another program or to restart itself, but there is no way to restart the current program at any point except the beginning; you cannot specify a line number option.

Converting Interpretive BASIC Programs to Turbo Basic

The first step in converting an Interpretive BASIC program to Turbo Basic is to save it to disk in ASCII format. For example, to save your current program, type

```
SAVE "progname.txt",A
```

The ",*A*" option causes Interpretive BASIC to write out a text (ASCII) file without performing *tokenizing*. This file will be directly readable by Turbo Basic, although if it is larger than 64K, you will have to subdivide it into separate main and include files before editing or compiling with Turbo Basic.

Extensions to the BASIC Language

Turbo Basic has added many new command features and extensions to the BASIC language. Several extensions are discussed here. (Refer to Chapter 5, "Turbo Basic Reference Directory," for further details.)

Structured Statements

In an enhancement to Interpretive BASIC, Turbo Basic uses IF/ELSEIF/ELSE/END IF and SELECT CASE statements to control program flow and to promote easy-to-read programs. The new block-structured statement DO/LOOP allows total control over program loops with testing at the beginning and end of the loop.

Binary File I/O

Turbo Basic supports a new BINARY mode of file input and output. The GET$, PUT$, and SEEK commands give the programmer a very low level of file control. The program can read and write bytes to a file, and position the file pointer at any byte.

Function and Procedure Definitions

In Turbo Basic, function definitions can be both single line, like standard Interpretive BASIC functions, and multiline, permitting a more structured subroutine mechanism. The SUB and END SUB statements allow the creation of procedures. (For more information see Chapter 4's section entitled "Subroutines, Functions, and Procedures.")

Turbo Basic supports recursive procedures and functions with true local variable support. Use the LOCAL statement to define which variables will be pushed on to the stack during recursive execution.

Assembly Language Interface

In Turbo Basic, the CALL statement has three forms: CALL *procname*, CALL INTERRUPT, and CALL ABSOLUTE. CALL INTERRUPT uses the REG command to pass data via a register buffer. INLINE assembly language bytes or .COM files can be embedded inside procedures using the $INLINE directive. (See Appendix C, "Assembly Language Interface," for more details.)

Built-in Functions

Unlike Interpretive BASIC, Turbo Basic's transcendental functions return double-precision results.

New Commands

Turbo Basic has many new commands, as well as new options for old ones. Table D-1 partially lists the enhancements to Interpretive BASIC.

If you inadvertently use some of these reserved words as variables, you will get a syntax error at compile-time. To compile correctly, do a Find and replace operation to change conflicting variable names.

Table D-1 Turbo Basic's Enhancements to BASIC

BIN$	Returns binary form of an integer
BINARY	New file mode for low-level access
CEIL, FIX	Floating point to integer functions
COMMAND$	Returns command line trailer
CVMS, CVMD, MKMS$, MKMD$	Translates existing Microsoft-format data
DECR/INCR	Alternate way to increment and decrement variables
DEFLNG, MKL$, CVL	Support for new numeric-type long integer
DELAY	Waits *n* seconds (for machine-independent delays)
DO/LOOP	Flexible ANSI standard looping construct
ERADR	Address of most recent error
EXIT	Leaves a FOR/NEXT, WHILE/WEND, or DO/LOOP loop, IF block, procedure, or function
EXP2, EXP10	Returns powers of 2 and 10
GET$	Reads data from BINARY mode files
IF/ELSEIF/ELSE/END IF	Performs multiple IF tests
INLINE	Inserts bytes directly into object code
INSTAT	Returns keyboard status
LCASE$	Converts string to lowercase.
LOCAL/SHARED/STATIC	Declares procedure and function variables
LOG2, LOG10	Returns logarithms of base 2 and base 10
MEMSET	Defines free space in high memory
MTIMER	Fine-resolution timer
PUT$	Writes data to BINARY mode files
REG	Reads/writes register buffer
SEEK	Determines file position in BINARY mode files
SELECT CASE	Powerful CASE statement testing facility
SUB/END SUB	Defines procedure
VARSEG	Returns segment address of variable or array element

Compiler Implementation

Compiler implementation will affect some existing BASIC programs and also allow greater control over program compilation and code generation. We have already discussed some of the differences and extensions; other important points that grew out of the powerful implementation of Turbo Basic will be discussed in this section.

The Editor and Large Programs

The editor integrated within Turbo Basic allows source programs to be no larger than 64K in size. The $INCLUDE directive allows programs larger than 64K to be compiled. If you have a source program that is larger than 64K, you will need to split it up into several separate files. Use the **Main** file option in the **File** pull-down menu to specify the program you want Turbo Basic to start compiling (if it is different from the file currently in the edit buffer).

The Turbo Basic editor supports lines up to 248 characters wide. Interpretive BASIC supports lines as wide as 255 characters. Lines that are longer than 248 will automatically be split with a carriage return after column 248. However, you'll still need to check whether the line formation is correct before loading your program into the Turbo Basic editor.

Turbo Basic also supports programs that are larger than 64K of executable code. The $SEGMENT directive specifies that a new code segment will be generated and all CALLs/GOTOs will be changed to far calls and jumps.

Random Files with Floating-Point Values

Because Turbo Basic uses the IEEE floating-point standard values and Interpretive BASIC uses Microsoft's nonstandard format for single- and double-precision variables, a Turbo Basic program must translate floating-point fields in existing random files created by Interpretive BASIC programs. The MKMS$ and MKMD$ functions create Microsoft-format numeric strings; the CVMS and CVMD functions take Microsoft-format strings and return Turbo Basic-format numeric data.

Note that this applies only to floating-point fields in random access files, not integer or string fields.

Floating-Point Considerations

Unlike Interpretive BASIC, Turbo Basic uses the IEEE standard floating-point conventions when representing real numbers. Turbo Basic's single-precision numbers use 6 bytes of memory each and double-precision numbers use 8 bytes. Interpretive BASIC uses 4 bytes for single precision; 6 bytes for double precision. Turbo Basic's use of the IEEE format increases the level of floating-point precision. (Note that the conversion functions MKMD$, MKMS$, CVMD, and CVMS convert any data from Turbo Basic format to Interpretive BASIC and vice versa.)

Also since Turbo Basic performs all of its math operations using the math coprocessor (or an emulator of the 8087), the rounding of a fractional part of a number is not always rounded up. So whenever Turbo Basic rounds any number containing a 5 in its fractional part, the number is rounded up or down to the closest even number. For example, 0.5 would be rounded to 0; 9.005 would be rounded to 9.01.

When running the following program, Turbo Basic will generate 0 0 and Interpretive BASIC will generate 0 1.

```
10 DEFINT A-Z
20 A = 1/2  ' integer division
```

```
30 B = 1/2  ' floating-point divison
40 PRINT A;B
```

Running in a Window

In the Turbo Basic environment, programs that output text can run in the Run window, which is a virtual 25-row-by-80-column screen. Use *Alt-F5* to zoom the Run window while your program is executing.

If the program does any special POKEs to set the cursor location or change color attributes while running in a window, the screen may not display correctly. However, if you zoom the Run window before execution, the display will be fine. Programs that output graphics will take over the entire screen.

Intermediate Floating-Point Precision

Because Turbo Basic uses the IEEE standard for floating point, intermediate results are calculated to full 80-bit precision. Some Interpretive BASIC programs handle limited floating-point precision by adding to certain calculations a "fudge factor" of 1 to elicit the correct result. Since Turbo Basic gives you extended precision, code that takes advantage of limited precision arithmetic may have to be modified.

Strings

String handling has been enhanced in Turbo Basic. The maximum string length has been expanded from 255 to 32,767 characters. Also, the "garbage collection" performed periodically by Interpretive BASIC has been done away with—so there's no good reason to use FRE intermittently to force this operation.

Improved Memory Use

Turbo Basic makes all your system's memory available to your programs, without the stingy 64K limitation of Interpretive BASIC. Programs can have an unlimited amount of code, up to 64K of scalar (nonarray) variables, up to 64K of string data, and an unlimited number of arrays, each up to 64K in length.

PEEK and POKE Locations

When in graphics mode, text color has been preserved in PEEK/POKE location 4E Hex offset in the BASIC data segment. PEEKs and POKEs of other locations may have unpredictable results.

A P P E N D I X **E**

Error Messages

There are two fundamental types of errors in Turbo Basic: *compile-time* and *run-time*. Compile-time errors are errors in syntax discovered by the compiler. Run-time errors are anomalies caught by error-detection mechanisms the compiler places in your object programs.

Most compile-time errors are errors of syntax, caused by missing symbols, misspelled commands, unbalanced parentheses, and so on. If the compiler finds something in a source program that it cannot understand or permit, you are automatically placed in the editor, with the cursor positioned at the point of the error. Press any key to clear the error message, then edit the offending statement and recompile.

At the bottom of the screen, Turbo Basic lists the error number and a brief description of the error. Compiler errors have error codes of 256 and above.

Run-time errors occur when a compiled program is executed. Examples include file-system errors (disk full or write-protected), improper function calls (graphics statements without a graphics adapter), trying to take the square root of −14, memory errors (usually, not enough), and a host of other problems.

Run-time errors can be trapped; that is, you can cause a designated error-handling subroutine to get control should an error occur using the ON ERROR statement. This routine can "judge" what to do next based on the type of error that occurs. File-system errors in particular (for example, disk full) are well-suited to handling such routines; they are the only errors that a thoroughly debugged program should have to deal with.

The ERROR statement can simulate run-time errors as a debugging technique for error-handling routines.

For more information about run-time error trapping, see the ON ERROR and ERROR statements and the ERR, ERL, and ERADR functions in Chapter 5, "Turbo Basic Reference Directory."

If run-time errors are not trapped by your program, then a Turbo Basic program aborts upon encountering an error condition and displays the error number and a brief message to describe the condition. If the program was executed from within Turbo Basic, the editor cursor is also positioned at the statement that caused the error. Run-time errors have error codes between 0 and 255; for example:

```
Error 5 Illegal function call at pgm-ctr: 761
```

Error messages aren't included in .EXE programs; therefore, run-time errors that occur in programs launched from DOS do not include error text, only numbers. Debug's Find run-time error option is able to translate the program counter value returned by a run-time error into the exact statement within the source file that caused the error. For example:

```
nnnError-description<CR/LF>
```

where *nnn* is a three-digit error code. (For more information, see Chapter 3, "The Debug Command.")

Run-time Errors

---

2 **Syntax error**
A run-time syntax error has been created by a READ statement trying to load string data into a numeric variable. Other syntax errors are caught by the compiler.

3 **RETURN without GOSUB**
A RETURN was encountered without a matching GOSUB; that is, there is nothing to RETURN from.

4 **Out of data**
A READ statement ran out of DATA statement values.

5 **Illegal function call**
This is a catch-all error related to passing an inappropriate argument to some statement or function. A few of the 101 things that can cause it:

- Too large a color or screen mode argument
- Issuing a graphics statement without a graphics adapter or setting the proper mode with the SCREEN statement

- Trying to perform invalid mathematical operations, such as taking the square root of a negative number.
- Too large (or negative) a record number in a GET or PUT.
- Attempting to use the WIDTH statement on a sequential file.

6 **Overflow**
An overflow is the result of a calculation producing a value too large to be represented in the indicated numeric type. For example, $x\% = 32767 + 1$ causes overflow because 32,768 can't be represented by an integer. Integer overflow error is not caught unless a program is compiled with the **O**verflow switch turned on in the **O**ptions menus; floating-point overflow is always caught.

7 **Out of memory**
Many different situations can cause this message, including dimensioning too large an array.

9 **Subscript out of range**
You attempted to use a subscript larger than the maximum value established when the array was DIMensioned. This error is not reported unless the compiler **O**ptions' **B**ounds switch is turned on.

10 **Duplicate definition**
You attempted to dynamically dimension an array for the second time, without first erasing it.

11 **Division by zero**
You attempted to divide by zero or to raise zero to a negative power.

13 **Type mismatch**
You used a string value where a numeric value was expected or vice versa. This can occur in PRINT USING, DRAW, or PLAY statements.

14 **Out of string space**
String storage space is exhausted; string memory is limited to 64K.

15 **String too long**
The string produced by a string expression is longer than 32,767 bytes.

19 **No RESUME**
Program execution ran to the physical end of the program while in an error-trapping routine. There may be a missing RESUME statement in an error handler.

20 **RESUME without error**
You executed a RESUME statement without an error occurring; that is, there is no error-handling subroutine to RESUME from.

24 Device time-out

The specified time-out value for a communication status line has expired. Time-out values can be specified for the ClearToSend, CarrierDetect, and DataSetReady status lines. The program should either abort execution or retry the communications operation. (See the OPEN COM statement in Chapter 5 for further information.)

25 Device fault

A hardware error has occurred; for example, with the printer interface or a communications adapter.

27 Out of paper

The printer interface indicates that the printer is out of paper. It may simply be turned off or have some other problem.

50 Field overflow

Given the file's record length, you attempted to define too long a set of field variables in a FIELD statement.

51 Internal error

A malfunction occurred within the Turbo Basic run-time system. Call Borland's Technical Support Group with information about your program.

52 Bad file number

The file number you gave in a file statement doesn't match one given in an OPEN statement or the file number may be out of the range of valid file numbers.

53 File not found

The file name specified could not be found on the indicated drive.

54 Bad file mode

You attempted a PUT or a GET (or PUT$ or GET$) on a sequential file.

55 File already open

You attempted to open a file that was already open or you tried to delete an open file.

57 Device I/O error

A serious hardware problem occurred when trying to carry out some command.

58 File already exists

The new name argument specified by the NAME command already exists.

61 Disk full

There isn't enough free space on the indicated or default disk to carry out a file operation. Make sure there is enough free disk space and retry your program.

62 Input past end
You tried to read more data from a file than it had to read. Use the EOF (end of file) function to avoid this problem. This error can also be caused by trying to read from a sequential file opened for output or append.

63 Bad record number
A negative number or one larger than 16,777,215 was specified as the record argument to a random file PUT or GET statement.

64 Bad file name
The file name specified in a FILES, KILL, or NAME statement contains invalid characters.

67 Too many files
This error can be caused either by trying to create too many files in a drive's root directory or by an invalid file name that affects the performance of DOS's Create File system call.

68 Device unavailable
You tried to OPEN a device file on a machine without that device; for example, COM1: on a system without a serial adapter or modem.

69 Communications buffer overflow
You executed a statement to INPUT characters into an already full communications buffer. Your program should either check and empty the buffer more often or provide a larger buffer size.

70 Permission denied
You tried to write to a write-protected disk.

71 Disk not ready
The door of a floppy disk drive is open or there is no disk in the indicated drive.

72 Disk media error
The controller board of a floppy or hard disk indicates a hard media error in one or more sectors.

74 Rename across disks
You can't rename a file across disks or directories. A file isn't moved by a NAME statement, it's only given a new title.

75 Path/File access error
During a command capable of specifying a path name (OPEN, RENAME, MKDIR, for example), you used a path inappropriately; for example, trying to OPEN a subdirectory or to delete an in-use directory.

76 Path not found
The path you specified during a CHDIR, MKDIR, OPEN, and so forth, can't be found.

202 Out of string temp space

A string expression required the use of too many temporary string buffers. This can be caused by an expression like MID$(LEFT$(MID$(RIGHT$(...). Try simplifying your string expressions by storing intermediate results in temporary string variables.

203 Mismatched common variables

You attempted to CHAIN between two program segments that did not contain matching COMMON statements. Turbo Basic checks the type and number of variables in COMMON statements.

204 Mismatched program options

You attempted to CHAIN between two program segments that were compiled with different program options (different math library, math coprocessor required, and so forth).

205 Mismatched program revisions

You attempted to CHAIN between two program segments that were created with different versions of the Turbo Basic compiler.

206 Invalid program file

You attempted to CHAIN or RUN a program segment that was not compiled with Turbo Basic.

242 String/array memory corrupt

The string memory area has been improperly overwritten. This could be caused by the improper action of an assembler subroutine, string array access outside of the dimensioned limits, or by an error within the Turbo Basic run-time system.

243 CHAIN/RUN from .EXE file only

You attempted to CHAIN or RUN a program segment from within the Turbo Basic environment. You must compile your program to disk using the compiler **O**ptions menu selection and then execute programs that use CHAIN or RUN from DOS.

Compiler Errors

401 Expression too complex

The expression contained too many operators/operands; break it down into two or more simplified expressions.

402 Statement too complex

The statement complexity caused an overflow of the internal compiler buffers; break the statement down into two or more simplified statements.

403 **$IF nesting overflow**
Conditional compilation blocks ($IF/$ELSE/$ENDIF) can only be nested up to 16 levels deep.

404 **$INCLUDE nesting overflow**
Include files may be nested up to five levels deep, including the main program itself. That allows the program to have four nested include files.

405 **Block nesting overflow**
Your program has too many statement block structures nested within each other. Turbo Basic block structures may be nested 255 levels deep.

406 **Compiler out of memory**
Available compiler memory for symbol space, buffers, and so on, has been exhausted. If no more memory is available, separate your program into a small main program that uses the $INCLUDE metastatement to include the rest of your program. If you are compiling your program to memory and get this error, try compiling the program to disk with the compiler **O**ptions menu.

407 **Program too large**
Your program contains more than 65,530 statements.

408 **Segment exceeds 64K**
Your program contains a segment that exceeds the 64K limitation. Add a $SEGMENT metastatement to your source program to force program code into another segment.

409 **Variables exceed 64K**
Scalar variables are limited to 64K total space. In this space we include pointers to strings, integers, long integers, and single- and double-precision reals. Get rid of any unused variables or split up your program into separate Main and CHAIN programs.

410 **"," expected**
The statement's syntax requires a comma (,).

411 **";" expected**
The statement's syntax requires a semicolon (;).

412 **"(" expected**
The statement's syntax requires a right parenthesis (( ).

413 **")" expected**
The statement's syntax requires a left parenthesis ( )).

414 **"=" expected**
The statement's syntax requires an equal sign (=).

415 **"-" expected**
The statement's syntax requires a hyphen (-).

416 Statement expected

A Turbo Basic statement was expected. Some character could not be identified as a command, a metacommand, or a variable.

417 Label/line number expected

A valid label or line number reference was expected in an IF, GOTO, GOSUB, or ON statement.

418 Numeric expression requires relational operator

The compiler has found a string operand in a position where a numeric operator should be.

419 String expression requires string operand

The compiler expected a string expression and found something else; for example:

```
X$ = A$ + B
```

420 Scalar variable expected

The compiler expected a scalar variable as a formal parameter to a user-defined function. Scalar variables include strings, integers, long integers, and single- and double-precision reals.

421 Array variable expected

An array variable was expected in a DIM statement or in the graphics GET and PUT statements.

422 Numeric variable expected

A numeric variable was expected in an INCR, DECR, or CALL ABSOLUTE offset specification.

423 String variable expected

A string variable was expected in a FIELD, GET$, PUT$ or LINE INPUT statement.

424 Variable expected

A variable was expected in a VARPTR, VARPTR$, or VARSEG function.

425 Integer constant expected

An integer constant was expected in a named constant assignment or a conditional compilation $IF/$ELSEIF.

426 Positive integer constant expected

A positive integer constant was expected in the array bounds for a DIM STATIC array or in the $COM, $SOUND, and $STACK metastatements.

427 String constant expected

A string constant was expected for the file name in an $INCLUDE metastatement.

428 **Numeric scalar variable expected**
Either an integer, long integer, or single- or double-precision real variable is expected; for example, in a FOR/NEXT loop.

429 **Integer scalar variable expected**
An integer variable was expected as a parameter in a CALL ABSOLUTE statement.

430 **Integer array variable expected**
An integer array variable was expected; for example, in a PALETTE statement.

431 **End of line expected**
No characters are allowed on a line (except for a comment) following a metastatement, END SUB, or a statement label.

432 **AS expected**
The AS reserved word is missing in either a FIELD or an OPEN statement. Check the syntax of the FIELD and OPEN statements in Chapter 5.

433 **DEF FN expected**
The compiler found a END FN or EXIT FN statement without a function defined. When defining a function, it must begin with a DEF FN statement.

434 **IF expected**
The compiler found an END IF or an EXIT IF statement without a beginning IF statement defined.

435 **DO LOOP expected**
The compiler found a LOOP or EXIT LOOP statement without a beginning DO statement defined.

436 **SELECT expected**
When defining a SELECT CASE statement, you either forgot to include the reserved word SELECT or the compiler ran into a END SELECT or EXIT SELECT without a beginning SELECT CASE statement. This error can also occur if you try to use the reserved word CASE as a variable name in your program.

437 **CASE expected**
When defining a SELECT CASE statement, you forgot to include the reserved word CASE. This error can also occur if you try to use the reserved word SELECT as a variable name in your program.

438 **FOR LOOP expected**
The compiler found an EXIT FOR statement without a beginning FOR statement defined.

439 SUB expected
The compiler found an END SUB or EXIT SUB statement without a subprocedure defined. You must define a subprocedure by beginning it with a SUB statement.

440 END DEF expected
A function wasn't terminated by a corresponding END DEF statement.

441 END IF expected
An IF block wasn't terminated by a corresponding END IF statement.

442 LOOP/WEND expected
A DO or WHILE loop was not terminated with a corresponding LOOP or WEND statement.

443 END SELECT expected
A SELECT CASE statement was not properly terminated with an END SELECT statement.

444 END SUB expected
A procedure was not properly terminated with an END SUB statement.

445 NEXT expected
A FOR loop was not properly terminated with a NEXT statement.

446 THEN expected
An IF statement is missing its accompanying THEN part.

447 TO expected
A FOR statement is missing its accompanying TO part.

448 GOSUB expected
An ON statement is missing its accompanying GOSUB part.

449 GOTO expected
An ON statement is missing its accompanying GOTO part.

450 $ENDIF expected
An $IF conditional compilation metastatement is missing its accompanying $ENDIF. Look for all $IF metastatements and find out where to put the associated $ENDIF.

451 Unmatched $ELSE
The compiler encountered an $ELSE metastatement that was missing a preceding $IF conditional compilation metastatement. Go back in the source code from the $ELSE and determine where to put the associated $IF.

452 Unmatched $ENDIF
The compiler encountered an $ENDIF metastatement that was missing a preceding $IF conditional compilation metastatement. Go back in the source code from the $ENDIF and determine where to put the associated $IF.

453 Undefined name constant
You used a named constant in your program without defining it. Define the named constant or use a literal constant in the statement.

454 Undefined function reference
You used a function name in an expression without defining the function. Check the name of the function for mistakes or provide a definition for the function.

455 Undefined subprogram reference
You used CALL to a subprogram, but you did not define the subprogram. Check the name of the subprogram for mistakes or provide the subprogram.

456 Undefined label/line reference
You used a line number or label in an IF, GOTO, GOSUB, or ON statement, but you did not define the label or line number. Check the label or line number for mistakes or provide a label.

457 Undefined array reference
An array was referenced but was never defined in a DIM statement. Check the array name for mistakes or provide a DIM statement for it.

458 Duplicate label/line number
The same line number was used twice or the same statement label name was defined twice. Check your program and any include files for duplicate line numbers or labels and change one or both of them.

459 Duplicate named constant
Two named constants were defined with the same name. Check your program and any include files for duplicate names and change one or both of them.

460 Duplicate function definition
Two DEF FN functions were defined with the same name. Check your program and any include files for duplicate names and change one or both of them.

461 Duplicate subprogram definition
Two SUB procedures were defined with the same name. Check your program and any include files for duplicate names and change one or both of them.

462 Duplicate common variable
Two variables with the same name were listed in a COMMON statement. Check your program and any include files for duplicate names and change one or both of them.

463 Duplicate variable declaration
Two variables with the same name have been declared with a LOCAL, STATIC, or SHARED statement. Check your program and any include files for duplicate names and change one or both of them.

464 Duplicate $COM definition
Only one $COM metastatement for each communications port can be used in your program. Check your program and any include files for $COM definitions and delete one of them.

465 Duplicate $SOUND definition
Only one $SOUND metastatement can be used in your program. Check your program and any include files for $SOUND definitions and delete one of them.

466 Duplicate $STACK definition
Only one $STACK metastatement can be used in your program. Check your program and any include files for $STACK definitions and delete one of them.

467 Invalid line number
Line numbers must be in the range 0 to 65535.

469 Metastatements not allowed here
Metastatements must be the first statement on the line.

470 Block/Scanned statements not allowed here
Block statements like WHILE/WEND, DO/LOOP, and SELECT CASE are not allowed in single line IF statements.

471 Unknown identifier/ syntax error
Something is incorrect on the line—the compiler could not determine a proper error message.

472 Array subscript error
You dimensioned an array with a number of subscripts and used it with another number of subscripts.

473 Array bounds error
For a static dimensioned array, your program referenced the array with a literal value that was out of the range.

474 Type mismatch
The variable types in a SWAP statement are not the same.

475 Parameter mismatch
The type or number of parameters does not correspond with the declaration of the function or procedure.

476 **CLEAR parameter error - use MEMSET/$STACK**
The additional parameters available to the CLEAR statement are not available in a BASIC compiler like Turbo Basic.

477 **LOCAL requires DEF FN/SUB**
You can only declare LOCAL variables in a function or procedure.

478 **SHARED requires DEF FN/SUB**
You can only declare SHARED variables in a function or procedure.

479 **STATIC requires DEF FN/SUB**
You can only declare STATIC variables in a function or procedure.

480 **COMMON arrays must be dynamic**
Arrays used in a COMMON statement must be declared DYNAMIC.

481 **LOCAL arrays must be dynamic**
Arrays defined as LOCAL cannot be defined as STATIC. Get rid of the STATIC specifier or move the array definition out of the procedure or function and into your main program.

482 **Parameter arrays cannot be altered**
You cannot ERASE and DIM an array used as a parameter in a function or subprocedure.

483 **Array is not STATIC**
A static array may not be DIMensioned using variables as the index descriptors. You must use either named constants or literal constants when specifying the indices of STATIC arrays.

484 **Array previously STATIC**
If you have two DIM statements in a program for the same array, the array is automatically declared as DYNAMIC. You then tried to declare the array STATIC in another place or your program tried to issue a DIM DYNAMIC to an array that was previously declared STATIC.

485 **Array name without "( )" expected**
When using the ERASE statement, you need not specify the parentheses with the array name.

486 **Array exceeds 64K**
The size of an array cannot exceed 64K (one data segment). If you need larger arrays, you can split up one array into several arrays.

487 **Arrays limited to eight dimensions**
The maximum number of dimensions that can be specified for an array is eight. This is an internal limit for the compiler.

488 **Invalid numeric format**
Your program declared a number with more than 36 digits or a floating-point number with an *E* component without the exponent value.

489 **Invalid function/procedure name**
In the case of a function, FN must be followed by a letter and then other letters, digits, and periods, optionally ended with a type identifier (%, &, !, #, or $). In the case of a procedure, the name must begin with a letter and may be followed by other letters, digits, and periods, but may not include a type identifier.

490 **No parameters with INLINE SUB**
You did not specify a formal parameter list in an INLINE SUB procedure declaration. The assembly language program is responsible for knowing the number and type of parameters being passed to it. No type-checking is done by the compiler.

491 **Only $INLINE allowed here**
Only $INLINE statements are allowed in a SUB procedure declared with the INLINE option.

492 **$INLINE requires SUB INLINE**
$INLINE statements can only be used in a SUB procedure with the INLINE option.

493 **$INCLUDE file not found**
An include file could not be found in the specified directory path, current directory, or in the path specified by **S**etup's **D**irectories option. Check the **D**irectories path or make sure that the specified include file name exists.

494 **$INCLUDE disk error**
When Turbo Basic tried to open the include file, a disk error was reported during compilation.

495 **$INCLUDE file too large**
Include files, like all files that can be loaded by the Turbo Basic editor, must be no larger than 64K.

496 **$INLINE file not found**
An INLINE file could not be found in the specified directory path or current directory. Make sure that the specified include file name exists.

497 **$INLINE disk read error**
When Turbo Basic tried to open the INLINE file, a disk error was reported during compilation.

498 **Temporary file access error**
While compiling to disk (an .EXE or a .TBC file), the compiler was unable to access its temporary file. Check the Turbo directory in the **D**irectories option of the **S**etup pull-down menu to make sure that the directory defined exists.

499 Destination file write error

While compiling to disk (an .EXE or a .TBC file), the compiler received a disk write error.

600–610 Internal Error

If this error occurs, report it immediately to Borland's Technical Support Group.

A P P E N D I X **F**

Reference Materials

This chapter is devoted to various reference materials, and includes an ASCII table, keyboard scan codes, and extended codes.

ASCII Codes

The American Standard Code for Information Exchange is code that translates alphabetic and numeric characters and symbols and control instructions into 7-bit binary code. Table F-1 shows both printable characters and control characters.

Table F-1 ASCII Table

D	H	Ch	Ctrl	Mne	D	H	Ch	D	H	Ch	D	H	Ch	D	H	Ch	D	H	Ch	D	H	Ch	D	H	Ch
00	00		@	NUL	32	20	SP	64	40	@	96	60	`	128	80	Ç	160	A0	á	192	C0	└	224	E0	∝
01	01	☺	A	SOH	33	21	!	65	41	A	97	61	a	129	81	ü	161	A1	í	193	C1	┴	225	E1	β
02	02	☻	B	STX	34	22	"	66	42	B	98	62	b	130	82	é	162	A2	ó	194	C2	┬	226	E2	Γ
03	03	♥	C	ETX	35	23	#	67	43	C	99	63	c	131	83	â	163	A3	ú	195	C3	├	227	E3	π
04	04	♦	D	EOT	36	24	$	68	44	D	100	64	d	132	84	ä	164	A4	ñ	196	C4	─	228	E4	Σ
05	05	♣	E	ENQ	37	25	%	69	45	E	101	65	e	133	85	à	165	A5	Ñ	197	C5	┼	229	E5	σ
06	06	♠	F	ACK	38	26	&	70	46	F	102	66	f	134	86	å	166	A6	ª	198	C6	╞	230	E6	µ
07	07	•	G	BEL	39	27	'	71	47	G	103	67	g	135	87	ç	167	A7	º	199	C7	╟	231	E7	τ
08	08	◘	H	BS	40	28	(	72	48	H	104	68	h	136	88	ê	168	A8	¿	200	C8	╚	232	E8	Φ
09	09	○	I	HT	41	29	)	73	49	I	105	69	i	137	89	ë	169	A9	⌐	201	C9	╔	233	E9	Θ
10	0A	◙	J	LF	42	2A	*	74	4A	J	106	6A	j	138	8A	è	170	AA	¬	202	CA	╩	234	EA	Ω
11	0B	♂	K	VT	43	2B	+	75	4B	K	107	6B	k	139	8B	ï	171	AB	½	203	CB	╦	235	EB	δ
12	0C	♀	L	FF	44	2C	,	76	4C	L	108	6C	l	140	8C	î	172	AC	¼	204	CC	╠	236	EC	∞
13	0D	♪	M	CR	45	2D	–	77	4D	M	109	6D	m	141	8D	ì	173	AD	¡	205	CD	═	237	ED	φ
14	0E	♫	N	SO	46	2E	.	78	4E	N	110	6E	n	142	8E	Ä	174	AE	«	206	CE	╬	238	EE	∈
15	0F	☼	ˆO	SI	47	2F	/	79	4F	O	111	6F	o	143	8F	Å	175	AF	»	207	CF	╧	239	EF	∩
16	10	►	ˆP	DLE	48	30	0	80	50	P	112	70	p	144	90	É	176	B0	░	208	D0	╨	240	F0	≡
17	11	◄	Q	DC1	49	31	1	81	51	Q	113	71	q	145	91	æ	177	B1	▒	209	D1	╤	241	F1	±
18	12	↕	R	DC2	50	32	2	82	52	R	114	72	r	146	92	Æ	178	B2	▓	210	D2	╥	242	F2	≥
19	13	‼	S	DC3	51	33	3	83	53	S	115	73	s	147	93	ô	179	B3	│	211	D3	╙	243	F3	≤
20	14	¶	T	DC4	52	34	4	84	54	T	116	74	t	148	94	ö	180	B4	┤	212	D4	╘	244	F4	⌠
21	15	§	U	NAK	53	35	5	85	55	U	117	75	u	149	95	ò	181	B5	╡	213	D5	╒	245	F5	⌡
22	16	▭	V	SYN	54	36	6	86	56	V	118	76	v	150	96	û	182	B6	╢	214	D6	╓	246	F6	÷
23	17	↨	ˆW	ETB	55	37	7	87	57	W	119	77	w	151	97	ù	183	B7	╖	215	D7	╫	247	F7	≈
24	18	↑	ˆX	CAN	56	38	8	88	58	X	120	78	x	152	98	ÿ	184	B8	╕	216	D8	╪	248	F8	°
25	19	↓	ˆY	EM	57	39	9	89	59	Y	121	79	y	153	99	Ö	185	B9	╣	217	D9	┘	249	F9	•
26	1A	→	Z	SUB	58	3A	:	90	5A	Z	122	7A	z	154	9A	Ü	186	BA	║	218	DA	┌	250	FA	·
27	1B	←	[	ESC	59	3B	;	91	5B	[	123	7B	{	155	9B	¢	187	BB	╗	219	DB	█	251	FB	√
28	1C	∟	\	FS	60	3C	<	92	5C	\	124	7C	¦	156	9C	£	188	BC	╝	220	DC	▄	252	FC	n
29	1D	↔	]	GS	61	3D	=	93	5D	]	125	7D	}	157	9D	¥	189	BD	╜	221	DD	▌	253	FD	²
30	1E	▲	∧	RS	62	3E	>	94	5E	∧	126	7E	~	158	9E	₧	190	BE	╛	222	DE	▐	254	FE	■
31	1F	▼	ˆ_	US	63	3F	?	95	5F	_	127	7F	△	159	9F	ƒ	191	BF	┐	223	DF	▀	255	FF	

D = decimal
H = hexadecimal
Ctrl = control character
Mne = mnemonic
Ch = character

Extended Key Codes

Extended key codes are returned by those keys or key combinations that cannot be represented by the standard ASCII codes listed in Table F-1.

The extended codes are returned by the system variable INKEY$. In a two-character string, a null character is returned as the first character. Generally, the second character is the scan code of the first key.

Table F-2 shows the second code and what it means.

Table F-2 *Extended Key Codes*

Second Code	Meaning
3	NUL (null character)
15	Shift Tab (— < ÷ ÷)
16–25	Alt-Q/W/E/R/T/Y/U/I/O/P
30–38	Alt-A/S/D/F/G/H/I/J/K/L
44–50	Alt-Z/X/C/V/B/N/M
59–68	Keys F1-F10 (disabled as softkeys)
71	Home
72	Up arrow
73	PgUp
75	Left arrow
77	Right arrow
79	End
80	Down arrow
81	PgDn
82	Ins
83	Del
84–93	F11-F20 (Shift-F1 to Shift-F10)
94–103	F21-F30 (Ctrl-F1 through F10)
104–113	F31-F40 (Alt-F1 through F10)
114	Ctrl-PrtSc
115	Ctrl-Left arrow
116	Ctrl-Right arrow
117	Ctrl-End
118	Ctrl-PgDn
119	Ctrl-Home

Table F-2 Extended Key Codes, continued

Second Code	Meaning
120–131	Alt-1/2/3/4/5/6/7/8/9/0/-/=
132	Ctrl-PgUp
133	F11
134	F12
135	Shift-F11
136	Shift-F12
137	Ctrl-F11
138	Ctrl-F12
139	Alt-F11
140	Alt-F12

Keyboard Scan Codes

Keyboard scan codes are the codes returned from the keys on the IBM PC keyboard, as they are seen by Turbo Basic. These keys are useful when you're working at the assembly language level. Note that the keyboard scan codes displayed in Table F-3 are in hexadecimal values.

Table F-3 Keyboard Scan Codes

Key	Scan Code in Hex	Key	Scan Code in Hex
Esc	01	Left/Right arrow	0F
!1	02	Q	10
@2	03	W	11
#3	04	E	12
$4	05	R	13
%5	06	T	14
^6	07	Y	15
&7	08	U	16
*8	09	I	17
(9	0A	O	18
)0	0B	P	19
_-	0C	{[	1A
+ =	0D	}]	1B
Backspace	0E	Enter	1C
Ctrl	1D	|\	2B
A	1E	Z	2C
S	1F	X	2D
D	20	C	2E
F	21	V	2F
G	22	B	30
H	23	N	31
J	24	M	32
K	25	<,	33
L	26	>.	34
:;	27	?/	35
"'	28	RightShift	36
~`	29	PrtScr*	37
LeftShift	2A	Alt	38
Spacebar	39	7Home	47
Caps Lock	3A	8Up arrow	48
F1	3B	9PgUp	49
F2	3C	–	4A
F3	3D	4Left arrow	4B
F4	3E	5	4C
F5	3F	6Right arrow	4D
F6	40	+	4E
F7	41	1End	4F
F8	42	2Down arrow	50
F9	43	3PgDn	51
F10	44	0Ins	52
F11	D9	Del	53
F12	DA		
Num Lock	45		
Scroll Lock	46		

APPENDIX G

A DOS Primer

If you are new to computers or to DOS, you may have trouble understanding certain terms used in this manual. This appendix provides you with a brief overview of the following DOS concepts and functions:

- What DOS is and does
- The proper way to load a program
- Directories, subdirectories, and the Path command
- Using AUTOEXEC.BAT files

This information is by no means a complete explanation of the DOS operating system. If you need more details, please refer to the MS-DOS™ or PC-DOS user's manual that came with your computer system.

Turbo Basic runs under the MS-DOS or PC-DOS operating system, version 2.0 or later.

What Is DOS?

DOS is shorthand for Disk Operating System. MS-DOS is Microsoft's version of DOS, while PC-DOS is IBM's rendition. DOS is the traffic coordinator, manager, and operator for the transactions that occur between the parts of the computer system and the computer system and you. DOS operates in the background, taking care of many of the menial computer tasks you wouldn't want to have to think about—for instance, the flow of characters between your keyboard and the computer, between the computer and your printer, and between your disk(s) and internal memory (RAM).

Other transactions are ones that you initiate by entering commands on the DOS command line; in other words, immediately after the DOS prompt. Your DOS prompt looks like one of the following:

```
A>
B>
C>
```

The capital letter refers to the active disk drive (the one DOS and you are using right now). For instance, if the prompt is A>, it means you are working with the files on drive *A*, and that the commands you give DOS will refer to this drive. When you want to switch to another disk, making it the active disk, all you do is type the letter of the disk, followed by a colon and *Enter*. For instance, to switch to drive *B*, just type B:*Enter*.

There are a few commands that you will use often with DOS, if you haven't already, such as

DEL or ERASE	To erase a file
DIR	To see a list of files on the logged disk
COPY	To copy files from one disk to another
TB	To load Turbo Basic

DOS doesn't care whether you type in uppercase or lowercase letters or a combination of both, so you can enter your commands however you like.

We'll assume you know how to use the first three commands listed; if you don't, refer to your DOS manual. Next, we will explain the proper way to load a program like Turbo Basic (see the last command on the list).

How to Load a Program

On your Turbo Basic system disk, you'll find the file name TB.EXE. This program file contains all the main BASIC functions. A file name with the "last name," or extension, .COM or .EXE means a program file that you can load and run (use) by typing only its "first name" on the DOS command line. So, to invoke the Turbo Basic program, you simply type TB and press *Enter* to load Turbo Basic into your computer's memory.

There's one thing you need to remember about loading Turbo Basic and other similar programs: *You must be logged on to the disk and directory where the program is located in order to load it*; unless you have set up a DOS path (described shortly), DOS won't know where to find the program.

Say your system disk with the TB.EXE program is in drive *A* but the prompt you see on your screen is B>. If you type TB and press **Enter**, DOS won't know what you're talking about and will give you the message "Bad command or file name."

In other words, you're in the wrong place.

So if you happen to get that DOS message, simply switch to drive *A* by typing A: and then press **Enter**. Then type TB and press **Enter** to load Turbo Basic.

You can set up a "path" to your Basic files so that DOS can find them using the DOS Path command. See the section, "The AUTOEXEC.BAT File," for more information.

Directories

A *directory* is a convenient way to organize your floppy or hard disk files. Directories allow you to subdivide your disk into sections, much the way you might put groups of manila file folders into separate file boxes. For instance, you might want to put all your file folders having to do with finance—for instance, a bank statement file, an income tax file, or the like—into a box labeled "Finances."

On your computer, it would be convenient to make a directory to hold all your Turbo Basic files, another for your SideKick files, another for your letters, and so on. That way, when you type DIR on the DOS command line, you don't have to wade through hundreds of file names looking for the file you want. You'll get a listing of only the files on the directory you're currently logged on to.

Although you can make directories on either floppy or hard disks, they are used most often on hard disks. This is because they can hold a greater volume of data; however, this also leads to a greater need for organization and compartmentalization of data.

When you're at the DOS level, rather than in Turbo Basic or another program, you can tell DOS to create directories, move files around between directories, and display which files are in a particular directory.

In the examples that follow, we assume you are using a hard disk system, and that you are logged on to the hard disk so that the prompt you see on your screen is C>. If you want to create directories on your floppy disks, just substitute *A* or *B* for *C* in the example.

To make a directory for your Turbo Basic files, do the following:

1. At the C> prompt, type MKDIR BASIC and press *Enter*. The MKDIR command tells DOS to make a directory called BASIC.
2. Type CHDIR BASIC and press *Enter*. The CHDIR command tells DOS to move you into the BASIC directory.
3. Now, put the Turbo Basic disk you want to copy from into one of your floppy drives—let's say *A* for this example—and type COPY A:*.* *Enter*. (The asterisks are *wildcards* that stand for *all files*.) The COPY command tells DOS to copy all files on the *A* drive to the BASIC directory on the *C* drive. As each file on the disk is copied, you will see it listed on the screen.

That's all there is to it. Treat a directory the same way you would a disk drive: To load Turbo Basic, you must be in the BASIC directory before typing TB and pressing *Enter*, or else DOS won't be able to find the program.

Subdirectories

If you are someone who really likes organization, you can further subdivide your directories into subdirectories. You can create as many directories and subdirectories as you like—just don't forget where you put your files!

A subdirectory is created the same way as a directory. To create a subdirectory from the BASIC directory (for instance, for storing your graphics files), do the following:

1. Be sure you are in the BASIC directory.
2. Type MKDIR GRAPH *Enter*.
3. Type CHDIR GRAPH. You are now in the GRAPH subdirectory.
4. If you already have BASIC graphics files you want to store in this subdirectory, copy them now. If the files are on a floppy disk with the extension .GRP, insert the disk in drive A and press *Enter*. If the files are in the root directory of your hard disk, type COPY *.GRP and press *Enter*.

Where Am I? The $p $g Prompt

You probably have noticed that when you change directories, you still see the C> prompt; there is no evidence of what directory or subdirectory you are in. This can be confusing, especially if you leave your computer for a while. It's easy to forget where you were when you left.

DOS gives you an easy way to find out. Just type

```
prompt=$p $g
```

and from now on (until you turn your computer off or reboot), the prompt will show you exactly where you are. Try it. If you are still in the GRAPH subdirectory, your DOS prompt should look like this:

```
C:\BASIC\GRAPH >
```

The AUTOEXEC.BAT File

To avoid typing the prompt command (discussed in the previous section) to see "where you are" every time you turn on your computer, you can set up an AUTOEXEC.BAT file to do it for you each time you turn on your computer.

The AUTOEXEC.BAT file is a useful tool and does much more than this, but rather than go into great detail here, we suggest referring to your DOS manual for more information. However, we will show you how to create an AUTOEXEC.BAT file that will automatically change your prompt so you know where you are in your directory structure, set a path to the BASIC directory, and then load Turbo Basic.

The DOS Path command tells your computer where to look for commands it doesn't recognize. DOS only recognizes programs in the current (logged) directory unless there is a path to the directory containing pertinent programs or files.

In the following example, we will set a path to the BASIC directory and a subdirectory called FILES.

If you have an AUTOEXEC.BAT file in your root directory, your computer will do everything in that file when you first turn your computer on. (The root directory is where you see the C> or C:\ prompt, with no directory names following it.)

Here's how to create an AUTOEXEC.BAT file.

1. Type CHDIR \ to get to the root directory.
2. Type COPY CON AUTOEXEC.BAT *Enter*. This tells DOS to copy whatever you type next into a file called AUTOEXEC.BAT.

3. Type

```
ECHO OFF
PROMPT=$P $G Enter
PATH=C:\BASIC;C:\BASIC\FILES
CHDIR\BASIC
\BASIC
Ctrl-Z Enter
```

The *Ctrl-Z* sequence saves your commands in the AUTOEXEC.BAT file.

To test your new AUTOEXEC.BAT file, reboot your computer by holding down the *Ctrl* and *Alt* keys and then pressing *Del*. You should see C:\BASIC > when your system comes up.

Changing Directories

How do you get from one directory to another? It depends on where you want to go. The basic DOS command for changing directories is CHDIR. Use it like this:

- **To move from one directory to another:** For example, to change from the BASIC directory to one called WP, type the following from the BASIC directory:

  C:\BASIC > `CHDIR \WP` *Enter*

  Notice the backslash (\) before the directory name. Whenever you are moving from one directory to another unrelated directory, type the name of the directory, preceded by a backslash.

- **To move from a directory to its subdirectory:** For example, to move from the BASIC directory to the GRAPH subdirectory, type the following from the BASIC directory:

  C:\BASIC > `CHDIR GRAPH` *Enter*

  In this case, you did not need the backslash, because the GRAPH directory is a direct offshoot of the BASIC directory. In fact, DOS would have misunderstood what you meant if you had used the backslash in this case. If you had included the backslash, DOS would have thought that GRAPH was a directory off the main (root) directory.

- **To move from a subdirectory to its parent directory:** For example, to move from the GRAPH subdirectory to the BASIC directory, type the following from the GRAPH subdirectory:

  C:\BASIC\GRAPH > `CHDIR ..` *Enter*

  DOS will move you back to the BASIC directory. Anytime you want to move back to the parent directory, use a space followed by two periods after the CHDIR command.

- **To move to the root directory:** The *root directory* is the original directory. It is the parent (or grandparent) of all directories (and subdirectories). When you are in the root directory, you see this prompt: C:\>.

  To move to the root directory from any other directory, simply type

  ```
  CHDIR \ Enter
  ```

  The backslash without a directory name signals DOS that you want to return to the root directory.

Setting Up an Operating Environment

If you have some special hardware needs or if you're a developer in need of a dynamic environment, being able to set *environment variables* will afford you some choices. Environment variables actually override compiler and/or program options, and are determined by using the SET command in DOS.

Environment variables have an effect on the entire environment in which a program is executed. Thus after setting a variable, it's in effect until you reset it to another value or turn off your machine. If you find yourself setting these values consistently one way, you may want to enter the SET command into a batch file or your AUTOEXEC.BAT file (see the earlier section detailing this file).

Turbo Basic's environment variables allow you to override compiler and runtime options for 8087 support and Color/Graphics Adapter (CGA) "snow" checking. For example, in the following example you're setting up your environment for 8087 use by typing at the DOS prompt

```
SET 87=yes
```

where *yes* means you have an 8087; *no* means even if you have an 8087 don't use it. The default setting is *yes*.

In the case of CGA snow-checking, you could type

```
SET CGASNOWCHK=no
```

where *no* doesn't do snow-checking and *yes* does snow-checking. The default setting is *yes*.

When your compiler begins executing or when a generated .EXE file starts executing, they actually search the *environment variable space* for these variables.

Though it's not necessary to set these variables, they're available when you need them. If you choose not to set them, the current directory searches for files and creates temporary ones to store the default variables.

This appendix presents only a quick look at DOS and some of its functions. Once you're familiar with the information given here, you may want to study your DOS manual and discover the many things you can do with your computer's operating system. There are many other DOS functions not mentioned here that can simplify and enhance your computer use.

APPENDIX **H**

Summary of Functions and Procedures

Use this appendix as a quick reference to operation-specific procedures and functions. For example, under the heading "String Operations," you'll find in particular the $BIN function that returns the binary string equivalent of a number, and in general other string-related operations.

Chaining

CHAIN	Invokes a Turbo Basic chain module (extension .TBC)
COMMON	Declares a variable(s) to be passed to a chained program
RUN	Restarts the program

Compiler Data

DIM	Declares arrays
LET	Assigns a value to a variable
LOCAL	Declares local variables in a procedure or function
OPTION BASE	Sets minimum value for array subscripts
REM	Delimits the programmer's remarks
SHARED	Declares shared (global) variables in a procedure or function
STATIC	Declares the static variables in a procedure or function
TRON/TROFF	Turns on and off execution trace

Devices

COM(*n*)	Controls the trapping of serial port events
INP	Reads from an I/O port
IOCTL/IOCTL$	Communicates with a device driver
OPEN COM	Opens and configures a communications port
OUT	Writes to an I/O port

DOS

CHDIR	Changes the current directory (DOS CD command)
KILL	Deletes a file (like the DOS DEL command)
MKDIR	Creates a subdirectory (like DOS's MKDIR command)
RMDIR	Removes the directory (like DOS's RMDIR command)
SHELL	Loads and executes child process (DOS 3.0 only)
SYSTEM	Terminates a program

Error Handling

ERADR	Returns the address of the most recent error
ERDEV/ERRDEV$	Returns device driver information
ERL/ERR	Returns the line and error code of the most recent error
ERROR	Simulates a run-time error

Files

BLOADS	Loads a BSAVEd file into memory
BSAVE	Saves a memory range to disk
CLOSE	Closes a file or device
EOF	Returns end-of-file status
FIELD	Defines field variables of a random file buffer
FILES	Displays the directory contents (like DOS's DIR command)
GET (files)	Reads a record from a random file
GET (graphics)	Reads all or part of the graphics screen into an array
LINE INPUT #	Reads a line from a sequential file into a string variable, ignoring delimiters
LOC	Returns the current file position
LOF	Returns the length of a file
LSET	Moves string data into the random file buffer
NAME	Renames a file (like DOS's REN function)
OPEN	Prepares a file or device for reading or writing
PRINT #, PRINT # USING	Writes formatted information to a file
PUT	Writes a record to a random file
PUT$	Writes a string to a binary mode file
RESET	Closes and flushes all disk files
RSET	Moves string data into the random file buffer
SEEK	Sets the position in a binary file for GET$ and PUT$
WRITE #	Outputs data to a sequential file

Flow Control

CALL	Invokes a procedure (subprogram)
CALL ABSOLUTE	Invokes an assembly language routine
CALL INTERRUPT	Calls the system interrupt
DEF FN/END DEF	Defines a function
DO/LOOP	Builds a loop with the test at the top and/or bottom
END	Terminates execution of a program or defines the end of a structured block
EXIT	Leaves a structure prematurely
FOR/NEXT	Defines an automatically incrementing (or decrementing) loop
GOSUB	Invokes a subroutine
GOTO	Sends program flow to the statement identified by *label*
IF	Tests a condition and alters program flow if the condition is met
IF BLOCK	Creates a series of IF statements
INLINE	Declares inline machine code
RESUME	Restarts execution after error handling
RETURN	Returns from the subroutine to the calling program
SELECT	Returns a general purpose testing statement
STOP	Halts the program
SUB/END SUB	Defines a procedure (subprogram)
WHILE/WEND	Builds a loop with the test at the top

Graphics

CIRCLE	Draws a circle or part of a circle
DRAW	Draws shapes onto the graphics screen
LINE	Draws a straight line or box
PAINT	Fills an enclosed area on the graphics screen with a selected color
PEEK	Returns the byte stored at the specified memory location
PEN (function)	Reads light-pen status
PEN (statement)	Controls the checking of light-pen events
PMAP	Translates physical coordinates to world coordinates and vice versa
POINT	Returns the color of a pixel or LPR information
POKE	Writes a byte to a specified address
PRESET	Plots a point on the graphics screen
PSET	Plots a point on the graphics screen
PUT	Plots the contents of a numeric array to the graphics screen
VIEW	Defines the active area (viewport) of the graphics screen
WINDOW	Defines the graphics coordinate system

Hardware Events

ON COM(*n*)	Declares trap subroutine for serial port events
ON ERROR	Specifies error-handling routine and turns on error trapping
ON/GOSUB	Calls one of several possible subroutines according to the value of a numeric expression
ON/GOTO	Sends program flow to one of several possible destinations based on the value of a numeric expression
ON KEY(*n*)	Declares the trap subroutine to get control if a specific key is pressed
ON PEN	Declares the trap subroutine to get control if light-pen activity occurs
ON PLAY	Declares the trap subroutine to get control if the background music buffer contains less than the specified number of notes
ON STRIG	Declares the trap subroutine for the joystick button
ON TIMER	Declares the trap subroutine to get control every *n* seconds
STICK	Returns joystick position information
STRIG (function)	Returns the status of the joystick buttons
STRIG (statement)	Controls the joystick button event checking
WAIT	Waits for the indicated hardware status condition

Input

INKEY$	Reads the keyboard
INPUT	Prompts the user for values to assign to one or more variables
INPUT #	Loads variables with data from a sequential file
INPUT$	Reads a specific number of characters from the keyboard or a file
INSTAT	Returns keyboard status
LINE INPUT	Reads a line from the keyboard into a string variable, ignoring delimiters
READ	Loads variables from DATA statement constants
RESTORE	Allows DATA statement constants to be read again

Keyboard Handling

KEY	Sets and displays function key contents and defines key trap values
KEY(*n*)	Turns trapping on or off for a specific key

Memory Management

CLEAR	Clears variable memory
DEF SEG	Defines the data segment to be used by BLOAD, BSAVE, CALL ABSOLUTE, PEEK, and POKE statements
ENDMEM	Returns the address of the end of physical memory
ERASE	Deletes dynamic arrays and resets static arrays
FRE	Returns the amount of free memory available to your program
MEMSET	Declares the upper memory limit
POKE	Writes a byte to a specified address
VARPTR	Returns the address of a variable
VARPTR$	Returns a pointer to a variable in string form
VARSEG	Returns the segment address of a variable

Metastatements

$COM	Allocates space for the serial port receive buffer
$DYNAMIC	Declares a default array allocation to be dynamic
$EVENT	Controls generation of event-trapping code
$IF/$ELSE/$ENDIF	Defines portions of a source program to be compiled or skipped
$INCLUDE	Includes a text file
$SEGMENT	Declares a new code segment
$SOUND	Declares the capacity of the background music buffer
$STACK	Declares the size of the run-time stack
$STATIC	Declares the default array allocation to be static

Miscellaneous

DATA	Declares constants for READ statements
DELAY	Inserts a pause
REG	Sets or returns a value in the register buffer
SWAP	Exchanges the values of two variables

Numeric

ABS	Returns an absolute value
ASC	Returns the ASCII code of a string's first character
ATN	Returns a trigonometric arctangent
CDBL	Converts a number to double-precision format
CEIL	Returns the largest integer greater than or equal to its argument
CINT	Converts to an integer
CLNG	Converts to a long integer
COS	Returns a trigonometric cosine
CSNG	Converts a numeric expression to its single-precision equivalent
CVI/CVL/CVS/CVD	Converts string data read from random files to numeric form
CVMD/CVMS	Converts string variables read from Microsoft-format random files to numeric form

DECR	Decrements a variable
DEFINT/DEFLNG/ DEFSNG/DEFDBL/ DEFSTR	Declares the default type of variable identifiers
EXP	Returns e^x
EXP2	Returns 2^x
EXP10	Returns 10^x
FIX	Truncates to integer
INCR	Increments a variable
INT	Converts a numeric expression to an integer
LOG	Returns the natural (base *e*) logarithm
LOG2	Returns the logarithm of base 2
LOG10	Returns the logarithm of base 10
MKI$/MKL$/ MKS$/MKD$	Converts numeric data into strings (for random file output)
MKMD$/MKMS$	Converts numeric data into Microsoft-format strings (for random file output)
RANDOMIZE	Seeds the random number generator
RND	Returns a random number
SGN	Returns the sign of a numeric expression
SIN	Returns a trigonometric sine
SQR	Returns a square root
TAN	Returns a trigonometric tangent

Output

PRINT	Sends data to the screen
PRINT USING	Sends formatted information to the screen
SPC	Skips *n* spaces (used in PRINT statement)
TAB	Tabs to a specified print position *n* (PRINT statement only)
WRITE	Sends comma-delimited data to the screen

Printer

LPOS	Returns the "cursor position" of the printer buffer
LPRINT, LPRINT USING	Sends data to the printer (LPT1:)

Screen

CLS	Clears the screen
COLOR	Sets text color
COLOR	Sets the colors for graphic operations
CSRLIN	Returns the current vertical cursor position (row number)
LOCATE	Positions the cursor and/or defines the cursor's shape
POS	Returns the cursor horizontal position (column number)
SCREEN (files)	Returns the ASCII code of the character at the specified row and column
SCREEN (graphics)	Sets the screen display mode
WIDTH	Sets the logical line size

Sound

PLAY (function)	Returns the number of notes in the background music buffer
PLAY (statement)	Returns the number of notes in the background music buffer
SOUND	Generates a tone of specified frequency and duration

String Operations

BIN$	Returns the binary string equivalent of a number
CHR$	Converts an ASCII code into a one-character string
GET$	Reads a string from a file opened in BINARY mode
HEX$	Converts a number into its hex string equivalent
INSTR	Searches a string for a pattern
LCASE$	Returns a lowercase-only string
LEFT$	Returns the left-most *n* characters of a string
LEN	Returns the length of a string
MID$	Returns a character string
MID$	Replaces string characters
OCT$	Returns a string representing the octal (base 8) form of an integer
RIGHT$	Returns the right-most *n* characters of the target string
SPACE$	Returns a string consisting of all spaces
STR$	Returns the string equivalent of a number
STRING$	Returns a string consisting of multiple copies of the indicated character
UCASE$	Returns an all-uppercase string
VAL	Returns the numeric equivalent of a string

A P P E N D I X **I**

Customizing Turbo Basic

The program TBINST.COM lets you do four things:

- set up a path to your help and setup files
- customize your keyboard
- modify your default edit modes
- set up your default screen mode

If you want to store your help (TBHELP.TBH) and/or setup files (TBCONFIG.TB) on a directory other than the one where you have TB.EXE, you'll need to use the Turbo Basic directory option to set a path to those files.

If you're either unfamiliar with Turbo Basic's editor or inexorably tied to another editor, you can use the **E**ditor commands option to reconfigure (customize) the editor keystrokes to your liking.

You can use the **D**efault edit mode option to set several defaults for the editor: insert or overwrite mode, tabs, and auto-indenting.

And, finally, you can set up the display mode that Turbo Basic will use when it is in operation.

Running TBINST

To get started, type TBINST at the DOS prompt. The first menu lets you select the Turbo Basic directory, **E**ditor commands, **D**efault edit modes, **S**creen mode, or **Q**uit. You can either press the highlighted capital letter of the preferred option or use the *Up* and *Down arrow* keys to move to your selection and then press *Enter*; for instance, press *D* to modify the **D**efault edit modes. In general, pressing *Esc* will eventually return you to the main screen.

The Turbo Basic Directory Option

The **T**urbo Basic directory option is really only useful for hard disk users. You'll use this option to specify a path to your configuration files, so that these files will be accessible from wherever you call up Turbo Basic (assuming that you set up a path statement for Turbo Basic).

When you select the **T**urbo Basic directory option, you're prompted to enter the full path to your Turbo directory. (This is where your configuration files are kept; see the **D**irectories option in the **S**etup pull-down menu in Chapter 3). For example, if you want to keep the configuration files in a subdirectory of Borland products, you might type for your path name

```
C:\BORLAND\BASIC
```

After entering a path, press *Enter* to accept it and the main menu will redisplay. When you exit the program, you're prompted whether or not to save the changes. Once you save the path, the location is written to disk. (Note that the 25th line tells you which keystrokes to use when you're in this screen.)

The Editor Command Option

This option allows you to change the default keys that you use while you're in the Turbo Basic editor. To modify the **E**ditor commands, press *E* or move the selection bar to the option and press *Enter*. The help line at the top of the screen shows you which keys to use to move around and make changes. Most of these commands are simply movement commands; however, the **R** option is useful when you want to restore the keystrokes to their factory defaults. You'll notice that you can only modify the secondary, or highlighted, keystrokes.

Once you press *Enter* to modify a keystroke(s), you'll see a selection bar next to the command you want to redefine. If you take another look at the top of the screen, you'll see the help line now lists the available commands:

```
← backspace  C clear  R restore  ↵ accept edit  <Scroll Lock> literal
```

Use the *Backspace* key to backspace and/or delete something in the keystroke box. The **C** option clears, or erases, the whole box. Use **R** to restore the original keystrokes before exiting from the screen. The ↵ accepts the keystroke modification you've made. And finally, the **<Scroll Lock>** is a toggle that lets you alternate between command and literal modes.

To explain the **<Scroll Lock>** option, let's take a look at the *Enter* key, which is used to modify and accept the editing of a key command. If you wanted to use *Enter* as part of, say, Find string's keystrokes (<CtrlQ> <CtrlF>), you would have to toggle *Scroll Lock* to literal mode so that when you press the *Enter* key, it will be interpreted literally as part of the new keystroke you are entering. Follow these steps:

1. Make sure **<Scroll Lock>** is toggled to command mode (check the upper right-hand corner of your screen).
2. Then press *Enter* at the Find string command line.
3. Press *Backspace* to delete the <CtrlF> part of the string.
4. Now toggle **<Scroll Lock>** to literal and press *Enter*—voilà.
5. Again, toggle **<Scroll Lock>** to command mode and then press *Enter* to accept.

After you've defined a new keystroke(s) for a command, press *Enter* to accept it. If you're finished making changes, press *Esc* to exit. If you still have more changes to make, then use the arrow keys to scroll up and down the list and select your next command.

At this point, if you've accidentally assigned a keystroke sequence that's been used as a control character sequence in the primary command column, the message

```
Command conflicts need to be corrected. Press Esc
```

will flash across the screen. Any duplicated sequences will be highlighted, which enables you to easily search for any disallowed items and reselect a sequence. If you change your mind, you can use the **R** option to restore the factory defaults.

The Default Edit Mode Option

Press *D* to bring up the **D**efault edit mode menu. There are three editor modes that can be installed: **I**nsert mode, **A**uto-indent mode, and **T**abs.

With **I**nsert mode on, anything you enter at the keyboard is inserted at the cursor position, pushing any text to the right of the cursor further right. Toggling **I**nsert mode off allows you to overwrite text at the cursor.

With **A**uto-indent mode on, the cursor returns to the starting column of the previous line. When toggled off, the cursor always returns to column one.

Toggle on **T**ab mode when you want to insert tabs; toggle off and the tab is automatically set to the beginning of the first word in the previous line.

When you load Turbo Basic, the default values for all three modes are on. You can change the defaults to suit your preferences and save them back to Turbo Basic. Of course, you'll still be able to toggle these modes from inside Turbo Basic's editor.

Look to the 25th line for directions on how to select these options: Either use the arrow keys to move the selection bar to the option and then press *Enter* or else press the key that corresponds to the highlighted capital letter of the option.

The Screen Mode Option

Press *S* to select **S**creen mode from the installation menu. A pull-down menu will appear from which you can select the screen mode Turbo Basic will use during operation. Your options include

- **D**efault
- **C**olor
- **B**lack and white
- **M**onochrome

Default Display Mode

By default, Turbo Basic will always operate in the mode that is active when you load it.

Color Display Mode

Turbo Basic will use color mode with 80 × 25 characters no matter what mode is active, switching back to the active mode when you exit.

Black and White Display Mode

Turbo Basic will use black and white mode with 80 × 25 characters no matter what mode is active, switching back to the active mode when you exit.

Monochrome Display Mode

Turbo Basic will use monochrome mode no matter what mode is active, switching back to the active mode when you exit.

Quitting the Program

Once you have finished making all desired changes, select **Q**uit at the main menu. The message "Save changes to TB.EXE?" will appear at the bottom of the screen. If you press *Y* (for Yes), all of the changes you have made will be permanently installed into Turbo Basic. (Of course, you can always run this program again if you want to change them.) If you press *N* (for No), your changes will be ignored and you will be returned to the operating system prompt.

If you decide you want to restore the original Turbo Basic factory defaults, simply copy TB.EXE from your master disk onto your work disk. You can also restore the **E**ditor commands by selecting the **E** option at the main menu, then press *R* (for Restore) and *Esc*.

Index

D

Q

R

S

T

U

V

W

X

Z

Borland Software

BORLAND
INTERNATIONAL

4585 Scotts Valley Drive, Scotts Valley, CA 95066

SIDEKICK®: THE DESKTOP ORGANIZER

Whether you're running WordStar,® Lotus,® dBASE,® or any other program, SideKick puts all these desktop accessories at your fingertips—Instantly!

A full-screen WordStar-like Editor to jot down notes and edit files up to 25 pages long.

A Phone Directory for names, addresses, and telephone numbers. Finding a name or a number is a snap.

An Autodialer for all your phone calls. It will look up and dial telephone numbers for you. (A modem is required to use this function.)

A Monthly Calendar from 1901 through 2099.

Appointment Calendar to remind you of important meetings and appointments.

A full-featured Calculator ideal for business use. It also performs decimal to hexadecimal to binary conversions.

An ASCII Table for easy reference.

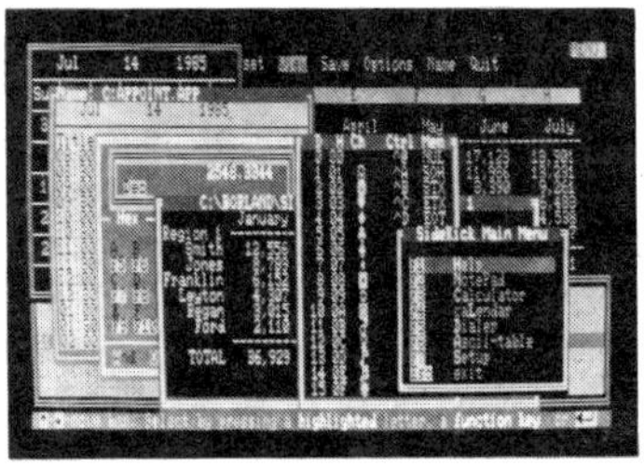

All the SideKick windows stacked up over Lotus 1-2-3.® From bottom to top: SideKick's "Menu Window," ASCII Table, Notepad, Calculator, Appointment Calendar, Monthly Calendar, and Phone Dialer.

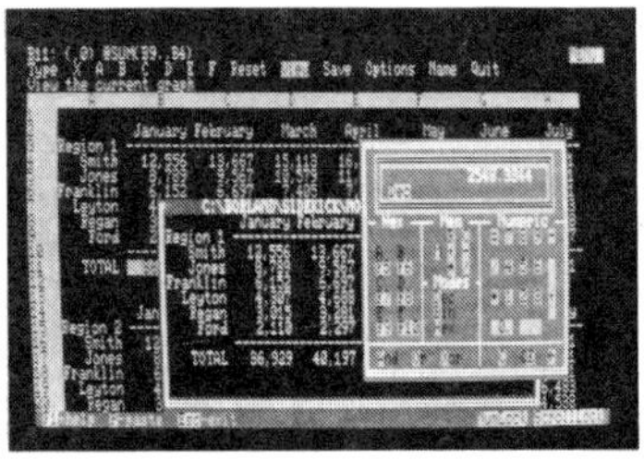

Here's SideKick running over Lotus 1-2-3. In the SideKick Notepad you'll notice data that's been imported directly from the Lotus screen. In the upper right you can see the Calculator.

The Critics' Choice

"In a simple, beautiful implementation of WordStar's block copy commands, SideKick can transport all or any part of the display screen (even an area overlaid by the notepad display) to the notepad."
—Charles Petzold, PC MAGAZINE

"SideKick deserves a place in every PC."
—Gary Ray, PC WEEK

"SideKick is by far the best we've seen. It is also the least expensive."
—Ron Mansfield, ENTREPRENEUR

"If you use a PC, get SideKick. You'll soon become dependent on it."
—Jerry Pournelle, BYTE

Suggested Retail Price: $84.95 (not copy protected)

Minimum system configuration: IBM PC, XT, AT, PCjr and true compatibles. PC-DOS (MS-DOS) 2.0 or greater. 128K RAM. One disk drive. A Hayes-compatible modem, IBM PCjr internal modem, or AT&T Modem 4000 is required for the autodialer function.

BORLAND
INTERNATIONAL

SUPERKEY® THE PRODUCTIVITY BOOSTER

RAM-resident
Increased productivity for IBM® PCs or compatibles

SuperKey's simple macros are electronic shortcuts to success. By letting you reduce a lengthy paragraph into a single keystroke of your choice, SuperKey eliminates repetition.

SuperKey turns 1,000 keystrokes into 1!
SuperKey can record lengthy keystroke sequences and play them back at the touch of a single key. Instantly. Like magic.

In fact, with SuperKey's simple macros, you can turn "Dear Customer: Thank you for your inquiry. We are pleased to let you know that shipment will be made within 24 hours. Sincerely," into the one keystroke of your choice!

SuperKey keeps your confidential files—confidential!
Without encryption, your files are open secrets. Anyone can walk up to your PC and read your confidential files (tax returns, business plans, customer lists, personal letters, etc.).

With SuperKey you can encrypt any file, *even* while running another program. As long as you keep the password secret, only *you* can decode your file correctly. SuperKey also implements the U.S. government Data Encryption Standard (DES).

- ☑ RAM resident—accepts new macro files even while running other programs
- ☑ Pull-down menus
- ☑ Superfast file encryption
- ☑ Choice of two encryption schemes
- ☑ On-line context-sensitive help
- ☑ One-finger mode reduces key commands to single keystroke
- ☑ Screen OFF/ON blanks out and restores screen to protect against "burn in"
- ☑ Partial or complete reorganization of keyboard
- ☑ Keyboard buffer increases 16 character keyboard "type-ahead" buffer to 128 characters
- ☑ Real-time delay causes macro playback to pause for specified interval
- ☑ Transparent display macros allow creation of menus on top of application programs
- ☑ Data entry and format control using "fixed" or "variable" fields
- ☑ Command stack recalls last 256 characters entered

Suggested Retail Price: $99.95 (not copy protected)

Minimum system configuration: IBM PC, XT, AT, PCjr, and true compatibles. PC-DOS (MS-DOS) 2.0 or greater. 128K RAM. One disk drive.

BORLAND INTERNATIONAL

BOR 0062C

REFLEX:® THE DATABASE MANAGER

The high-performance database manager that's so advanced it's easy to use!

Lets you organize, analyze and report information faster than ever before! If you manage mailing lists, customer files, or even your company's budgets—Reflex is the database manager for you!

Reflex is the acclaimed, high-performance database manager you've been waiting for. Reflex extends database management with business graphics. Because a picture is often worth a 1000 words, Reflex lets you extract critical information buried in mountains of data. With Reflex, when you look, you see.

The ***REPORT VIEW*** allows you to generate everything from mailing labels to sophisticated reports. You can use database files created with Reflex or transferred from Lotus 1-2-3,® dBASE,® PFS: File,® and other applications.

Reflex: The Critics' Choice

". . . if you use a PC, you should know about Reflex . . . may be the best bargain in software today."
Jerry Pournelle, BYTE

"Everyone agrees that Reflex is the best-looking database they've ever seen."
Adam B. Green, InfoWorld

"The next generation of software has officially arrived." ***Peter Norton, PC Week***

Reflex: don't use your PC without it!
Join hundreds of thousands of enthusiastic Reflex users and experience the power and ease of use of Borland's award-winning Reflex.

Suggested Retail Price: $149.95 (not copy protected)

Minimum system configuration: IBM PC, XT, AT, and true compatibles. 384K RAM minimum. IBM Color Graphics Adapter, Hercules Monochrome Graphics CArd, or equivalent. PC-DOS (MS-DOS) 2.0 or greater. Hard disk and mouse optional. Lotus 1-2-3, dBASE, or PFS: File optional.

BORLAND
I N T E R N A T I O N A L

If you use an IBM® PC, you need

TURBO Lightning®

Turbo Lightning teams up with the Random House Concise Word List to check your spelling as you type!

Turbo Lightning, using the 80,000-word Random House Dictionary, checks your spelling *as you type*. If you misspell a word, it alerts you with a "beep." At the touch of a key, Turbo Lightning opens a window on top of your application program and suggests the correct spelling. Just press one key and the misspelled word is instantly replaced with the correct word.

Turbo Lightning works hand-in-hand with the Random House Thesaurus to give you instant access to synonyms

Turbo Lightning lets you choose just the right word from a list of alternates, so you don't say the same thing the same way every time. Once Turbo Lightning opens the Thesaurus window, you see a list of alternate words; select the word you want, press ENTER and your new word will instantly replace the original word. Pure magic!

If you ever write a word, think a word, or say a word, you need Turbo Lightning

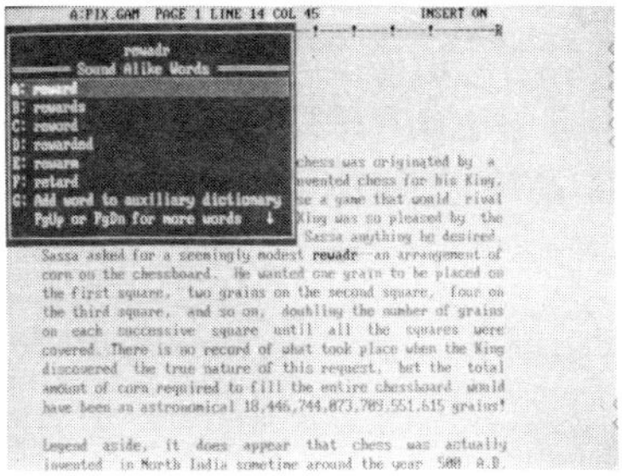

The Turbo Lightning Proofreader

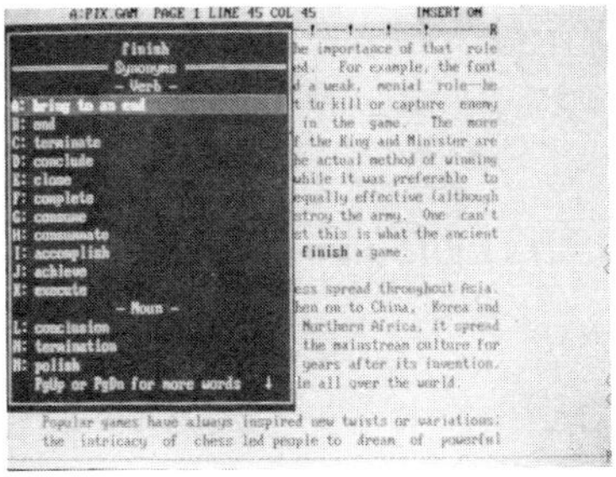

The Turbo Lightning Thesaurus

You can teach Turbo Lightning new words

You can *teach* your new Turbo Lightning your name, business associates' names, street names, addresses, correct capitalizations, and any specialized words you use frequently. Teach Turbo Lightning once, and it knows forever.

Turbo Lightning is the engine that powers Borland's Turbo Lightning Library®

Turbo Lightning brings electronic power to the Random House Concise Word List and Random House Thesaurus. They're at your fingertips—even while you're running other programs. Turbo Lightning will also "drive" soon-to-be-released encyclopedias, extended thesauruses, specialized dictionaries, and many other popular reference works. You get a head start with this first volume in the Turbo Lightning Library.

Suggested Retail Price: $99.95 (not copy protected)

Minimum system configuration: IBM PC, XT, AT, PCjr, and true compatibles with 2 floppy disk drives. PC-DOS (MS-DOS) 2.0 or greater. 256K RAM. Hard disk recommended.

BORLAND INTERNATIONAL

TURBO PASCAL

GRAPHIX TOOLBOX®

A Library of Graphics Routines for Use with Turbo Pascal®

High-resolution graphics for your IBM™ PC, AT,™ XT,™ PCjr™, true PC compatibles, and the Heath Zenith Z-100.™ Comes complete with graphics window management.

Even if you're new to Turbo Pascal programming, the Turbo Pascal Graphix Toolbox will get you started right away. It's a collection of tools that will get you right into the fascinating world of high-resolution business graphics, including graphics window management. You get immediate, satisfying results. And we keep Royalty out of American business because you don't pay any—even if you distribute your own compiled programs that include all or part of the Turbo Pascal Graphix Toolbox procedures.

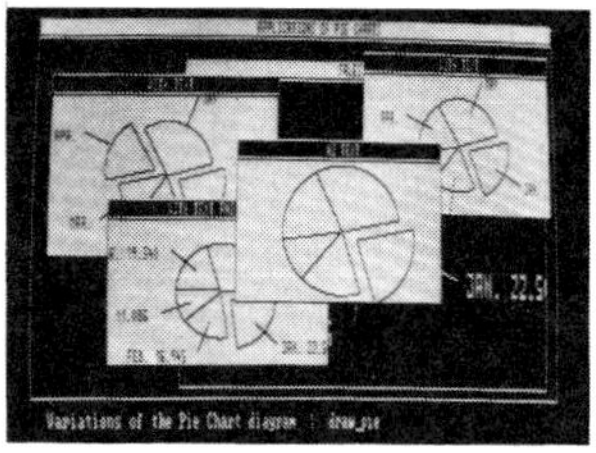

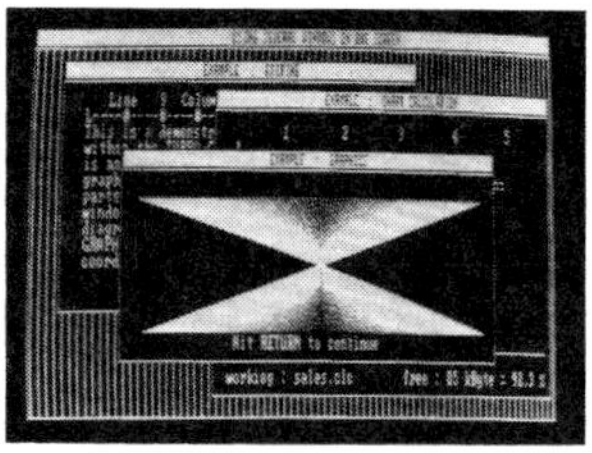

What you get includes:

- Complete commented source code on disk.
- Tools for drawing simple graphics.
- Tools for drawing complex graphics, including curves with optional smoothing.
- Routines that let you store and restore graphic images to and from disk.
- Tools allowing you to send screen images to Epson®-compatible printers.
- Full graphics window management.
- Two different font styles for graphic labeling.
- Choice of line-drawing styles.
- Routines that will let you quickly plot functions and model experimental data.
- And much, much more . . .

"While most people only talk about low-cost personal computer software, Borland has been doing something about it. And Borland provides good technical support as part of the price."

John Markov & Paul Freiberger, syndicated columnists.

If you ever plan to create Turbo Pascal programs that make use of business graphics or scientific graphics, you need the Turbo Pascal Graphix Toolbox.

Suggested Retail Price: $69.95 (not copy protected)

Minimum system configuration: IBM PC, XT, AT, PCjr, true compatibles and the Heath Zenith Z-100. Turbo Pascal 3.0 or later. 192K RAM minimum. Two disk drives and an IBM Color Graphics Adapter (CGA), IBM Enhanced Graphics Adapter (EGA), Hercules Graphics Card or compatible.

BORLAND
INTERNATIONAL

TURBO PASCAL EDITOR TOOLBOX®

It's All You Need To Build Your Own Text Editor Or Word Processor

Build your own lightning-fast editor and incorporate it into your Turbo Pascal® programs. Turbo Editor Toolbox gives you easy-to-install modules. Now you can integrate a fast and powerful editor into your own programs. You get the source code, the manual, and the know-how.

Create your own word processor. We provide all the editing routines. You plug in the features you want. You could build a WordStar®-like editor with pull-down menus like Microsoft's® Word, and make it work as fast as WordPerfect.®

To demonstrate the tremendous power of Turbo Editor Toolbox, we give you the source code for two sample editors:

Simple Editor A complete editor ready to include in your programs. With windows, block commands, and memory-mapped screen routines.

MicroStar A full-blown text editor with a complete pull-down menu user interface, plus a lot more. Modify MicroStar's pull-down menu system and include it in your Turbo Pascal programs.

The Turbo Editor Toolbox gives you all the standard features you would expect to find in any word processor:

- Wordwrap
- UN-delete last line
- Auto-indent
- Find and Find/Replace with options
- Set left and right margin
- Block mark, move, and copy
- Tab, insert and overstrike modes, centering, etc.

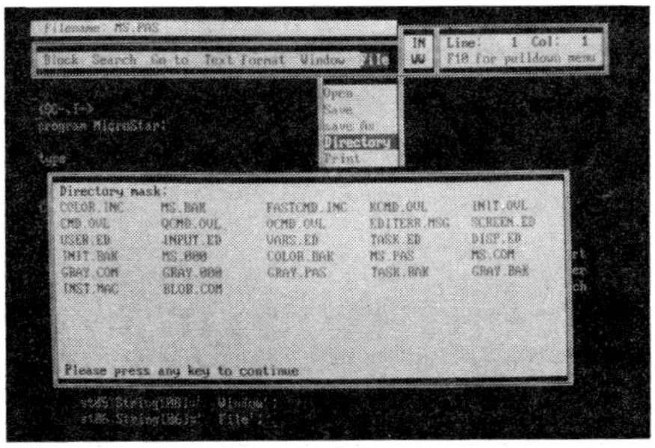

MicroStar's pull-down menus.

And Turbo Editor Toolbox has features that word processors selling for several hundred dollars can't begin to match. Just to name a few:

- ☑ ***RAM-based editor***. You can edit very large files and yet editing is lightning fast.
- ☑ ***Memory-mapped screen routines.*** Instant paging, scrolling, and text display.
- ☑ ***Keyboard installation.*** Change control keys from WordStar-like commands to any that you prefer.
- ☑ ***Multiple windows.*** See and edit up to eight documents—or up to eight parts of the same document—all at the same time.
- ☑ ***Multitasking.*** Automatically save your text. Plug in a digital clock, an appointment alarm—see how it's done with MicroStar's "background" printing.

Best of all, **source code is included for everything in the Editor Toolbox.**

Suggested Retail Price: $69.95 (not copy protected)

Minimum system configuration: IBM PC, XT, AT, 3270, PCjr, and true compatibles. PC-DOS (MS-DOS) 2.0 or greater. 192K RAM. You must be using Turbo Pascal 3.0 for IBM and compatibles.

BORLAND
INTERNATIONAL

STEP-BY-STEP TUTORIAL AND DEMO PROGRA WITH SOURCE CODE INCLUDED!

TURBO PROLOG™

the natural language of Artificial Intelligence

Turbo Prolog brings fifth-generation supercomputer power to your IBM®PC!

Turbo Prolog takes programming into a new, natural, and logical environment

With Turbo Prolog, because of its natural, logical approach, both people new to programming *and* professional programmers can build powerful applications such as expert systems, customized knowledge bases, natural language interfaces, and smart information management systems.

Turbo Prolog is a *declarative* language which uses deductive reasoning to solve programming problems.

Turbo Prolog provides a fully integrated programming environment like Borland's Turbo Pascal,® the *de facto* worldwide standard.

You get the complete Turbo Prolog programming system

You get the 200-page manual you're holding, software that includes the lightning-fast Turbo Prolog six-pass compiler and interactive editor, and the free GeoBase natural query language database, which includes commented source code on disk, ready to compile. (GeoBase is a complete database designed and developed around U.S. geography. You can modify it or use it "as is.")

Turbo Prolog's development system includes:

- ☐ A complete Prolog compiler that is a variation of the Clocksin and Mellish Edinburgh standard Prolog.
- ☐ A full-screen interactive editor.
- ☐ Support for both graphic and text windows.
- ☐ All the tools that let you build your own expert systems and **AI** applications with unprecedented ease.

Minimum system configuration: IBM PC, XT, AT, Portable, 3270, PCjr and true compatibles. PC-DOS (MS-DOS) 2.0 or later. 384K RAM minimum.

Suggested Retail Price: $99.95
(not copy protected)

BORLAND
INTERNATIONAL

EUREKA: THE SOLVER™

The solution to your most complex equations—in seconds!

If you're a scientist, engineer, financial analyst, student, teacher, or any other professional working with equations, Eureka: The Solver can do your Algebra, Trigonometry and Calculus problems in a snap.

Eureka also handles maximization and minimization problems, plots functions, generates reports, and saves an incredible amount of time. Even if you're not a computer specialist, Eureka can help you solve your real-world mathematical problems fast, without having to learn numerical approximation techniques. Using Borland's famous pull-down menu design and context-sensitive help screens, Eureka is easy to learn and easy to use—as simple as a hand-held calculator.

X + exp(X) = 10 solved instantly instead of eventually!
Imagine you have to "solve for X," where X + exp(X) = 10, and you don't have Eureka: The Solver. What you do have is a problem, because it's going to take a lot of time guessing at "X." With Eureka, there's no guessing, no dancing in the dark—you get the right answer, right now. (PS: X = 2.0705799, and Eureka solved that one in .4 of a second!)

How to use Eureka: The Solver

It's easy.

1. Enter your equation into the full-screen editor
2. Select the "Solve" command
3. Look at the answer
4. You're done

You can then tell Eureka to

- Evaluate your solution
- Plot a graph
- Generate a report, then send the output to your printer, disk file or screen
- Or all of the above

Some of Eureka's key features

You can key in:

- ☑ A formula or formulas
- ☑ A series of equations—and solve for all variables
- ☑ Constraints (like X has to be < or = 2)
- ☑ A function to plot
- ☑ Unit conversions
- ☑ Maximization and minimization problems
- ☑ Interest Rate/Present Value calculations
- ☑ Variables we call "What happens?," like "What happens if I change this variable to 21 and that variable to 27?"

Eureka: The Solver includes

- ☑ A full-screen editor
- ☑ Pull-down menus
- ☑ Context-sensitive Help
- ☑ On-screen calculator
- ☑ Automatic 8087 math co-processor chip support
- ☑ Powerful financial functions
- ☑ Built-in and user-defined math and financial functions
- ☑ Ability to generate reports complete with plots and lists
- ☑ Polynomial finder
- ☑ Inequality solutions

Minimum system configuration: IBM PC, AT, XT, Portable, 3270 and true compatibles. PC-DOS (MS-DOS) 2.0 and later. 384K.

Suggested Retail Price: $99.95*
(not copy protected)

BORLAND
INTERNATIONAL

SIDEKICK®: THE DESKTOP ORGANIZER Release 2.0

Macintosh™

The most complete and comprehensive collection of desk accessories available for your Macintosh!

Thousands of users already know that SideKick is the best collection of desk accessories available for the Macintosh. With our new Release 2.0, the best just got better.

We've just added two powerful high-performance tools to SideKick—Outlook™: The Outliner and MacPlan™: The Spreadsheet. They work in perfect harmony with each other and *while* you run other programs!

Outlook: The Outliner

- It's the desk accessory with more power than a stand-alone outliner
- A great desktop publishing tool, Outlook lets you incorporate both text and graphics into your outlines
- Works hand-in-hand with MacPlan
- Allows you to work on several outlines at the same time

MacPlan: The Spreadsheet

- Integrates spreadsheets and graphs
- Does both formulas and straight numbers
- Graph types include bar charts, stacked bar charts, pie charts and line graphs
- Includes 12 example templates free!
- Pastes graphics and data right into Outlook creating professional memos and reports, complete with headers and footers.

SideKick: The Desktop Organizer, Release 2.0 now includes

- ☑ Outlook: The Outliner
- ☑ MacPlan: The Spreadsheet
- ☑ Mini word processor
- ☑ Calendar
- ☑ PhoneLog
- ☑ Analog clock
- ☑ Alarm system
- ☑ Calculator
- ☑ Report generator
- ☑ Telecommunications (new version now supports XModem file transfer protocol)

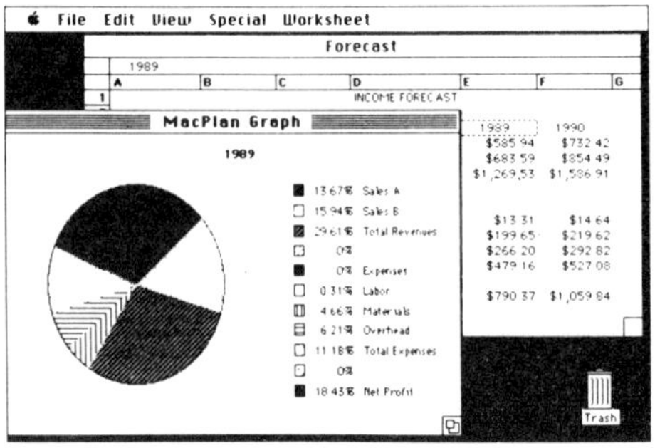

MacPlan does both spreadsheets and business graphs. Paste them into your Outlook files and generate professional reports.

Suggested Retail Price: $99.95 (not copy protected)

Minimum system configurations: Macintosh 512K or Macintosh Plus with one disk drive. One 800K or two 400K drives are recommended. With one 400K drive, a limited number of desk accessories will be installable per disk.

BORLAND INTERNATIONAL

BOR 0069D

REFLEX®: THE DATABASE MANAGER

The easy-to-use relational database that thinks like a spreadsheet. Reflex for the Mac lets you crunch numbers by entering formulas and link databases by drawing on-screen lines.

5 free ready-to-use templates are included on the examples disk:

- A sample 1040 tax application with Schedule A, Schedule B, and Schedule D, each contained in a separate report document.
- A portfolio analysis application with linked databases of stock purchases, sales, and dividend payments.
- A checkbook application.

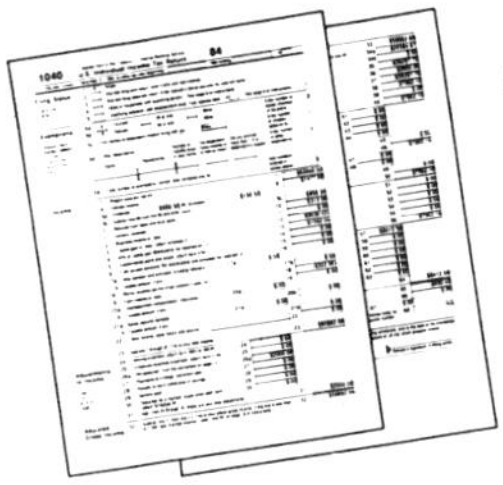

- A client billing application set up for a law office, but easily customized by any professional who bills time.
- A parts explosion application that breaks down an object into its component parts for cost analysis.

Reflex for the Mac accomplishes all of these tasks without programming—using spreadsheet-like formulas. Some other Reflex for the Mac features are:

- Visual database design.
- "What you see is what you get" report and form layout with pictures.
- Automatic restructuring of database files when data types are changed, or fields are added and deleted.
- Display formats which include General, Decimal, Scientific, Dollars, Percent.
- Data types which include variable length text, number, integer, automatically incremented sequence number, date, time, and logical.
- Up to 255 fields per record.
- Up to 16 files simultaneously open.
- Up to 16 Mac fonts and styles are selectable for individual fields and labels.

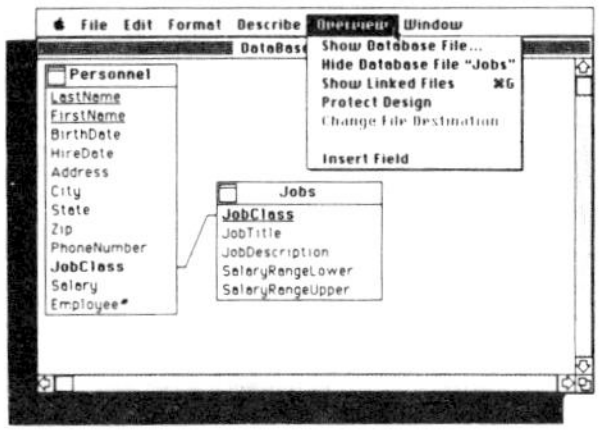

After opening the "Overview" window, you draw link lines between databases directly onto your Macintosh screen.

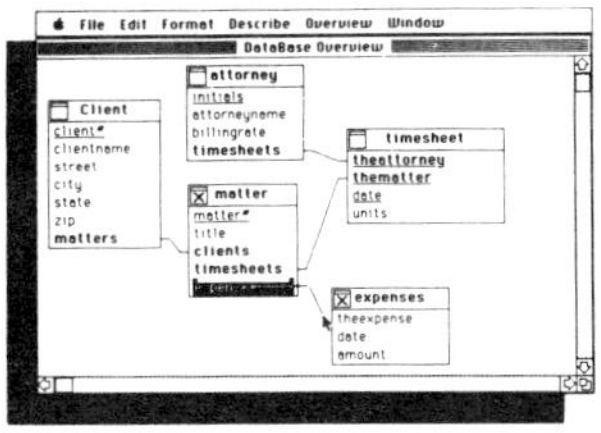

The link lines you draw establish both visual and electronic relationships between your databases.

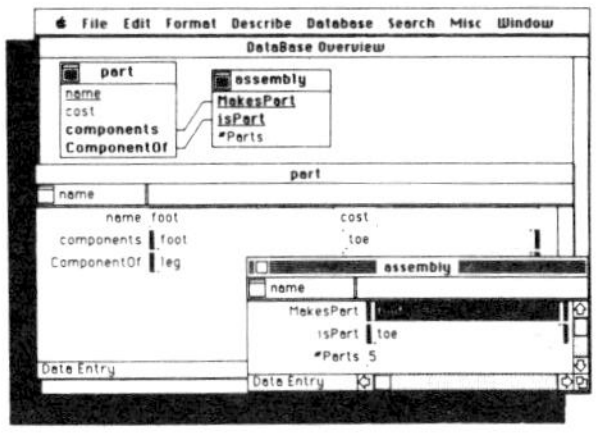

You can have multiple windows open simultaneously to view all members of a linked set—which are interactive and truly relational.

Critic's Choice

". . . a powerful relational database . . . uses a visual approach to information management." ***InfoWorld***

". . . gives you a lot of freedom in report design; you can even import graphics." ***A+ Magazine***

". . . bridges the gap between the pretty programs and the power programs." **Stewart Alsop, *PC Letter***

BORLAND INTERNATIONAL

Suggested Retail Price: $99.95*
(not copy protected)

Minimum system configuration: *Macintosh 512K or Macintosh Plus with one disk drive. Second external drive recommended.*

BOR0149A

*Introductory price expires July 1, 1987